3 Practice Tests for the

ACT®

The Princeton Review®

3 Practice Tests for the

ACT®

The Staff of The Princeton Review

PrincetonReview.com

Random House, Inc. New York

The Princeton Review, Inc.
111 Speen Street, Suite 550
Framingham, MA 01701
E-mail: editorialsupport@review.com

Some content in this book previously appeared
in *Cracking the ACT*, 2013 Edition, and *1,296 ACT
Practice Questions*, 3rd Edition, both published by
Random House as trade paperbacks in 2013.

ISBN: 978-0-307-94603-4

ACT is a registered trademark of ACT, Inc., which
does not sponsor or endorse this product.

The Princeton Review is not affiliated with Princeton
University.

Editor: Meave Shelton
Production Editor: Melissa Duclos-Yourdon
Production Artist: Deborah A. Silvestrini

Editorial
Rob Franek, Senior VP, Publisher
Mary Beth Garrick, Director of Production
Selena Coppock, Senior Editor
Calvin Cato, Editor
Kristen O'Toole, Editor
Meave Shelton, Editor
Alyssa Wolff, Editorial Assistant

Random House Publishing Team
Tom Russell, Publisher
Nicole Benhabib, Publishing Director
Ellen L. Reed, Production Manager
Alison Stoltzfus, Managing Editor

Acknowledgments

The completion of this book would not have been possible without the help and dedication of several individuals. We would like to thank Melissa Hendrix in particular for her hard work revising and updating the included material.

Contents

Foreword

Welcome to *3 Practice Tests for the ACT*! The ACT is not a test of aptitude, how good of a person you are, or how successful you will be in life. The ACT simply tests how well you take the ACT. And performing well on the ACT is a skill, one that can be learned like any other. The Princeton Review was founded more than 20 years ago on this very simple idea, and—as our students' test scores show—our approach is the one that works.

Sure, you want to do well on the ACT, but you don't need to let the test intimidate you. As you prepare, remember these two important things:

- The key to raising your ACT score does not lie in memorizing dozens of math theorems, the periodic table of elements, or obscure rules of English grammar. There's more to mastering this test that just improving math, verbal, and science skills. At its root, the ACT measures academic achievement. It doesn't pretend to measure your analytic ability or your intelligence. The people at ACT admit that you can increase your score by preparing for the test, and by spending just a little extra time preparing for the ACT, you can substantially change your score.

- If there is any flaw in the ACT, it is that, in its attempt to be fair, it has become a little, well, predictable. The ACT tests the same information the same way, year after year. For example, there are always 14 plane geometry questions on the ACT. Not 13, not 15—exactly 14. There are exactly 10 questions on punctuation. You can count on it. Even the way the test asks the questions is predictable, based on the need for a standardized product.

We have included in this book three complete practice ACT exams. Rest assured that these tests are modeled closely on actual ACT exams and questions, with the proper balance of questions reflective of what the ACT actually tests. We at The Princeton Review spend millions of dollars every year improving our methods and materials, and our books contain the most accurate, up-to-date information available. We're always ready for the ACT, and we'll get you ready too.

However, there is no magic pill: Just buying this book isn't going to improve your scores. Solid score improvement takes commitment and effort from you. Read the book carefully and learn our strategies. Take full-length practice tests under actual timed conditions. Analyze your performance and focus your efforts where you need improvement. Visit PrincetonReview.com to find a tutoring, small group, or classroom instruction program near you. Study with a friend to stay motivated.

This test is challenging, but you're on the right track. We'll be with you all the way.

Good luck!

The Staff of The Princeton Review

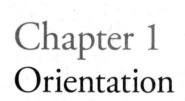

Chapter 1
Orientation

GENERAL INFORMATION ABOUT THE ACT

You may have bought this book because you know nothing about the ACT, or perhaps you took the test once and want to raise your score. Either way, it's important to know about the test and the people who write it. Let's take a second to discuss some ACT facts; some of them may surprise you.

What Does the ACT Test?

The ACT does not measure intelligence, nor does it predict your ultimate success or failure as a human being. No matter how high or how low you score on this test initially, and no matter how much you may increase your score through preparation, you should *never* consider the score you receive on this or any other test a final judgment of your abilities.

WHO PUTS THE TEST OUT?

The ACT is written by a company that used to call itself American College Testing but now just calls itself ACT. The company's main offices are in Iowa City, Iowa. The people at ACT have been writing a version of this test since 1959. Even if you aren't looking forward to taking the ACT this year, you would probably prefer it to the version they used to give. In the old days, the test included detailed questions about topics like the Constitution of the United States, electrostatic forces, and planets in the solar system.

The people at ACT also write a number of other tests, including a test for professional golfers and a test for dieticians. They provide a broad range of services to educational agencies and business institutions.

WHAT'S ON IT?

The ACT is a multiple-choice standardized exam that is supposed to measure your knowledge of some of the subjects taught in high school. The ACT takes about three and a half hours and has one break. It is divided into four tests, which are always given in the same order. (ACT calls them tests, but we may also use the term "sections" in this book to avoid confusion.)

1. English Test (45 minutes—75 questions)

In this section, you will see five essays on the left side of the page. Some words or phrases will be underlined. On the right side of the page, you will be asked whether the underlined portion is correct as written or whether one of the three alternatives listed would be better. This is a test of grammar, punctuation, sentence structure, and rhetorical skills. Throughout each essay, commonly known as a "passage," there will also be questions about overall organization and style or perhaps about how the writing could be revised or strengthened.

Power Booking
If you were getting ready to take a history test, you'd study history. If you were preparing for a basketball game, you'd practice basketball. So if you're preparing for the ACT, study the ACT!

2. Math Test (60 minutes—60 questions)

These are the regular, multiple-choice math questions you've been doing all your life. The easier questions, which test basic math proficiency, *tend* to come first, but the folks at the ACT try to mix in easy, medium, and difficult problems throughout the Math test. A good third of the test covers pre-algebra and elementary algebra. Slightly less than a third covers intermediate algebra and coordinate geometry (graphing). Regular geometry accounts for less than a quarter of the questions, and there are four questions that cover trigonometry.

3. Reading Test (35 minutes—40 questions)

In this test, there will be four reading passages of about 750 words each—the average length of a *People* magazine article but maybe not as interesting. There is always one prose fiction passage, one social science passage, one humanities passage, and one natural science passage, and they are always in that order. After reading each passage, you have to answer 10 questions.

4. Science Test (35 minutes—40 questions)

No specific scientific knowledge is necessary for the Science test. You won't need to know the chemical makeup of hydrochloric acid or any formulas. Instead, you will be asked to understand six sets of scientific information presented in graphs, charts, tables, and research summaries, and you will have to make sense of one disagreement between two or three scientists. (Occasionally, there are more than three scientists.)

There may be one additional, experimental section on the ACT. This section typically comes at the end of the test and is usually very easy to recognize, as it is much shorter than a regular section—just 10 to 15 minutes long. In other words, it's not a big deal. This section usually shows up on the June exam, and it won't count toward your score.

5. Optional Writing Test (30 minutes)

The ACT contains an "optional" writing test featuring a single essay. We recommend you take the "ACT Plus Writing," version of the test because some schools require it. While on test day you may think you don't need it, you might later decide to apply to a school that requires a writing score. The last thing you want is to be forced into taking the whole ACT all over again…this time *with* the writing test. The essay consists of a prompt "relevant" to high school students on which you will be asked to write an essay stating your position on the prompt. Two people will then grade your essay on a scale of 1 to 6 for a total score of 2 to 12. In this book, we will teach you how to write the best possible essay for the ACT.

More great titles by The Princeton Review

Check out *Math and Science Workout for the ACT* and *English and Reading Workout for the ACT* for targeted, subject-based reviews and practice tests.

SCORING

Scores for each of the four tests are reported on a scale of 1 to 36 (36 being the highest score possible). The four scores are averaged to yield your composite score, which is the score colleges and universities primarily use to determine admission. Next to each score is a percentile ranking. Percentile ranking refers to how you performed on the test relative to other people who took it at the same time. For instance, a percentile ranking of 87 indicates that you scored higher than 87 percent of the people who took the test and 13 percent scored higher than you.

Some of the scores have subcategories. English is broken down into Usage/Mechanics and Rhetorical Skills. The subcategories may be of some marginal use to colleges; they are much more useful to you if you decide to take the test again, because they pinpoint your strengths and weaknesses. In these subcategories, scores are reported on a scale of 1 to 18 (18 being the highest score possible). They are also reported as percentiles.

If you decide to take the ACT Plus Writing test, you will receive standard ACT scores plus two additional scores. One will be a scaled score from 1 to 36, which combines your performance on the Writing test and the English test. The other will be a subscore, ranging from 2 to 12, which reflects how you did on your essay. Neither score contributes to your composite score. The Writing test costs an additional $15, which you will be charged when you sign up for the ACT. The ACT with the Essay section is more expensive than the ACT without the Essay section. Check www.act.org for current costs.

Three to seven weeks after you take the ACT, you and the colleges you have selected, if any, will receive your ACT scores in the mail. If you want, you can pay to see your scores a bit earlier (about 10 to 14 days after your test date).

Who Actually Receives the Scores?

You might think that your scores will be mailed directly to your home, but this is not always the case. If you take the June administration of the test, scores are mailed to colleges and to you. For all other administrations, scores are sent to colleges and to your high school counselor, not directly to you, unless your high school has given ACT permission to send them to you. You then get the scores from the counselor. We've checked with ACT, and the people we talked to there said that if you choose not to provide a High School Code, your scores simply won't be sent to your high school. So, if you want your scores sent to your home (and not your high school), leave the High School Code blank. All colleges you list will get copies of your score regardless of whether you leave the High School Code blank.

There is one potential downside to not reporting your scores to your high school: If you're likely to receive a state-awarded scholarship on the basis of your ACT score, such a score is usually reported to the state's scholarship-awarding entity through—you guessed it—the high school. If you anticipate receiving such a score and are counting on such a scholarship (taking at least one test as a reality check is a good idea), go ahead and provide your High School Code. As the owners of your transcript, you and your parents can go to your high school and have a score removed from it later if you feel the score doesn't reflect your abilities. In any event, because ACT allows score choice (sending scores from just one testing date to colleges), the test scores on your high school transcript ultimately don't matter that much.

THE ACT VS. THE SAT

You may have to take the ACT anyway, but most of the schools in which you're interested also accept the SAT. We think the SAT is nowhere near as fair a test as the ACT. Whereas the ACT says it measures "achievement" (which we believe *can* be measured), the SAT says it measures "ability" (which we don't think can be measured at all; and if it can, the SAT sure isn't doing it).

More great titles by The Princeton Review

ACT or SAT? Choosing the Right Exam For You

What Exactly Are the Differences?

The SAT tends to be less time-pressured than the ACT. However, many of the questions on the SAT are trickier than those on the ACT. The SAT Verbal sections have a stronger emphasis on vocabulary than do the ACT English and Reading tests. The SAT Math section tests primarily algebra and plane geometry and includes no trigonometry at all.

Both tests include an Essay section, although ACT has made this new essay optional because some colleges require it while others do not. ACT doesn't want to force students to take (and pay for) a test they don't need. The implication then is that many students can ignore the new Writing Test altogether depending on what the schools to which they are applying require.

To find out if the schools in which you are interested require the ACT essay, visit the ACT writing test page at www.actstudent.org/writing or contact the schools directly.

While we are obviously not tremendously fond of the SAT, you should know that some students end up scoring substantially higher on the SAT than they do on the ACT and vice versa. It may be to your advantage to take a practice test for each one and see which is more likely to get you a better score.

Chapter 2
Strategy

The first step to cracking the ACT is to know how best to approach the test. The ACT is not like the tests you've taken in school, so you need to learn to look at it in a different way. This chapter will show test-taking strategies that immediately improve your score.

How Questions Are Organized

Wouldn't it be great if all the questions on the ACT were arranged in order of difficulty? Then you could do the easiest questions first and move on from there. That way you wouldn't waste a lot of time trying to answer difficult questions before you had answered all the easy questions, which count for the same number of points anyway.

Unfortunately, the ACT is not organized that way.

According to the ACT writers we interviewed, the English section of the test is not in any order of difficulty. In the Math test, according to ACT literature, "most people find the first questions on the test easier... than the ones that come later," but these are only very rough guidelines. Many Princeton Review students find that some questions toward the end of the test are easier than many of the questions in the beginning.

Oh. But What If...

But what if the Science Reasoning and Reading *passages* were arranged in order of difficulty? Some of the other test-preparation books maintain that they are. According to one ACT writer, this is true, "...only in an average sense. We believe in the philosophy that if students are running out of time, the questions they don't get to should be ones they would have difficulty with anyway. But students will find plenty of exceptions." So by its own admission, ACT does not use a definite order of difficulty in the Science Reasoning or Reading tests.

Oh. But...

But nothing! On the ACT, if you want to do the easy questions first, you're going to have to find them for yourself. We have a good way to think about this. We call it "triage."

TRIAGE

Triage is the medical term that describes the technique used by emergency-room doctors when they have several emergencies at the same time. To save the most lives, doctors separate patients into three groups: those who will die regardless of intervention, those who require immediate medical attention, and those who can afford to wait a little while. The routine patients are left until last.

In ACT triage, you adapt this strategy somewhat. See that really tough algebra problem sitting over there? Forget it; it's a goner. How about that problem on frequency and amplitude? That would take far too long, and even if you got it right, it would still only be worth one point. Now this problem involving basic arithmetic—this is something different altogether. It's an easy question, so you should do it right away.

See that tough, horrible-looking passage about European authoritarianism during the nineteenth century? Let's see if it's still breathing after we finish the one about Ronald Reagan's election in 1980.

More great titles by The Princeton Review

For more great strategies, helpful lessons, and a thorough review of all ACT subjects, check out *Cracking the ACT*.

For more help check out our academic tutoring offers at PrincetonReview.com

Just One More Minute…

If you find yourself stuck on a question, waiting for divine inspiration, it's time to move on to another, easier problem. Save your time and live to fight another day (or question, that is). The temptation to get stubborn and stay with a particular problem can be very strong, especially when you've already invested some time on it. Nonetheless, you need to move on. Why stick with a question that's giving you problems when there are easier questions to be answered?

"Oh, Yeah!"

We've all had the experience of riding home in the car and suddenly slapping our hand to our forehead as we finally realized exactly how to do question number five. By using triage, you can sometimes have this sudden revelation *before* the test is over, when you can still do something about it. So how does triage work exactly?

Now, Later, Never

Do you want to do the problem *now*? That is the question you should constantly be asking yourself during the exam. If you finish reading a problem and immediately know how to solve it, then of course you should do it right away.

But what if you finish reading a problem and you aren't really certain how to begin? If you think you might be able to figure it out on your second pass, circle the question number and move on. This might seem hard to do at first, but it is one of the central tenets of good test taking, and it gets easier with practice. You aren't necessarily skipping the problem forever. You're just putting it at the back of the line.

However, if the problem is a goner and you're sure you'll never figure it out, fill in your guess answer and forget it. There are other problems out there waiting for you; don't worry about the ones you just *can't* do.

Two Passes

We want you to do each section in two passes. During the first pass, the object is to nail every single question you can answer. By answering all the questions of which you're sure, you will never have to hear the words, "Okay, pencils down," and know that there were several more questions you could have done if only there had been more time. You will have already done them.

What Happens if I Think I Know How to Do It, but Then I Realize I Was Wrong?

Nobody's right all the time. As soon as you realize you're stuck, you should put a big circle around the question and move on. This is the time when people tend to get stubborn. They think, "But I've already spent so much time on this question. It would be a waste to skip it now."

You Haven't Wasted the Time; You've Invested It

When you come back to this question on the second pass, you won't be starting from scratch. You'll already have read the question once. You may have made some notes in the margin. Perhaps reading it again will make you realize an important point you missed the first time. If not, throw it to the back of

First Pass, Second Pass
On the first pass, do the questions you know how to do and guess on the questions that you have no idea how to do. On the second pass, answer all the questions that are doable but likely to take you more time.

the line and count your blessings: You could still be back there working on question number five!

The Second Pass

After you've finished everything you can do on the first pass and bubbled in your Letter of the Day on all questions that you're sure you can't do, come back to the questions you circled for a second pass. Again, think ACT triage. Most of the "patients" in your emergency room have now been handled. Look over the remaining problems and ask yourself the same question: Which one do I want to do *now*? Obviously, none of them struck you as easy the first time or you would have answered on the first pass. On the contrary, among the remaining problems, some are probably more likely bets than others.

Sometimes when you read a question again, you suddenly realize what the point of the question really is. This will save you from having that "Oh, yeah!" revelation on the car ride home. But other times when you re-read a question, you suddenly realize that you will hate this question for the rest of your life and you never, ever want to see it again. Fine. Throw it to the back of the list and keep looking. These are "never" questions: Do them only if you have time to spare.

Sometimes you reject a question initially because you think it will take too much time. Well, now you have time. You've already locked in all the sure points, so maybe this is the question to do now.

Scoring More Points with ACT Triage

Deciding whether you will do a question *now*, *later*, or *never* is a crucial part of improving your results on the ACT. The whole point of ACT triage is to help you invest your time more profitably. By utilizing the two-pass approach and the concept of triage, you will, unlike most test takers, spend the majority of your time working on questions that seem easy or at least doable. As a result, you will score more points.

NO PENALTY FOR GUESSING

You've done all the questions you know how to do and all the questions you think you know how to do. Now what? You guess.

Imagine for a moment that you are a game show contestant. It's the final, big deal of the day. The host asks you, "Do you want curtain number one, curtain number two, or curtain number three?" As you carefully weigh your options, the members of the audience are screaming out their suggestions, but you can bet there is one suggestion no one in the audience is going to shout at you.

"Skip the question!"

It wouldn't make sense. You have a one-in-three shot of winning, and there is no penalty for guessing wrong. (Okay, you might have to cart home a lifetime supply of toilet paper.)

On the ACT, you don't even have to worry about the toilet paper because there is no guessing penalty at all.

Be Test Smart
Many students with good grades get below-average scores because they refuse to guess.

You Must Fill in an Answer for Every Single Question on the ACT

There are 215 questions on the ACT. If you went into the test room, filled out your name, and then went to sleep for the entire test, your composite score would be just about what you might expect: 0.

If, however, you went into the test room, filled out your name, went to sleep for most of the time, then woke up and picked answer choice (B) or (G) 215 times, your composite score would be a 12!

We would not recommend random guessing as an overall strategy (unless all you need is a 12, and that's only the first percentile), but you can see that it is in your interest to guess on every question you either can't answer or don't get to in time.

Ah, but there's guessing, and then there's *guessing*.

How to Score Higher on the ACT

Try the following question:

Multiple Choice
The ACT is a multiple-choice test. This means you don't have to come up with an answer; you just have to identify the correct one from among the four or five choices provided.

1. What is the French word for "eggplant"?

What? You don't know? Well then, you'd better guess at random. (By the way, there are no questions about vegetables, French or otherwise, on the ACT. We're just using this question to make a point.)

If you really don't know the answer to a question, of course, you should always guess. But before you choose an answer at random, take a look at the problem the way you would see it on the ACT.

1. What is the French word for "eggplant?"

   A. のみもの
   B. すきやき
   C. Aubergine
   D. デザート

Suddenly the question looks a lot easier, doesn't it? You may not have known the correct answer to this question, but you certainly knew three answers that were incorrect.

PROCESS OF ELIMINATION (POE)

The Process of Elimination (POE for short) enables you to make your guesses really count. Incorrect answer choices are often easier to spot than correct ones. Sometimes they are logically absurd; sometimes they are the opposite of the correct answer. If you find a wrong answer, eliminate it. While you will rarely be able to eliminate all of the incorrect answer choices, it is often possible to eliminate one or two, and each time you can eliminate an answer choice, your odds of guessing correctly get better.

Try another question.

1. What is the capital of Malawi?

   A. New York
   B. Lilongwe
   C. Paris
   D. Kinshasa

This time you could probably eliminate only two of the answer choices. However, that meant you were down to a fifty-fifty guess—much better than random guessing.

The Process of Elimination is a tremendously powerful tool. We refer to it in every single chapter of this book, and explain how to use it on a variety of specific types of questions.

Letter of the Day

Which makes more sense—guessing the same letter every time or switching around? If you think you're better off switching around, think again. As counterintuitive as it may seem, you will pick up more points consistently if you always guess the same letter. Sure, you won't get all of your random guesses correct, but you'll get some points. On the contrary, if you vary your guess answer, you might get some correct, but you might miss all of them just as easily.

It doesn't matter what letter you pick as your Letter of the Day. Contrary to popular opinion, you won't get more questions right if you guess choice (C) rather than any other choice. Go crazy, guess choice (A) or (F) on the next ACT you take. Just be consistent.

Chapter 3
Practice Test 1

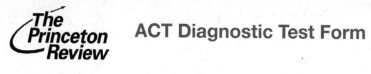

ACT Diagnostic Test Form

Use a No. 2 pencil only. Be sure each mark is dark and completely fills the intended oval. Completely erase any errors or stray marks.

1. **YOUR NAME:** _____
   (Print)   Last   First   M.I.

   SIGNATURE: _____   **DATE:** _____ / _____ / _____

   HOME ADDRESS: _____
   (Print)   Number and Street

   _____
   City   State   Zip

   E-MAIL: _____

   PHONE NO.: _____
   (Print)

   SCHOOL: _____

   CLASS OF: _____

IMPORTANT: Please fill in these boxes exactly as shown on the back cover of your tests book.

2. **TEST FORM**

   _____

3. TEST CODE

⓪	⓪	⓪	⓪
①	①	①	①
②	②	②	②
③	③	③	③
④	④	④	④
⑤	⑤	⑤	⑤
⑥	⑥	⑥	⑥
⑦	⑦	⑦	⑦
⑧	⑧	⑧	⑧
⑨	⑨	⑨	⑨

4. PHONE NUMBER

⓪	⓪	⓪	⓪	⓪	⓪	⓪
①	①	①	①	①	①	①
②	②	②	②	②	②	②
③	③	③	③	③	③	③
④	④	④	④	④	④	④
⑤	⑤	⑤	⑤	⑤	⑤	⑤
⑥	⑥	⑥	⑥	⑥	⑥	⑥
⑦	⑦	⑦	⑦	⑦	⑦	⑦
⑧	⑧	⑧	⑧	⑧	⑧	⑧
⑨	⑨	⑨	⑨	⑨	⑨	⑨

5. YOUR NAME

First 4 letters of last name | FIRST INIT | MID INIT

				FIRST INIT	MID INIT
Ⓐ	Ⓐ	Ⓐ	Ⓐ	Ⓐ	Ⓐ
Ⓑ	Ⓑ	Ⓑ	Ⓑ	Ⓑ	Ⓑ
Ⓒ	Ⓒ	Ⓒ	Ⓒ	Ⓒ	Ⓒ
Ⓓ	Ⓓ	Ⓓ	Ⓓ	Ⓓ	Ⓓ
Ⓔ	Ⓔ	Ⓔ	Ⓔ	Ⓔ	Ⓔ
Ⓕ	Ⓕ	Ⓕ	Ⓕ	Ⓕ	Ⓕ
Ⓖ	Ⓖ	Ⓖ	Ⓖ	Ⓖ	Ⓖ
Ⓗ	Ⓗ	Ⓗ	Ⓗ	Ⓗ	Ⓗ
Ⓘ	Ⓘ	Ⓘ	Ⓘ	Ⓘ	Ⓘ
Ⓙ	Ⓙ	Ⓙ	Ⓙ	Ⓙ	Ⓙ
Ⓚ	Ⓚ	Ⓚ	Ⓚ	Ⓚ	Ⓚ
Ⓛ	Ⓛ	Ⓛ	Ⓛ	Ⓛ	Ⓛ
Ⓜ	Ⓜ	Ⓜ	Ⓜ	Ⓜ	Ⓜ
Ⓝ	Ⓝ	Ⓝ	Ⓝ	Ⓝ	Ⓝ
Ⓞ	Ⓞ	Ⓞ	Ⓞ	Ⓞ	Ⓞ
Ⓟ	Ⓟ	Ⓟ	Ⓟ	Ⓟ	Ⓟ
Ⓠ	Ⓠ	Ⓠ	Ⓠ	Ⓠ	Ⓠ
Ⓡ	Ⓡ	Ⓡ	Ⓡ	Ⓡ	Ⓡ
Ⓢ	Ⓢ	Ⓢ	Ⓢ	Ⓢ	Ⓢ
Ⓣ	Ⓣ	Ⓣ	Ⓣ	Ⓣ	Ⓣ
Ⓤ	Ⓤ	Ⓤ	Ⓤ	Ⓤ	Ⓤ
Ⓥ	Ⓥ	Ⓥ	Ⓥ	Ⓥ	Ⓥ
Ⓦ	Ⓦ	Ⓦ	Ⓦ	Ⓦ	Ⓦ
Ⓧ	Ⓧ	Ⓧ	Ⓧ	Ⓧ	Ⓧ
Ⓨ	Ⓨ	Ⓨ	Ⓨ	Ⓨ	Ⓨ
Ⓩ	Ⓩ	Ⓩ	Ⓩ	Ⓩ	Ⓩ

6. DATE OF BIRTH

MONTH	DAY		YEAR	
○ JAN				
○ FEB				
○ MAR	⓪	⓪	⓪	⓪
○ APR	①	①	①	①
○ MAY	②	②	②	②
○ JUN	③	③	③	③
○ JUL		④	④	④
○ AUG		⑤	⑤	⑤
○ SEP		⑥	⑥	⑥
○ OCT		⑦	⑦	⑦
○ NOV		⑧	⑧	⑧
○ DEC		⑨	⑨	⑨

7. SEX

○ MALE
○ FEMALE

8. OTHER

1 Ⓐ Ⓑ Ⓒ Ⓓ Ⓔ
2 Ⓐ Ⓑ Ⓒ Ⓓ Ⓔ
3 Ⓐ Ⓑ Ⓒ Ⓓ Ⓔ

OpScan *i*NSIGHT™ forms by Pearson NCS EM-255315-1:654321   Printed in U.S.A.

THIS PAGE INTENTIONALLY LEFT BLANK

The Princeton Review
Diagnostic ACT Form

Completely darken bubbles with a No. 2 pencil. If you make a mistake, be sure to erase mark completely. Erase all stray marks.

ENGLISH

1 Ⓐ Ⓑ Ⓒ Ⓓ	21 Ⓐ Ⓑ Ⓒ Ⓓ	41 Ⓐ Ⓑ Ⓒ Ⓓ	61 Ⓐ Ⓑ Ⓒ Ⓓ
2 Ⓕ Ⓖ Ⓗ Ⓙ	22 Ⓕ Ⓖ Ⓗ Ⓙ	42 Ⓕ Ⓖ Ⓗ Ⓙ	62 Ⓕ Ⓖ Ⓗ Ⓙ
3 Ⓐ Ⓑ Ⓒ Ⓓ	23 Ⓐ Ⓑ Ⓒ Ⓓ	43 Ⓐ Ⓑ Ⓒ Ⓓ	63 Ⓐ Ⓑ Ⓒ Ⓓ
4 Ⓕ Ⓖ Ⓗ Ⓙ	24 Ⓕ Ⓖ Ⓗ Ⓙ	44 Ⓕ Ⓖ Ⓗ Ⓙ	64 Ⓕ Ⓖ Ⓗ Ⓙ
5 Ⓐ Ⓑ Ⓒ Ⓓ	25 Ⓐ Ⓑ Ⓒ Ⓓ	45 Ⓐ Ⓑ Ⓒ Ⓓ	65 Ⓐ Ⓑ Ⓒ Ⓓ
6 Ⓕ Ⓖ Ⓗ Ⓙ	26 Ⓕ Ⓖ Ⓗ Ⓙ	46 Ⓕ Ⓖ Ⓗ Ⓙ	66 Ⓕ Ⓖ Ⓗ Ⓙ
7 Ⓐ Ⓑ Ⓒ Ⓓ	27 Ⓐ Ⓑ Ⓒ Ⓓ	47 Ⓐ Ⓑ Ⓒ Ⓓ	67 Ⓐ Ⓑ Ⓒ Ⓓ
8 Ⓕ Ⓖ Ⓗ Ⓙ	28 Ⓕ Ⓖ Ⓗ Ⓙ	48 Ⓕ Ⓖ Ⓗ Ⓙ	68 Ⓕ Ⓖ Ⓗ Ⓙ
9 Ⓐ Ⓑ Ⓒ Ⓓ	29 Ⓐ Ⓑ Ⓒ Ⓓ	49 Ⓐ Ⓑ Ⓒ Ⓓ	69 Ⓐ Ⓑ Ⓒ Ⓓ
10 Ⓕ Ⓖ Ⓗ Ⓙ	30 Ⓕ Ⓖ Ⓗ Ⓙ	50 Ⓕ Ⓖ Ⓗ Ⓙ	70 Ⓕ Ⓖ Ⓗ Ⓙ
11 Ⓐ Ⓑ Ⓒ Ⓓ	31 Ⓐ Ⓑ Ⓒ Ⓓ	51 Ⓐ Ⓑ Ⓒ Ⓓ	71 Ⓐ Ⓑ Ⓒ Ⓓ
12 Ⓕ Ⓖ Ⓗ Ⓙ	32 Ⓕ Ⓖ Ⓗ Ⓙ	52 Ⓕ Ⓖ Ⓗ Ⓙ	72 Ⓕ Ⓖ Ⓗ Ⓙ
13 Ⓐ Ⓑ Ⓒ Ⓓ	33 Ⓐ Ⓑ Ⓒ Ⓓ	53 Ⓐ Ⓑ Ⓒ Ⓓ	73 Ⓐ Ⓑ Ⓒ Ⓓ
14 Ⓕ Ⓖ Ⓗ Ⓙ	34 Ⓕ Ⓖ Ⓗ Ⓙ	54 Ⓕ Ⓖ Ⓗ Ⓙ	74 Ⓕ Ⓖ Ⓗ Ⓙ
15 Ⓐ Ⓑ Ⓒ Ⓓ	35 Ⓐ Ⓑ Ⓒ Ⓓ	55 Ⓐ Ⓑ Ⓒ Ⓓ	75 Ⓐ Ⓑ Ⓒ Ⓓ
16 Ⓕ Ⓖ Ⓗ Ⓙ	36 Ⓕ Ⓖ Ⓗ Ⓙ	56 Ⓕ Ⓖ Ⓗ Ⓙ	
17 Ⓐ Ⓑ Ⓒ Ⓓ	37 Ⓐ Ⓑ Ⓒ Ⓓ	57 Ⓐ Ⓑ Ⓒ Ⓓ	
18 Ⓕ Ⓖ Ⓗ Ⓙ	38 Ⓕ Ⓖ Ⓗ Ⓙ	58 Ⓕ Ⓖ Ⓗ Ⓙ	
19 Ⓐ Ⓑ Ⓒ Ⓓ	39 Ⓐ Ⓑ Ⓒ Ⓓ	59 Ⓐ Ⓑ Ⓒ Ⓓ	
20 Ⓕ Ⓖ Ⓗ Ⓙ	40 Ⓕ Ⓖ Ⓗ Ⓙ	60 Ⓕ Ⓖ Ⓗ Ⓙ	

MATHEMATICS

1 Ⓐ Ⓑ Ⓒ Ⓓ Ⓔ	16 Ⓕ Ⓖ Ⓗ Ⓙ Ⓚ	31 Ⓐ Ⓑ Ⓒ Ⓓ Ⓔ	46 Ⓕ Ⓖ Ⓗ Ⓙ Ⓚ
2 Ⓕ Ⓖ Ⓗ Ⓙ Ⓚ	17 Ⓐ Ⓑ Ⓒ Ⓓ Ⓔ	32 Ⓕ Ⓖ Ⓗ Ⓙ Ⓚ	47 Ⓐ Ⓑ Ⓒ Ⓓ Ⓔ
3 Ⓐ Ⓑ Ⓒ Ⓓ Ⓔ	18 Ⓕ Ⓖ Ⓗ Ⓙ Ⓚ	33 Ⓐ Ⓑ Ⓒ Ⓓ Ⓔ	48 Ⓕ Ⓖ Ⓗ Ⓙ Ⓚ
4 Ⓕ Ⓖ Ⓗ Ⓙ Ⓚ	19 Ⓐ Ⓑ Ⓒ Ⓓ Ⓔ	34 Ⓕ Ⓖ Ⓗ Ⓙ Ⓚ	49 Ⓐ Ⓑ Ⓒ Ⓓ Ⓔ
5 Ⓐ Ⓑ Ⓒ Ⓓ Ⓔ	20 Ⓕ Ⓖ Ⓗ Ⓙ Ⓚ	35 Ⓐ Ⓑ Ⓒ Ⓓ Ⓔ	50 Ⓕ Ⓖ Ⓗ Ⓙ Ⓚ
6 Ⓕ Ⓖ Ⓗ Ⓙ Ⓚ	21 Ⓐ Ⓑ Ⓒ Ⓓ Ⓔ	36 Ⓕ Ⓖ Ⓗ Ⓙ Ⓚ	51 Ⓐ Ⓑ Ⓒ Ⓓ Ⓔ
7 Ⓐ Ⓑ Ⓒ Ⓓ Ⓔ	22 Ⓕ Ⓖ Ⓗ Ⓙ Ⓚ	37 Ⓐ Ⓑ Ⓒ Ⓓ Ⓔ	52 Ⓕ Ⓖ Ⓗ Ⓙ Ⓚ
8 Ⓕ Ⓖ Ⓗ Ⓙ Ⓚ	23 Ⓐ Ⓑ Ⓒ Ⓓ Ⓔ	38 Ⓕ Ⓖ Ⓗ Ⓙ Ⓚ	53 Ⓐ Ⓑ Ⓒ Ⓓ Ⓔ
9 Ⓐ Ⓑ Ⓒ Ⓓ Ⓔ	24 Ⓕ Ⓖ Ⓗ Ⓙ Ⓚ	39 Ⓐ Ⓑ Ⓒ Ⓓ Ⓔ	54 Ⓕ Ⓖ Ⓗ Ⓙ Ⓚ
10 Ⓕ Ⓖ Ⓗ Ⓙ Ⓚ	25 Ⓐ Ⓑ Ⓒ Ⓓ Ⓔ	40 Ⓕ Ⓖ Ⓗ Ⓙ Ⓚ	55 Ⓐ Ⓑ Ⓒ Ⓓ Ⓔ
11 Ⓐ Ⓑ Ⓒ Ⓓ Ⓔ	26 Ⓕ Ⓖ Ⓗ Ⓙ Ⓚ	41 Ⓐ Ⓑ Ⓒ Ⓓ Ⓔ	56 Ⓕ Ⓖ Ⓗ Ⓙ Ⓚ
12 Ⓕ Ⓖ Ⓗ Ⓙ Ⓚ	27 Ⓐ Ⓑ Ⓒ Ⓓ Ⓔ	42 Ⓕ Ⓖ Ⓗ Ⓙ Ⓚ	57 Ⓐ Ⓑ Ⓒ Ⓓ Ⓔ
13 Ⓐ Ⓑ Ⓒ Ⓓ Ⓔ	28 Ⓕ Ⓖ Ⓗ Ⓙ Ⓚ	43 Ⓐ Ⓑ Ⓒ Ⓓ Ⓔ	58 Ⓕ Ⓖ Ⓗ Ⓙ Ⓚ
14 Ⓕ Ⓖ Ⓗ Ⓙ Ⓚ	29 Ⓐ Ⓑ Ⓒ Ⓓ Ⓔ	44 Ⓕ Ⓖ Ⓗ Ⓙ Ⓚ	59 Ⓐ Ⓑ Ⓒ Ⓓ Ⓔ
15 Ⓐ Ⓑ Ⓒ Ⓓ Ⓔ	30 Ⓕ Ⓖ Ⓗ Ⓙ Ⓚ	45 Ⓐ Ⓑ Ⓒ Ⓓ Ⓔ	60 Ⓕ Ⓖ Ⓗ Ⓙ Ⓚ

The Princeton Review
Diagnostic ACT Form

READING

1 Ⓐ	Ⓑ	Ⓒ	Ⓓ	11 Ⓐ	Ⓑ	Ⓒ	Ⓓ	21 Ⓐ	Ⓑ	Ⓒ	Ⓓ	31 Ⓐ	Ⓑ	Ⓒ	Ⓓ
2 Ⓕ	Ⓖ	Ⓗ	Ⓙ	12 Ⓕ	Ⓖ	Ⓗ	Ⓙ	22 Ⓕ	Ⓖ	Ⓗ	Ⓙ	32 Ⓕ	Ⓖ	Ⓗ	Ⓙ
3 Ⓐ	Ⓑ	Ⓒ	Ⓓ	13 Ⓐ	Ⓑ	Ⓒ	Ⓓ	23 Ⓐ	Ⓑ	Ⓒ	Ⓓ	33 Ⓐ	Ⓑ	Ⓒ	Ⓓ
4 Ⓕ	Ⓖ	Ⓗ	Ⓙ	14 Ⓕ	Ⓖ	Ⓗ	Ⓙ	24 Ⓕ	Ⓖ	Ⓗ	Ⓙ	34 Ⓕ	Ⓖ	Ⓗ	Ⓙ
5 Ⓐ	Ⓑ	Ⓒ	Ⓓ	15 Ⓐ	Ⓑ	Ⓒ	Ⓓ	25 Ⓐ	Ⓑ	Ⓒ	Ⓓ	35 Ⓐ	Ⓑ	Ⓒ	Ⓓ
6 Ⓕ	Ⓖ	Ⓗ	Ⓙ	16 Ⓕ	Ⓖ	Ⓗ	Ⓙ	26 Ⓕ	Ⓖ	Ⓗ	Ⓙ	36 Ⓕ	Ⓖ	Ⓗ	Ⓙ
7 Ⓐ	Ⓑ	Ⓒ	Ⓓ	17 Ⓐ	Ⓑ	Ⓒ	Ⓓ	27 Ⓐ	Ⓑ	Ⓒ	Ⓓ	37 Ⓐ	Ⓑ	Ⓒ	Ⓓ
8 Ⓕ	Ⓖ	Ⓗ	Ⓙ	18 Ⓕ	Ⓖ	Ⓗ	Ⓙ	28 Ⓕ	Ⓖ	Ⓗ	Ⓙ	38 Ⓕ	Ⓖ	Ⓗ	Ⓙ
9 Ⓐ	Ⓑ	Ⓒ	Ⓓ	19 Ⓐ	Ⓑ	Ⓒ	Ⓓ	29 Ⓐ	Ⓑ	Ⓒ	Ⓓ	39 Ⓐ	Ⓑ	Ⓒ	Ⓓ
10 Ⓕ	Ⓖ	Ⓗ	Ⓙ	20 Ⓕ	Ⓖ	Ⓗ	Ⓙ	30 Ⓕ	Ⓖ	Ⓗ	Ⓙ	40 Ⓕ	Ⓖ	Ⓗ	Ⓙ

SCIENCE REASONING

1 Ⓐ	Ⓑ	Ⓒ	Ⓓ	11 Ⓐ	Ⓑ	Ⓒ	Ⓓ	21 Ⓐ	Ⓑ	Ⓒ	Ⓓ	31 Ⓐ	Ⓑ	Ⓒ	Ⓓ
2 Ⓕ	Ⓖ	Ⓗ	Ⓙ	12 Ⓕ	Ⓖ	Ⓗ	Ⓙ	22 Ⓕ	Ⓖ	Ⓗ	Ⓙ	32 Ⓕ	Ⓖ	Ⓗ	Ⓙ
3 Ⓐ	Ⓑ	Ⓒ	Ⓓ	13 Ⓐ	Ⓑ	Ⓒ	Ⓓ	23 Ⓐ	Ⓑ	Ⓒ	Ⓓ	33 Ⓐ	Ⓑ	Ⓒ	Ⓓ
4 Ⓕ	Ⓖ	Ⓗ	Ⓙ	14 Ⓕ	Ⓖ	Ⓗ	Ⓙ	24 Ⓕ	Ⓖ	Ⓗ	Ⓙ	34 Ⓕ	Ⓖ	Ⓗ	Ⓙ
5 Ⓐ	Ⓑ	Ⓒ	Ⓓ	15 Ⓐ	Ⓑ	Ⓒ	Ⓓ	25 Ⓐ	Ⓑ	Ⓒ	Ⓓ	35 Ⓐ	Ⓑ	Ⓒ	Ⓓ
6 Ⓕ	Ⓖ	Ⓗ	Ⓙ	16 Ⓕ	Ⓖ	Ⓗ	Ⓙ	26 Ⓕ	Ⓖ	Ⓗ	Ⓙ	36 Ⓕ	Ⓖ	Ⓗ	Ⓙ
7 Ⓐ	Ⓑ	Ⓒ	Ⓓ	17 Ⓐ	Ⓑ	Ⓒ	Ⓓ	27 Ⓐ	Ⓑ	Ⓒ	Ⓓ	37 Ⓐ	Ⓑ	Ⓒ	Ⓓ
8 Ⓕ	Ⓖ	Ⓗ	Ⓙ	18 Ⓕ	Ⓖ	Ⓗ	Ⓙ	28 Ⓕ	Ⓖ	Ⓗ	Ⓙ	38 Ⓕ	Ⓖ	Ⓗ	Ⓙ
9 Ⓐ	Ⓑ	Ⓒ	Ⓓ	19 Ⓐ	Ⓑ	Ⓒ	Ⓓ	29 Ⓐ	Ⓑ	Ⓒ	Ⓓ	39 Ⓐ	Ⓑ	Ⓒ	Ⓓ
10 Ⓕ	Ⓖ	Ⓗ	Ⓙ	20 Ⓕ	Ⓖ	Ⓗ	Ⓙ	30 Ⓕ	Ⓖ	Ⓗ	Ⓙ	40 Ⓕ	Ⓖ	Ⓗ	Ⓙ

The Princeton Review
Diagnostic ACT Form

ESSAY

Begin your essay on this side. If necessary, continue on the opposite side.

Continue on the opposite side if necessary.

The Princeton Review
Diagnostic ACT Form

Continued from previous page.

The Princeton Review
Diagnostic ACT Form

Continued from previous page.

The Princeton Review
Diagnostic ACT Form

Continued from previous page.

THIS PAGE INTENTIONALLY LEFT BLANK

ACT ENGLISH TEST
45 Minutes—75 Questions

DIRECTIONS: In the five passages that follow, certain words and phrases are underlined and numbered. In the right-hand column, you will find alternatives for each underlined part. In most cases, you are to choose the one that best expresses the idea, makes the statement appropriate for standard written English, or is worded most consistently with the style and tone of the passage as a whole. If you think the original version is best, choose "NO CHANGE." In some cases, you will find in the right-hand column a question about the underlined part. You are to choose the best answer to the question.

You will also find questions about a section of the passage or the passage as a whole. These questions do not refer to an underlined portion of the passage but rather are identified by a number or numbers in a box.

For each question, choose the alternative you consider best and blacken the corresponding oval on your answer document. Read each passage through once before you begin to answer the questions that accompany it. For many of the questions, you must read several sentences beyond the question to determine the answer. Be sure that you have read far enough ahead each time you choose an alternative.

PASSAGE I

The Record

The moment I had been anticipating finally came on a seemingly routine Monday. I arrived home to find a flat package; left by the delivery man casually leaning against the front screen door. Reading the words *Caution! Do not bend!*

scrawled on the top of the box, I immediately recognized my uncle's sloppy handwriting. I quickly ushered the box

inside, and my heart skipping a beat (or two). I knew what the box contained but still felt as anxious as a child on Christmas morning. Could this *really* be the old vinyl record?

My hands trembled as I opened the box, of which I was thrilled to see that it did indeed contain the record I had been seeking for years. To an outsider, this dusty disc with its faded hand-written label would seem inconsequential. To others, on the other hand, it was worth something far greater. The record was a compilation from the greatest musician I had ever known—my grandfather.

1. A. NO CHANGE
   B. package, left by the delivery man
   C. package; left by the delivery man,
   D. package, left by the delivery man,

2. F. NO CHANGE
   G. were scrawled on
   H. scrawl on
   J. scrawled

3. A. NO CHANGE
   B. inside,
   C. inside and
   D. inside, when

4. F. NO CHANGE
   G. box that
   H. box, and
   J. box

5. Given that all the choices are true, which one would most effectively illustrate the difference between outsiders' perception of the record and its actual significance to the writer's family?

   A. NO CHANGE
   B. In fact, the recording was not heard by many people outside my family.
   C. To my family, however, it was a precious heirloom.
   D. The disc would be in better condition had my uncle stored it in a sleeve.

GO ON TO THE NEXT PAGE.

Several years before he married my grandmother, Papa would make his living as a folk singer in a
₆

band. Performing in music halls and local festivals. He recorded
₇

a single album produced by Great Sounds Records before
₈
giving up his professional music career to pursue business. This

record was all that remained of his life's passion—in fact, there
₉

had been only one surviving copy since Papa's death 10 years
₁₀

earlier. It took many years of begging and pleading to convince
₁₁
my uncle to pass the record down to me.

I brought out my old record player from the attic and gently placed the disc on the turntable. As soft, twanging notes filled the room, I was transported to my grandfather's cabin, located at the foot the mountains. My cousins and I would
₁₂
gather around the campfire every night to roast marshmallows, cook hotdogs, and listen to my grandfather's old stories.

Of the many familiar favorites, Papa would pick up his guitar
₁₃
and play all of our familiar tunes.
₁₃

When the record started playing one of my favorite songs, I struggled to hold back my tears. It was a bittersweet reminder of

6. **F.** NO CHANGE
   G. would have made
   H. would have been making
   J. had made

7. **A.** NO CHANGE
   B. band; performing
   C. band, which he had performed
   D. band, performing

8. **F.** NO CHANGE
   G. album, produced by Great Sounds Records,
   H. Great Sounds Records album
   J. album

9. **A.** NO CHANGE
   B. even so,
   C. since,
   D. for example,

10. **F.** NO CHANGE
    G. had been about
    H. is
    J. was to be

11. **A.** NO CHANGE
    B. begging
    C. pleadingly begging
    D. begging the plea

12. At this point in the essay, the writer wants to suggest the significance of his grandfather's cabin to the writer's upbringing. Given that all the choices are true, which one would best accomplish that purpose?
    F. NO CHANGE
    G. where I had spent many childhood summers.
    H. which I still remembered well.
    J. a family property for many generations.

13. **A.** NO CHANGE
    B. Playing all of our favorite songs, the many familiar tunes and guitar would be picked up by Papa.
    C. Papa would also pick up his guitar and strum familiar tunes, playing all of our favorite songs, of which there were many.
    D. Picking up his guitar, Papa would also play strumming familiar tunes all of our favorite, of which there were many, songs.

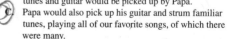

GO ON TO THE NEXT PAGE.

the man I loved and <u>missed,</u> Papa's gentle voice on the record,
₁₄

however, assured <u>me,</u> that he was still with me, both in spirit
₁₅
and in song.

14. F. NO CHANGE
   G. missed for
   H. missed.
   J. missed

15. A. NO CHANGE
   B. me
   C. me—
   D. me;

Passage II

Road Trips Back Home

During my junior year of college, it became a kind of ritual

for a group of us to hop in a car and "discover" a new suburb

every month. At first, we all agreed, we had come to college in

this major city to escape what we thought were our boring lives

in our various places of origin, but after a time, we realized that

it would be impossible for us to turn our backs on our old <u>lives</u>
₁₆

completely. <u>I grew up in Pennsylvania, many parts of which</u>
₁₇
<u>look like the ones we drove to.</u>
₁₇

The first stop was typically some old diner, which

reminded each of us of one from our various hometowns. There

we'd usually sit, chat with the restaurant's <u>owners</u> drink a cup
₁₈
of coffee, and figure out which new and exciting place we'd

be driving to next. Even now I can remember one diner in

Maryland, whose sign we could see flickering from the highway

as we turned off <u>looking forward to it in anticipation.</u> Although
₁₉
we had all agreed that it had to be a new town each time, we

16. F. NO CHANGE
   G. lives,
   H. live's
   J. lives'

17. Given that all the choices are true, which one best supports
the point that the narrator and his friends all shared a common background?

   A. NO CHANGE
   B. Many suburbs have become as populous as the cities
they surround.
   C. The first major migration of families from the city to
the suburbs occurred in the late 1940s and early 1950s.
   D. Our hometowns were all over the map, but they all
shared a palpable likeness.

18. F. NO CHANGE
   G. owners;
   H. owners'
   J. owners,

19. A. NO CHANGE
   B. in anticipation.
   C. excited and looking forward to it.
   D. in anticipation and expectation.

GO ON TO THE NEXT PAGE.

tacitly agreed a few times to break the rules and come back to
this place. [20]

After we had taken nourishment (usually a grilled cheese
sandwich, a patty melt, or something similarly nutritious
that could be ordered from the menu) for our "big night out,"
21
we would then drive on. We got to know the lay of the land
so well that we could usually just follow our noses to the
kinds of places we liked to visit in these towns, typically
stopping by the biggest retailer we could find. There we'd
buy industrial-sized packs from childhood of instant noodles,
22
huge packs of soda, and other types of foods we all remembered
but which we were either too embarrassed to buy in front
of other people at the University market, or which were too

expensive in the city, where there is a lot more variety.
23

Going to as many places like this as we could, we were always
24
sure to happen upon something strangely familiar to us. The
place—whether it was one of a million grocery stores, movie

theaters, or fast-food restaurants—were unimportant; it seemed
25
that everywhere had something special for at least one of us,

---

20. At this point, the writer is considering adding the following true statement:

> Many diners have been forced to shut down to make way for larger, national chain restaurants.

Should the writer make the addition here?

- **F.** Yes, because it provides important contextual information relevant to the passage.
- **G.** Yes, because it helps readers to see why the narrator was drawn to this particular diner.
- **H.** No, because it interrupts the flow of the paragraph, which is primarily a personal reflection.
- **J.** No, because it alters the focus of the paragraph from a discussion of driving to a discussion of specific places.

21. **A.** NO CHANGE
- **B.** whom could be ordered from
- **C.** whom could order
- **D.** that were ordering

22. The best placement for the underlined phrase would be:
- **F.** where it is now
- **G.** after the word *noodles.*
- **H.** after the word *soda.*
- **J.** after the word *remembered*

23. Which choice most effectively supports and elaborates on the description in an earlier part of this sentence?
- **A.** NO CHANGE
- **B.** where prices for such basic foods were steep.
- **C.** where we didn't like to drive the car.
- **D.** where most of us had only small refrigerators.

24. Which of the following alternatives to the underlined portion would NOT be acceptable?
- **F.** As we went
- **G.** While going
- **H.** While we went
- **J.** We went

25. **A.** NO CHANGE
- **B.** was
- **C.** have been
- **D.** are

GO ON TO THE NEXT PAGE.

and <u>even now, many years on, I still think of these trips fondly.</u>
₂₆

    Looking back, I'm still not sure why we took these trips.

<u>Nevertheless,</u> I have been living in an urban environment
₂₇
now for almost eight years, and should I ever have to move

back to the suburbs, I will certainly go reluctantly. Sometimes,

though, even now that I live in a different city, I'll still sneak

out to those kinds of places once in a while and just drive

<u>about the town.</u> I guess, in a way, many of those early memories
₂₈
are like that diner sign we could see from the highway; most

people would never notice that old sign, but to those of us who

<u>cherish it in our hearts</u> and what it represents, we all harbored
₂₉
a great hope that it would still be burning the same as we

remembered every time we drove by or <u>came back.</u>
₃₀

26. Given that all the choices are true, which one most effectively signals the shift in focus that occurs when moving from this paragraph to the next?
F. NO CHANGE
G. we all remained friends until we graduated.
H. I regret not having spent more time in the city when I had the chance.
J. I haven't been back to any of those places since I graduated.

27. A. NO CHANGE
B. Therefore,
C. Nonetheless,
D. DELETE the underlined portion.

28. Which of the following alternatives to the underlined portion would NOT be acceptable?
F. among the town.
G. about.
H. around.
J. around the town.

29. A. NO CHANGE
B. have a great fondness for it
C. have strong feelings of adoration for it
D. cherish it

30. F. NO CHANGE
G. we were coming back.
H. were returning.
J. there was a return by us.

GO ON TO THE NEXT PAGE.

Passage III

> The following paragraphs may or may not be in the most logical order. Each paragraph is numbered in brackets, and question 45 will ask you to choose where Paragraph 3 should most logically be placed.

The Palio of Siena

[1]

Siena is an old, picturesque city located in the hills of Tuscany. <u>Even though</u> its inhabitants live modern lives, many historical markers from as far back as medieval Italy still

remain throughout the city. [32] Another remnant from Siena's rich history that still plays a very prominent role today is the tradition of *Il Palio*.

[2]

Il Palio di Siena is <u>a biannual horse race that is held twice a year,</u> once in July and once in August. A field of ten bareback horses races three laps around a dangerously steep track circling the city's central plaza, the *Piazza del Campo*, <u>each with two dreaded right-angle turns.</u> Even though *Il Palio*

31. Which of the following alternatives to the underlined portion would be LEAST acceptable?

  A. Although
  B. While
  C. Though
  D. When

32. Which of the following true statements, if inserted here, would best connect the first part of Paragraph 1 with the last part while illustrating the main idea of this paragraph?

  F. Like most Italian cities, Siena is very serious about soccer, a modern sport codified in England in the 1800s.
  G. Cobblestone streets and Gothic architecture are blended with modern sidewalk cafes and trendy designer stores.
  H. The city of Siena is certainly a mixture of ancient and contemporary practices.
  J. Siena is a major cultural center that offers numerous examples of art and architecture by Renaissance masters.

33. A. NO CHANGE
  B. a biannual race that is held two times a year,
  C. a horse race that is held twice a year,
  D. a biannual horse race, held

34. Assuming that a period will always be placed at the end of the sentence, the best placement for the underlined phrase would be:

  F. where it is now.
  G. after the words *horses race* (setting the phrase off with commas).
  H. after the word *laps* (setting the phrase off with commas).
  J. after the word *plaza* (setting the phrase off with commas).

GO ON TO THE NEXT PAGE.

lasted only about 90 seconds, its importance in Siena goes far
₃₅
beyond the race itself.

[3]

Members are fiercely committed emotionally, socially,
and financially to their own *contrada*. Because the members
₃₆
voluntarily tax themselves to support their own *contrada* and to
invest in a good horse and jockey for the biannual race. Jockey
salaries for a single race often exceed 250,000 euros! This
is, however, a small price to pay to achieve victory at *Il Palio*.
₃₇
Seeing the colors and arms of their *contrada* in the winner's
circle is the most glorious event—even more so than getting

married for many Sienese citizens. Old men weep openly out of
₃₈

sheer joy, and elated adults and children parade. Throughout the
₃₉
city with their newly won silk banner, also called the *palio*.

[4]

The brief race is a spectacular culmination of an entire way
of life in Siena. Every citizen belongs to one of seventeen city
districts, collectively known as the *Contrade*. *Contrada* is the
₄₀
term for a single district that has its own color and arms, such
as the *Aquila* (the eagle) or *Bruco* (the caterpillar). A *contrada*
is the source of so much local patriotism that every important
event; from baptisms to food festivals, is celebrated only within
₄₁

one's own *contrada* and fellow members, who become more
₄₂
like family.

[5]

After the actual race day, the *Palio* festivities continue for a
minimum of two weeks. Thousands of visitors from around the

35. A. NO CHANGE
    B. will last
    C. lasts
    D. had lasted

36. F. NO CHANGE
    G. Though this
    H. In addition, they
    J. They

37. A. NO CHANGE
    B. moreover,
    C. for instance,
    D. therefore,

38. F. NO CHANGE
    G. married—for
    H. married, for
    J. married; for

39. A. NO CHANGE
    B. parade; throughout
    C. parade throughout
    D. parade throughout,

40. F. NO CHANGE
    G. *Contrade*
    H. *Contrade*,
    J. *Contrade* yet

41. A. NO CHANGE
    B. event, from
    C. event: from
    D. event—from

42. F. NO CHANGE
    G. for whose
    H. whose
    J. whom

GO ON TO THE NEXT PAGE.

world travel to Siena during the <u>summer; not</u> only to witness
₄₃

43. A. NO CHANGE
   B. summer. Not
   C. summer not
   D. summer, not

the exciting race but also to attend the after-parties <u>were thrown</u>
₄₄
by the locals. While the *Palio* is not as important to outsiders
who do not live in Siena as it is to the Sienese, the race and the
festivities that follow are a spectacular experience.

44. F. NO CHANGE
   G. thrown
   H. were threw
   J. threw

> Question 45 asks about the preceding passage as a whole.

45. For the sake of the logic and coherence of this essay, the best placement for Paragraph 3 would be:

   A. where it is now.
   B. before Paragraph 1.
   C. before Paragraph 2.
   D. before Paragraph 5.

> The following paragraphs may or may not be in the most logical order. Each paragraph is numbered in brackets, and question 59 will ask you to choose where Paragraph 2 should most logically be placed.

Sherwood Anderson the Pioneer

[1]

Sherwood Anderson saw his first novel, *Windy McPherson's Son*, published in 1916, but it was not until 1919 with the publication of his masterpiece *Winesburg, Ohio* that Anderson was pushed to the forefront of <u>it</u> in American
₄₆
literature. The latter book, something between a short-story

46. F. NO CHANGE
   G. this
   H. a new movement
   J. a thing

collection and a novel, <u>helping</u> to inaugurate an age of a truly
₄₇
homespun American Modernism.

47. A. NO CHANGE
   B. which helped
   C. helped
   D. was helped

GO ON TO THE NEXT PAGE.

[2]

As other writers began to supplant him in the popular imagination, Anderson tireless continued his literary
48
experimentation until his death in 1941. In the contemporary

popular imagination, Anderson's influence often appears to be
49
diminishing. But it takes only a few pages of *Winesburg, Ohio* or many of his other short stories, articles, and novels to see that Anderson is still very much with us today and that much of what we understand about ourselves as Americans was made clear to us only by the pen of the advertising man from Ohio.

[3]

Sherwood Anderson would be seen by a new generation of American writers as the first author to take a real step until
50
creating a type of literature that was in tune with something previously only associated with Europe. Anderson was able to

fuse his sense of the passing of the Industrial Age in America
51
with a type of uniquely American expression that sought to replace previous literary conventions with more local expressions of fragmentation and alienation.

[4]

With *Winesburg, Ohio*, Anderson inspired a younger group
52
of writers, among whose ranks were Ernest Hemingway and William Faulkner, to embrace their American experiences and to express them in ways separate from those being expressed by

European writers or American expatriates, as American writers
53
living abroad were known. When *Winesburg, Ohio* finally
53

48. The best placement for the underlined word would be:

F. where it is now.
G. before the word *death*.
H. after the word *experimentation*.
J. before the word *literary*.

49. Which of the following alternatives to the underlined portion would NOT be acceptable?

A. can seem to be
B. appeared to be
C. seems to be
D. can appear to be

50. F. NO CHANGE
G. at
H. toward
J. DELETE the underlined portion.

51. A. NO CHANGE
B. fuse;
C. fuse:
D. fuse,

52. Which of the following alternatives to the underlined portion would be LEAST acceptable?

F. encouraged
G. motivated
H. forced
J. emboldened

53. A. NO CHANGE
B. expatriates, as American writers living abroad, were known.
C. expatriates as American writers living abroad were known.
D. expatriates as American writers living abroad, were known.

GO ON TO THE NEXT PAGE.

appeared in 1919, its general reception was <u>positive, but limited</u>
₅₄

to those who were able to find copies of the book. <u>Anderson's</u>
₅₅
<u>later books, such as *Dark Laughter*, would go on to sell many</u>
₅₅
<u>more copies.</u>
₅₅

[5]

    In the 1920s, Anderson wrote some direct responses to the
more explicit examples of literary Modernism in Europe. In

the 1930s, Anderson wrote *Beyond Desire* [56] But Anderson's
most important contributions in the 1920s and 1930s are best

felt indirectly through the works <u>of the various writers</u> he
₅₇
inspired. Anderson was among the first to explore the troubled
relationship between the city and the rural town, the direct

style to which we so often apply the <u>name, "American," and</u>
₅₈
the idea that deeply intellectual concerns can be relevant to
everyday people as much as they can to academics. Even
today, Anderson's initial treatment of these themes remains
an important starting point for anyone interested in
American culture.

54. F. NO CHANGE
   G. positive but limited,
   H. positive; but limited
   J. positive but limited

55. Given that all the choices are true, which one best supports
the point that although Anderson's book was difficult to
find, those who read it were very impressed?
   A. NO CHANGE
   B. Many critics still preferred the older European models
of writing.
   C. *Winesburg, Ohio* remains one of Anderson's best-loved
books.
   D. Those who did secure a copy of *Winesburg, Ohio* felt
that it inaugurated a new age in American literature.

56. Given that all the following are true, which one, if added
here, would provide the clearest and most effective indication that Anderson was doing things that had not been
done before in American literature?
   F. , which addressed social questions that only social
scientists and propagandists dared touch.
   G. , which was heavily influenced by the literature of the
Southern Populist movement.
   H. , which has been named by many literary critics as a
highlight from Anderson's later work.
   J. , which was not as highly revered as *Winesburg, Ohio*.

57. The best placement for the underlined phrase would be:
   A. where it is now.
   B. after the word *contributions*.
   C. after the word *1930s*.
   D. after the word *inspired* (ending the sentence with a
period).

58. F. NO CHANGE
   G. name "American,"
   H. name "American"
   J. name, "American"

GO ON TO THE NEXT PAGE.

Questions 59 and 60 ask about the preceding passage as a whole.

59. For the sake of the logic and coherence of this essay, Paragraph 2 should be placed:

   A. where it is now.
   B. after Paragraph 3.
   C. after Paragraph 4.
   D. after Paragraph 5.

60. Suppose the writer's goal was to draft an essay that would show the influence of one American author on the work of future authors. Does this essay successfully accomplish this goal?

   F. Yes, because it describes an interesting group of authors and focuses on the literature of a particular country.
   G. Yes, because it gives a brief description of Sherwood Anderson's writing career and discusses his influence on writers whom his work inspired.
   H. No, because it limits the focus to the contrasts between American writing and European writing.
   J. No, because it refers only to events that took place in the twenties and thirties.

PASSAGE V

Women at Work

World War II offered numerous employment opportunities for women in the United States. As the men headed to the war front, the work force <u>retracted and diminished</u> on the
₆₁

home front, and women <u>begun</u> to take over responsibilities
₆₂

traditionally assigned to men. <u>These</u> responsibilities included
₆₃
work previously deemed inappropriate for women.

The government realized that participation in the war <u>but</u>
₆₄
required the use of all national resources. American industrial facilities were turned into war production factories, and the government targeted the female population as an essential source of labor. Women worked in factories and shipyards

61. A. NO CHANGE
   B. retracted diminishingly
   C. diminished
   D. DELETE the underlined portion.

62. F. NO CHANGE
   G. has began
   H. would of begun
   J. began

63. A. NO CHANGE
   B. The traditionally male
   C. Which
   D. That

64. F. NO CHANGE
   G. and it
   H. although it
   J. DELETE the underlined portion.

GO ON TO THE NEXT PAGE.

as riveters, welders, and <u>machinists making</u> everything from
₆₅
uniforms to munitions to airplanes, they directly contributed

to the war effort. The number of women in the <u>workforce</u>
₆₆
increased from 12 million in 1940 to 18 million in 1944. By
1945, 36% of the laborers were women.

Women's increased presence in wartime workforces <u>were</u>
₆₇

not limited to factories and shipyards. ⬜₆₈ Thousands moved
to Washington D.C. to fill government jobs exclusively held by
men before the war. Some women engaged in farm labor, and
others joined the military as field nurses. The shortage of men

also led to openings in non-traditional fields, <u>such as day-care.</u>
₆₉
Since many players had been drafted into the armed services,
Major League Baseball parks around the country were on the
verge of collapse when a group of Midwestern businessmen
devised a brilliant solution to the player shortage.

The All-American Girls Professional Baseball League was
created in 1943 and offered a unique blend of baseball and
softball suitable for female players. <u>Founder, Philip K. Wrigley</u>
₇₀
<u>and League president,</u> Ken Sells promoted the new league with
aggressive advertising campaigns that promoted the physical
attractiveness of female athletes. Photographs displayed women

65. **A.** NO CHANGE
    B. machinists, making
    C. machinists. Making
    D. machinists, who made

66. **F.** NO CHANGE
    G. workforce, for example in factories and shipyards,
    H. workforce, such as factories and shipyards,
    J. factory and shipyard workforce

67. **A.** NO CHANGE
    B. are
    C. was
    D. have been

68. At this point, the writer is considering adding the following true statement:

> The marriage rate increased significantly during
> the war, as did the rate of babies born to unmarried
> women.

Should the writer add this sentence here?

    F. No, because it does not echo the style and tone that has
already been established in the essay.
    G. No, because it is not relevant to the essay's focus on
the changing roles of women during World War II.
    H. Yes, because it contributes to the essay's focus on
women's roles in the home during World War II.
    J. Yes, because it provides a contrast between women in
the home and women in the workplace.

69. Given that all the choices are true, which one provides the
most logical transition to the information presented in the
rest of this essay?

    A. NO CHANGE
    B. the most notable of which was baseball.
    C. which many women had to give up after the war.
    D. shaking American society to the core.

70. **F.** NO CHANGE
    G. Founder Philip K. Wrigley and League president
    H. Founder Philip K. Wrigley, and, League president
    J. Founder, Philip K. Wrigley, and League president,

GO ON TO THE NEXT PAGE.

players with pretty smiles on their faces and baseball mitts
in their hands. Their silk shorts, fashionable knee-high socks,
₇₁

red lipstick, having flowing hair directly contrasted with the
₇₂
competitive, masculine nature of the game. These

photographs are indicative of the delicate balance between

feminine appeal and masculine labor that was expected

of all women throughout World War II. 73 Although

its' success lasted only a decade, the All-American Girls
₇₄
Professional Baseball League's role in expanding opportunities

for women during World War II and thereafter is everlasting. 75

---

71. Given that all the choices are true, which one most effectively helps the writer's purpose of helping readers visualize the players in the photographs?
- **A.** NO CHANGE
- **B.** at the plate during a live game.
- **C.** clearly focused on playing well.
- **D.** showing close camaraderie.

72. **F.** NO CHANGE
- **G.** their
- **H.** with
- **J.** and

73. If the writer were to delete the words *silk*, *fashionable*, and *red* from the preceding sentence, it would primarily lose:
- **A.** details that have already been presented in the vivid imagery of the previous sentence.
- **B.** a digression from the focus of this paragraph on the athletic talent of the players.
- **C.** description of what was written in the captions accompanying the photographs.
- **D.** details that highlight the femininity of the players in contrast to the masculinity of the game.

74. **F.** NO CHANGE
- **G.** it's
- **H.** their
- **J.** its

Question 75 asks about the preceding passage as a whole.

75. Suppose the writer's goals were to write an essay that would illustrate the range of non-traditional activities women pursued during wartime. Does this essay achieve that goal?
- **A.** Yes, because it explains the impact of the All-American Girls Professional Baseball Team on public perception of women.
- **B.** Yes, because it gives several examples of women performing jobs during World War II that were typically filled by men.
- **C.** No, because it limits its focus to the type of work women engaged in during World War II.
- **D.** No, because it explains that women's importance in the workforce, especially in baseball, lasted only several years.

END OF TEST 1
STOP! DO NOT TURN THE PAGE UNTIL TOLD TO DO SO.

NO TEST MATERIAL ON THIS PAGE.

MATHEMATICS TEST

60 Minutes—60 Questions

DIRECTIONS: Solve each problem, choose the correct answer, and then darken the corresponding oval on your answer document.

Do not linger over problems that take too much time. Solve as many as you can; then return to the others in the time you have left for this test.

You are permitted to use a calculator on this test. You may use your calculator for any problems you choose,

but some of the problems may best be done without using a calculator.

Note: Unless otherwise stated, all of the following should be assumed:

1. Illustrative figures are NOT necessarily drawn to scale.
2. Geometric figures lie in a plane.
3. The word *line* indicates a straight line.
4. The word *average* indicates arithmetic mean.

---

1. In the hiking trail shown below, X marks the trail's halfway point. If $\overline{YZ}$ measures 24 kilometers and is $\frac{1}{3}$ the length of $\overline{XZ}$, what is the total length, in kilometers, of the trail?

DO YOUR FIGURING HERE.

A. 144
B. 104
C. 96
D. 72
E. 48

2. What is the value of x when $\frac{4x}{5} + 7 = 6$?

F. $\frac{5}{4}$

G. $-\frac{4}{5}$

H. -1

J. $-\frac{5}{4}$

K. -5

GO ON TO THE NEXT PAGE.

44 | 3 Practice Tests for the ACT

DO YOUR FIGURING HERE.

3. Cyclist A averages 80 pedal revolutions per minute, and Cyclist B averages 61 pedal revolutions per minute. At these rates, how many more minutes does Cyclist B need than Cyclist A to make 9,760 pedal revolutions?

A.   19
B.   38
C.   122
D.   141
E.   160

4. The perimeter of a square is 36 inches. What is the area of the square, in square inches?

F.   6
G.   9
H.   18
J.   36
K.   81

5. For the rectangle shown in the standard (x,y) coordinate plane below, what are the coordinates of the unlabeled vertex?

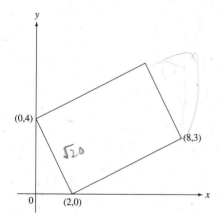

A. $(4,5)$

B. $(4,7)$

C. $\left(5, \dfrac{7}{2}\right)$

D. $(6,7)$

E. $(10,4)$

GO ON TO THE NEXT PAGE.

6. Carla has 5 times as many notebooks as her brother does. If they have 42 notebooks between them, how many notebooks does Carla have?

    F. 30
    G. 33
    H. 35
    J. 37
    K. 47

DO YOUR FIGURING HERE.

$5x = y$

$x + y = 42$

$6x = 42$

$x = 7$

✓

7. If *G* is in the interior of right angle $\angle DEF$, then which of the following could be the measure of $\angle GEF$?

    A. 85°
    B. 95°
    C. 105°
    D. 115°
    E. 125°

    ✓

8. Susie has three T-shirts: one red, one blue, and one black. She also has three pairs of shorts: one red, one blue, and one black. How many different combinations are there for Susie to wear exactly one T-shirt and one pair of shorts?

    F. 3
    G. 6
    H. 8
    J. 9
    K. 27

    ✓

9. 20% of 20 is equal to 50% of what number?

    A. 2
    B. 4
    C. 8
    D. 10
    E. 200

    ✓

10. There are 45 musicians in an orchestra, and all play two instruments. Of these musicians, 36 play the piano, and 22 play the violin. What is the maximum possible orchestra members who play both the piano and the violin?

    F. 9
    G. 13
    H. 22
    J. 23
    K. 36

    ✓

GO ON TO THE NEXT PAGE.

11. What is the largest value of m for which there exists a real value of n such that $m^2 = 196 - n^2$?

- **A.** 14
- **B.** 98
- **C.** 182
- **D.** 196
- **E.** 392

DO YOUR FIGURING HERE.

12. Phil earned \$800 at his summer job and saved all of his earnings. He wants to buy a deluxe drum kit that is regularly priced at \$925 but is on sale for $\frac{1}{5}$ off. The drum kit is subject to 5% sales tax after all discounts are applied. If Phil buys the kit on sale and gives the sales clerk his entire summer earnings, how much change should he receive?

- **F.** \$23
- **G.** \$37
- **H.** \$40
- **J.** \$77
- **K.** None; Phil still owes \$171.25.

13. Which of the following numbers is an imaginary number?

- **A.** $\sqrt{64}$
- **B.** $\sqrt{11}$
- **C.** $-\dfrac{4}{\sqrt{3}}$
- **D.** $-\sqrt{-64}$
- **E.** $-\sqrt{64}$

14. Which of the following correctly factors the expression $25x^4 - 16y^8$?

- **F.** $(25 - 16)(x^2 - y^4)(x^2 + y^4)$
- **G.** $(5x^2 - 4y^4)(5x^2 + 4y^4)$
- **H.** $(25x^2 - y^4)(x^2 + 16y^4)$
- **J.** $(5x^4 - 4y^8)(5x^4 + 4y^8)$
- **K.** $(5x^4 - 8y^8)(5x^4 + 2y^8)$

GO ON TO THE NEXT PAGE.

15. The figure below shows a portion of a tile floor from which the shaded polygon will be cut in order to make a repair. Each square tile has sides that measure 1 foot. Every vertex of the shaded polygon is at the intersection of 2 tiles. What is the area, in square feet, of the shaded polygon?

DO YOUR FIGURING HERE.

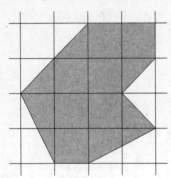

- **A.** 9.5
- **B.** 10.0
- **C.** 10.5
- **D.** 11.0
- **E.** 11.5

16. The percent P of a population that has completed 4 years of college is given by the function $P(t) = -0.001t^2 + 0.4t$ where t represents time, in years. What percent of the population have completed four years of college after 20 years, to the nearest tenth?

- **F.** 0.1
- **G.** 7.6
- **H.** 8.0
- **J.** 8.4
- **K.** 160.0

17. At Fatima's Fruits, a bag of eight grapefruits costs $4.40. At Ernie's Edibles, a bag of three grapefruits costs $1.86. How much cheaper, per grapefruit, is the cost at Fatima's Fruits than at Ernie's Edibles?

- **A.** $0.07
- **B.** $0.35
- **C.** $0.59
- **D.** $1.17
- **E.** $2.54

18. Which of the following is equivalent to $(x^4 - 4)(x^4 + 4)$?

- **F.** $2x^4$
- **G.** $x^8 - 16$
- **H.** $x^8 + 16$
- **J.** $x^{16} - 16$
- **K.** $x^8 - 8x^4 - 16$

GO ON TO THE NEXT PAGE.

DO YOUR FIGURING HERE.

19. Wade is making a tile mosaic. He begins the project by laying tile at a speed of 50 pieces per hour for 3.5 hours. He is then interrupted from his work for 60 minutes. He resumes working and lays tile at a speed of 35 pieces per hour, until he has laid 280 pieces of tile total. How many hours did Wade spend working on the mosaic after he was interrupted?

A. 2.5
B. 3
C. 3.5
D. 4
E. 4.5

20. Point C (1,2) and point D (7,–10) lie in the standard coordinate plane. What are the coordinates of the midpoint of $\overline{CD}$?

F. (1, 8)
G. (3,–6)
H. (4,–4)
J. (4,–6)
K. (7,–4)

21. Michael is planning to put fencing along the edge of his rectangular backyard, which is 22 yards by 16 yards. One long side of the backyard is along his house, so he will need to fence only 3 sides. How many yards of fencing will Michael need?

A. 38
B. 54
C. 60
D. 76
E. 352

22. What is the y-intercept of the line given by the equation $7x - 3y = 21$?

F. –7

G. $-\dfrac{7}{3}$

H. $\dfrac{7}{3}$

J. 7

K. 21

GO ON TO THE NEXT PAGE.

DO YOUR FIGURING HERE.

23. On April 8th, a flower at Blooming Acres Florist was 15.0 centimeters tall. On April 16th, the flower was 17.4 centimeters tall. If the flower grew at a constant rate, on what day was the flower 16.5 centimeters tall?

   A. April 11th
   B. April 12th
   C. April 13th
   D. April 14th
   E. April 15th

24. Which of the following expressions is equivalent to the expression given below?

   $(2x^3 - x - 1) - 3(x^4 + 2x^3 - 2x^2 - x + 3)$

   F. $x^{14} - 3$
   G. $-3x^{14}$
   H. $-3x^4 + 8x^3 - 6x^2 - 4x + 8$
   J. $-3x^4 + 4x^3 - 2x^2 - 2x - 3$
   K. $-3x^4 - 4x^3 + 6x^2 + 2x - 10$

25. The playground equipment shown below has a ladder that is 6 feet tall and a diagonal slide that is 7 feet long. If the ladder makes a right angle with the ground, approximately how many feet is the base of the slide from the base of the ladder?

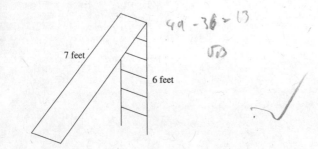

7 feet

6 feet

   A. 2
   B. 4
   C. 6
   D. 8
   E. 10

26. In a data set of 5 points, the mean, median, and mode are each equal to 8. Which of the following could be the data set?

   F. {5, 7, 8, 8, 12}
   G. {7, 7, 8, 8, 12}
   H. {7, 8, 8, 8, 12}
   J. {7, 8, 8, 10, 12}
   K. {7, 8, 8, 12, 12}

GO ON TO THE NEXT PAGE.

27. In a certain sequence of numbers, each term after the 1st term is the result of adding 2 to the previous term and multiplying that sum by 3. If the 4th term in the sequence is 186, what is the 2nd term?

- A.   2
- B.   4
- C.   18
- D.   60
- E.   174

DO YOUR FIGURING HERE.

$186 = 3(a_3 + 2)$

$62 = a_3 + 2$

28. Which of the following values of x does NOT satisfy the inequality $|x-3| \geq 12$?

- F.   −15
- G.   −12
- H.   −9
- J.   9
- K.   15

29. For all real numbers s, t, u, and v, such that $s + t + u = 29$ and $s < v$, which of the following statements is true?

- A. $s + t + v < 29$
- B. $t + u + v > 29$
- C. $s + t + v = 29$
- D. $s + u + v = 29$
- E. $s + t + v > 29$

30. In the figure below, rectangle $ABCD$ shares $\overline{CD}$ with $\triangle CDE$, diagonal $\overline{BD}$ of the rectangle extends in a straight line beyond D to E to create $\overline{DE}$, and the measure of $\angle CDE$ is 155°. What is the measure of $\angle CBD$?

- F.   25
- G.   55
- H.   65
- J.   90
- K.   155

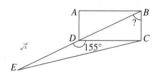

31. If a, b, and c are positive prime numbers, in the equation $a - b = c$, either b or c must represent which number?

- A.   13
- B.   11
- C.   7
- D.   5
- E.   2

GO ON TO THE NEXT PAGE.

32. Pierre competes in a triathlon, along a course as shown in the figure below. He begins swimming at starting point S and swims straight across the lake, gets on his bicycle at station A, bikes to station B, and then runs to finishing line F. The judges use a stopwatch to record his elapsed times of t_A, t_B, and t_F hours from point S to points A, B, and F, respectively. If the distance, in miles, between points S and A along the racecourse is denoted by SA, then what is Pierre's average speed for this race, in miles per hour?

DO YOUR FIGURING HERE.

F. $\dfrac{SA}{t_A}$

G. $\dfrac{SB}{t_B}$

H. $\dfrac{SF}{t_F}$

J. $\dfrac{SA}{t_F}$

K. $\dfrac{SF}{t_A}$

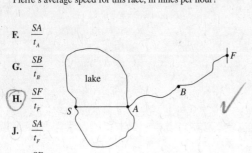

33. The triangle shown below has a hypotenuse with a length of 13 feet. The measure of $\angle A$ is 20° and the measure of $\angle B$ is 70°. Which of the following is closest to the length, in feet, of $\overline{BC}$?

(Note: sin 70° ≈ 0.9397
cos 70° ≈ 0.3420
tan 70° ≈ 2.747)

A. 4.4
B. 5.0
C. 12.0
D. 12.2
E. 35.7

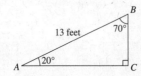

34. What is the value of $\dfrac{8}{y^2} - \dfrac{x^2}{y}$ when $x = -3$ and $y = -4$?

F. $-\dfrac{11}{4}$

G. $-\dfrac{7}{4}$

H. $\dfrac{7}{4}$

J. $\dfrac{11}{4}$

K. $\dfrac{56}{9}$

GO ON TO THE NEXT PAGE.

35. As shown in the figure below, with angles as marked, a ramp is being designed that will have a vertical height of 4 feet. Which of the following is closest to the horizontal length of the ramp, in feet?

DO YOUR FIGURING HERE.

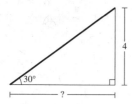

A. 5
B. 6
C. 7
D. 8
E. 9

36. In the diagram below, $\triangle ABC$ is isosceles and $\triangle BCD$ is equilateral. $\overline{AB} = \overline{BC}$ and the measure of $\angle ABC$ is half the measure of $\angle BAC$. What is the measure of $\angle ABD$?

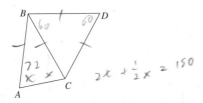

F. 36°
G. 60°
H. 72°
J. 96°
K. 150°

GO ON TO THE NEXT PAGE.

Use the following information to answer questions 37–39.

The coordinates of the vertices of △*MON* are shown in the standard (*x,y*) coordinate plane below. Rectangle *MPQR* is shown shaded. Point *P* lies on $\overline{MO}$, point *Q* lies on $\overline{ON}$, and point *R* lies on $\overline{MN}$.

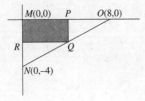

37. What is the slope of $\overline{ON}$?

   A. −2
   B. $-\dfrac{1}{2}$
   C. 0
   D. $\dfrac{1}{2}$
   E. 2

38. Which of the following is closest to the perimeter, in coordinate units, of △*MON* ?

   F. 12.0
   G. 16.9
   H. 18.0
   J. 20.9
   K. 92.0

39. What is the value of cos (∠*MNO*) ?

   A. $\dfrac{8}{\sqrt{80}}$
   B. $\dfrac{4}{\sqrt{80}}$
   C. 2
   D. $\dfrac{1}{2}$
   E. $\dfrac{\sqrt{80}}{8}$

GO ON TO THE NEXT PAGE.

40. In a Spanish class there are *m* students, of which *n* did NOT pass the last exam. Which of the following is a general expression for the fraction of the class that did receive a passing grade?

F. $\dfrac{m-n}{m}$

G. $\dfrac{m}{n}$

H. $\dfrac{m-n}{n}$

J. $\dfrac{n-m}{n}$

K. $\dfrac{n-m}{m}$

DO YOUR FIGURING HERE.

41. The solution set of $5x + 9 \geq 2(3x + 4) + 7$ is shown by which of the following number line graphs?

A.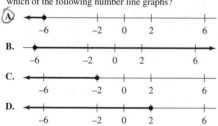
B.
C.
D.
E.

$5x + 9 \geq 6x + 15$

$5x \geq 6x + 6$

$-x \geq 6$

$x \leq -6$

42. An artist wants to cover the entire outside of a rectangular box with mosaic tiles. The dimensions of the box shown below are given in centimeters. If each tile is exactly one square centimeter, and the artist lays the tiles with no space between them, how many tiles will he need?

F. 75
G. 96
H. 108
J. 126
K. 150

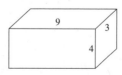

GO ON TO THE NEXT PAGE.

43. In the figure shown below, $\overline{BC}$ and $\overline{EF}$ are parallel and $\overline{AE} = \overline{FD}$. If $\angle ABC$ is 130° and $\angle BAE$ is 22°, what is the measure of $\angle AEF$?

DO YOUR FIGURING HERE.

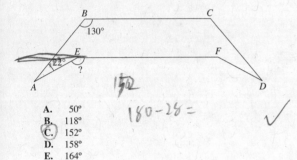

152

$180 - 28 =$

✓

- A.   50°
- B.   118°
- C.   152°
- D.   158°
- E.   164°

44. Given the figure below, what is the area of the trapezoid, in square inches?

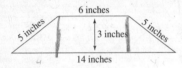

6 inches

5 inches   3 inches   5 inches

14 inches

✓

- F.   18
- G.   30
- H.   42
- J.   50
- K.   52

45. What is the solution set of $\sqrt[3]{x^2 + 4x} = 2$?

- A.   {4}
- B.   {8}
- C.   {−4, 8}
- D.   {−8, 4}
- E.   {−2, ±2√2}

$x^2 + 4x = 32$

$x^2 + 4x - 32$

)

GO ON TO THE NEXT PAGE.

46. As shown in the figure below, a skateboard ramp leading from the top of a boulder is 10 feet long and forms a 32° angle with the level ground. Which of the following expressions represents the height, in feet, of the boulder?

DO YOUR FIGURING HERE.

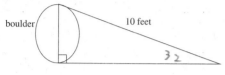
boulder   10 feet

32

F.   10 tan 32°

G. $\dfrac{\sin 32°}{10}$

H. $\dfrac{10}{\cos 32°}$

J.   10 sin 32°

K.   10 cos 32°

47. The 4 integers j, j, k, and n have an average of 0. Which of the following equations *must* be true?

A. $k = n$
B. $k = -j$
C. $k + n = -2j$
D. $k + n = 0$
E. $k + n = j$

48. If $f(x) = \sqrt{x}$ and the composite function

$f(g(x)) = \sqrt{4x^2 - 5}$, which of the following could be $g(x)$?

F. $\sqrt{4x^4 - 5}$

G. $\sqrt{16x^4 - 25}$

H. $2x^2 - 25$

J. $4x^2 - 5$

K. $16x^4 - 5$

GO ON TO THE NEXT PAGE.

DO YOUR FIGURING HERE.

Use the following information to answer questions 49–51.

In the qualifying rounds for a race, Rusty and Dale drive their cars around a 6,000-foot oval track. Rusty and Dale each drive 8 laps in the qualifying rounds in lanes of identical length.

49. On day one of the qualifying rounds, Rusty and Dale start from the same point, but their cars are reversed and each drives opposite ways. Rusty drives at a constant speed that is 8 feet per second faster than Dale's constant speed. Rusty passes Dale for the first time in 150 seconds. Rusty drives at a constant rate of how many feet per second?

    A. 16
    B. 20
    C. 24
    D. 32
    E. 40

50. In the qualifying rounds, Rusty averages 180 seconds per lap until he begins the last lap. He then goes into a lower gear. He averages 190 seconds per lap for this qualifying round. How many seconds does Rusty take to drive the final lap?

    F. 155
    G. 160
    H. 185
    J. 200
    K. 260

51. Dale drives 6 laps in 90 minutes. At what average rate, in feet per hour, does Dale drive these 6 laps?

    A. 400
    B. 5,400
    C. 10,000
    D. 24,000
    E. 48,000

    6 laps   36000 ft

    1.5 hrs   1.5 hrs

52. Circle *A* has its center at point (−5,2) with a radius of 2, and circle *B* is represented by the equation $(x + 4)^2 + (y - 2)^2 = 9$. Where is point (−2,2) located?

    F. Inside circle *A* only
    G. Inside circle *B* only
    H. Inside both circle *A* and circle *B*
    J. Outside both circle *A* and circle *B*
    K. Cannot be determined from given information

GO ON TO THE NEXT PAGE.

53. A heart-shaped ornament is made from a square and two semicircles, each of whose diameter is a side of the square. The ornament is shown in the standard (x,y) coordinate plane below, where 1 coordinate unit represents 1 inch. The coordinates of six points on the border of the ornament are given. What is the perimeter, in inches, of the ornament?

DO YOUR FIGURING HERE.

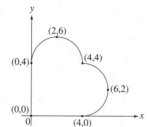

A. $4 + 2\pi$
B. $8 + 4\pi$
C. $8 + 8\pi$
D. $16 + 4\pi$
E. $16 + 8\pi$

54. A function $f(x)$ is defined as even if and only if $f(x) = f(-x)$ for all real values of x. Which one of the following graphs represents an even function $f(x)$?

F.

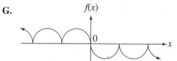

G.

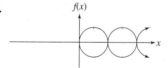

H.

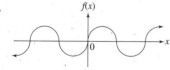

J.

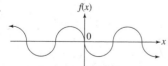

K.

GO ON TO THE NEXT PAGE.

55. In the standard (x,y) coordinate plane, point A is located at $(w,w + 5)$ and point B is located at $(4w,w - 5)$. In coordinate units, what is the distance between A and B ?

DO YOUR FIGURING HERE.

A. $\sqrt{9w^2 + 2w + 10}$

B. $\sqrt{9w^2 + 100}$

C. $9w^2 + 100$

D. $|w|\sqrt{11}$

E. $|w|$

56. RST is a right triangle with side lengths of r, s, and t, as shown below. What is the value of $\cos^2 S + \cos^2 R$?

F. 1

G. $\sqrt{2}$

H. $\sqrt{3}$

J. $\dfrac{\sqrt{2}}{2}$

K. $\dfrac{1+\sqrt{2}}{3}$

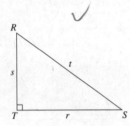

57. In isosceles triangle ABC below, the measures of $\angle BAC$ and $\angle BCA$ are equal and $\overline{DE} \parallel \overline{AC}$. The diagonals of trapezoid $DECA$ intersect at F. The lengths of $\overline{DF}$ and $\overline{EF}$ are 6 centimeters, the length of $\overline{DE}$ is 9 centimeters, and the length of $\overline{AC}$ is 27 centimeters. What is the length, in centimeters, of $\overline{FC}$?

A. 12
B. 15
C. 18
D. 33
E. 36

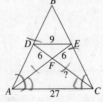

GO ON TO THE NEXT PAGE.

58. Which of the following represents the product of the matrices below?

$$\begin{bmatrix} 4 & -2 \\ 3 & -6 \end{bmatrix} \times \begin{bmatrix} 0 \\ 2 \end{bmatrix}$$

$\begin{bmatrix} -4 \\ -12 \end{bmatrix}$

F. $\begin{bmatrix} -4 \\ -12 \end{bmatrix}$

G. $\begin{bmatrix} -12 \\ 0 \end{bmatrix}$

H. $\begin{bmatrix} -6 \end{bmatrix}$

J. $\begin{bmatrix} 6 & -12 \end{bmatrix}$

K. $\begin{bmatrix} -4 & -12 \end{bmatrix}$

DO YOUR FIGURING HERE.

59. If $\dfrac{(n+1)!}{(n-1)!} = 20$, then $n! = ?$

A. 6
B. 10
C. 12
D. 24
E. 120

$n \cdot (n+1) = 20$

$n^2 + n = 20$

$n^2 + n = 20 = 0$

60. What is the ratio of a circle's radius to its circumference?

F. $2\pi{:}1$
G. $2{:}1$
H. $\pi{:}1$
J. $1{:}\pi$
K. $1{:}2\pi$

$2\pi r = C$

END OF TEST 2
STOP! DO NOT TURN THE PAGE UNTIL TOLD TO DO SO.
DO NOT RETURN TO THE PREVIOUS TEST.

READING TEST
35 Minutes—40 Questions

DIRECTIONS: There are four passages in this test. Each passage is followed by several questions. After reading each passage, choose the best answer to each question and blacken the corresponding oval on your answer document. You may refer to the passages as often as necessary.

Passage I

PROSE FICTION: This passage is adapted from the short story "Ruby" by Tristan Ivory (©2007 by Tristan Ivory).

Ruby's Downhome Diner was an institution. If you only spent one night in Franklin, Texas, someone would inevitably direct you right off Highway 79 and Pink Oak Road to Ruby's Downhome Diner, Ruby's, or The Downhome; whatever
5　name the locals gave you, there was always something there that you would enjoy.

Ruby's was named after Ruby Sanders, my grandmother. She had opened the diner with money she saved from cleaning houses and with personal loans from friends. By the time
10　I was born, Ruby's did enough business to pay off all debts and obligations. It didn't take long before my grandmother was a person of considerable stature in and around Robertson County, just like the restaurant that bore her name.

Ever since I was knee-high, I spent each sweltering
15　summer with my grandmother. This, truth be told, meant that for all practical purposes I lived at Ruby's Downhome. Time familiarized me with all nuances within the diner: there were five steps and four ingredients that separated peach preserves from peach cobbler filling; Deputy Sheriff Walter Mayes
20　preferred his eggs, always cooked over-easy, to finish cooking on the top of his ham before it was transferred to his plate; Mr. Arnold delivered the milk and the buttermilk on Mondays, Thursdays, and Saturdays; and there were days when I would need to go to the general store to pick up whatever was in
25　short supply. By the time I entered high school, I could have run the diner from open to close if my Grandmother were absent, but she never was.

Perhaps the single greatest contributing factor to the success of Ruby's Diner was the omnipresent personality of
30　its namesake. Even the most hopelessly spun-around visitor who happened inside those doors would know who Ms. Ruby was. There were no sick days, vacations, or holidays. Between 5 a.m. and 9 p.m., you knew where Ruby Sanders could be found. If the diner were a sort of cell, then my grandmother was
35　its nucleus; without the nucleus, the cell would surely perish.

The people who worked at Ruby's were as dedicated as Ruby herself. There were the regulars: Del (short for Delmont) did double duty as a short-order cook and janitor,

while Marlene and Deborah waited tables. Extra help would
40　be hired from time to time depending on the season and individual need. No matter how long those extra helpers stayed, they and everyone else who worked at the Downhome were family, and no one ever fell out of touch.

Ruby's did the things you'd expect a diner to do, as
45　well as the things you wouldn't. You could stop in and get yourself a nice cool drink for the road. Or you could pull up a stool at the counter and grab a steaming hot bowl of red pepper chili with a slice of corn pone or a dish of chilled and creamy homemade ice cream. Or better still, you could
50　grab a booth and try any number of full-plate entrees made to order. But you could also order a wedding cake a week in advance, take a weekend course in food preparation, or, when the time came, have your wake catered with dignity and grace.

When I was very young, I would spend most of my time
55　exploring every inch of Ruby's until the entire layout was printed indelibly in my mind. I could walk blindfolded from the basement where the dry goods were kept, up to the kitchen with the walk-in refrigerator chocked full of perishables, over to the main restaurant with row after row of booths and counter and stools,
60　well-worn but always cleaned after each patron had finished, and finally to the front porch, with its old wooden swing. I can see my grandmother moving from her station near the door to the kitchen, over to the counter and tables, and then back to the front again. Even now, I can see Del speedily making a double
65　order of hash, Deborah picking up a generous tip, and Marlene topping off a customer's sweet tea. Every summer sunset from that porch seemed to be more magnificent than the last.

As I got older, I took on more responsibility. There were fewer sunsets to watch and more work to be done. It was hard
70　but never dull work. The company kept me coming back despite the increasing allure of summer football leagues and idle moments with friends or girls. After all, the woman who built Ruby's was strong enough to make me forget those things, if only for the summer. I didn't know that I would never return
75　after my sophomore year of college, and for that, I am glad—I could not have asked for a better end to my long history at Ruby's. It warms my heart when I think of the last memory of Ruby Sanders: tying her silver hair into a tight bun, hands vigorously wiping down tables with a rag, enjoying a story
80　and a laugh as we closed for the night.

GO ON TO THE NEXT PAGE.

1. The narrator's point of view can most correctly be described as that of an adult:

   A. remembering the events that brought a particular place
   into existence.
   B. analyzing how different his current life is from how
   things were when he was younger.
   C. thinking about the qualities of his grandmother and
   her restaurant that made her well-respected in the
   community.
   D. curious as to how many people's lives were positively
   impacted by his grandmother and her diner.

2. One of the main purposes of the first part of the passage
(lines 1–27) is to:

   F. explain how Ruby got the money to pay for the diner
   and her eventual success in paying off her debts.
   G. state that the diner had taken its name from the narrator's grandmother although many of the locals called it
   by different names.
   H. explain how Ruby was able to become the most important person in Franklin and that her restaurant was the
   best place for visitors to the city.
   J. introduce the primary setting of the story and to describe a central character.

3. Based on the narrator's characterization, Ruby Sanders
would best be described as:

   A. always at the diner, though she often preferred to be
   absent.
   B. the main force holding the diner and its employees
   together.
   C. carefree, particularly when it came to hearing humor-
   ous stories.
   D. the only woman the narrator had ever respected.

4. Information in the last paragraph most strongly suggests
that the narrator felt his last summer at the diner to be:

   F. disappointing because he didn't know it would be his
   last.
   G. something he was forced to do when he would rather
   have been playing football.
   H. pleasant although he did not know it would be his last.
   J. exhausting because of all his new responsibilities.

5. According to the narrator, working at Ruby's Diner was:

   A. easy but tedious.
   B. difficult but enjoyable.
   C. hard and monotonous.
   D. unpredictable and overwhelming.

6. According to the narrator, his grandmother was like the
diner in that she had:

   F. a position of high standing within the community at
   large.
   G. a desire to make all people feel comfortable no matter
   who they were.
   H. an ability to make money within the community.
   J. a refusal to settle for anything but the best.

7. The statement in lines 44–45 most strongly suggests that
the Downhome Diner:

   A. served the community in ways beyond simple dining.
   B. was the most significant place within Robertson County.
   C. gave the people who worked there great importance in
   Robertson County.
   D. was a place where the waiting times were often
   unpredictable.

8. The narrator describes Ruby's Downhome Diner as providing all of the following EXCEPT:

   F. cooking classes.
   G. football leagues.
   H. wedding cakes.
   J. corn pone.

9. The passage indicates that one of the ways in which the
narrator was familiar with Ruby's Downhome Diner was
shown by his:

   A. ability to teach the cooking classes held on the premises.
   B. awareness of the habits of visitors to Robertson
   County.
   C. detailed memory of the layout of the kitchen and the
   restaurant.
   D. unwillingness to leave at the end of each summer
   before his return to school.

10. According to the narrator, which of the following most
accurately represents the reason he was able to forget the
summer activities outside while working at his grandmother's restaurant?

   F. His tips and wages helped to contribute to his college
   tuition.
   G. His grandmother's restaurant was chronically
   understaffed.
   H. It helped him to gain stature in and around the
   community.
   J. He admired his grandmother's strength.

GO ON TO THE NEXT PAGE.

Passage II

SOCIAL SCIENCE: This passage is adapted from the entry "Happiness" from *The Psychologist's Scientific Encyclopedia* (© 2004 by The Scientific Press of Illinois).

Lee D. Ross, a psychologist at Stanford University, has a friend who lost both her parents in the Holocaust. According to the woman, the awful events of the Holocaust taught her that it was inappropriate to be upset about trivial things in
5 life and important to enjoy human relationships. Even though the circumstances of her life were tragic, the woman was extremely happy, perhaps due to an innate sense of well-being.

According to psychologists, most of our self-reported level of happiness, a measure researchers call "subjective
10 well-being," seems to be genetically predetermined, rather than caused by experience. A study carried out by Auke Tellegen and David Lykken of the University of Minnesota compared the subjective well-being scores of both fraternal and identical twins, some who were raised together and some who were
15 separated and raised in different families. By comparing the scores of the twins, Tellegen and Lykken determined that most of the differences in people's levels of happiness are determined by differences in genetic makeup.

A genetic predisposition toward a certain level of hap-
20 piness means that regardless of what happens in a person's life, he or she will eventually adjust to the new circumstances and report the same level of subjective well-being as before. The tendency for people to maintain a consistent level of happiness despite their circumstances, known as "hedonic
25 adaptation," benefits those whose life-experiences are beset by adverse conditions, such as permanent disability or sudden loss of income. Because they return to a "genetic set point," they eventually feel just as happy as they did before the unfortunate event.

30 However, hedonic adaptation also affects the happiness of people who experience positive changes in their lives. For example, in one study conducted in the 1970s among lottery winners, it was found that a year after the winners received their money, they were no happier than non-winners.

35 Despite the quantity of research that supports hedonic adaptation, there is still some debate within the scientific community over how much people can change their baseline happiness. Kennon M. Sheldon, a psychologist at the University of Missouri-Columbia, explains that many research
40 psychologists hypothesized that certain behaviors, such as choosing particular goals in life, could affect long-term happiness. However, scientific literature suggests that these behaviors provide only a temporary increase in subjective well-being.

45 Sheldon worked alongside Sonja Lyubomirsky of the University of California at Riverside and David A. Schkade of the University of California at San Diego to determine exactly what is known about the science of happiness. They compiled the findings of existing scientific studies in the field
50 of happiness and determined that 50 percent of subjective well-being is predetermined by the genetic set point, while only about 10 percent is influenced by circumstances.

However, people are not completely at the mercy of their genes. Lyubomirsky notes that 40 percent of what contributes
55 to people's happiness is still unexplained, and she believes that much of this may be attributable to what she calls "intentional activity," which includes mental attitudes and behaviors that people can modify and improve. Conscious choices such as demonstrating kindness, fostering optimism, and expressing
60 gratitude may work to influence subjective well-being in much the same way that diet and exercise can affect a person's inherited predisposition toward heart disease. Lyubomirsky hopes to learn the specific mechanisms by which these conscious strategies counteract genetic forces. She and Sheldon are cur-
65 rently expanding their study of subjective well-being to large groups of subjects to be observed over extended periods of time. Using these longitudinal studies, the researchers hope to discover the inner workings of the correlations between behaviors and mood.

70 Lyubomirsky and Sheldon's studies have found that simply choosing "happy" activities may not be the most effective way to increase happiness. Lyubomirsky says that other factors, such as variation and timing of intentional activities, are crucial in influencing happiness. For example, one study
75 has shown that subjects who varied their acts of kindness from one day to the next experienced greater happiness than those who repeated the same kind act many times. Another study demonstrated that writing a list of things to be grateful for only once a week was more effective in improving levels of
80 happiness than keeping a gratitude journal every day.

The study of happiness is still a relatively new area of psychological research. Traditionally, much more psychological research focused on depression and other disorders associated with destructive mental health, leading some psychologists
85 to suspect that overall levels of subjective well-being are low. But now that more studies are focused on positive psychology, there is evidence to the contrary. Researchers have discovered not only that personal choices improve subjective well-being from a genetic set point, but also that this level is higher than
90 traditionally expected. According to surveys conducted by the University of Chicago, only about one in ten people claim to be "not too happy." Most Americans describe themselves as "pretty happy," and 30 percent as "very happy," even without using intentional activities specifically to improve
95 their well-being.

GO ON TO THE NEXT PAGE.

11. The passage's focus is primarily on the:

- **A.** search for the specific genes known to cause hedonic adaptation.
- **B.** scientific studies investigating various influences on happiness.
- **C.** attempts by experimental psychologists to develop cures for depression.
- **D.** conflicting opinions of psychologists regarding the influence of genes on happiness.

12. Based on the passage, the subjects in the studies by Tellegen and Lykken and the subjects in studies by Lyubomirsky and Sheldon were similar in that both groups were:

- **F.** part of large groups studied over an extended time.
- **G.** intentionally engaged in acts of kindness.
- **H.** asked to describe their own subjective well-being.
- **J.** either identical or fraternal twins.

13. Which of the following questions is NOT answered by the passage?

- **A.** To what extent is a person's level of happiness determined by his or her circumstances?
- **B.** According to Lyubomirsky and Sheldon's studies, what are some specific things people can do to improve their subjective well-being?
- **C.** Does the choice of specific life goals affect happiness over a lifetime?
- **D.** According to Tellegen and Lykken, were twins who were raised together happier than twins who were raised apart?

14. The passage most strongly suggests that the primary goal of Lyubomirsky and Sheldon's research is to:

- **F.** discover the specific mechanisms that may help people overcome the level of happiness determined by their genetic set point.
- **G.** contradict Tellegen and Lykken's findings that genes are the primary determinant in a person's overall level of happiness.
- **H.** find out whether keeping a gratitude journal or engaging in kind acts is more effective at improving happiness.
- **J.** determine which behaviors most completely eliminate hedonic adaptation.

15. Which of the following statements best summarizes the findings of the University of Chicago surveys on happiness?

- **A.** Earlier psychologists were mistaken to believe people are generally depressed and experience low levels of happiness.
- **B.** Depression and other destructive mood disorders are uncommon in America.
- **C.** People are happier if they do not try to improve their subjective well-being by writing in a gratitude journal.
- **D.** Most people report a level of happiness higher than was traditionally expected by psychologists and researchers.

16. According to the passage, all of the following are true of the Lykken and Tellegen study EXCEPT:

- **F.** The subjects were paired groups of twins.
- **G.** Subjects rated their happiness.
- **H.** The twins studied were all raised together.
- **J.** The study found happiness is genetic.

17. According to the passage, "hedonic adaptation" (lines 24–25) is a useful trait because it can help people to:

- **A.** restore levels of happiness that have been interrupted or altered by tragic events.
- **B.** forget that they have suffered a permanent disability or loss of income.
- **C.** adjust quickly to positive circumstances like winning the lottery and become happier.
- **D.** identify with immediate family members who share their genes and choose those who are more inclined to be happy.

18. If the author were to delete the first paragraph, the passage would primarily lose:

- **F.** the idea that events people experience are not the least important factor influencing their subjective well-being.
- **G.** a useful illustration of the idea that there may be little relationship between a person's circumstances and his or her level of happiness.
- **H.** a clear and complete articulation of the essay's main point regarding hedonic adaptation.
- **J.** all examples of adverse conditions people may overcome because of their genetic predisposition to happiness.

19. The main purpose of the final paragraph is to:

- **A.** conclude that psychological researchers make many errors and tend to focus on the negative.
- **B.** disprove the idea suggested by Ross's anecdote by showing that Americans are also happy.
- **C.** cite a specific study that gives a positive view of people's overall levels of happiness.
- **D.** undermine Lyubomirsky and Sheldon's studies indicating that people need to apply effort in order to become happier.

20. According to the passage, which of the following researchers have an ongoing collaboration?

- **F.** Tellegen and Lykken
- **G.** Sheldon and Schkade
- **H.** Sheldon and Lyubomirsky
- **J.** Schkade and Lykken

GO ON TO THE NEXT PAGE.

Passage III

HUMANITIES: This passage is adapted from the memoir *Literary Tourism* by Krista Prouty (© 2002 by Krista Prouty).

Just recently, I visited the House of the Seven Gables, in Salem, Massachusetts. Up until the moment I looked through my travel guide, I hadn't even known that there was an actual house, much less that it was in Salem. We had intended only
5 to visit the Salem Witch Memorials, but since I've been a Nathaniel Hawthorne fan since junior high, a side trip to the building that had inspired one of his greatest works seemed to be in order.

Let me back up a bit to explain. Ever since I was a
10 little girl, I've loved to read. Classics, in particular, thrilled me, taking me back in time to worlds that hadn't existed for hundreds of years. I knew, of course, that real people wrote these books, but somehow the authors didn't interest me very much. The whole point of reading was to explore other reali-
15 ties, and while I had a great deal of respect for anyone who could create those worlds, their life stories didn't hold much appeal. In college, I opted to major in literature, assuming that this would involve reading scores of wonderful books, which it did. It also meant, however, spending hours, days,
20 and weeks studying the people behind the books. Completing my professors' assignments, I felt more like a detective than a reader, scouring personal letters for hints of relationship problems, familial tragedies, or even fond memories that seemed reminiscent of storylines. I would analyze how authors'
25 childhood traumas might have influenced their writing, and I would try to discover any hidden secrets and vices. In inspired moments, I felt the advantage of this depth of knowledge—a piece that had been opaque to me would suddenly open up, as I grasped the personal truth the author was trying to convey.
30 More often, though, I found myself losing sight of the books in the forest of biographical details.

By the time I graduated, I was heartily sick of the whole business. Casting aside all previous plans of continued study, I gave away or sold all of my textbooks, keeping only a few
35 of my favorite books for pleasure reading. Over the years, I regressed to my natural habits—when I read, I did so with blinders on. My focus was solely on the book itself, and I gave no thought to the writer, aside from admiration for his or her skill. Reading this way was more enjoyable, and with
40 no professors watching, I was free to do as I pleased.

It was in this frame of mind that I learned of the existence of the actual House of the Seven Gables, so my enthusiasm had more to do with visiting a site featured in one of my favorite books than with visiting the former home of a famous
45 author. We found the house, parked the car, and walked in. The woman staffing the entrance desk informed us that visitors were allowed only as part of a tour. Although my plans had not included being herded through a rambling old house, I acceded and the tickets were duly purchased. As we waited
50 for the tour to begin, we wandered through the gardens, which were desolate during the winter months. Several buildings were clustered around the central garden area, and each structure had a sign explaining its historical relevance. The main building had been the original inspiration for <u>The House of the Seven</u>
55 <u>Gables</u>, another a counting house, and another the home of Nathaniel Hawthorne's family. As I gazed at the signs, a bit confused, having assumed that Hawthorne had lived in the main house, our guide arrived and ushered us all indoors.

For the next hour, we were inundated with facts about
60 Nathaniel Hawthorne's life. We learned that he had not, in fact, lived in the famous house. His family had struggled financially, and even the small house that bore his name on a plaque had ultimately proven too expensive. The guide told us about Hawthorne's troubled youth, the untimely death of
65 his father, his psychological battles, and his ultimate redemption through marriage with a woman he loved deeply. As I listened, for the first time I began to see Nathaniel Hawthorne not just as a talented writer but as a real person with a life as rich and complicated as my own. Maybe it was visiting his
70 home, maybe it was hearing the right words at the right moment, but whatever the cause, something clicked. The writer's personal dossier and his literary work no longer seemed to get in the way of each other, but instead blended seamlessly into a varicolored, complex, and beautiful tapestry. The work itself
75 is indeed the frame, but when we weave the threads of the author's life around that base, we are able to see the interactions between text and author, as they join to create a pattern more complete than either would be on its own.

GO ON TO THE NEXT PAGE.

21. The author of the passage indicates that she has learned that the personal details of an author's life:

   A. get in the way of the literary work.
   B. are always discussed in the author's works.
   C. contribute to a reader's appreciation of the author's works.
   D. help a reader understand his or her own familial tragedies and childhood traumas.

22. As it is used in line 22, the word *scouring* most nearly means:

   F. purifying.
   G. obliterating.
   H. scrutinizing.
   J. cleansing.

23. It can reasonably be inferred that the author of the passage visited the House of the Seven Gables because she wanted to:

   A. explore in person a location she had read about in a novel.
   B. take advantage of all the tourist attractions in Salem.
   C. gain a deeper understanding of how the details of Hawthorne's past influenced his writing.
   D. learn what Hawthorne endured during the Salem Witch Trials.

24. According to the author of the passage, the college professors referred to in line 21 most likely believe that:

   F. the interactions between an author's life and work provide the reader with a more complete understanding than does the text alone.
   G. learning about an author's life is more important than reading his books.
   H. knowledge of the background of an author interferes with enjoyment of the text.
   J. reading for pleasure is less useful than is reading for cultural analysis.

25. According to the second paragraph (lines 9–31), the author of the passage chose to study literature in college in order to:

   A. scour personal letters for an author's secret vices.
   B. read a great number of literary works.
   C. demonstrate the falsity of the scholars' approach.
   D. better grasp the connection between an author and his work.

26. According to the author of the passage, the likely result of following her professors' assignments was:

   F. "to explore other realities" (lines 14–15).
   G. grasping "the personal truth the author was trying to convey" (line 29).
   H. "losing sight of the books in the forest of biographical details" (lines 30–31).
   J. "to see the interactions between text and author" (lines 76–77).

27. It can reasonably be inferred from the passage that "the building that had inspired one of his greatest works" (lines 6–7) refers to:

   A. the home inhabited by relatives of Nathaniel Hawthorne.
   B. a popular attraction for tourists in Salem.
   C. the site of historically important events.
   D. a site that has fallen into a state of disrepair.

28. As it is used in line 75, the word *frame* most nearly means the:

   F. isolated goal.
   G. ultimate purpose.
   H. auxiliary data.
   J. focal point.

29. Following her visit to Salem, the author's attitude toward studying the lives of writers could best be described as:

   A. incredulous disdain.
   B. healthy timidity.
   C. keen acceptance.
   D. resigned frustration.

30. If the third paragraph (lines 32–40) were omitted from the passage, how would the structure of the passage be affected?

   F. The transition from the author's past to the present would be less explicit.
   G. The reasons for the author's trip would not be clear.
   H. The introduction to the discussion of literature in the final paragraph would be lost.
   J. There would no longer be definite evidence supporting the author's conclusion.

GO ON TO THE NEXT PAGE.

Passage IV

NATURAL SCIENCE: This passage is adapted from the article "A Tree Frog Grows Up in Hawaii" by Ashley C. Tulliver (© 2005 by Ashley Tulliver).

As night falls on Hawaii's Big Island, a low, jarring sound begins. It is a faint murmur at first, but as the darkness deepens, the sound grows louder, rending the stillness of the evening. These deep cries, from male *E. coqui* frogs, are met with
5 lower, guttural croaks from their prospective mates; during this time, the sound for which the coqui is named (ko-KEE) fills the air. This sound has become the theme song of a growing environmental problem: invasive species' threat to ecological biodiversity.

10 Native to Puerto Rico, the small tree frogs—measuring about five millimeters long—probably arrived in Hawaii as passengers aboard potted plants imported from the Caribbean. Once coquis explored their new environment, they found an abundance of food, including insects, tiny spiders, and mites.
15 In addition, they faced little ecological competition, as there are no other amphibians native to the islands, nor are there the snakes, tarantulas, or other Caribbean hunters that usually serve to keep the coqui population in check.

The way the coqui hatch also gives the coqui an advan-
20 tage in Hawaii's ecosystem. Frogs usually hatch into tadpoles, which require a consistent and substantial amount of water to survive. By contrast, the coqui emerges from the egg as a tiny but fully formed frog, which allows it to thrive in saturated moss, the dampened plastic that importers wrap around plants,
25 or even a drop of water on a plant leaf. Moreover, young coquis don't begin to emit their signature calls until they are about a year old; consequently, avian predators are unable to locate the tiny frogs by sound.

Perhaps the coqui's most noteworthy feature is its ex-
30 tremely loud calling song. To a listener one to two feet away, a single coqui can produce a mating call up to 100 decibels. The unusual volume of the frog's call is compounded by two other factors. First, coquis congregate closely on relatively small parcels of land; one recent survey found 400 adult frogs
35 in one 20-by-20-meter plot. This degree of concentration amplifies the sound the frogs make. Second, coquis tend to overlap their calls, with a single coqui seeking to fill gaps in other frogs' songs with its own effort to attract a mate. As a result, coquis create a "wall of sound" that is even more
40 pronounced because Hawaii boasts few other night-calling species. For these reasons, human residents of Hawaii tend to regard coquis as nuisances, polluting the air with their incessant noise.

Conservationists worry about other ramifications of the
45 coqui's invasion of the Hawaiian ecosystem. One problem is that while the coqui receives the bulk of residents' attention because of its nocturnal serenades, another, quieter genus of the frog—the greenhouse frog—represents an equal threat to the biodiversity of the island. As voracious insectivores,
50 coquis and greenhouse frogs are threatening the survival of arthropods (invertebrate animals with jointed legs, including insects, scorpions, crustaceans, and spiders), whose populations are already close to extirpation due to other foreign predators. Ornithologists fear that depleting the insect population
55 could result in serious consequences for Hawaii's food web, especially considering that the birds native to the islands are also insectivores.

Symbiotic interactions between the coqui and other invasive species pose another ecological threat. The presence
60 of coquis could permit the flourishing of other so-called "dissonant" species, such as non-native snakes that prey upon the frogs. Herpetologists have speculated that nematodes and other types of vertebrate parasites can be transported with coquis and can infect indigenous fauna. Furthermore, many
65 ecologists believe the proliferation of these frogs will further homogenize the island's biota.

Debate persists about how best to reduce or even eradicate the population of coquis and their cousins in Hawaii. Hand-capturing the tiny frogs is probably the most environmentally
70 sensitive way to remove them from their habitat, but their sheer number renders this approach inefficient. The maximum concentration of pesticides that would not damage fauna or flora has not been potent enough to kill the frogs. Seeking a more creative solution, scientists have had some success treating the
75 frogs with caffeine citrate, a drug typically prescribed to treat breathing and metabolic abnormalities in humans. Caffeine citrate can penetrate the coqui's moist skin, and the drug's high acidity essentially poisons the animal and inactivates its nervous systems. From a biodiversity standpoint, this
80 technique has the added benefit of posing almost no danger to plants, which lack a nervous system, or to insects, which have an impenetrable, hard exoskeleton.

Even if new techniques finally exterminate the coqui, experts are skeptical that the invader's current effects on the
85 1,000 acres of Hawaii's ecosystem can be reversed. This patch of land is not expansive in comparison to Hawaii's total 4.1 million acres, yet it is an indication of potential widespread disaster: since the habitat and its native residents have thus far been able to adjust to the presence of coquis, eliminating the
90 frogs could yield unintended and far-reaching consequences to the biodiversity of the habitat beyond arthropods. For now, scientists are likely to continue the delicate balancing act of limiting the coqui's population growth while preventing further damage to Hawaii's ecosystem.

GO ON TO THE NEXT PAGE.

31. Which of the following questions is NOT answered by this passage?

    A. On an annual basis, how often do coqui frogs mate and produce offspring?

    B. Which predators native to Puerto Rico are absent in the Hawaiian islands?

    C. What behavorial factors influence the volume of the coqui's calls?

    D. How could the coqui potentially disrupt the food chain on the islands it inhabits?

32. It is most reasonable to infer from the passage that the lack of amphibian life in Hawaii:

    F. benefits coquis, which don't have to compete for food and space.

    G. provides little opportunity for coquis to form symbiotic relationships.

    H. forces coquis to build their own nests in order to mate and breed.

    J. is a result of invasive species' attacks on the biodiversity of the islands.

33. Which of the following statements about the noise levels produced by the coqui is supported by the passage?

    A. The coqui males have lower, guttural croaks than do females of the species.

    B. Calls are louder when coquis are defending their territory than when they are mating.

    C. The calls of coqui sound particularly loud because there are no gaps of silence.

    D. Coqui are noisier at dawn and dusk than at other times of day.

34. The primary purpose of the third paragraph (lines 19–28) is to:

    F. describe wet weather conditions in Hawaii necessary for the coqui to breed.

    G. provide a physical description of the coqui's habitat in Hawaii compared to that in Puerto Rico.

    H. explain the ecological and behavioral advantages that permit the coqui to thrive in Hawaii.

    J. give an overview of the amphibian life cycle, from the tadpole to frog stage.

35. Compared to the language of the first paragraph, the language of the sixth paragraph (lines 58–66) is more:

    A. opinionated.

    B. scientific.

    C. optimistic.

    D. casual.

36. As it is used in line 53, the word *extirpation* most nearly means:

    F. competition.

    G. extinction.

    H. overpopulation.

    J. pursuit.

37. Which of the following ideas is presented in the passage as theory and not fact?

    A. Coqui frogs cluster together in high concentrations, amplifying the sound they make.

    B. Store-bought poisons, in permissible doses, are not strong enough to kill the frogs.

    C. The exoskeleton of insects is a better defense against caffeine citrate than the skin of amphibians.

    D. A decrease in Hawaii's insect population causes a decrease in bird populations.

38. The passage states that coquis often carry parasites called:

    F. nematodes.

    G. arthropods.

    H. scorpions.

    J. arachnids.

39. Which of the following statements best reflects the information provided in the passage about the relevance of the greenhouse frog to the discussion of the coqui?

    A. The greenhouse frog lives primarily indoors, whereas the coqui lives primarily in island rain forests.

    B. The greenhouse frog is less prominent than the coqui but can be equally damaging to the Hawaiian ecosystem.

    C. The greenhouse frog does not pose as dangerous a threat to the Hawaiian ecosystem as the coqui does.

    D. It is easier to locate and eliminate the coqui because the greenhouse frog does not produce loud mating calls.

40. The phrase "1,000 acres" (line 85) refers to which type of land in Hawaii?

    F. Caribbean ecosystem

    G. Bird sanctuary

    H. Rain forest

    J. Coqui habitat

END OF TEST 3.
STOP! DO NOT TURN THE PAGE UNTIL TOLD TO DO SO.
DO NOT RETURN TO A PREVIOUS TEST

SCIENCE REASONING TEST

35 Minutes—40 Questions

DIRECTIONS: There are seven passages in the following section. Each passage is followed by several questions. After reading a passage, choose the best answer to each question and blacken the corresponding oval on your answer sheet. You may refer to the passages as often as necessary.

You are NOT permitted to use a calculator on this test.

Passage I

A group of students studied the frictional forces involved on stationary objects.

In a series of experiments, the students used rectangular shaped objects of various materials that all had identical masses. One end of a plastic board coated with a polymer film was fastened to a table surface by a hinge so the angle θ between the board and table could be changed, as shown in Figure 1.

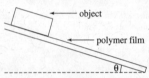

Figure 1

Objects were placed on the opposite end of the board, and the angle θ at which the object started to slide was recorded. The tangent of this angle represents the coefficient of static friction between the object and the polymer surface. This coefficient is proportional to the force required to move a stationary object. Higher coefficients mean that greater forces of friction must be overcome to initiate movement.

The dimensions of the objects gave them 3 distinct *faces* of unequal area as shown in Figure 2. Unless otherwise stated, the objects were placed on the ramp with Face A down.

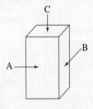

Figure 2

Experiment 1

Four objects made of different materials were placed on the ramp at a temperature of 25°C. The ramp was gradually raised and as soon as the object started to move, the angle θ of the ramp was recorded in Table 1.

Table 1	
Object material	θ (degrees)
Granite	12.1
Copper	16.8
Wood	22.0
Brick	31.1

Experiment 2

The procedure for Experiment 1 was repeated with the wooden object, varying which face was placed down on the ramp. Results were recorded in Table 2.

Table 2	
Face	θ (degrees)
A	22.0
B	22.0
C	22.0

GO ON TO THE NEXT PAGE.

Experiment 3

The procedure for Experiment 1 was repeated with the wooden object, varying the temperature of the polymer ramp. Results for 5 temperatures were recorded in Table 3.

Table 3	
Temperature (°C)	θ (degrees)
0	18.5
25	22.0
50	25.4
75	29.0
100	32.5

Experiment 4

The procedure for Experiment 1 was repeated with multiple wooden objects. For each trial, the objects were stacked on top of each other before raising the ramp. The angle θ where the stack started to slide was recorded in Table 4.

Table 4	
Number of objects	θ (degrees)
2	22.0
3	22.0
4	22.0

1. If the procedure used in Experiment 3 had been repeated at a temperature of 62.5°C, the angle required for the object to start moving down the ramp most likely would have been closest to which of the following?

   A. 27.2 degrees
   B. 29.2 degrees
   C. 30.3 degrees
   D. 31.4 degrees

2. Suppose the students had placed the 4 objects used in Experiment 1 on the ramp when it was flat and pushed each of the objects, such that the amount of force applied to each object gradually increased until it moved. Based on the results of Experiment 1, the object made of which material would most likely have taken the *greatest* amount of force to start moving?

   F. Brick
   G. Wood
   H. Copper
   J. Granite

3. Based on the results of Experiments 1 and 4, what was the effect, if any, of the weight of the object on the coefficient of static friction?

   A. The coefficient of static friction always increased as the object's weight increased.
   B. The coefficient of static friction always decreased as the object's weight increased.
   C. The coefficient of static friction increased and then decreased as the object's weight increased.
   D. The coefficient of static friction was not affected by the weight of the object.

4. In Experiment 1, the reason the students used objects made of different materials was most likely to vary the amount of frictional force between the:

   F. plastic board and the polymer surface.
   G. various objects and the polymer surface.
   H. objects made of different materials when brought into contact with each other.
   J. stacked objects, so that the objects would not fall over when the angle of the ramp was raised high enough to cause motion.

5. Which of the following ranks the different types of objects used, in order, from the material that presented the greatest resistance to movement to the material that presented the least resistance to movement?

   A. Granite, copper, wood, brick
   B. Copper, wood, granite, brick
   C. Granite, wood, brick, copper
   D. Brick, wood, copper, granite

6. The main purpose of Experiment 3 was to determine the effects of temperature on which of the following variables?

   F. Coefficient of static friction between wood and wood
   G. Coefficient of static friction between wood and polymer
   H. Mass of the wooden object
   J. Total frictional force of the polymer on all objects placed on the ramp

GO ON TO THE NEXT PAGE.

Passage II

Despite a global campaign since 1988 to eradicate *polio-myelitis* (polio), the virus that causes this disease continues to be endemic in four countries. This polio virus, which can exist as Type 1, Type 2, or Type 3, is most often transmitted through water that is contaminated by human waste. People can be immunized from this virus with a highly effective vaccine, which can be administered orally or by injection. Recent analyses of polio virus transmission have focused on the four polio-endemic countries India, Pakistan, Afghanistan, and Nigeria.

Study 1

In 2004, a temporary ban on polio vaccines was instituted in Nigeria in response to concerns that they were contaminated. Researchers reviewed World Health Organization (WHO) records to determine the number of Type 1 polio virus infections that were reported in Nigeria in 2004 and tallied their findings by month (see Figure 1). The World Health Organization has noted that in polio-endemic countries, official records underestimate the number of people actually infected, because numerous infected individuals do not report their symptoms to clinics or rely on local therapists who are not surveyed. In a polio-endemic country, for every person who has reported an infection, as many as ten people may actually be infected in the local population.

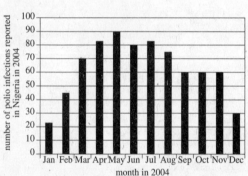

Figure 1

Study 2

Although polio eradication efforts have been most consistent in the urban areas of polio-endemic countries, these areas also have a high risk for a reemergence of polio, especially when the large urban populations are exposed to water contaminated with wastes that harbor the polio virus. In 2007, researchers analyzed the number of people who reported infections with Type 3 polio virus in the five largest cities in India. These cities were Mumbai in western India, New Delhi and Kolkata in northern India, and Chennai and Hyderabad in southern India. The analysis was undertaken in the months of June and August. June 2007 was chosen as a representative month for the dry summer season in India, during which there was minimal rainfall. August 2007 was chosen as a representative month for the wet monsoon season in India, during which there was daily rainfall. The results of the findings are shown in Figure 2.

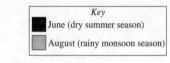

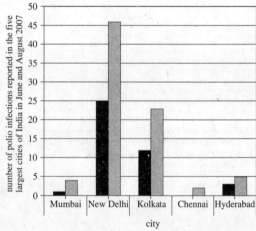

Figure 2

GO ON TO THE NEXT PAGE.

7. According to Figure 1, the greatest increase in the number of reported polio infections in Nigeria occurred between which two months?

    A. January and February
    B. February and March
    C. April and May
    D. November and December

8. It is estimated that for every person infected with the polio virus in an endemic country, there are 200 people at risk for contracting the virus. Given the results of Study 1, how many people would have been at risk for becoming infected with the polio virus in Nigeria in June 2004 ?

    F. 80
    G. 200
    H. 800
    J. 16,000

9. Given the information in Figure 2, which of the following might explain the difference in reported cases of polio in major Indian cities between June and August of 2007 ?

    A. Water is more likely to become contaminated with polio-infected human waste in periods of high rainfall.
    B. Water is less likely to become contaminated with polio-infected human waste in periods of high rainfall.
    C. The polio virus infects more people in India during the summer and monsoon seasons than during the autumn and winter seasons.
    D. Those diagnosed with the polio virus in June are able to recover by August.

10. Which of the following hypotheses was most likely tested in Study 2 ?

    F. The number of reported cases of polio infections varies significantly between Nigeria and India.
    G. Most cases of polio infections are not reported to medical authorities in India.
    H. Poliomyelitis infections affect more people in certain regions in India than in other regions.
    J. The number of reported cases of polio infections in India is greatest during the summer and least during the winter.

11. Polio-endemic countries are located in warm climates that harbor many mosquitoes. Would the presence of mosquitoes directly affect the transmission of the polio virus?

    A. Yes, because the polio virus is primarily transmitted through mosquitoes.
    B. Yes, because the polio virus is primarily transmitted through human waste.
    C. No, because the polio virus is primarily transmitted through mosquitoes.
    D. No, because the polio virus is primarily transmitted through human waste.

12. The comparison of reported polio infections in India in 2007, as shown in Figure 2, indicates that relative to the number of people in Kolkata infected with polio in June, the number of people infected with polio in Kolkata in August was approximately:

    F. half as much.
    G. the same.
    H. twice as much.
    J. ten times as much.

GO ON TO THE NEXT PAGE.

Passage III

Osmotic pressure (Π) is the amount of pressure, in atm, required to maintain equilibrium of a solvent across a semipermeable membrane. At a constant temperature, osmotic pressure is dependent only on a solute's ability to dissociate or ionize in the solvent (*van 't Hoff factor*, *i*) and the concentration of solute particles. The osmotic pressure is determined by the equation:

$$\Pi = iMRT$$

M represents the concentration (in molarity, *M*), *R* is the ideal gas constant (0.0821 L atm mol^{-1} K^{-1}), and *T* (300 K) is the temperature in Kelvin (K). The value of *R* is assumed to be a constant for all osmotic pressure calculations.

The dissociation of a solute depends on its unique chemical properties. The van 't Hoff factors for some common substances are displayed in Table 1. Higher van 't Hoff factors correlate with greater dissociation or ionization. The effect of the van 't Hoff factor on the osmotic pressure may be seen in Figure 1.

Table 1	
Substance	van 't Hoff factor *
sucrose	1.0
NaCl	1.9
MgCl$_2$	2.7
FeCl$_3$	3.4
*Values at 300 K	

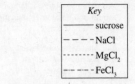

Key
— sucrose
--- NaCl
······ MgCl$_2$
-·-·- FeCl$_3$

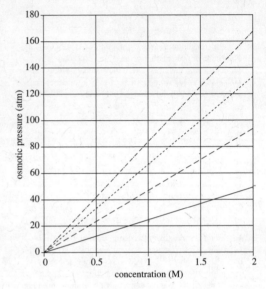

Figure 1

GO ON TO THE NEXT PAGE.

13. According to Figure 1, which of the following solutions would exhibit the *least* osmotic pressure?

   A. 1.0 M FeCl₃ solution
   B. 1.0 M MgCl₂ solution
   C. 2.0 M NaCl solution
   D. 2.0 M sucrose solution

14. If 1.0 M solutions of various solutes were prepared, which of the following solutions would have the highest level of ionization?

   F. Sucrose
   G. NaCl
   H. MgCl₂
   J. FeCl₃

15. Which of the following solutions would exhibit the closest osmotic pressure to that of a 1.5 M NaCl solution at 300 K, if the gas constant is 0.0821 L atm/ mol⁻¹ K⁻¹ ?

   A. 1.0 M NaCl solution ($i = 1.9$)
   B. 2.0 M NaCl solution ($i = 1.9$)
   C. 2.9 M Sucrose solution ($i = 1.0$)
   D. 3.5 M Sucrose solution ($i = 1.0$)

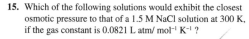

16. Based on Figure 1, as the concentration of solute decreases, the pressure required to hold solvent concentration across a membrane at equilibrium will:

   F. increase only.
   G. decrease only.
   H. remain constant.
   J. increase, then remain constant.

17. A scientist recently discovered a compound that ionizes readily in solution ($i = 3.8$) and results in low osmotic pressures. Are the findings of this scientist consistent with Figure 1 ?

   A. Yes, because FeCl₃ causes higher osmotic pressure than sucrose.
   B. No, because sucrose causes higher osmotic pressure than FeCl₃.
   C. Yes, because FeCl₃ causes lower osmotic pressure than sucrose.
   D. No, because sucrose causes lower osmotic pressure than FeCl₃.

GO ON TO THE NEXT PAGE.

Passage IV

Soil salinity is the concentration of potentially harmful salts dissolved in the groundwater that fills soil pores. Salinity is determined by measuring a soil's *electrical conductivity (EC)* and *exchangeable sodium percentage (ESP)*. High EC indicates a high concentration of dissolved salt particles; ESP indicates the proportion of electrical conductivity that is due to dissolved sodium ions.

Soil samples were collected from five different distances west of a particular river. Figure 1 shows the electrical conductivity of the soil samples at four different depth ranges measured in milli-Siemens per centimeter (mS/cm).

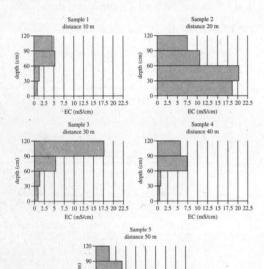

Figure 1

Figure 2 shows the exchangeable sodium percentage of the five sites at different depths.

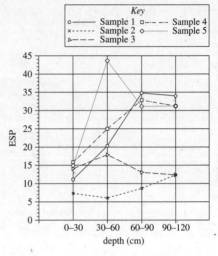

Figure 2

18. Figure 2 indicates that, compared with the soil tested in Sample 1, the soil tested in Sample 4 contains:

  F. a higher percentage of sodium ions throughout.
  G. a lower percentage of sodium ions throughout.
  H. a higher percentage of sodium ions at shallower depths only.
  J. a lower percentage of sodium ions at shallower depths only.

19. According to Figure 2, in the soil collected in Sample 3 at a depth of 30–60 cm, approximately what percent of the soil conductivity is due to sodium ions?

  A. 14%
  B. 17%
  C. 24%
  D. 44%

20. Based on Figures 1 and 2, the electrical conductivity due to sodium ions in the sample collected 40 m west of the river was:

  F. greatest at a depth of 90–120 cm.
  G. greatest at a depth of 0–30 cm.
  H. least at a depth of 30–60 cm.
  J. least at a depth of 0–30 cm.

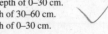

GO ON TO THE NEXT PAGE.

21. Based on Figure 2, which of the following figures best represents the exchangeable sodium percentage for the five soil samples collected at a depth of 90–120 cm?

A.

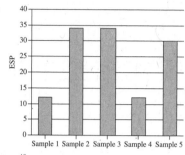

B.

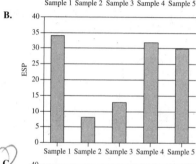

C.

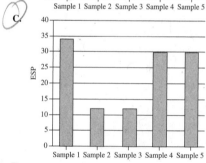

D.

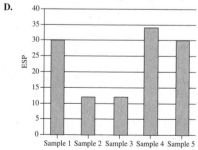

22. A student claimed that as soil moves away from a major water source, such as a river, the salinity of the soil increases. Is this claim supported by Figures 1 and 2 ?

F. No; the electrical conductivity and exchangeable sodium percentage both decreased from Sample 1 to Sample 5.

G. No; there was no consistent trend for electrical conductivity and exchangeable sodium percentage.

H. Yes; the electrical conductivity and exchangeable sodium percentage both increased from Sample 1 to Sample 5.

J. Yes; the electrical conductivity increased and exchangeable sodium percentage decreased from Sample 1 to Sample 5.

GO ON TO THE NEXT PAGE.

Passage V

A group of researchers performed the following study in order to investigate declines in primarily carnivorous polar bear populations in the Arctic over a 10-year period.

Study

The researchers obtained previously collected data from several areas previously identified as polar bear habitats. From this data, the researchers selected sixty 5 km × 5 km blocks that do not overlap with one another. The blocks were selected to fall into six groups, each with a different set of conditions selected in order to conform to criteria for listing animals as threatened species. Previous research has indicated that Arctic sea ice and available food are among the factors which may affect polar bear populations.

Table 1 identifies each of the groups utilized in the study. Conditions other than the ones listed were considered to be normal.

Table 1	
Group	Conditions
1	These areas had significantly decreased populations of marine mammals consumed by polar bears.
2	These areas had significantly increased populations of seaweed commonly consumed by marine mammals.
3	These areas had been subject to excess thawing of Arctic sea ice.
4	These areas were subject to the same conditions as Groups 1 and 3.
5	These areas were subject to the same conditions as Groups 2 and 3.
6	Unaffected polar bear habitat.

Data for each of the plots was collected, and the population density of polar bears was calculated in terms of adult polar bears/km². Table 2 shows the population density of the blocks in Group 6.

Table 2	
Area Label	Population density of Group 6 areas (polar bears/km²)
A	0.93
B	2.10
C	0.21
D	0.72
E	0.88
F	0.72
G	0.91
H	0.53
I	1.12
J	0.74

The data collected was analyzed to find the *average population density ratio* for each group. The researchers defined the average population density ratio of a given group as being equal to the result of the following expression:

$$\frac{\text{average population density of the group's areas}}{\text{average population density of Group 6 areas}}$$

Figure 1 shows the average population density ratio of Groups 1–5.

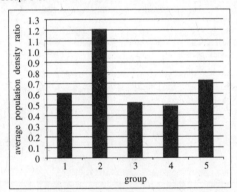

Figure 1

GO ON TO THE NEXT PAGE.

23. Which of the following statements provides the best explanation for why the researchers collected data for Group 6 in their study?

   A. Group 6 provided data indicating the types of predators which most threaten polar bears in their natural habitat.
   B. Group 6 provided a standard by which the other groups could be compared in order to determine how each set of conditions affected polar bear populations.
   C. Group 6 provided a means by which the researchers could carefully identify and select the conditions for the remaining five groups.
   D. Group 6 provided a means of determining the greatest number of polar bears that would be likely to survive in an area of 25 km².

24. Which one of the following is a question that most likely explains why Group 2 areas were included in the study?

   F. Does an increase in the food source of their prey affect the population density of polar bears?
   G. If additional masses of seaweed were to be introduced to the Arctic, would polar bears be increasingly omnivorous?
   H. If additional masses of seaweed were to be introduced to the Arctic, would prey population density increase?
   J. Does an increase in the number of prey animals living in the same area as polar bears affect the amount of Arctic ice?

25. Which of the following correctly ranks Groups 1–5 from the group where the conditions are *most* conducive to polar bear population density in the study to the group where the conditions are *least* conducive?

   A. Group 1, Group 2, Group 3, Group 4, Group 5
   B. Group 4, Group 3, Group 1, Group 5, Group 2
   C. Group 2, Group 5, Group 1, Group 3, Group 4
   D. Group 2, Group 1, Group 5, Group 3, Group 4

26. Which of the following is most likely an organism that the researchers identified as exhibiting a significantly decreased population when defining Group 1 ?

   F. Snowy owl
   G. Seal
   H. Salmon
   J. Polar bear

27. *Synergy* between two effects is said to exist when their combined effect is greater than the sum of each effect considered separately. The study appears to be designed such that the researchers can investigate possible synergy in which of the following two groups?

   A. Groups 1 and 2
   B. Groups 1 and 4
   C. Groups 4 and 5
   D. Groups 1 and 3

28. Before performing their analysis of the data, the researchers developed four different hypotheses. Each one of the four hypotheses below is supported by the results of the study EXCEPT:

   F. Declining prey populations have had some effect on polar bear populations.
   G. The melting of Arctic sea ice has a greater effect on polar bear populations than declining prey populations.
   H. Declining prey populations have a greater effect on polar bear populations than the melting of Arctic sea ice.
   J. The melting of Arctic sea ice has had some effect on polar bear populations.

GO ON TO THE NEXT PAGE.

Passage VI

Methane (CH_4) is an important energy source and a powerful greenhouse gas. CH_4 levels in the atmosphere are increasing, largely as a result of increasing livestock populations and energy emissions. Two scientists debate possible consequences of rising levels of atmospheric methane.

Scientist 1

Increasing CH_4 levels are a serious concern because, in the atmosphere, CH_4 can be converted into *formaldehyde* (H_2CO). H_2CO is a dangerous chemical, banned in some countries and used as an embalming fluid in others.

When *ozone* (O_3) is struck by solar radiation (light) in the presence of water, *hydroxyl radicals* ($\cdot OH$) are created (Reaction 1):

$$light + O_3 + H_2O \rightarrow 2 \cdot OH + O_2$$

When OH comes into contact with CH_4, another radical, $\cdot CH_3$, is formed (Reaction 2):

$$OH + CH_4 \rightarrow \cdot CH_3 + H_2O$$

In the presence of oxygen (O_2) and nitric oxide (NO), the highly reactive $\cdot CH_3$ is converted into H_2CO (Reaction 3):

$$\cdot CH_3 + NO + 2O_2 \rightarrow H_2CO + NO_2 + HO_2$$

The product HO_2 is unstable and reacts with NO, yielding more $\cdot OH$ (Reaction 4):

$$HO_2 + NO \rightarrow NO_2 + \cdot OH$$

Together, Reactions 2–4 are called a *chain reaction* because the OH formed in Reaction 4 can react with another CH_4 molecule in Reaction 2:

$$\cdot OH + CH_4 \rightarrow \cdot CH_3 + H_2O$$

$$\cdot CH_3 + NO + 2O_2 \rightarrow H_2CO + NO_2 + HO_2$$

$$HO_2 + NO \rightarrow NO_2 + \cdot OH$$

As a result, one $\cdot OH$ can convert a great deal of CH_4. At current CH_4 levels, this chain reaction is the primary fate of atmospheric $\cdot OH$, making the formation of H_2CO an urgent concern.

Scientist 2

H_2CO is a dangerous chemical, but atmospheric formaldehyde levels will not increase dramatically due to methane emissions. *Carbon monoxide* (CO) generation may be the greater concern. Hydroxyl radicals can break down methane, leading to the formation of H_2CO and nitric oxide, as in Reactions 1–4; in the presence of light, however, H_2CO quickly decomposes to CO and *hydrogen,* H_2 (Reaction 5):

$$H_2CO \rightarrow H_2 + CO$$

Furthermore, the OH generated by Reactions 1 and 4 will react rapidly with any H_2CO in the atmosphere to produce CO and water: (Reaction 6)

$$H_2CO + 2 \cdot OH \rightarrow CO + 2H_2O$$

In addition to reducing the amount of H_2CO by breaking down the H_2CO molecule, this reaction removes OH from the atmosphere, inhibiting the chain reaction of Reactions 2–4.

29. Which of the following substances do the two scientists agree must be present in order for $\cdot CH_3$ to be generated by atmospheric methane?

A. H_3O^+
B. NO_2
C. HNO_3
D. O_3

GO ON TO THE NEXT PAGE.

30. Which of the following graphs reflects Scientist 1's hypothesis of how levels of H_2CO in the atmosphere will change as more CH_4 is released into the atmosphere?

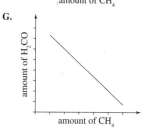

F.

G.

H.

J.

31. A student suggested that the molecular mass of either product in Reaction 5 would be greater than the molecular mass of the reactant in Reaction 5. Is he correct?

A. No; H_2CO is composed not of molecules, but of atoms.
B. Yes; the mass of a molecule of H_2CO is greater than the mass of either reactant.
C. No; the mass of a molecule of H_2CO is greater than the mass of either product.
D. Yes; the mass of a molecule of CO is greater than the mass of a molecule of H_2.

32. In certain parts of the atmosphere, the amount of O_3 is decreasing. As O_3 levels decrease, which of the following would Scientist 1 *most strongly agree with* regarding the levels of $\cdot CH_3$ and H_2CO in the atmosphere?

F. The amount of $\cdot CH_3$ would increase and the amount of H_2CO would decrease.
G. The amount of $\cdot CH_3$ would decrease and the level of H_2CO would remain constant.
H. The amounts of $\cdot CH_3$ and H_2CO would both decrease.
J. The amounts of $\cdot CH_3$ and H_2CO would both increase.

33. Of the following statements, with which would Scientist 2 *most strongly disagree*?

A. O_3 is involved in the generation of H_2CO in the atmosphere.
B. $\cdot OH$ is contributing to the formation of carbon monoxide in the atmosphere.
C. Solar radiation contributes to the break down of CH_4.
D. As CH_4 emissions increase, levels of H_2CO will rise dramatically.

34. After examining Scientist 1's hypothesis, Scientist 2 claimed that Reaction 3 would lead to increased levels of carbon monoxide. By which of the following explanations would Scientist 2 most likely support this argument?

F. Reaction 3 reduces the amount of NO present, inhibiting Reaction 4.
G. Reaction 3 produces H_2CO, which can react in Reaction 5 and Reaction 6.
H. Reaction 3 produces HO_2, which can react with H_2CO to produce CO.
J. Reaction 3 reduces the amount of O_2 present, making it more difficult for CO to form.

35. Further investigation has shown that Reaction 6 occurs on a large scale. Which of the following statements explains how the new evidence *most* weakens the argument of Scientist 1 ?

A. The OH produced in Reaction 4 reacts with CH_4.
B. The OH produced in Reaction 4 reacts with H_2CO.
C. The H_2O produced in Reaction 6 reacts with light and O_3.
D. The OH produced in Reaction 6 reacts with H_2CO.

GO ON TO THE NEXT PAGE.

Passage VII

A *Carnot heat engine* is an engine which runs by compressing and expanding a gas and transferring heat.

Figures 1 and 2 show the changes in pressure, P, and volume, V, that occur as two Carnot heat engines, A and B, run. For every gas, $PV = \Omega T$, where Ω is a constant and T represents the time.

The cycle begins as the gas is at its highest temperature and pressure. First, the gas expands, so volume increases while pressure decreases. As the gas expands, it can do work, such as pushing a piston. After the gas has run out of thermal energy and can no longer do work it is at its lowest temperature and pressure and the gas begins to be compressed, for instance a piston falling back down on the gas. As the gas is compressed, pressure increases while volume decreases and temperature begins to rise. In every Carnot heat engine, the gas ends at the same pressure, temperature, and volume as it began, thus completing a cycle.

Carnot Heat Engine B

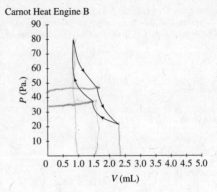

Figure 2

Carnot Heat Engine A

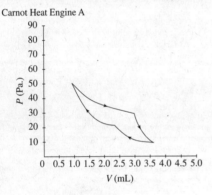

Figure 1

36. According to Figure 2, for Carnot heat engine B, when V was decreasing from its largest value and had a value of 1.5 mL, P had a value closest to:

F. 10 Pa.
G. 30 Pa.
H. 50 Pa.
J. 70 Pa.

GO ON TO THE NEXT PAGE.

37. For a new Carnot heat engine, F, a partial graph of V versus P is obtained.

If Carnot heat engine F behaves like Carnot heat engines A and B, the remainder of the graph of V versus P for Carnot heat engine F will look most like which of the following?

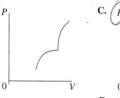

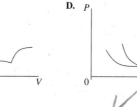

38. For Carnot heat engine A, the minimum value of P was obtained at a V closest to:

F. 0.5 mL.
G. 2.0 mL.
H. 3.5 mL.
J. 5.0 mL.

39. Consider the largest value of V and the smallest value of V on the graph in Figure 2. How are these values related?

A. The smallest value of V is –1 times the largest value of V.
B. The smallest value of V is 1/3 times the largest value of V.
C. The smallest value of V is 1 times the largest value of V.
D. The smallest value of V is 2 times the largest value of V.

40. The *reversible isothermal expansion* step of a Carnot heat engine cycle takes place when P is decreased from its highest value and V is increased from its lowest value. According to Figure 1, the *reversible isothermal expansion* step for Carnot heat engine A begins when V is closest to:

F. 1.0 mL.
G. 2.25 mL.
H. 3.0 mL.
J. 3.5 mL.

END OF TEST 4
STOP! DO NOT RETURN TO ANY OTHER TEST.

Directions

This is a test of your writing skills. You will have thirty (30) minutes to write an essay. Before you begin planning and writing your essay, read the writing prompt carefully to understand exactly what you are being asked to do. Your essay will be evaluated on the evidence it provides of your ability to express judgments by taking a position on the issue in the writing prompt; to maintain a focus on the topic throughout your essay; to develop a position by using logical reasoning and by supporting your ideas; to organize ideas in a logical way; and to use language clearly and effectively according to the conventions of standard written English.

You may use the unlined pages in this test booklet to plan your essay. These pages will not be scored. *You must write your essay on the lined pages in the answer folder.* Your writing on those lined pages will be scored. You may not need all the lined pages, but to ensure you have enough room to finish, do NOT skip lines. You may write corrections or additions neatly between the lines of your essay, but do NOT write in the margins of the lined pages. *Illegible essays cannot be scored, so you must write (or print) clearly.*

If you finish before time is called, you may review your work. Lay your pencil down immediately when time is called.

DO NOT OPEN THIS BOOK UNTIL YOU ARE TOLD TO DO SO.

ACT Assessment Writing Test Prompt

A number of health organizations are lobbying the Motion Picture Association of America (MPAA) to incorporate cigarette smoking into the criteria for a restricted, or R, rating for films. Since the R rating requires anyone under the age of 17 to be accompanied by a parent or guardian, supporters of this policy believe it would reduce the exposure youths may have to smoking as a glamorous habit and make these teens less likely to smoke as a result. Opponents of the policy believe it would curtail the creative freedom of the filmmakers. In your opinion, should movies be rated R if they contain cigarette smoking?

In your essay, take a position on this question. You may write about either one of the two points of view given, or you may present a different point of view on this question. Use specific reasons and examples to support your position.

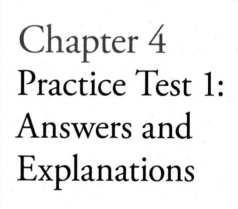

Chapter 4
Practice Test 1:
Answers and
Explanations

TEST 1 ENGLISH ANSWERS

1.	D	36.	J
2.	F	37.	A
3.	B	38.	G
4.	H	39.	C
5.	C	40.	F
6.	J	41.	B
7.	D	42.	F
8.	J	43.	D
9.	A	44.	G
10.	F	45.	D
11.	B	46.	H
12.	G	47.	C
13.	C	48.	J
14.	H	49.	B
15.	B	50.	H
16.	F	51.	A
17.	D	52.	H
18.	J	53.	A
19.	B	54.	J
20.	H	55.	D
21.	A	56.	F
22.	J	57.	A
23.	B	58.	G
24.	J	59.	D
25.	B	60.	G
26.	F	61.	C
27.	D	62.	J
28.	F	63.	A
29.	D	64.	J
30.	F	65.	C
31.	D	66.	F
32.	G	67.	C
33.	D	68.	G
34.	H	69.	B
35.	C	70.	G

71. A	26. F
72. J	27. C
73. D	28. J
74. J	29. B
75. B	30. H
	31. E
	32. H
	33. A
	34. J

TEST 1 MATH ANSWERS

1. A		35. C
2. J		36. J
3. B		37. D
4. K		38. J
5. D		39. B
6. H		40. F
7. A		41. A
8. J		42. K
9. C		43. C
10. H		44. G
11. A		45. D
12. F		46. J
13. D		47. C
14. G		48. J
15. D		49. C
16. G		50. K
17. A		51. D
18. G		52. G
19. B		53. B
20. H		54. F
21. B		55. B
22. F		56. F
23. C		57. C
24. K		58. F
25. B		59. D
		60. K

TEST 1 READING ANSWERS

1.	C	21.	C
2.	J	22.	H
3.	B	23.	A
4.	H	24.	F
5.	B	25.	B
6.	F	26.	H
7.	A	27.	B
8.	G	28.	J
9.	C	29.	C
10.	J	30.	F
11.	B	31.	A
12.	H	32.	F
13.	D	33.	C
14.	F	34.	H
15.	D	35.	B
16.	H	36.	G
17.	A	37.	D
18.	G	38.	F
19.	C	39.	B
20.	H	40.	J

TEST 1 SCIENCE ANSWERS

1.	A	21.	C
2.	F	22.	G
3.	D	23.	B
4.	G	24.	F
5.	D	25.	C
6.	G	26.	G
7.	B	27.	D
8.	J	28.	H
9.	A	29.	D
10.	H	30.	F
11.	D	31.	C
12.	H	32.	H
13.	D	33.	D
14.	J	34.	G
15.	C	35.	B
16.	G	36.	G
17.	D	37.	C
18.	H	38.	H
19.	B	39.	B
20.	J	40.	F

TEST 1 ENGLISH EXPLANATIONS

1. **D** The phrase *left by the delivery man* is an unnecessary detail added to the sentence and should be off-set by two commas, making choice (D) the best answer. The semicolon in choices (A) and (C) creates a fragment in the second half of the sentence.

2. **F** The sentence uses *scrawled* as an adjective to describe the words, not as a verb, so you can eliminate (G). Choice (H) uses the wrong form of *scrawl*, and choice (J) is the wrong idiomatic expression.

3. **B** The phrase *my heart skipping a beat (or two)* is incomplete and cannot be linked to the complete phrase with *and,* eliminating choices (A) and (C). *When* changes the meaning of the sentence, making (B) the best answer.

4. **H** The two halves of this sentence are both complete, eliminating choice (J). Since the second half already uses the pronoun it to refer to the box, *that* and *which* are unnecessary, making choice (C) the best answer.

5. **C** Since the question asks you to make a contrast, you can eliminate choices (B) and (D). Choice (C) better describes the people for whom the record holds value than choice (A).

6. **J** The verb should be in past perfect tense to show that he made his living as a musician before marrying, making choice (J) the only possible answer. Choices (F), (G), and (H) all use *would*, which is the conditional tense of will.

7. **D** The phrase *performing in music hall and local festivals* is incomplete and must be linked to the previous thought, eliminating choices (A) and (B). By using *which* to link the ideas, choice (C) makes it sound as if the grandfather performs the band, rather than the band performing.

8. **J** The best answer is (J) because it is the most concise of the choices. It is unnecessary to the meaning of the sentence to mention who produced the album.

9. **A** The phrase after the dash is adding further details to how rare the record truly is, making choice (A) the best answer. Choice (B) is a contrasting transition, and choices (C) and (D) use transition words that confuse the meaning of the sentence.

10. **F** The verb should be in past perfect tense because it is describing how long one copy had existed before the writer received the record in the mail, eliminating choices (H) and (J). Choice (G) uses the incorrect expression.

11. **B** The words *beg* and *plead* are synonyms, so it is redundant to use both. Choice (B) is the most concise answer.

12. **G** Since the question asks you to discuss the significance to the writer's upbringing, you can eliminate choices (F) and (H). Choice (G) is more personal to the writer than choice (J), making it the best answer.

13. **C** Choice (C) is the only answer that clearly expresses the writer's intended meaning. Choices (A), (B), and (C) all misplace phrases throughout the sentence, confusing who and what are being described.

14. **H** The punctuation should separate two complete ideas, eliminating choices (F) and (J). Choice (G) is an unnecessary transition word, because *however* is already used in the following sentence.

15. **B** The phrase *that he was still with me* is an incomplete thought and should be linked to the previous complete thought, eliminating choice (D). Since the sentence explains what the author feels reassured of, punctuation between *me* and *that* creates an unnecessary pause, making choice (B) the best answer.

16. **F** This question requires that you determine whether an apostrophe or additional punctuation mark is required. No apostrophe is needed because the word *lives* is not possessing anything, so eliminate choices (H) and (J). No pause is required between the words *lives* and *completely*, so eliminate choice (G), which interrupts the sentence unnecessarily. The sentence is correct as written, so the best choice is (F).

17. **D** The question asks for a line that indicates some similarity between the narrator and his friends. Choice (A) discusses only the narrator; choices (B) and (C) contain information that is much too general to discuss only the narrator and his friends. Only choice (D) has all the appropriate elements, particularly as presented in the words *palpable likeness*.

18. **J** This question requires that you determine whether an apostrophe or additional punctuation mark is required. No apostrophe is needed because there is no indication that owners are possessing anything (hint: don't get thrown off by the phrase *restaurant's owners* in which the word appears), so you can eliminate choice (H). Only choice (J) has the appropriate comma placement to situate *chat with the restaurant's owners* within a list (the other items in this list are *sit, drink a cup of coffee,* and *figure out which new and exciting place we'd be driving to next*). A semicolon is inappropriate here because the semicolon is a punctuation mark used to separate two complete ideas, and the context indicates that it is not used to separate the items in this list.

19. **B** The sentence as written contains the phrase *looking forward to it in anticipation*, which is redundant, so you can eliminate choice (A). Choices (C) and (D) contain the same error. Only choice (B) preserves the meaning in a concise, non-redundant way. In addition, the word *it* in choices (A) and (C) is ambiguous.

20. **H** This question asks whether the writer's proposed addition would be appropriately placed at the end of this paragraph. If you're not sure whether to answer Yes or No, look at the reasons. Choice (F) must be eliminated because the proposed addition is too general and is consequently not relevant to other, more personal information in the passage. Choice (G) must be eliminated because it is too general and gives no indication why the narrator should choose a *specific* diner.

Choice (J) suggests that the primary focus of the paragraph up to this point has been *driving*, which it has not; rather, the primary focus of the paragraph is the stop at the diner and the things the narrator and his friends did there. Accordingly, only choice (H) appropriately recognizes the personal tone of the paragraph and correctly advises not to include the proposed addition.

21. **A** The first place you should look in this question is to whether *that* or *whom* is an appropriate first word. *Whom* is the objective form of *who*, which is used to refer only to people. The word here refers back to *something*, not a person, so eliminate choices (B) and (C). Choice (D) changes the meaning of the sentence to suggest that something is doing the ordering, rather than being ordered. The sentence is correct as written, so NO CHANGE is required.

22. **J** This question asks you to determine which word would be most appropriately modified by the phrase *from childhood*. To place the phrase after any of the words in choices (F), (G), or (H) is to break the flow of the sentence and to make the meaning of the sentence unclear. Only choice (J) establishes the proper link between the underlined and non-underlined portions of the sentence in the phrase *remembered from childhood*.

23. **B** In an earlier part of the sentence, the narrator refers to the food in the city as *too expensive*. Only choice (B) supports and modifies this idea. Read the question closely: While the other choices may be true, the best answer will be one that supports and modifies a specific part of the passage.

24. J   In EXCEPT/LEAST/NOT questions, the underlined portion of the sentence is correct. Compare your answer choices. What do words like *as* and *when* do to the first part of the sentence? They make it an introductory idea and an incomplete thought. When the first part of the sentence is incomplete, the comma after the word *could* sets this first part off from the complete idea after it. By contrast, if the first part of the sentence is made complete as it is in choice (J), this creates a comma splice, wherein two complete ideas are insufficiently separated by a comma.

25. B   Identify the subject of the verb. Although the word *restaurants* is closest to the verb, it is not the subject; rather, the subject is the word *place*, a singular subject that requires a singular verb. Since choices (A), (C), and (D) all contain plural verbs, eliminate them. Only choice (B) remains, and the verb *was* does agree in number with the word *place*.

26. F   We need an idea that will signal the transition between the paragraph above, which is a recollection of the trips, and the paragraph below, which fast forwards to the present and discusses the narrator's life now. Only choice (F) contains this transition. Choice (G) deals only with the narrator's friends who are not mentioned in the last paragraph. Choice (H) deals only with the past, and choice (J) deals only with the narrator's life after graduation. Only choice (F) has both the past and present components it needs to transition from one paragraph to the next.

27. D   This question asks you to determine whether you need a transition between the first and second sentences of this last paragraph. Choices (A) and (C) suggest a disagreement between the two ideas where none exists. Choice (B) suggests a cause-and-effect relationship between the two sentences where none exists. Only choice (D) makes sense in the context, where no transition is needed.

28. **F** In EXCEPT/LEAST/NOT questions, the underlined portion of the sentence is correct. To answer this question, you need to determine which prepositions work idiomatically with the verb *drive*. Choice (G) contains the same preposition, *about*, used in the underlined portion, and although not a particularly common usage, *drive about* is idiomatically correct. The same goes for the more familiar *drive around*, as it is used in choices (H) and (J). Accordingly, only choice (F) does not work in the context of the sentence because it is incorrect usage to say *drive among the town*.

29. **D** All the answer choices mean roughly the same thing; each just presents a different way to say it. In situations such as this one, the most concise answer that preserves the meaning is the best. Accordingly, choices (A), (B), and (C) are all too wordy in comparison with choice (D).

30. **F** This question too asks you to determine which choice presents the most concise alternative that preserves the meaning of the sentence. Eliminate choices (G) and (J) because each presents an awkward, wordy alternative to the original. Choice (H) is as concise as choice (F), but note the context: Your answer will need to be parallel to other verbs in the sentence. In this case, only *came back* is parallel with the tense and tone of *drove by*, making the best choice (F).

31. **D** In EXCEPT/LEAST/NOT questions, the underlined portion of the sentence is correct. The original sentence uses *even though* to introduce two contrasting ideas. Choices (A), (B), and (C) are all contrasting transition words and are acceptable. Choice (D) indicates that the ideas are similar and, therefore, is not an acceptable alternative.

32. **G** The best connecting statement should continue the previous idea that Siena has both ancient and modern elements, eliminating choices (F) and (J). The following sentence begins with *Another remnant*, which means the inserted sentence should already list specific examples and makes choice (G) better than (H).

33. **D** It is redundant to describe the horse race as *biannual* and as *held twice a year*, eliminating choices (A) and (B). Choice (D) is better than choice (C) because it is more concise.

34. **H** The phrase *dreaded right-angle turns* describes an obstacle racers must face as they complete each lap, therefore it must immediately follow *laps* to clarify meaning. Choices (F), (G), and (J) do not provide logical sentences because the phrase does not describe *horses*, *track*, or *plaza*.

35. **C** Choice (C) correctly agrees with the present tense of the other verb in the sentence. Choices (A), (B), and (D) do not agree in tense and alter the meaning of the sentence.

36. **J** *Because* introduces an incomplete thought, so choice (F) creates a sentence fragment. Choice (G) suggests contrasting rather than similar ideas. Choice (H) is incorrect because the preceding sentence has already mentioned *financial* commitments, so voluntary taxation cannot be considered an additional act by members.

37. **A** The previous sentence illustrates the enormous cost to hire a jockey, which contrasts with the idea that it is a small price to pay, so the best transition word is choice (A). Choices (B), (C), and (D) all indicate a similar relationship, which is not consistent with the passage.

38. **G** The phrase *even more so than getting married* is an unnecessary description within the sentence and should be offset by either two commas or dashes, eliminating choice (F). Since the non-underlined portion uses a dash before *even*, the best answer is choice (G) not choice (H). Choice (J) creates a sentence fragment, since a semicolon can separate only complete ideas.

39. **C** The word *throughout* begins an incomplete idea, and the phrase cannot stand on its own as a sentence, eliminating choice (A). Choice (C) connects the incomplete phrase to the complete idea before it with the smoothest transition. The comma in choice (D) creates an unnecessary pause. Since a semicolon is generally used to separate two complete sentences, choice (B) is also incorrect.

40. **F** The word *Contrade* ends a complete thought, and *Contrada* begins a second complete thought, so you need a period making choice (F) the best answer. Choices (G), (H), and (J) all create run-on sentences because they do not separate complete ideas.

41. **B** The phrase *from baptisms to food festivals* is an unnecessary description within the sentence and should be offset by either two commas or dashes, eliminating choice (A). Since the non-underlined portion uses a comma after festivals, the best answer is choice (B) not choice (D). Choice (C) incorrectly uses a colon, which can be used only after a complete idea.

42. **F** The correct pronoun is *who* because *members* is the subject for the verb *become*. Choices (G) and (H) use possessive rather than subject case, and choice (J) is object case and does not indicate which noun become describes.

43. **D** The second half of the sentence is an incomplete idea and must be linked to the complete thought, eliminating choices (A), (B), and (C).

44. **G** The passage is written in the present tense, eliminating choices (F) and (H). Since the parties are *thrown* by the locals, you need the passive form for the verb (also called the past participle) not the past tense verb *threw*.

45. **D** The best location for Paragraph 3 is before Paragraph 5, choice (D), because Paragraph 4 introduces and defines the *contrada* discussed in the first sentence of Paragraph 3. There is also a logical sequence from winning the *Palio* at the end of Paragraph 3 to the celebration in the beginning of Paragraph 5.

46. **H** As written, the pronoun *it* in the underlined portion has no clear referent. Choices (G) and (J) do not fix the problem. Only choice (H) replaces the ambiguous pronoun with a clear referent.

47. **C** The sentence as written is a fragment. Choice (B) is also a fragment. Choices (C) and (D) both fix the sentence fragment, but choice (D) changes the meaning of the sentence.

48. **J** The sentence as written is incorrect because the adjective *tireless* cannot modify the verb *continued*. Choices (G) and (H) do not make sense in the given context. Only choice (J) links the word *tireless* with its appropriate noun, *literary experimentation*.

49. **B** In EXCEPT/LEAST/NOT questions, the underlined portion of the sentence is correct. Since the verbs *to seem* and *to appear* are synonyms, look for differences among the answer choices. Note that the original sentence and choices (A), (C), and (D) all contain the present tense, appropriately matched to the word *contemporary* used earlier in this sentence. Only choice (B) changes the tense to past, making choice (B) the LEAST acceptable substitution.

50. **H** The sentence as written is idiomatically incorrect. The prepositions *until* and *at*, as in choice (G), are incorrectly linked to the phrase *take a real step*. Only the word *toward* completes this phrase appropriately to create *take a real step toward*. Deleting the underlined portion, as in choice (J), makes the sentence unclear and changes its meaning.

51. **A** Choices (B), (C), and (D) all incorrectly separate the verb *fuse* from its objects. NO CHANGE is required here because no punctuation is necessary between the verb and its objects.

52. **H** In EXCEPT/LEAST/NOT questions, the underlined portion of the sentence is correct. Note the similarities between the words. *Encouraged*, *motivated*, and *emboldened*, in choices (F), (G), and (J) are all synonyms for the verb *inspired*. Only the word *forced* in choice (H) changes the meaning of the sentence and is thus the LEAST acceptable substitution.

53. **A** Since the phrase *as American writers living abroad were known* is a descriptive phrase that plays no essential role in determining the meaning of the sentence, it must be set off by a comma as it is in the sentence as written. Choices (B) and (D) introduce new punctuation that loses the clarity of the original sentence. Choice (C) suggests that

the phrase is a portion necessary to preserve the meaning of the sentence and should not be set off from the rest. This is incorrect because *as American writers living abroad were known* is merely a phrase that clarifies and defines the word before it, *expatriates*.

54. **J** For two ideas to be separated by a comma and a coordinating conjunction such as *but*, the ideas on either side of this punctuation and conjunction must be complete. The sentence as written is incorrect because the phrase *limited to those who were able to find copies of the book* is not a complete idea. Choice (H) is incorrect because a semicolon is also a punctuation mark that requires that the two ideas on either side of it be complete. Choice (G) creates an unnecessary pause in the sentence. Accordingly, only choice (J), which removes all punctuation marks, maintains the proper flow of the sentence and correctly treats *positive but limited to those who were able to find copies of the book* as a modifying phrase for the word *reception*.

55. **D** The sentence as written discusses the reception of a different book, not the one discussed in the previous sentence. Choice (C) refers to the current reputation of the book, and choice (B) is too general to be said to refer to only the specific book mentioned in this paragraph. Only choice (D) contains the reaction of critics to the appropriate work and the idea that the book was difficult to obtain.

56. **F** This question asks you to identify which answer best indicates that the novel *Beyond Desire* had presented something new in American literature. Choice (G) suggests that this book had other influences and does not say whether Anderson was the first to incorporate these influences. Choices (H) and (J) discuss the reactions of critics and readers to the book, not the book itself.

57. **A** Choice (B) is idiomatically incorrect—the preposition used with the word *contributions* in this context should be *to,* rather than *from.* Choices (C) and (D) are unclear in creating the phrases *the 1930s of the various writers* and *he influenced of the various writers*, respectively. Only choice (A) properly links the noun and the proper prepositional phrase in *works of the various writers.*

58. **G** To keep the sentence as written is to suggest the word *American* is not an essential piece of the sentence, but without this information, the words *the name* are undefined and unclear. Choices (H) and (J) omit the necessary comma before the conjunction *and*, which, in this case, is separating the items in a list: *the troubled relationship, the direct style*, and *the idea* are the main nouns used in this list. Only choice (G) indicates the importance of the word *American* to the meaning of the sentence and sets this portion of the sentence in a list appropriately.

59. **D** Pay close attention to the years discussed in each of these paragraphs. Paragraph 2 discusses Anderson's death in *1941* and his influence *today*. It should be logically placed after the paragraph discussing the time period most directly before that. Paragraph 5 is appropriate here because it discusses the 1920s and the 1930s, the periods closest to 1941 in this passage.

60. **G** Pay close attention to the reasons given in each of these answer choices. Choice (F) is too general and does not accurately reflect the content of the passage. Choice (H) erroneously says that the passage is primarily about a difference between two large groups when in fact it is about only a single author and his influence on a group of other authors. Choice (J) suggests that the passage only discusses the 1920s and the 1930s when the years 1919 and 1941 are mentioned explicitly.

61. **C** Choice (C) is the clearest and most concise option. The verbs *retracted* and *diminished* essentially mean the same thing, thus choices (A) and (B) are redundant. Choice (D) is incorrect, because without a verb the sentence is incomplete.

62. J   The passage is written in past tense, eliminating choices (G) and (H). The correct past tense form of *to begin* is *began*, making choice (J) the best answer. The form *begun* is used after a helping verb.

63. A   *These responsibilities* refer to the previous sentence, which describes the responsibilities to be *traditionally assigned to men*. Choice (B), therefore, is redundant. Choice (C) creates a sentence fragment. Choice (D) does not agree in number with the plural *responsibilities*.

64. J   Choice (J) eliminates the word *but*, fixing the sentence fragment that is created by the pronoun *that*. Choices (F), (G), and (H) incorrectly add conjunctions that create incomplete sentences.

65. C   The two words *machinists* and *making* should be separated by a period because the sentence has two complete ideas, making choice (C) the best answer. Choices (A) and (D) create run-on sentences. A comma cannot separate two complete ideas, eliminating choice (B).

66. F   The previous sentence already mentions factories and shipyards, making choices (G) and (H) redundant. Choice (J) changes the meaning of the sentence, therefore the best answer is choice (F).

67. C   Choice (C) provides the correct verb, *was*, that agrees with the singular subject of the sentence, *presence*. Choices (A), (B), and (D) all incorrectly use a plural verb.

68. G   Choice (G) is correct because the addition distracts the reader from the topic at hand, which is the changing role of women in the workforce during World War II. Choice (F) is wrong because although it suggests not adding the information, its reasoning is incorrect. The proposed sentence is consistent in style and tone with the rest of the essay. Choices (H) and (J) incorrectly recommend adding a sentence that is irrelevant to the essay.

69. B   The rest of the essay is about the women's baseball league, therefore the best transition is choice (B). Choices (A) and (C) do not reflect the focus of the essay, and choice (D) is too extreme.

70. **G** *Philip K. Wrigley* is necessary to clarify who the *Founder* is and should not be off-set by commas, eliminating choice (J). Choices (F) and (H) have unnecessary pauses due to too many commas; therefore, choice (G) is the clearest answer.

71. **A** Choice (A) describes a specific visual with *pretty smiles* and *baseball mitts in their hands*. Choices (B), (C), and (D) are incorrect because the added information does not qualify as descriptive detail that helps the reader visualize the photographs.

72. **J** The sentence lists different feminine characteristics but does not make clear where the list ends, usually indicated by *and* before the last item. The best answer, therefore, is choice (J). Choices (F) and (G) don't list the items in parallel form. Choice (H) uses the wrong linkage for a list of things.

73. **D** The following sentence states that the photographs of the female players exemplify the *balance between feminine appeal and masculine labor* of women during WWII, making choice (D) the best explanation. Choice (A) is incorrect because the previous sentence suggests the physical attractiveness of the players but does not give specific details about what they look like. Choice (B) is incorrect because women's athleticism is not the focus of the paragraph. Choice (C) is incorrect because the captions of the photographs are never discussed.

74. **J** Choice (J) is the correct answer because the correct form of the possessive pronoun is *its*. The correct possessive form of the pronoun does not use apostrophes, eliminating choices (F) and (G). Choice (H) uses the plural pronoun *their*, which incorrectly replaces the singular antecedent *All-American Girls Professional Baseball League*.

75. **B** The essay directly describes various jobs that women held during World War II, all of which were roles traditionally filled by men, eliminating choices (C) and (D). Choice (A)'s reasoning only addresses the *All-American Girl's Baseball League*, which is the focus of Paragraph 4 but not the essay as a whole.

TEST 1 MATH EXPLANATIONS

1. **A** Since $\overline{YZ}$ is $\dfrac{1}{3}$ the length of $\overline{XZ}$, $\overline{XZ}$ will be $3 \times 24 = 72$ kilometers.

   Since X is the halfway point of the trail, the trail's entire length will be

   twice $\overline{XZ}$, or $72 \times 2 = 144$ kilometers.

2. **J** To find the value of x, first subtract 7 from both sides to get $\dfrac{4x}{5} = -1$.

   Next, multiply both sides by 5 to get $4x = -5$. Finally, divide both

   sides by 4 to give you choice (J). Choice (F) neglects the negative sign.

   Choice (G) is the reciprocal of the correct answer. Choices (H) and

   (K) are partial answers.

3. **B** Determine how many minutes it takes each cyclist to make 9,760 pedal revolutions. Cyclist A takes 9,760 rev ÷ 80 rev/min = 122 minutes. Cyclist B takes 9,760 rev ÷ 61 rev/min = 160 minutes. So, Cyclist B takes 160 – 122 = 38 more minutes than Cyclist A. Notice that Choices (C) and (E) are partial answers. Choice (D) is the sum of each cyclist's rate, and Choice (A) is the difference of their rates.

4. **K** The perimeter of a square is $4s$, so one side of this square is $\dfrac{36}{4} = 9$

   inches. The area of the square is $s^2 = 9^2 = 81$. Choice (F) is the length

   of one side if the square had an *area* of 36. Choice (G) is the length

   of one side rather than the area. Choice (H) is the result of 9 + 9.

   Choice (J) is the result of 6^2, rather than 9^2.

5. **D** From the figure, you can see that the *y*-coordinate must be greater than 4, eliminating choice (C), and the *x*-coordinate must be less than 8, eliminating choice (E). Since the figure is a rectangle, opposite sides must be parallel and thus have the same slope. The slope from (2,0) to (8,3) is 3 units up and 6 units right. You can now calculate the fourth vertex from the point (0,4): (0+6, 4+3), which gives you (6,7). Choices (A) and (B) have an *x*-coordinate of 4, which is halfway between 0 and 8.

6. **H** If Carla's brother has *x* notebooks, Carla has $5x$ notebooks, so $5x + x = 42$. Since $x = 7$ and Carla has $5x$ notebooks, she has $5(7) = 35$. You can also use the answer choices to solve this problem: divide the answer choices by 5 to calculate how many notebooks Carla's brother has and determine when Carla (the answer) and Carla's brother (the answer ÷ 5) add up to 42. A calculation error of $x = 6$ leads to choice (F). Choices (J) and (K) add and subtract numbers from the problem without answering the question asked.

7. **A** A right angle has a measure of 90°; therefore, any angle contained within a right angle must be smaller than 90°, leaving only choice (A).

8. **J** You have to count the number of different ways Susie can choose her one T-shirt and her one pair of shorts. She has 3 options for her T-shirt and 3 options for her pair of shorts. She can combine any of the T-shirts with any of the pairs of shorts, so there are 3×3, or 9, combinations. Choices (F) and (G) do not account for all possible combinations. Choice (H) is 2^3 rather than 3^2.

9. **C** Use the words in the problem to create an equation: *percent* means "divide by 100," *of* means "multiply," and *what number* means "use a variable." The resulting equation is $\frac{20}{100} \times 20 = \frac{50}{100} \times y$. Solve to find that $y = 8$. Be careful of choices (B), which is 20% of 20, and (D), which is 50% of 20.

10. **H** The number of piano players exceeds the number of violin players; thus the number of musicians who play both instruments cannot exceed the number who play violin, eliminating choices (J) and (K). Since all 22 musicians who play the violin could also play the piano, choice (H) gives the maximum possible number.

11. **A** In order to make m^2 (and therefore m) as large as possible, make n^2 as small as possible. The square of any real number can't be negative, so the smallest that n^2 can be is 0. This makes $m^2 = 196$, so m equals either –14 or 14. Choices (B), (C), (D), and (E) are based on multiplication, division, or subtraction, not taking a square root.

12. **F** To solve this problem, break it down into manageable pieces. $\frac{1}{5} \times \$925 = \$185$, so the sale price of the drum kit is $\$925 - \$185 = \$740$. Since the sales tax is $.05 \times \$740 = \$37$, the total owed is $\$740 + \$37 = \$777$. Phil receives back the amount he gave the sales clerk minus the amount he owes: $\$800 - \$777 = \$23$. Choice (G) is the amount of tax paid. Choices (H) and (J) resemble numbers from steps within the problem and choice (K) calculates the taxed price without applying the sale discount.

13. **D** Taking the square root of a negative number yields an imaginary number. If you picked choice (C), be careful—this number is not *rationalized*, but that does not mean it is not a *real number*.

14. **G** The general quadratic expression $a^2 - b^2$ equals $(a - b)(a + b)$. In this question, take the square root of $25x^4$ and the square root of $16y^8$; thus $a = 5x^2$ and $b = 4y^4$. Choice (F) correctly factors the variables but not the coefficients, introducing an incorrect factor of the coefficients. Choices (H) and (K) incorrectly factor the coefficients. Choice (J) incorrectly factors the variables.

15. D Use the formula *Shaded Area = Total Area – Unshaded Area*. In this case, the *Total Area* is the area of the square, which is $4^2 = 16$. To find the *Unshaded Area*, add up the areas of the 4 unshaded triangles. Starting at the lower left of the figure and going clockwise, those areas are: $\frac{1}{2}(1 \times 2) + \frac{1}{2}(2 \times 2) + \frac{1}{2}(2 \times 1) + \frac{1}{2}(1 \times 2) = 5$. So, the *Shaded Area* = $16 - 5 = 11$.

16. G To find the percent *P*, substitute 20 for *t* to calculate $-0.001(20)^2 + 0.4(20) = 7.6$. Choice (F) is the rounded value of 0.076%, which is not equivalent to 7.6%. Choices (H) and (J) result if you don't pay attention to PEMDAS or distribution of the negative sign. Choice (K) results if t^2 and *t* are switched.

17. A Find the cost per grapefruit at each store by dividing the cost of each bag by the number of grapefruits in each bag. The cost per grapefruit at Fatima's is $\$4.40 \div 8 = \$0.55$, while the cost per grapefruit at Ernie's is $\$1.86 \div 3 = \$0.62$. Find the difference: $\$0.62 - \$0.55 = \$0.07$. Choice (B) comes from multiplying $0.07 by the difference in the number of grapefruits ($8 - 3 = 5$). Choice (C) comes from averaging $0.55 and $0.62. Choice (D) comes from adding $0.55 and $0.62. Choice (E) is the difference in costs of the two bags.

18. G In order to multiply factors, you need to FOIL (First, Outer, Inner, Last). Remember to *add* exponents when multiplying numbers with the same base and watch your signs carefully: $x^8 + 4x^4 - 4x^4 - 16 = x^8 - 16$. Choice (F) adds rather than multiplies the factors. Choice (J) multiplies the exponents instead of adding them. Choices (H) and (K) confuse the signs.

19. B First, calculate the number of tile pieces laid in the first period of work: $\frac{50 \text{ pieces}}{1 \text{ hour}} \times 3.5 \text{ hours} = 175 \text{ pieces}$. Next, since you are looking for the time Wade spends working after the interruption, you'll need to figure out how many tile pieces he laid during that time. Subtract 280 pieces – 175 pieces = 105 pieces. Calculate the number of hours he spends in the second work session by dividing $\dfrac{105 \text{ pieces}}{35 \text{ pieces per hour}} =$ 3 hours. If you chose choice (D), be careful—you may have included the 60 minutes during which Wade is interrupted, but the question is looking for the time it took Wade to complete his work *after he was interrupted*.

20. **H** To find the midpoint of a line, you must take the average of the x-coordinates, $\dfrac{x_1 + x_2}{2}$, and the average of the y-coordinates of the endpoints, $\dfrac{y_1 + y_2}{2}$. Choices (F), (G), and (K) incorrectly average the x-coordinates. Choice (J) incorrectly averages the y-coordinates.

21. **B** You might want to draw a picture to see what is happening. Add the lengths of the two short sides of the backyard and one long side: 16 + 16 + 22 = 54. Choice (C) is the sum of two long sides and one short side. Choice (D) is the perimeter of the backyard but the problem says the fencing is needed only on 3 sides. Choice (E) is the area of the backyard.

22. **F** One way to solve this problem is to rewrite the equation in the slope-intercept form, $y = mx + b$, by subtracting $7x$ and dividing by –3 on both sides. The resulting equation is $y = \dfrac{7}{3}x - 7$, where –7 is the value of b, the y-intercept. Another way to solve this problem is to remember that the y-intercept occurs at $x = 0$ and calculate $7(0) - 3y = 21$. Choice (H) is the slope of the line, and the other choices do not modify the equation correctly.

23.   **C**   Find the flower's growth rate by dividing the total growth by the number of days. This is the same thing as finding the slope: $\frac{17.4 - 15.0}{16 - 8} = \frac{2.4}{8} = 0.3$ cm per day. You want to know when the flower was 16.5 cm tall, which means it has grown 16.5 − 15.0 = 1.5 cm: 1.5 cm ÷ 0.3 cm/day = 5 days after April 8th, which is April 13th.

24.   **K**   To subtract, you must first distribute −3 to each term in the second parentheses. You get $2x^3 - x - 1 - 3x^4 - 6x^3 + 6x^2 + 3x - 9$. Combine like terms to get $-3x^4 - 4x^3 + 6x^2 + 2x - 10$. Choices (H) and (J) incorrectly distribute the −3. Choices (F) and (G) incorrectly combine terms and exponents.

25.   **B**   The slide makes a right triangle, as shown in the picture. Use the Pythagorean Theorem ($a^2 + b^2 = c^2$) to solve $7^2 = 6^2 + x^2$. $49 = 36 + x^2$, $x^2 = 13$, $x \approx 3.61$, which rounds to 4. Choice (A) is too small, and choice (C) is too large.

26.   **F**   You're looking for a set in which the mean (average), median ("middle" value), and mode (number that appears most often) all equal 8. All five answer choices have a median of 8, but you can eliminate (G) and (K), because their modes are not 8. You can then eliminate (H) and (J) by calculating their means—8.6 and 9, respectively. That leaves you with (F).

27.   **C**   The easiest approach to this problem is to test out the answer choices. For choice (C), if the 2nd term is 18, then the 3rd term is (18 + 2) × 3 = 60, and the 4th term is (60 + 2) × 3 = 186. You could also work backwards: if the 4th term is 186, then the 3rd term is (186 ÷ 3) − 2 = 60, and the 2nd term is (60 ÷ 3) − 2 = 18. Be sure to read the problem carefully. Choices (B) and (D) are the 1st and 3rd terms of the sequence, respectively.

28. J The easiest approach to this problem is to test all the answer choices. $|9 - 3| \geq 12$ is false; thus the correct answer is choice (J). You could also solve algebraically by solving the equation where $(x - 3) \geq 12$ and $-(x - 3) \geq 12$. The other choices solve the inequality with wrong direction of signs, choice (K), or confusion of positive/negative values within the absolute value.

29. B Given that v is larger than s, then $t + u + v$ must be larger than $s + t + u$, since $t + u$ are equal in both expressions. Because $s + t + u = 29$, $t + u + v$ must be larger than 29. Choices (A), (C), (D), and (E) are not necessarily true, because you don't know anything about the relationships of t, u, and v. Another way to approach this question is to make up your own numbers for the variables: for example, let $s = 20$, $t = 5$, $u = 4$, and $v = 21$. Using these numbers, choices (A), (C), and (D) are false. Now make up different numbers: $s = 5$, $t = 4$, $u = 20$, and $v = 6$. Choice (B) is still true (30 > 29), but choice (E) is now false (15 > 29).

30. H You can eliminate choices (J) and (K) immediately since $\angle CBD$ is clearly less than 90° in the figure. Since $\overline{BE}$ is a straight line, $\angle CDE + \angle BDC = 180°$, $\angle BDC = 180° - 155° = 25°$. $\overline{AB}$ and $\overline{CD}$ are opposite sides of a rectangle, so the line segments are parallel. Extend line segments $\overline{AB}$, $\overline{CD}$, and $\overline{BE}$ to reveal that the two parallel lines are crossed by a transversal, which means $\angle BDC$ and $\angle ABD$ are congruent. Thus, $\angle ABD = 25°$. $\angle ABD$ and $\angle CBD$ make up one of the right angles of rectangle $ABCD$; thus $\angle CBD = 90° - 25° = 65°$. Choices (F), (J), and (K) are all angles within the figure, but do not answer the question.

31. E Test the prime numbers from the answer choices in the equation. Since all the numbers in the equation $a - b = c$ must be positive prime numbers, the only possible result for c can be 2 (e.g., $13 - 11 = 7 - 5 = 2$). The only exceptions to $c = 2$ are $5 - 2 = 3$, $13 - 2 = 11$, and $7 - 2 = 5$. Even so, the only number common to all of these equations is 2, answer choice (E).

32.   H   You can determine Pierre's average speed, in miles per hour, by dividing his total mileage by his total time. The total number of miles he covers is the distance from starting point S to finish line F, which is SF. You can eliminate choices (F), (G), and (J) because they don't include the entire length of the racecourse. The total elapsed time from point S to point F is t_F. You can eliminate choices (F), (G), and (K) because they don't use the elapsed time clocked at the end of the race.

33.   A   Since you know the hypotenuse of the triangle and need to find the adjacent side of $\angle ABC$, use SOHCAHTOA: $\dfrac{\overline{BC}}{13}$ = cos (70°). So, $\overline{BC}$ = 13 cos (70°) ≈ 4.4. Choices (D) and (E) are the answers that you would get if you used either the sine or the tangent functions in the equation above. If you chose either choice (B) or (C), you might have assumed that the triangle was a 5:12:13 right triangle.

34.   J   When x = –3 and y = –4, then $\dfrac{8}{(-4)^2} - \dfrac{(-3)^2}{(-4)} = \dfrac{1}{2} - (-\dfrac{9}{4}) = \dfrac{11}{4}$. Choices (F), (G) and (J) all confuse the signs. Choice (K) switches x and y.

35.   C   The ramp forms a 30°-60°-90° triangle with side lengths in a ratio of $1:\sqrt{3}:2$. Since the shortest leg measures 4, the other leg of the triangle will be $\sqrt{3}$ times the short side: $4\sqrt{3} = 6.92 ≈ 7$. Choice (D) gives the length of the ramp itself, not the horizontal length.

36.   J $\triangle BCD$ is equilateral, so $\angle CBD$ is 60°. $\angle ABD$ must be larger than 60°, eliminating choices (F) and (G). Choice (J) would mean $\angle ABC$ is 96° – 60° = 36°. Since $\angle ABC$ is half the measure of $\angle BAC$ and $\angle BAC = \angle BCA$, each base angle of the isosceles triangle would be

$(180° - 36°) \div 2 = 72°$, which works within $\triangle ABC$: $36° + 72° + 72° = 180$. Choice (K) mistakenly calculates $\angle ABC$ to be twice, rather than half, the measure of $\angle BAC$.

37. **D** Use the standard slope formula with points (8,0) and (0,–4): $m = \dfrac{y_2 - y_1}{x_2 - x_1} = \dfrac{(-4) - (0)}{(0) - (8)} = \dfrac{-4}{-8} = \dfrac{1}{2}$. If you selected choice (E), you may have flipped the x and the y when you calculated the slope. If you selected choice (A), you may have confused some of the negative signs.

38. **J** Find the hypotenuse with the Pythagorean theorem: $a^2 + b^2 = c^2$. With the values given in the figure, this becomes $(8)^2 + (4)^2 = c^2$, and $c^2 = 80$, so $c \approx 8.9$. Accordingly, the sides of this triangle have lengths of 4, 8, and 8.9. To find the perimeter, add these sides together to get 20.9.

39. **B** The formula for cosine is as follows: $\cos\theta = \dfrac{adjacent}{hypotenuse}$. Since you are dealing with $\angle MNO$, the adjacent side will be 4, and the hypotenuse (the same whether you're dealing with sine or cosine) is $\sqrt{80}$. Accordingly, the cosine is $\dfrac{4}{\sqrt{80}}$. Choice (A) gives the sine of $\angle MNO$, and choice (C) gives the tangent.

40. **F** The fraction is equal to $\dfrac{\text{\# of students who passed}}{\text{total \# of students}}$. If there are m students in the class, m must be the denominator, so you can eliminate choices (G), (H), and (J). The number of students who received a passing grade is calculated by subtracting the number who didn't pass the last exam, n, from the total number of students, m. Choice (K) would give a negative fraction, which is not possible.

41. **A** To solve the inequality, distribute the 2 on the right side of the inequality: $5x + 9 \geq 6x + 8 + 7$. Then combine like terms to get: $-x \geq 6$. Remember to flip the sign when you divide by -1 for x to give you the range $x \leq -6$. Choice (B) forgets to flip the sign. Choices (C) and (D) are the result if you forget to distribute 2 to the 4 in the first step. Choice (E) results if you missed a negative sign.

42. **K** The tiles must equal the surface area of the box, which is the sum of the areas of all 6 faces. There are three sets of faces: front/back, top/bottom, and the two sides: $2 (4 \times 9) + 2 (3 \times 9) + 2 (3 \times 4) = 24 + 72 + 54 = 150$. Because each tile covers 1 cm^2, the artist must have 150 cm$^2 \div 1$ cm$^2 = 150$, choice (K). Choice (F) finds the area of only three faces, and choices (G) and (J) account for only two of the three pairs of faces. Choice (H) finds the volume of the box.

43. **C** Draw in $\overline{AD}$, which is parallel to both $\overline{BC}$ and $\overline{EF}$, to find $\angle BAD$. The interior angles of two parallel lines add up to 180°, so you can subtract $\angle ABC$ (130°) from 180° to yield $\angle BAD = 50°$. Subtract $\angle BAE$ from the larger angle $\angle BAD$ to get $\angle EAD = 50° - 22° = 28°$. Since $\angle AEF$ and $\angle EAD$ are also interior angles of two parallel lines, subtract: $180° - \angle EAD = 180° - 28° = 152° = \angle AEF$. You could also extend $\overline{AE}$ to $\overline{BC}$ and find the third angle of the triangle. The same rule will apply—the third angle of this triangle will be equal to $\angle AEF$ because $\overline{BC}$ and $\overline{EF}$ are parallel.

44. **G** To find the area of a trapezoid, multiply the height by the average of the bases. The bases are 6 and 14 , so their average is 10. Don't confuse the height of the trapezoid with the length of one of the slanted sides, which would give you choice (J). Choices (F) and (H) are the results when you multiply the length of only one of the bases by the height. You can also solve this problem by breaking the trapezoid apart into one central rectangle and right triangles on either side.

45. **D** First, raise both sides of the equation to the fifth power to get rid of the fifth root: $\left(\sqrt[5]{x^2 + 4x}\right)^5 = 2^5$ becomes $x^2 + 4x = 32$. Then, subtract 32 from both sides to get a standard quadratic form: $x^2 + 4x - 32 = 0$. Factor the quadratic to get $(x + 8)(x - 4) = 0$. So, $x = -8$ or $x = 4$. You could also test the answers until you find all the numbers that satisfy the equation. Choice (A) gives only one of the possible values for x. Choice (C) reverses the signs. Be careful of choice (E)—that's what you get if you only square the 2 and use the quadratic formula!

46. **J** Since you know the length of the *hypotenuse* (the ramp) and are solving for the height *opposite* the angle of 32°, use SOHCAHTOA:

$\sin A = \dfrac{\text{opposite}}{\text{hypotenuse}}$. By process of elimination, you can get rid of choices (F), (H), and (K). If $\sin 32° = \dfrac{\text{height}}{10}$, the height h is 10 sin 32°.

47. **C** Since average is $\dfrac{\text{sum}}{\text{\# of terms}}$, the sum of $j + j + k + n$ must equal 0 to make the average equal 0. Combining like terms gives you $2j + k + n = 0$. Subtracting $2j$ from both sides, you get $k + n = -2j$. Choices (A) and (B) are not necessarily true (for example, if $j = -3$, k could equal 4 and n could equal 2). Choices (D) and (E) are only true when j is equal to 0.

48.   J   In the composite function $f(g(x))$, the value of $g(x)$ is the input x value in $f(x)$; therefore $f(x)$ is taking the square root of $g(x)$. When $g(x) = 4x^2 - 5$, its square root is $\sqrt{4x^2 - 5}$. Choices (G) and (K) make errors in taking the square root of $4x^2 - 5$. Choices (F) and (G) reverse the composite and use $g(f(x))$.

49.   C   Start with the rate formula: $d = rt$. In this problem, $t = 150$ s, and you'll want to set up equations for as much as you can. If r_r is Rusty's rate and d_r is Rusty's distance, the equation will be $d_r = r_r t$. When the two cars meet, their combined distances will equal the length of the entire track, 6,000 m. Therefore, you can use the relationships given in the problem to set up an equation as follows: $6000 \text{ ft} = r_r t + (r_r - 8 \text{ ft/s})(t)$. Since t is constant at 150 s throughout this problem, substitute it into the equation to get $6000 \text{ ft} = (150 \text{ s})(r_r) + (150 \text{ s})(r_r - 8)$. The (150 s) is common to both terms so you can factor it out and divide both sides by 150 s to get this: $\dfrac{6{,}000\,ft}{150s} = r_r + r_r - 8$ and $40\,ft\,/\,s = 2r_r - 8\,ft\,/\,s$. Manipulate the equation to isolate and find $r_r = \dfrac{48\,ft\,/\,s}{2} = 24\,ft\,/\,s$. If you selected choice (A), be careful—this is Dale's rate!

50. **K** Since Rusty drives the first 7 laps at an average time of 180 s, you can multiply these values together to find that he drives the first 7 laps in a total time of 1,260 s. Complete the same operation for the second set of numbers: since Rusty drives 8 laps at an average time of 190 s, multiply these values together to find that he drives all 8 laps in a total time of 1,520 s. Since you know the two total times, you can simply find the difference between them to find the time of the last lap: 1,520 s – 1,260 s = 260 s. If you selected choice (H), be careful—this is the average of 180 and 190, but it doesn't take into account that Rusty drives 7 laps at an average of 180 s and only one lap at an average of 190 s.

51. **D** Dale drives 6 laps, each of which is 6,000 ft, for a total of 36,000 ft in 90 minutes. The question asks for this value in feet per hour, so convert the 90 minutes to 1.5 hours. 36,000 ft ÷ 1.5 hrs = 24,000 ft/hr. If you selected choice (A), you may have forgotten to change the 90 minutes to 1.5 hours.

52. **G** The equation of a circle is $(x - h)^2 + (y - k)^2 = r^2$, where (h, k) is the center of the circle and r is the radius. Thus, circle B has its center at $(-4,2)$ with a radius of 3. If you draw a diagram, you'll find that point $(-2,2)$ lies outside circle A and inside circle B.

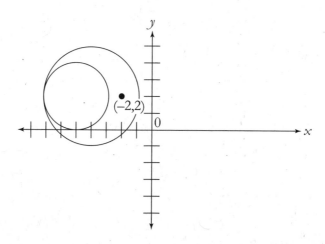

53. **B** The perimeter is the distance of the shape's outline. There are two straight lines: from (0,0) to (0,4) and from (0,0) to (4,0), each with a length of 4. The straight lines total 8, eliminating choices (A), (D), and (E). The curved parts are two semicircles and two semicircles make one complete circle, so find the circumference of one circle with radius 2: $C = 2\pi r = 2\pi(2) = 4\pi$. Eliminate choice (C) and pick choice (B). If you picked choice (D), you may have found the area instead of the perimeter.

54. **F** An even function is defined in the question as a function for which the value of $f(x) = f(-x)$. This means that $f(x)$ has the same value for both x and $-x$. If you fold the graph of an even function along the $f(x)$ axis, the two sides of the graph will be mirror reflections of each other. Choices (G), (J), and (K) are odd functions, in which $f(-x) = -f(x)$ for all values of x. Odd functions rotate 180° about the point (0, 0). Choice (H) is not a function, because it does not pass the vertical line test; the same x value yields two values for $f(x)$.

55. **B** Use the distance formula: $d = \sqrt{(x_2 - x_1)^2 + (y_2 - y_1)^2}$. $d = \sqrt{(4w - w)^2 + (w - 5 - (w + 5))^2} = \sqrt{9w^2 + 100}$.

56. **F** In a right triangle with angle A, $\cos A = \dfrac{\text{length of adjacent side}}{\text{length of hypotenuse}}$. In this triangle, $\cos S = \dfrac{r}{t}$ and $\cos R = \dfrac{s}{t}$. So $\cos^2 S + \cos^2 R = \dfrac{r^2}{t^2} + \dfrac{s^2}{t^2}$, or $\dfrac{r^2 + s^2}{t^2}$. Since ΔRST is a right triangle, use the Pythagorean Theorem to determine that $r^2 + s^2 = t^2$. You're left with $\cos^2 S + \cos^2 R = \dfrac{t^2}{t^2} = 1$.

57. **C** Trapezoid *DECA* is isosceles because $\triangle ABC$ is isosceles and, since $\overline{DE} \| \overline{AC}$, line segments $\overline{AD}$ and $\overline{CE}$ have equal lengths. Since the trapezoid is isosceles, the diagonals are congruent. Thus, $\triangle DFE$ and $\triangle AFC$ are similar. Set up a proportion to find the missing side: $\frac{9}{6} = \frac{27}{FC}$. So, $\overline{FC} = 18$. Choice (A) is the short side of $\triangle DFE$ multiplied by 2. Choice (B) is 9 + 6. Choice (D) is 27 + 6 and choice (E) is 27 + 9. Remember that hard problems typically require more work than just adding together some of the numbers from the problem!

58. **F** The dimensions of a matrix product are determined by the number of rows in the first matrix and the number of columns in the second matrix, in this case 2 × 1. Thus, choices (H), (J), and (K) have the wrong dimensions. To find the product value, multiply rows by columns and add the products of one row-column: $(4 \times 0) + (-2 \times 2) = -4$ and $(3 \times 0) + (-6 \times 2) = -12$.

59. **D** An ! symbol denotes a factorial, which is the product of decreasing consecutive integers starting from the integer in front of the ! sign. (For example, $5! = 5 \times 4 \times 3 \times 2 \times 1 = 120$.) You can simplify this expression if you separate the two largest factors in the numerator; in other words, write $(n + 1)!$ as $(n + 1) \times (n) \times (n - 1)!$ Canceling $(n - 1)!$ from numerator and denominator leaves you with $(n + 1)(n)$. So $(n + 1)(n) = 20$, which means that $n + 1 = 5$ and $n = 4$. Finally, the question asks for $n! = 4! = 4 \times 3 \times 2 \times 1 = 24$. Choice (A) is 3! Choice (B) is half of 20. Choice (C) is half of 24. Choice (E) is 5!

60. **K** To simplify this abstract problem, substitute a value in for the circle's radius. If the radius is 3, the circumference is $2\pi r = 2(\pi)(3) = 6\pi$. $\dfrac{radius}{circumference} = \dfrac{3}{6\pi} = \dfrac{1}{2\pi}$. Choice (F) gives the ratio of the circumference to the radius. Choices (H) and (J) work with the diameter instead of the radius, and choice (G) finds the ratio of the diameter to the radius.

TEST 1 READING EXPLANATIONS

1. **C** Choice (C) points to the portion of the passage in which the narrator says that his grandmother had gained considerable stature in Robertson County and, more importantly, refers to information concerning the story's principal character. The main topic of the passage is Ruby and her diner, so you can safely assume there will be a connection between the main topic and the correct answer. Choice (A) focuses on information that occurs only in the beginning of the story and choices (B) and (D) are too general and not directly supported by information in the passage.

2. **J** The second paragraph begins by introducing the character of Ruby Sanders, the narrator's grandmother. This indicates that the paragraph will explain who she is and why she is important. Choices (F) and (G) point out topics in the beginning of the passage, but they do not serve to cover the character of Ruby. Finally, choice (H) is an overstatement, so we have to dismiss it as a viable choice in light of choice (J).

3. **B** Only choice (B) contains an answer that refers correctly to a part of the text—*If the diner were a sort of cell, then my grandmother was its nucleus; without the nucleus, the cell would surely perish.* The other answer choices contain words from the passage as well, but the things stated in those answer choices are either untrue or not supported by the passage.

4. **H** Choice (H) should be selected in this instance because the question asks you to make an inference, and inferences must always be supported by the facts within the area in question. The end of the paragraph directly states that the narrator was glad that he didn't know that he wouldn't return to the diner after his last summer there. Choices (F), (G), and (J) force us to make unfounded assumptions as to how the narrator would feel.

5. **B** Locate where the author talks about working at the diner (paragraph 8). The narrator mentions that the work was *hard but never dull*. Therefore, you should select choice (B). Although each of the others contains individual characteristics that may be true, both characteristics listed in the correct answer must be true.

6. **F** Note the sentence at the end of the second paragraph: *It didn't take long before my grandmother was a person of considerable stature in and around Robertson County, just like the restaurant that bore her name.* From this sentence, you can easily infer that both Ruby and her restaurant were popular in and around the community. If you chose one of the other answers, be careful—these refer to either Ruby or the restaurant, but never to both.

7. **A** The lines in question provide the introduction to this paragraph, which details the ways in which Ruby's was significant to the community in ways other than as a restaurant—choice (A). Choice (B) is not supported in the text, and choice (D) gives a too literal interpretation of the lines referred to in the passage and misreads the word *expect*. Choice (C) is deceptive—the passage does suggest that Ruby herself had risen to prominence, but it does not mention anyone else in this regard.

8. **G** The author speaks of choices (F), (H), and (J) in the sixth paragraph. He mentions football leagues in the last paragraph, but as something he had to forego to continue to work at the restaurant. Accordingly, the passage mentions all of the things as being available at the diner EXCEPT the football leagues, choice (G).

9. **C** In the seventh paragraph, the author vividly describes the physical details of the restaurant. In this paragraph, he gives a detailed description of the grounds, down to the furniture and the locations of some minor items. Choices (A), (B), and (D) use words from the passage, but the information in these choices is not supported.

10. J In the last paragraph, the narrator says, *After all, the woman who built Ruby's was strong enough to make me forget those things, if only for the summer.* It can therefore be inferred that the narrator is impressed by his grandmother's strength. None of the other answer choices are supported by evidence in the passage.

11. B The passage is about studies on several different factors that contribute to happiness. According to the second paragraph, Tellegen and Lykken state that genes play a part in happiness, but no specific genes have been found that cause hedonic adaptation, eliminating choice (A). Although an account of Lyubomirsky and Sheldon's studies indicates that there may be ways to improve happiness levels (lines 70–80), there is no discussion of the cure for depression mentioned in choice (C). No scientist in the passage disagrees that genes have an influence on happiness levels, eliminating choice (D).

12. H All the studies in the passage involve subjects telling researchers how happy they are, which is the same as *subjective well-being* as defined in lines 8–11. Only Lyubomirsky and Sheldon's study made specific note of studying their subjects' levels of happiness *over time* (lines 64–67), eliminating choice (F), or involved subjects engaging in *acts of kindness* (line 75), eliminating choice (G). Only Tellegen and Lykken's study mentioned using *identical twins* (lines 13–14), eliminating choice (J).

13. D Tellegen and Lykken's study of twins that had been *separated and raised in different families* (line 15) does not indicate whether separated twins were less happy. The question presented by choice (A) can be answered by the statistic on line 52, which says *10 percent is influenced by circumstances.* Descriptions of Lyubomirsky and Sheldon's studies suggest that people who *varied their acts of kindness* (line 75) and who wrote *a list of things to be grateful for* (line 78) can improve their subjective well-being, which answers the question posed in choice (B). In lines 43–44, Sheldon explains that scientific literature suggests that behaviors such as choosing the right goals *provide only a temporary increase in subjective well-being*, answering the question in choice (C).

14. **F** Lyubomirsky hopes to show how *conscious strategies counteract genetic forces* (lines 63–64)—in other words help people to overcome their genetic predispositions. You can eliminate choice (J) because the passage never indicates that hedonic adaptation can be eliminated entirely. Sheldon and Lyubomirsky also agree that *50 percent of subjective well-being is predetermined by the genetic set point* (lines 50–51), which confirms, rather than contradicts, Tellegen and Lykken's study, eliminating choice (G). Determining which intentional act is more effective is not the primary purpose of their research, eliminating choice (H).

15. **D** The statistics cited in the last sentence of the passage best support choice (D). Though the passage indicates that some psychologists' emphasis caused them to *suspect that overall levels of subjective well-being are low* (line 85), this does not summarize the University of Chicago studies, so eliminate choice (A). Though Americans are mostly happy people, this does not mean that depression is *uncommon*, as choice (B) states. You can also eliminate choice (C), because it suggests that happiness levels are actually harmed by attempts to improve them.

16. **H** The Lykken and Tellegen study is discussed in paragraph two. Choice (H) is correct, as the passage clearly states that only some of the twins were raised together, not all of them. The paragraph states that the members of the study were both fraternal and identical twins and that researchers compared the scores of the twins, making choice (F) true. Choice (G) is true because the study compared the twins' subjective well-being, which is described as our self-reported level of happiness in the first sentence. Choice (J) is found in the final sentence of the paragraph, which states that most of the difference in people's levels of happiness are determined by differences in genetic makeup.

17. **A** Hedonic adaptation is useful because it benefits people who experience adverse conditions in their lives (line 25). Although these adverse

conditions may include *permanent disability or sudden loss of income* (lines 26–27), hedonic adaptation does not cause people to *forget* about these problems, as indicated in choice (B). It is not useful to adjust to the higher level of happiness caused by *winning the lottery,* eliminating choice (C). Hedonic adaptation helps people to adjust their levels of happiness back to their own genetic set point, not to identify better with family members, eliminating choice (D).

18. G If you deleted the first paragraph, you wouldn't get a detailed story about a particular person whose life shows that happiness and life events, in this case the Holocaust, are not necessarily correlated, as in choice (G). The passage mentions in the third paragraph that circumstances are not a large contributor to happiness, so eliminate choice (F). The first paragraph includes an example that is relevant to establishing the main idea of the passage, eliminating choice (H). Lines 26–27 mention *permanent disability or sudden loss of income* as specific examples of adverse conditions people may experience, so you can eliminate choice (J).

19. C The topic sentence of the last paragraph suggests that its purpose is to focus on people's generally positive assessment of their own happiness. The researchers mentioned in the paragraph had an incorrect suspicion, which is different from making *many errors,* so you can eliminate choice (A). Choice (B) can be eliminated because Ross's anecdote in the first paragraph is not meant to suggest that Americans are unhappy. Lyubomirsky and Sheldon's findings that certain behaviors may improve happiness are still valid even if people are already generally happy, eliminating choice (D).

20. H Lines 64–65 state that Lyubomirsky and Sheldon *are currently expanding their study.* Though it is possible that the researchers mentioned in choices (F), (G), and (J) may still collaborate, the passage never explicitly gives this information, making choice (H) the best answer.

21. **C** This question asks what the author has learned. Since the author ended the passage by explaining her new theory of the connectedness of fiction and biography, you want something that agrees with that, which choice (C) does nicely. Choices (A) and (D) both use deceptive language from the passage but do not reflect what the author has learned. Choice (B) is extreme.

22. **H** The passage states that studying literature in college involved *scouring personal letters for hints of relationship problems, familial tragedies, or even fond memories that seemed reminiscent of storylines*. Since the prior part of the sentence discussed the intensive research that the author did, *scouring* is being used to mean something like *researching*. Choice (F), *purifying*, is not supported. The author is studying, so choice (G), *obliterating*, is not supported. Choice (J), *cleansing*, is one meaning for *scouring*, but it is not supported in this context.

23. **A** The author states, *since I've been a Nathaniel Hawthorne fan since junior high, a side trip to the building that had inspired one of his greatest works seemed to be in order*. While the passage states that the author was visiting Salem's tourist attractions, choice (A) is better supported by the text than choice (B). The author had not originally sought to learn the personal details of Hawthorne's life, making choice (C) incorrect. Choice (D) is deceptive, since there is no proof that Hawthorne lived during the Salem Witch Trials.

24. **F** While the college professors are mentioned in line 21, we do not learn until the last paragraph that the author has finally understood that *when we weave the threads of the author's life around that base, we are able to see the interactions between text and author, as they join to create a pattern more complete than either would be on its own*. The passage does not state that one is more necessary than the other, as choices (G) and (J) do. Choice (H) is too strong, since the professors are referring to understanding, not enjoyment.

25. **B** The passage tells us that the author *opted to major in literature, assuming that this would involve reading scores of wonderful books.* Although the author disagrees with her professors, there is no evidence that she chose her field of study in order to disprove their theories, as stated in choice (C), and choices (A) and (D) incorrectly state that she agrees with the professors' approach.

26. **H** The author's ultimate conclusion regarding the purpose of literary studies is most clearly outlined in the final paragraph, as quoted in choice (J), but that does not answer this question. Choice (F) refers to her earlier aim when reading, and choice (G) refers to what she gleaned in inspired moments. Choice (H) correctly refers to what the author experienced *more often* and thus was the most likely result of completing her professors' assignments.

27. **B** The House of the Seven Gables is discussed mainly in the fourth and fifth paragraphs. The passage does not state precisely who lived there, just that Nathaniel Hawthorne did not, eliminating choice (A). Although it may have been an important historical site, the passage does not tell us if anything actually took place there, as choice (C) states. The garden is described as *desolate* due to the season but there is no evidence that the house is in poor repair, as in choice (D). Since the author must buy tickets and take part in a tour in order to visit the house, it is reasonable to infer that it is now a tourist attraction, as in choice (B).

28. **J** The passage closes with the statement that *The work itself is indeed the frame, but when we weave the threads of the author's life around that base…* In this context, the *frame* is referring to the novel, which the author believes is the *base* of our understanding. Choice (F) incorrectly states that the novel is the *isolated goal.* Choice (G) likewise treats the novel as the *purpose* as opposed to the *base.* Choice (H) refers to the novel as extra, or *auxiliary,* information. Choice (J) correctly identifies the novel as the *focal,* or central, point.

29. **C** Choice (C) most closely matches the author's final opinion of studying authors' lives as discussed in the final paragraph, where she states that *we are able to see their interactions,* as they join to become something *more complete than either would be on its own.* Choice (A) does not address the author's ultimate conclusion that this study can be worthwhile. Neither *timidity,* choice (B), nor *frustration,* choice (D), is supported by the passage.

30. **F** The third paragraph tells us what happened after the author finished school, connecting the second paragraph, which details her childhood and schooling, to the fourth paragraph, which brings us back to the visit to Salem. The reasons for her trip, choice (G), are mentioned in the first paragraph. The study of literature, choice (H), was discussed in the second paragraph as well as the third, and the evidence for the author's final conclusion, choice (J), is found in the last paragraph.

31. **A** Although the passage mentions that the frogs' calls concern mating behavior, it doesn't specify how often they mate, so choice (A) is the best answer. Choice (B) is addressed in line 17, choice (C) is answered in lines 29–43, and choice (D) is answered in lines 54–57.

32. **F** Lines 15–16 state that the coqui faces almost no ecological competition because there are no other native amphibians; thus, choice (F) is the best answer. Choice (G) is contradicted in lines 58–62.

33. **C** Paragraph 4 (lines 29–43) states that the *volume of the frog's call is compounded by two other factors,* one of which is the *wall of sound* produced by overlapping calls, making choice (C) the best answer. Choice (A) is contradicted by lines 4–5. Choices (B) and (D) refer to facts that aren't supported by the passage.

34. **H** This paragraph states that the coqui thrives because it doesn't need as much water as it would if it were born a tadpole. The end of the paragraph also implies that the coqui faces little predatorial threat before it has matured. The paragraph does describe the environmental conditions in Hawaii, but description of the habitat isn't the primary

purpose of the paragraph, eliminating choices (F) and (G). Choice (J) is not the primary purpose of the paragraph, nor does it accurately describe the coqui.

35. B The first paragraph is a descriptive, evocative passage that attempts to capture the sound of the frog calls in the night. By contrast, the sixth paragraph explains specifically how scientists believe these frogs could endanger the local environment, so choice (B) is the best description of the change in the language's tone. Nothing in the passage suggests the *author's* opinion, so choice (A) doesn't fit. The sixth paragraph talks about the frogs as a potential threat, so you wouldn't select choice (C) or (D) as the best option.

36. G Earlier in the sentence, the coqui populations are described as *threatening the survival of arthropods*, which indicates that the arthropod population is struggling, eliminating choices (H) and (J). The word *pursuit* doesn't fit as well as *extinction*, making choice (G) the best answer.

37. D The last sentence of the fifth paragraph (lines 54–57) begins with the phrase *Ornithologists fear*, which means that the potential outcome hasn't happened yet. Choice (A) is stated as factual information in lines 33–34, choice (B) in lines 71–73, and choice (C) in lines 81–82.

38. F The passage states that *nematodes and other types of vertebrate parasites could be transported with coquis and infect indigenous fauna*, making choice (F) the best answer. Choices (G) and (H) refer to the frogs' food sources, not parasites; *arachnids* in choice (J) aren't mentioned specifically in the passage, although they are a member of the arthropod class.

39. **B** The fifth paragraph states that *another quieter genus of the frog—the greenhouse frog—represents an equal threat to the biodiversity of the island*, which is best summarized by choice (B). Choice (C) incorrectly states that the greenhouse frog is less, rather than equally, dangerous. It is true that the greenhouse frog is relatively quiet, but that characteristic isn't necessarily what makes the frog hard to eliminate, eliminating choice (D). Although the name *greenhouse frog* points to an indoor habitat, the passage doesn't support that assumption, so you can rule out choice (A).

40. **J** The last paragraph mentions *1,000 acres* in the first sentence and continues in the next sentence to describe the land as the habitat in which the coqui has adopted as its home in Hawaii, making choice (J) the best answer. There is no evidence in the passage to support choices (F), (G), and (H).

TEST 1 SCIENCE EXPLANATIONS

1. **A** The data in Table 3 indicate that for every increase of 25°C, there is a corresponding increase in θ of approximately 3.5 degrees. A temperature of 62.5°C falls halfway between 50°C and 75°C, so the corresponding angle should fall halfway between 25.4 and 29.0 degrees. Only choice (A) has a value anywhere within this range.

2. **F** According to Table 1, the object made of brick required the largest ramp angle θ before any movement took place. Therefore, it is the most resistant to movement. Raising the angle of the ramp accomplishes the same thing as applying increasing force to the object to eventually overcome friction.

3. **D** In Experiments 1 and 4, the angle θ where the wooden object starts to move stays the same, no matter how many objects are stacked on top of each other. Since any change to this angle will signal a change to the coefficient of static friction, you can confidently say that if the angle doesn't change, the coefficient of friction will not change.

4. **G** The interaction of interest is between the various objects and the polymer coating of the ramp. The polymer coating is what comes into contact with the objects, while the underlying plastic board is not participating, eliminating choice (F). Objects of different material are not brought into contact during the experiment, eliminating choice (H). Objects are not stacked until Experiment 4, eliminating choice (J).

5. **D** The object with the largest angle θ is the object that is most resistant to movement. According to Table 1, this is brick. Only choice (D) ranks brick as the most resistant to movement, eliminating all other answer choices.

6. **G** The data in Table 3 indicate that when temperature increases, the corresponding θ increases. The passage states that the *tangent of this angle represents the coefficient of static friction between the object and the polymer surface.* The experiment is not exploring the interaction

between wood and wood, eliminating choice (F). The mass of the object is constant, eliminating choice (H). Only wooden objects are used in Experiment 3, eliminating choice (J).

7. B   The transition from April to May shows a small increase in the number of reported polio infections, and the transition from November to December shows a decrease, so neither choices (C) nor (D) would be the correct answer. There are large increases in the number of reported cases from January to February and from February to March, but upon close inspection, the transition from February to March is larger. Therefore, choice (B) is the best answer.

8. J   In June 2004, 80 cases of polio infection were reported, so $80 \times 200 = 16,000$ people would have been at risk for contraction of the infection.

9. A   In all the Indian cities, there are more reported cases of polio virus infections in August than in June. Choices (B) and (D) are consistent with *decreases*, not increases, in the reported polio cases. The study described by Figure 2 only covers the dry summer and rainy monsoon season, not the autumn or winter, so the explanation given in choice (C) is unsupported. Choice (A) is the best answer because the month of August is expected to have more rainfall, and therefore is more likely to feature water contamination.

10. H   Figure 2 presents findings that are applicable only to India, not Nigeria, so (F) is incorrect. The findings only present information on reported infections during June and August 2007, not on unreported infections (choice (G) is wrong) nor on winter months (choice (J) is wrong). The findings do, however, show a stark contrast between the small number of reported cases in the cities in western and southern India (Mumbai, Chennai, and Hyderabad) and the large number of cases in the northern cities (New Delhi and Kolkata), making (H) the best answer.

11. **D** The passage states that the polio virus is most often transmitted through water contaminated with human waste and makes no mention of the role (or the lack thereof) that other life forms play in the transmission of the virus. The answer that summarizes this is choice (D).

12. **H** In June 2007, there were between 10 and 15 reported polio infections in Kolkata, while in August 2007, there were between 20 and 25 reported polio infections. This is an approximate doubling of the number of reported infections, so choice (H) is the best answer.

13. **D** The solution with the *least osmotic pressure* will have the smallest value from Figure 1. The pressure for choice (A) is 85 atm; choice (B) is 70 atm; choice (C) is 90 atm; choice (D) is 50 atm. Therefore, a 2.0 M sucrose solution has the least osmotic pressure.

14. **J** The introduction states that *higher van't Hoff factors correlate with greater dissociation or ionization.* According to Table 1, $FeCl_3$ exhibits the greatest van't Hoff factor, which means the highest degree of ionization.

15. **C** Examine the equation given in the introduction: $\Pi = iMRT$. Since the values of R and T remain constant among all the answer choices as seen in the question, osmotic pressure is determined by the product of M and i. The product of concentration of solute particles and van't Hoff factor for a 1.5 M NaCl solution is $1.5 \times 1.9 = 2.85$. The product for the solution in choice (A) is $1.0 \times 1.9 = 1.9$; choice (B) is $2.0 \times 1.9 = 3.8$; choice (C) is $2.9 \times 1.0 = 2.9$; choice (D) is $3.5 \times 1.0 = 3.5$. Choice (C) has the closest product to 2.85.

16. **G** The pressure required to maintain solvent equilibrium across a membrane is the solution's osmotic pressure, as discussed in the introduction. Figure 1 shows a linear relationship between solute concentration and osmotic, eliminating choices (H) and (J). As concentration of solute decreases, the osmotic pressure will also decrease, eliminating choice (F).

17. **D** Comparing different solutes in Figure 1 at a given concentration greater than $M = 0$, you will determine that $FeCl_3$ always has greater osmotic pressure than sucrose, eliminating choices (B) and (C). The trend in Figure 1 predicts that a substance with $i = 3.8$ would have a greater osmotic pressure than $FeCl_3$, which does *not* support the scientist's findings.

18. **H** Examine the relationship between the line for Sample 1 and the line for Sample 4. Between the 30–60-cm depth range and the 60–90-cm depth range, the line for Sample 1 crosses over to become higher than the line for Sample 4. Choices (F) and (G) suggest that the lines would never cross over, while choice (J) incorrectly states that Sample 4's shallower sodium concentrations were lower than Sample 1's.

19. **B** On the line for Sample 3 in Figure 2, the second data point most closely matches 17%. Choice (A) would describe the earliest data point for Sample 3, from a soil depth of 0–30 cm; choices (C) and (D) describe Samples 4 and 5 at this depth, respectively.

20. **J** Use Sample 4, because the question asks you for soil 40 m away from the river. Remember the definitions given for EC and ESP: EC is the total electrical conductivity of the soil, while ESP is the percentage of that amount which is due to sodium ions. To find the total EC due to sodium ions, you would need to multiply the total EC by the percentage due to sodium. Since the total EC for Sample 4 is significantly less at the 90–120 cm depth than at the 60–90 cm depth, while the ESP is roughly the same, (H) is incorrect; similarly, the low total EC at the 0–30 cm depth rules out the possibility of it having the greatest total EC due to sodium ions. Since the EC at the 0–30 cm depth and 30–60 cm depth are nearly the same, the much lower ESP at the 0–30 cm depth makes (J) the correct answer.

21. **C** This question is essentially asking you to convert one set of data points on a line graph into a bar graph. Choice (C) does this correctly, while choice (A) inverts the values, making small values large and large

values small. Choice (B) measures the wrong data point—it would be accurate for a sample depth of 60–90 cm, not 90–120 cm. Choice (D) is very close, but mixes up the values for Sample 4 and Sample 1.

22. **G** Compare all five samples in Figure 1 using a common depth such as 30–60 cm. In Sample 1, the EC is approximately 1 mS/cm; 20 mS/cm in Sample 2; 1 mS/cm in Sample 3; 0.5 mS/cm in Sample 4; 8 mS/cm in Sample 5. Thus, there is no consistent trend in the electrical conductivity, which means salinity does not increase with consistency with distance from the river, eliminating choices (H) and (J). The explanation in choice (F) is also not supported by passage.

23. **B** Examine the conditions associated with each group in Table 1. Group 6 is the only group which does not include data from an area affected by habitat loss or declines in prey population. It therefore allows the researchers to compare areas affected by these factors to one unaffected by them. Choices (A), (C), and (D) suggest that Group 6 provides information to the researchers that is not included in the passage.

24. **F** Examine the conditions associated with Group 2. These areas have additional seaweed which is consumed by marine mammals, the likely prey of the primarily carnivorous polar bear. Choice (G) implies that polar bears may prefer to eat seaweed, but there is nothing in the passage to support this statement. Choice (H) is eliminated because the study does not directly measure the population density of prey animals. Choice (J) would require additional information which links the population of prey animals to Arctic sea ice.

25. **C** A greater average population density ratio for a certain group indicates that more polar bears are living in areas that are a part of that group. Choice (C) correctly lists the groups by average population density ratio as given in Figure 1.

26. **G** Group 1 exhibits declines in the number of marine mammals consumed by polar bears. Choices (F) and (H) are not mammals so they are eliminated. Choice (J) is eliminated because the population of

polar bears is the outcome being studied as a result of some other environmental change, and there is nothing in the passage to suggest that polar bears consume other polar bears. Only choice (G) is a marine mammal that is likely consumed by a polar bear.

27. **D** You can use the process of elimination with the definitions in Table 1 to find the correct answer for this problem. Choice (A) includes Groups 1 and 2; these are likely to cause effects in opposite directions, not the same direction. Choices (B) and (C) each include Group 4; as Group 4 is simply a combination of Groups 1 and 3, the researchers are never directly comparing the effects of Group 4 conditions to any other conditions. Choice (D) lists Groups 1 and 3, both groups where there have been conditions likely to make it difficult for polar bears to survive. This is confirmed by data in Figure 1.

28. **H** Choices (F) and (J) are both true. As seen in Figure 1, average polar bear population ratios for both Groups 1 and 3 are not equal to 1. If they were equal to 1, this would indicate that there is no difference between those areas with the conditions listed and those without. Choice (H) reverses the relationship between Groups 1 and 3 in Figure 1, which means it is not supported. Choice (G) states the relationship from (H) correctly, which means (G) is supported and therefore not the correct answer.

29. **D** Scientist 2 says "*the $\cdot OH$ generated by Reactions 1 and 4 will react rapidly with any H_2CO,*" indicating that she does agree those reactions occur; the dispute is what formaldehyde decomposes to after Reaction 3. So according to both scientists, O_3 leads to the formation of $\cdot OH$ (Reaction 1), and OH leads to the formation of $\cdot CH_3$ (Reaction 2).

30. **F** As methane (CH_4) levels increase, CH_3 levels will increase (Reaction 2). As $\cdot CH_3$ levels increase, H_2CO levels will increase (Reaction 3). Therefore the correct graph should show low levels of H_2CO when methane levels are low, and high levels of H_2CO when methane levels are high. Choice (F) is the only graph that reflects this direct relationship.

31. **C** Remember: reactants on the left; products on the right. From that you can eliminate answer choices (B) and (D). For choice (A), it is true that H_2CO is composed of atoms (it *is* a molecule); however, composition is not mentioned in the question. Since there are no other reactants, the mass of H_2CO (the reactant) must be exactly the mass of the products (H_2 and CO). Therefore, the molecular mass of each of the products must be less than that of H_2CO.

32. **H** According to Scientist 1, the first step in the production of formaldehyde requires ozone (O_3). Follow the reactions: if O_3 levels decrease, $\cdot OH$ levels would decrease (Reaction 1), leading to a decrease in $\cdot CH_3$ levels (Reaction 2), which in turn would lead to a decrease in H_2CO levels (Reaction 3). Thus, both $\cdot CH_3$ and H_2CO levels would decrease.

33. **D** Scientist 2 says Reactions 1–4 do occur, which support choices (A) and (C). Choice (B) is Scientist 2's central argument: that the $\cdot OH$ produced by Reactions 1 and 4 can react with H_2CO to form CO (Reaction 6). While Scientist 2 does say that some H_2CO may form from CH_4 and O_3, she says that "H_2CO quickly decomposes" and that the chain reaction of Reactions 2–4 is inhibited. Thus, she would *not* expect an increase in CH_4 levels to cause levels of H_2CO to rise dramatically.

34. **G** If Reaction 4 were inhibited, the amount of H_2CO generated would be reduced, and therefore, according to Scientist 2, the amount of CO generated would be reduced, not increased, so choice (F) is incorrect. $\cdot OH$ can react with H_2CO to form CO, but there is no evidence of HO_2 reacting with H_2CO, as in choice (H). O_2 is not involved in the generation of CO, so choice (J) cannot be correct. Answer choice (G) is Scientist 2's hypothesis: the H_2CO generated in Reaction 3 will react in Reactions 5 and 6 to produce CO.

35.	**B**	Reaction 6 shows •OH reacting with H_2CO in the atmosphere, which weakens Scientist 1's hypothesis in 2 ways: it reduces the level of H_2CO, which Scientist 1 says is *increasing* in the atmosphere, and consumes •OH, inhibiting the chain reaction (Reactions 2–4), which is central to Scientist 1's hypothesis. Thus, choice (B) is the best explanation. The •OH produced in Reaction 4 reacts with CH_4 (in Reaction 2) agrees with Scientist 1's argument, so choice (A) is incorrect. The H_2O produced in Reaction 6 may react with light and O_3, as in Reaction 1, but again, does not weaken Scientist 1's argument, so choice (C) is incorrect. For choice (D), •OH is not produced in Reaction 6, it is a reactant.

36.	**G**	To solve this problem, you must be sure to read the question carefully: you are looking at the section of the graph where V is *decreasing* from its largest value. First, find the largest value of V; this is the point on the curve that is furthest to the right, since V increases left to right. Once you are looking in the right place, you just draw a line up from 1.5 mL on the V-axis to where it meets the curve, then draw a line over to the P-axis to get your answer: 30 Pa, choice (G).

37.	**C**	From the passage and Figures 1 and 2, you know that both ends of the second half of the curve must meet the ends of the first half to complete the cycle, so P must be higher on the left side than on the right side. Choices (A) and (B) cannot be correct because P is higher on the right side than on the left side. Choice (D) is simply the wrong shape to complete the cycle, so it cannot be correct. Choice (C) has P higher on the left side than on the right side, so it must be correct.

38.	**H**	Looking at Figure 1, all you need to do is find the lowest point on the curve, then draw a line down to the V-axis. Choice (H), 3.5 mL is the closest answer.

39.   B   To solve this question, you must first locate the approximate lowest and highest values of *V* on Figure 2. The lowest value is about 0.75 mL and the highest value is about 2.25 mL, so the lowest value is about 1/3 times the highest value, choice (B). Another way to solve this problem is to check the answer choices against the graph. Choice (A) cannot be correct because there are no negative numbers on the graph. Choice (C) doesn't really make sense because if the lowest value were 1 times the highest value, it would have to be the same number as the highest value, and then there wouldn't be a highest or lowest. Choice (D) doesn't make sense either because if the lowest value were 2 times the highest value, the lowest value would have to be higher than the highest value. Choice (B) is the only choice which could work because it is the only choice which is not negative and would make the lowest value actually lower than the highest value.

40.   F   This question is actually just an easy question with tricky wording. All it asks is this: What is the value of *V* when *P* is at its highest value? Find the highest value of *P*, and then find the value of *V*: 1.0 mL, choice (F).

WRITING TEST

Essay Checklist

1. The Introduction
   Did you
   o start with a topic sentence that paraphrases or restates the prompt?
   o clearly state your position on the issue?

2. Body Paragraph 1
   Did you
   o start with a transition/topic sentence that discusses the opposing side of the argument?
   o give an example of a reason that one might agree with the opposing side of the argument?
   o clearly state that the opposing side of the argument is wrong or flawed?
   o show what is wrong with the opposing side's example or position?

3. Body Paragraphs 2 and 3
   Did you
   o start with a transition/topic sentence that discusses your position on the prompt?
   o give one example or reason to support your position?
   o show the grader how your example supports your position?
   o end the paragraph by restating your thesis?

4. Conclusion
   Did you
   o restate your position on the issue?
   o end with a flourish?

5. Overall
   Did you
   o write neatly?
   o avoid multiple spelling and grammar mistakes?
   o try to vary your sentence structure?
   o use a few impressive-sounding words?

SCORING YOUR PRACTICE EXAM

Step A
Count the number of correct answers for each section and record the number in the space provided for your raw score on the Score Conversion Worksheet below.

Step B
Using the Score Conversion Chart on the next page, convert your raw scores on each section to scaled scores. Then compute your composite ACT score by averaging the four subject scores. Add them up and divide by four. Don't worry about the essay score; it is not included in your composite score.

Score Conversion Worksheet		
Section	Raw Score	Scaled Score
1	_____/75	_____
2	_____/60	_____
3	_____/40	_____
4	_____/40	_____

SCORE CONVERSION CHART

Scaled Score	Raw Score			
	English	Mathematics	Reading	Science Reasoning
36	75	60	39–40	40
35	74	59	38	39
34	72–73	58	37	38
33	71	57	36	—
32	70	55–56	35	37
31	69	53–54	34	36
30	67–68	52	33	—
29	65–66	50–51	32	35
28	62–64	46–49	30–31	33–34
27	59–61	43–45	28–29	31–32
26	57–58	41–42	27	30
25	55–56	39–40	26	29
24	52–54	37–38	25	28
23	50–51	35–36	24	27–26
22	49	33–34	23	25
21	48	31–32	21–22	24
20	45–47	29–30	20	23
19	43–44	27–28	19	22
18	40–42	24–26	18	20–21
17	38–39	21–23	17	18–19
16	35–37	18–20	16	16–17
15	32–34	16–17	15	15
14	29–31	13–15	14	13–14
13	27–28	11–12	12–13	12
12	24–26	9–10	11	11
11	21–23	7–8	9–10	10
10	18–20	6	8	9
9	15–17	5	7	7–8
8	13–14	4	—	6
7	11–12	—	6	5
6	9–10	3	5	—
5	7–8	2	4	4
4	5–6	—	3	3
3	3–4	1	2	2
2	2	—	1	1
1	0	0	0	0

Chapter 5
Practice Test 2

The Princeton Review

ACT Diagnostic Test Form

Use a No. 2 pencil only. Be sure each mark is dark and completely fills the intended oval. Completely erase any errors or stray marks.

1. YOUR NAME: _____
(Print)   Last   First   M.I.

SIGNATURE: _____ DATE: _____ / _____ / _____

HOME ADDRESS: _____
(Print)   Number and Street

_____
City   State   Zip

E-MAIL: _____

PHONE NO.: _____
(Print)

SCHOOL: _____

CLASS OF: _____

IMPORTANT: Please fill in these boxes exactly as shown on the back cover of your tests book.

2. TEST FORM

_____

3. TEST CODE

⓪	⓪	⓪	⓪
①	①	①	①
②	②	②	②
③	③	③	③
④	④	④	④
⑤	⑤	⑤	⑤
⑥	⑥	⑥	⑥
⑦	⑦	⑦	⑦
⑧	⑧	⑧	⑧
⑨	⑨	⑨	⑨

4. PHONE NUMBER

⓪	⓪	⓪	⓪	⓪	⓪	⓪
①	①	①	①	①	①	①
②	②	②	②	②	②	②
③	③	③	③	③	③	③
④	④	④	④	④	④	④
⑤	⑤	⑤	⑤	⑤	⑤	⑤
⑥	⑥	⑥	⑥	⑥	⑥	⑥
⑦	⑦	⑦	⑦	⑦	⑦	⑦
⑧	⑧	⑧	⑧	⑧	⑧	⑧
⑨	⑨	⑨	⑨	⑨	⑨	⑨

5. YOUR NAME

First 4 letters of last name				FIRST INIT	MID INIT
Ⓐ	Ⓐ	Ⓐ	Ⓐ	Ⓐ	Ⓐ
Ⓑ	Ⓑ	Ⓑ	Ⓑ	Ⓑ	Ⓑ
Ⓒ	Ⓒ	Ⓒ	Ⓒ	Ⓒ	Ⓒ
Ⓓ	Ⓓ	Ⓓ	Ⓓ	Ⓓ	Ⓓ
Ⓔ	Ⓔ	Ⓔ	Ⓔ	Ⓔ	Ⓔ
Ⓕ	Ⓕ	Ⓕ	Ⓕ	Ⓕ	Ⓕ
Ⓖ	Ⓖ	Ⓖ	Ⓖ	Ⓖ	Ⓖ
Ⓗ	Ⓗ	Ⓗ	Ⓗ	Ⓗ	Ⓗ
Ⓘ	Ⓘ	Ⓘ	Ⓘ	Ⓘ	Ⓘ
Ⓙ	Ⓙ	Ⓙ	Ⓙ	Ⓙ	Ⓙ
Ⓚ	Ⓚ	Ⓚ	Ⓚ	Ⓚ	Ⓚ
Ⓛ	Ⓛ	Ⓛ	Ⓛ	Ⓛ	Ⓛ
Ⓜ	Ⓜ	Ⓜ	Ⓜ	Ⓜ	Ⓜ
Ⓝ	Ⓝ	Ⓝ	Ⓝ	Ⓝ	Ⓝ
Ⓞ	Ⓞ	Ⓞ	Ⓞ	Ⓞ	Ⓞ
Ⓟ	Ⓟ	Ⓟ	Ⓟ	Ⓟ	Ⓟ
Ⓠ	Ⓠ	Ⓠ	Ⓠ	Ⓠ	Ⓠ
Ⓡ	Ⓡ	Ⓡ	Ⓡ	Ⓡ	Ⓡ
Ⓢ	Ⓢ	Ⓢ	Ⓢ	Ⓢ	Ⓢ
Ⓣ	Ⓣ	Ⓣ	Ⓣ	Ⓣ	Ⓣ
Ⓤ	Ⓤ	Ⓤ	Ⓤ	Ⓤ	Ⓤ
Ⓥ	Ⓥ	Ⓥ	Ⓥ	Ⓥ	Ⓥ
Ⓦ	Ⓦ	Ⓦ	Ⓦ	Ⓦ	Ⓦ
Ⓧ	Ⓧ	Ⓧ	Ⓧ	Ⓧ	Ⓧ
Ⓨ	Ⓨ	Ⓨ	Ⓨ	Ⓨ	Ⓨ
Ⓩ	Ⓩ	Ⓩ	Ⓩ	Ⓩ	Ⓩ

6. DATE OF BIRTH

MONTH	DAY		YEAR	
○ JAN				
○ FEB				
○ MAR	⓪	⓪	⓪	⓪
○ APR	①	①	①	①
○ MAY	②	②	②	②
○ JUN	③	③	③	③
○ JUL		④	④	④
○ AUG		⑤	⑤	⑤
○ SEP		⑥	⑥	⑥
○ OCT		⑦	⑦	⑦
○ NOV		⑧	⑧	⑧
○ DEC		⑨	⑨	⑨

7. SEX

○ MALE
○ FEMALE

8. OTHER

1 Ⓐ Ⓑ Ⓒ Ⓓ Ⓔ
2 Ⓐ Ⓑ Ⓒ Ⓓ Ⓔ
3 Ⓐ Ⓑ Ⓒ Ⓓ Ⓔ

OpScan /NSIGHT™ forms by Pearson NCS EM-255315-1:654321   Printed in U.S.A.

THIS PAGE INTENTIONALLY LEFT BLANK

The Princeton Review
Diagnostic ACT Form

ENGLISH

1 Ⓐ	Ⓑ	Ⓒ	Ⓓ	21 Ⓐ	Ⓑ	Ⓒ	Ⓓ	41 Ⓐ	Ⓑ	Ⓒ	Ⓓ	61 Ⓐ	Ⓑ	Ⓒ	Ⓓ
2 Ⓕ	Ⓖ	Ⓗ	Ⓙ	22 Ⓕ	Ⓖ	Ⓗ	Ⓙ	42 Ⓕ	Ⓖ	Ⓗ	Ⓙ	62 Ⓕ	Ⓖ	Ⓗ	Ⓙ
3 Ⓐ	Ⓑ	Ⓒ	Ⓓ	23 Ⓐ	Ⓑ	Ⓒ	Ⓓ	43 Ⓐ	Ⓑ	Ⓒ	Ⓓ	63 Ⓐ	Ⓑ	Ⓒ	Ⓓ
4 Ⓕ	Ⓖ	Ⓗ	Ⓙ	24 Ⓕ	Ⓖ	Ⓗ	Ⓙ	44 Ⓕ	Ⓖ	Ⓗ	Ⓙ	64 Ⓕ	Ⓖ	Ⓗ	Ⓙ
5 Ⓐ	Ⓑ	Ⓒ	Ⓓ	25 Ⓐ	Ⓑ	Ⓒ	Ⓓ	45 Ⓐ	Ⓑ	Ⓒ	Ⓓ	65 Ⓐ	Ⓑ	Ⓒ	Ⓓ
6 Ⓕ	Ⓖ	Ⓗ	Ⓙ	26 Ⓕ	Ⓖ	Ⓗ	Ⓙ	46 Ⓕ	Ⓖ	Ⓗ	Ⓙ	66 Ⓕ	Ⓖ	Ⓗ	Ⓙ
7 Ⓐ	Ⓑ	Ⓒ	Ⓓ	27 Ⓐ	Ⓑ	Ⓒ	Ⓓ	47 Ⓐ	Ⓑ	Ⓒ	Ⓓ	67 Ⓐ	Ⓑ	Ⓒ	Ⓓ
8 Ⓕ	Ⓖ	Ⓗ	Ⓙ	28 Ⓕ	Ⓖ	Ⓗ	Ⓙ	48 Ⓕ	Ⓖ	Ⓗ	Ⓙ	68 Ⓕ	Ⓖ	Ⓗ	Ⓙ
9 Ⓐ	Ⓑ	Ⓒ	Ⓓ	29 Ⓐ	Ⓑ	Ⓒ	Ⓓ	49 Ⓐ	Ⓑ	Ⓒ	Ⓓ	69 Ⓐ	Ⓑ	Ⓒ	Ⓓ
10 Ⓕ	Ⓖ	Ⓗ	Ⓙ	30 Ⓕ	Ⓖ	Ⓗ	Ⓙ	50 Ⓕ	Ⓖ	Ⓗ	Ⓙ	70 Ⓕ	Ⓖ	Ⓗ	Ⓙ
11 Ⓐ	Ⓑ	Ⓒ	Ⓓ	31 Ⓐ	Ⓑ	Ⓒ	Ⓓ	51 Ⓐ	Ⓑ	Ⓒ	Ⓓ	71 Ⓐ	Ⓑ	Ⓒ	Ⓓ
12 Ⓕ	Ⓖ	Ⓗ	Ⓙ	32 Ⓕ	Ⓖ	Ⓗ	Ⓙ	52 Ⓕ	Ⓖ	Ⓗ	Ⓙ	72 Ⓕ	Ⓖ	Ⓗ	Ⓙ
13 Ⓐ	Ⓑ	Ⓒ	Ⓓ	33 Ⓐ	Ⓑ	Ⓒ	Ⓓ	53 Ⓐ	Ⓑ	Ⓒ	Ⓓ	73 Ⓐ	Ⓑ	Ⓒ	Ⓓ
14 Ⓕ	Ⓖ	Ⓗ	Ⓙ	34 Ⓕ	Ⓖ	Ⓗ	Ⓙ	54 Ⓕ	Ⓖ	Ⓗ	Ⓙ	74 Ⓕ	Ⓖ	Ⓗ	Ⓙ
15 Ⓐ	Ⓑ	Ⓒ	Ⓓ	35 Ⓐ	Ⓑ	Ⓒ	Ⓓ	55 Ⓐ	Ⓑ	Ⓒ	Ⓓ	75 Ⓐ	Ⓑ	Ⓒ	Ⓓ
16 Ⓕ	Ⓖ	Ⓗ	Ⓙ	36 Ⓕ	Ⓖ	Ⓗ	Ⓙ	56 Ⓕ	Ⓖ	Ⓗ	Ⓙ				
17 Ⓐ	Ⓑ	Ⓒ	Ⓓ	37 Ⓐ	Ⓑ	Ⓒ	Ⓓ	57 Ⓐ	Ⓑ	Ⓒ	Ⓓ				
18 Ⓕ	Ⓖ	Ⓗ	Ⓙ	38 Ⓕ	Ⓖ	Ⓗ	Ⓙ	58 Ⓕ	Ⓖ	Ⓗ	Ⓙ				
19 Ⓐ	Ⓑ	Ⓒ	Ⓓ	39 Ⓐ	Ⓑ	Ⓒ	Ⓓ	59 Ⓐ	Ⓑ	Ⓒ	Ⓓ				
20 Ⓕ	Ⓖ	Ⓗ	Ⓙ	40 Ⓕ	Ⓖ	Ⓗ	Ⓙ	60 Ⓕ	Ⓖ	Ⓗ	Ⓙ				

MATHEMATICS

1 Ⓐ	Ⓑ	Ⓒ	Ⓓ	Ⓔ	16 Ⓕ	Ⓖ	Ⓗ	Ⓙ	Ⓚ	31 Ⓐ	Ⓑ	Ⓒ	Ⓓ	Ⓔ	46 Ⓕ	Ⓖ	Ⓗ	Ⓙ	Ⓚ
2 Ⓕ	Ⓖ	Ⓗ	Ⓙ	Ⓚ	17 Ⓐ	Ⓑ	Ⓒ	Ⓓ	Ⓔ	32 Ⓕ	Ⓖ	Ⓗ	Ⓙ	Ⓚ	47 Ⓐ	Ⓑ	Ⓒ	Ⓓ	Ⓔ
3 Ⓐ	Ⓑ	Ⓒ	Ⓓ	Ⓔ	18 Ⓕ	Ⓖ	Ⓗ	Ⓙ	Ⓚ	33 Ⓐ	Ⓑ	Ⓒ	Ⓓ	Ⓔ	48 Ⓕ	Ⓖ	Ⓗ	Ⓙ	Ⓚ
4 Ⓕ	Ⓖ	Ⓗ	Ⓙ	Ⓚ	19 Ⓐ	Ⓑ	Ⓒ	Ⓓ	Ⓔ	34 Ⓕ	Ⓖ	Ⓗ	Ⓙ	Ⓚ	49 Ⓐ	Ⓑ	Ⓒ	Ⓓ	Ⓔ
5 Ⓐ	Ⓑ	Ⓒ	Ⓓ	Ⓔ	20 Ⓕ	Ⓖ	Ⓗ	Ⓙ	Ⓚ	35 Ⓐ	Ⓑ	Ⓒ	Ⓓ	Ⓔ	50 Ⓕ	Ⓖ	Ⓗ	Ⓙ	Ⓚ
6 Ⓕ	Ⓖ	Ⓗ	Ⓙ	Ⓚ	21 Ⓐ	Ⓑ	Ⓒ	Ⓓ	Ⓔ	36 Ⓕ	Ⓖ	Ⓗ	Ⓙ	Ⓚ	51 Ⓐ	Ⓑ	Ⓒ	Ⓓ	Ⓔ
7 Ⓐ	Ⓑ	Ⓒ	Ⓓ	Ⓔ	22 Ⓕ	Ⓖ	Ⓗ	Ⓙ	Ⓚ	37 Ⓐ	Ⓑ	Ⓒ	Ⓓ	Ⓔ	52 Ⓕ	Ⓖ	Ⓗ	Ⓙ	Ⓚ
8 Ⓕ	Ⓖ	Ⓗ	Ⓙ	Ⓚ	23 Ⓐ	Ⓑ	Ⓒ	Ⓓ	Ⓔ	38 Ⓕ	Ⓖ	Ⓗ	Ⓙ	Ⓚ	53 Ⓐ	Ⓑ	Ⓒ	Ⓓ	Ⓔ
9 Ⓐ	Ⓑ	Ⓒ	Ⓓ	Ⓔ	24 Ⓕ	Ⓖ	Ⓗ	Ⓙ	Ⓚ	39 Ⓐ	Ⓑ	Ⓒ	Ⓓ	Ⓔ	54 Ⓕ	Ⓖ	Ⓗ	Ⓙ	Ⓚ
10 Ⓕ	Ⓖ	Ⓗ	Ⓙ	Ⓚ	25 Ⓐ	Ⓑ	Ⓒ	Ⓓ	Ⓔ	40 Ⓕ	Ⓖ	Ⓗ	Ⓙ	Ⓚ	55 Ⓐ	Ⓑ	Ⓒ	Ⓓ	Ⓔ
11 Ⓐ	Ⓑ	Ⓒ	Ⓓ	Ⓔ	26 Ⓕ	Ⓖ	Ⓗ	Ⓙ	Ⓚ	41 Ⓐ	Ⓑ	Ⓒ	Ⓓ	Ⓔ	56 Ⓕ	Ⓖ	Ⓗ	Ⓙ	Ⓚ
12 Ⓕ	Ⓖ	Ⓗ	Ⓙ	Ⓚ	27 Ⓐ	Ⓑ	Ⓒ	Ⓓ	Ⓔ	42 Ⓕ	Ⓖ	Ⓗ	Ⓙ	Ⓚ	57 Ⓐ	Ⓑ	Ⓒ	Ⓓ	Ⓔ
13 Ⓐ	Ⓑ	Ⓒ	Ⓓ	Ⓔ	28 Ⓕ	Ⓖ	Ⓗ	Ⓙ	Ⓚ	43 Ⓐ	Ⓑ	Ⓒ	Ⓓ	Ⓔ	58 Ⓕ	Ⓖ	Ⓗ	Ⓙ	Ⓚ
14 Ⓕ	Ⓖ	Ⓗ	Ⓙ	Ⓚ	29 Ⓐ	Ⓑ	Ⓒ	Ⓓ	Ⓔ	44 Ⓕ	Ⓖ	Ⓗ	Ⓙ	Ⓚ	59 Ⓐ	Ⓑ	Ⓒ	Ⓓ	Ⓔ
15 Ⓐ	Ⓑ	Ⓒ	Ⓓ	Ⓔ	30 Ⓕ	Ⓖ	Ⓗ	Ⓙ	Ⓚ	45 Ⓐ	Ⓑ	Ⓒ	Ⓓ	Ⓔ	60 Ⓕ	Ⓖ	Ⓗ	Ⓙ	Ⓚ

The Princeton Review
Diagnostic ACT Form

READING

1 Ⓐ	Ⓑ	Ⓒ	Ⓓ	11 Ⓐ	Ⓑ	Ⓒ	Ⓓ	21 Ⓐ	Ⓑ	Ⓒ	Ⓓ	31 Ⓐ	Ⓑ	Ⓒ	Ⓓ
2 Ⓕ	Ⓖ	Ⓗ	Ⓙ	12 Ⓕ	Ⓖ	Ⓗ	Ⓙ	22 Ⓕ	Ⓖ	Ⓗ	Ⓙ	32 Ⓕ	Ⓖ	Ⓗ	Ⓙ
3 Ⓐ	Ⓑ	Ⓒ	Ⓓ	13 Ⓐ	Ⓑ	Ⓒ	Ⓓ	23 Ⓐ	Ⓑ	Ⓒ	Ⓓ	33 Ⓐ	Ⓑ	Ⓒ	Ⓓ
4 Ⓕ	Ⓖ	Ⓗ	Ⓙ	14 Ⓕ	Ⓖ	Ⓗ	Ⓙ	24 Ⓕ	Ⓖ	Ⓗ	Ⓙ	34 Ⓕ	Ⓖ	Ⓗ	Ⓙ
5 Ⓐ	Ⓑ	Ⓒ	Ⓓ	15 Ⓐ	Ⓑ	Ⓒ	Ⓓ	25 Ⓐ	Ⓑ	Ⓒ	Ⓓ	35 Ⓐ	Ⓑ	Ⓒ	Ⓓ
6 Ⓕ	Ⓖ	Ⓗ	Ⓙ	16 Ⓕ	Ⓖ	Ⓗ	Ⓙ	26 Ⓕ	Ⓖ	Ⓗ	Ⓙ	36 Ⓕ	Ⓖ	Ⓗ	Ⓙ
7 Ⓐ	Ⓑ	Ⓒ	Ⓓ	17 Ⓐ	Ⓑ	Ⓒ	Ⓓ	27 Ⓐ	Ⓑ	Ⓒ	Ⓓ	37 Ⓐ	Ⓑ	Ⓒ	Ⓓ
8 Ⓕ	Ⓖ	Ⓗ	Ⓙ	18 Ⓕ	Ⓖ	Ⓗ	Ⓙ	28 Ⓕ	Ⓖ	Ⓗ	Ⓙ	38 Ⓕ	Ⓖ	Ⓗ	Ⓙ
9 Ⓐ	Ⓑ	Ⓒ	Ⓓ	19 Ⓐ	Ⓑ	Ⓒ	Ⓓ	29 Ⓐ	Ⓑ	Ⓒ	Ⓓ	39 Ⓐ	Ⓑ	Ⓒ	Ⓓ
10 Ⓕ	Ⓖ	Ⓗ	Ⓙ	20 Ⓕ	Ⓖ	Ⓗ	Ⓙ	30 Ⓕ	Ⓖ	Ⓗ	Ⓙ	40 Ⓕ	Ⓖ	Ⓗ	Ⓙ

SCIENCE REASONING

1 Ⓐ	Ⓑ	Ⓒ	Ⓓ	11 Ⓐ	Ⓑ	Ⓒ	Ⓓ	21 Ⓐ	Ⓑ	Ⓒ	Ⓓ	31 Ⓐ	Ⓑ	Ⓒ	Ⓓ
2 Ⓕ	Ⓖ	Ⓗ	Ⓙ	12 Ⓕ	Ⓖ	Ⓗ	Ⓙ	22 Ⓕ	Ⓖ	Ⓗ	Ⓙ	32 Ⓕ	Ⓖ	Ⓗ	Ⓙ
3 Ⓐ	Ⓑ	Ⓒ	Ⓓ	13 Ⓐ	Ⓑ	Ⓒ	Ⓓ	23 Ⓐ	Ⓑ	Ⓒ	Ⓓ	33 Ⓐ	Ⓑ	Ⓒ	Ⓓ
4 Ⓕ	Ⓖ	Ⓗ	Ⓙ	14 Ⓕ	Ⓖ	Ⓗ	Ⓙ	24 Ⓕ	Ⓖ	Ⓗ	Ⓙ	34 Ⓕ	Ⓖ	Ⓗ	Ⓙ
5 Ⓐ	Ⓑ	Ⓒ	Ⓓ	15 Ⓐ	Ⓑ	Ⓒ	Ⓓ	25 Ⓐ	Ⓑ	Ⓒ	Ⓓ	35 Ⓐ	Ⓑ	Ⓒ	Ⓓ
6 Ⓕ	Ⓖ	Ⓗ	Ⓙ	16 Ⓕ	Ⓖ	Ⓗ	Ⓙ	26 Ⓕ	Ⓖ	Ⓗ	Ⓙ	36 Ⓕ	Ⓖ	Ⓗ	Ⓙ
7 Ⓐ	Ⓑ	Ⓒ	Ⓓ	17 Ⓐ	Ⓑ	Ⓒ	Ⓓ	27 Ⓐ	Ⓑ	Ⓒ	Ⓓ	37 Ⓐ	Ⓑ	Ⓒ	Ⓓ
8 Ⓕ	Ⓖ	Ⓗ	Ⓙ	18 Ⓕ	Ⓖ	Ⓗ	Ⓙ	28 Ⓕ	Ⓖ	Ⓗ	Ⓙ	38 Ⓕ	Ⓖ	Ⓗ	Ⓙ
9 Ⓐ	Ⓑ	Ⓒ	Ⓓ	19 Ⓐ	Ⓑ	Ⓒ	Ⓓ	29 Ⓐ	Ⓑ	Ⓒ	Ⓓ	39 Ⓐ	Ⓑ	Ⓒ	Ⓓ
10 Ⓕ	Ⓖ	Ⓗ	Ⓙ	20 Ⓕ	Ⓖ	Ⓗ	Ⓙ	30 Ⓕ	Ⓖ	Ⓗ	Ⓙ	40 Ⓕ	Ⓖ	Ⓗ	Ⓙ

The Princeton Review
Diagnostic ACT Form

ESSAY

Begin your essay on this side. If necessary, continue on the opposite side.

The Princeton Review
Diagnostic ACT Form

Continued from previous page.

PLEASE PRINT
YOUR INITIALS

First	Middle	Last

The Princeton Review
Diagnostic ACT Form

Continued from previous page.

_____

_____

_____

_____

_____

_____

_____

_____

_____

_____

_____

_____

_____

_____

_____

_____

_____

_____

_____

_____

_____

_____

_____

_____

_____

**PLEASE PRINT
YOUR INITIALS**

| First | Middle | Last |

The Princeton Review
Diagnostic ACT Form

Continued from previous page.

THIS PAGE INTENTIONALLY LEFT BLANK

ACT ENGLISH TEST
45 Minutes—70 Questions

DIRECTIONS: In the five passages that follow, certain words and phrases are underlined and numbered. In the right-hand column, you will find alternatives for each underlined part. In most cases, you are to choose the one that best expresses the idea, makes the statement appropriate for standard written English, or is worded most consistently with the style and tone of the passage as a whole. If you think the original version is best, choose "NO CHANGE." In some cases, you will find in the right-hand column a question about the underlined part. You are to choose the best answer to the question.

You will also find questions about a section of the passage or the passage as a whole. These questions do not refer to an underlined portion of the passage but rather are identified by a number or numbers in a box.

For each question, choose the alternative you consider best and blacken the corresponding oval on your answer document. Read each passage through once before you begin to answer the questions that accompany it. For many of the questions, you must read several sentences beyond the question to determine the answer. Be sure that you have read far enough ahead each time you choose an alternative.

PASSAGE I

> The following paragraphs may or may not be in the most logical order. Each paragraph is numbered in brackets, and question 14 will ask you to choose where Paragraph 5 should most logically be placed.

A Window into History

[1]

One very long summer during high school, my mom volunteered me to help Grandpa research our family tree. Great, I thought, imagining hours spent pawing through dusty, rotting boxes and listening to boring stories about people I didn't know. "You'll be surprised," my mom promised. "Family histories can be very interesting."

[2]

In truth, Grandpa didn't want to limit my work to just research. Hoping to also preserve our family memories. He'd discovered a computer program that helps digitally scan old pictures, and letters to preserve their contents before they crumble from old age. Grandpa wanted me to help him connect

1. Given that all the choices are true, which one best conveys the author's initial expectations and effectively leads into her mother's comments?
   A. NO CHANGE
   B. bonding with the grandfather I barely knew.
   C. remembering fun times I had with relatives.
   D. trying to operate an unfamiliar machine.

2. F. NO CHANGE
   G. research. Hope to also preserve
   H. research, that hope to also preserve
   J. research, hoping to also preserve

3. A. NO CHANGE
   B. pictures, and, letters
   C. pictures and letters,
   D. pictures and letters

GO ON TO THE NEXT PAGE.

the scanner and set up the computer program. He could type documents and send <u>emails, but he had</u> never used a scanner.
₄

[3]

[1] Instead of sorting through dusty boxes as I had imagined, we spent a lot of time in my grandpa's bright, tidy computer room. [2] The scanner hummed happily, turning my <u>relatives precious memories</u> into permanent digital images.
₅
[3] A scanner is a device which makes electronic copies of actual items. [4] I worked happily while Grandpa shared stories that turned out not to be boring at all. [6]

[4]

Perusing through <u>her</u> belongings, I felt I was opening a
₇
window into the world of my relatives, a world long since gone.

Grandpa showed me a bundle of yellowed letters he <u>had send</u>
₈
to Grandma from the front lines of World War II, and I could almost smell the gunpowder. I turned the brittle pages of my great-grandmother's recipe book and could envision her sitting in her immaculate <u>kitchen penning</u> meticulously every entry. All
₉
of the people who had been merely names to me now had faces to match and lives lived.

[5]

I asked Grandpa to tell the story behind every picture and letter we scanned. <u>Besides, the</u> stories helped me not only
₁₀
understand but also relate to my relatives. Like me, they had celebrated achievements, overcome failures, pulled silly pranks, played <u>sports, and,</u> attended concerts. I became so hungry for
₁₁
more information that Grandpa needed additional props to keep

---

4. Which of the following choices is NOT an acceptable substitute for the underlined portion?
   F. emails but having
   G. emails, yet he had
   H. emails; however, he had
   J. emails but had

5. A. NO CHANGE
   B. relatives precious memory's
   C. relatives' precious memories
   D. relatives' precious memory's

6. Which of the following sentences in this paragraph is LEAST relevant to the progression of the narrative and therefore could be deleted?
   F. Sentence 1
   G. Sentence 2
   H. Sentence 3
   J. Sentence 4

7. A. NO CHANGE
   B. their
   C. one's
   D. there

8. F. NO CHANGE
   G. send
   H. has sent
   J. had sent

9. A. NO CHANGE
   B. kitchen, penning
   C. kitchen, which penned
   D. kitchen that penned

10. F. NO CHANGE
    G. Because the
    H. Therefore, the
    J. The

11. A. NO CHANGE
    B. sports, and
    C. sports and,
    D. sports and

GO ON TO THE NEXT PAGE.

me satisfied. He showed me a chest filled with random stuff, all

covered in dust. [12].

[6]

   As the new school year approached, Grandpa admitted, "I

probably could have done this project myself. I just wanted

someone to share it with." I can't thank him enough for sharing

the experience and making me appreciate the family members

who have made me the person I am. I will cherish family

memories and mementoes and hope that someday, I will be able
                                                            13
to pass them down to my own grandchildren.
                                        13

12. Which of the following true statements, if added at the beginning of this paragraph, would most successfully introduce readers to the information relayed in the paragraph?

   F. My family has been around for generations, so there were a lot of names to remember.
   G. My grandfather inundated me with items to catalogue on the computer.
   H. As I learned more about some relatives, I forgot about others.
   J. As the summer progressed, I became fascinated with my relatives' lives.

13. Which of the following provides the best conclusion to the paragraph and the essay as a whole?

   A. NO CHANGE
   B. My grandpa will teach me something new next summer.
   C. I never have to tell my mother she was right that family history isn't tedious and boring.
   D. I can figure out other ways to use my computer.

Questions 14 and 15 ask about the preceding passage as a whole.

---

14. Where should the author place Paragraph 5 in order to have a logical, coherent essay?

   F. Where it is now
   G. Before Paragraph 2
   H. Before Paragraph 3
   J. Before Paragraph 4

15. Suppose the writer's purpose had been to write an essay about some of the benefits of genealogical research. Does this essay succeed in achieving that purpose?

   A. Yes, because it describes the technological skills gained in the process of researching one's relatives.
   B. Yes, because it provides an example of how one person gained personal insights from her family history.
   C. No, because it provides only one person's research, which is susceptible to bias and cannot be reliable.
   D. No, because genealogical research require statistics in order to prove there were benefits.

PASSAGE II

Moving to a New Life

   I stand on the corner of Elm Avenue and Main Street by

me, watching my parents walk away and feeling nothing but
    16

apprehension about adjusting to this new town. I try not to show

the passersby just how scared I really am, but it's not possible.

16. F. NO CHANGE
   G. me watching
   H. myself, watching
   J. myself. Watching

GO ON TO THE NEXT PAGE.

My tears start to flow, and I quickly run to my new, cold,
₁₇
bedroom.

I know I am making a complete spectacle of myself, but I
₁₈

can't help it. I am an only child whom has never been more
₁₉
than 30 minutes away from her parents, yet here I am, on the
other side of the country, moving in to my new college dorm.

We all want to take responsibility for one's own lives. I just
₂₀
never realized that in order to do so, I would have to leave my
family. No longer will I wake up to Mom's Sunday breakfast of

non-pasteurized milk, and fresh orange juice, fluffy scrambled
₂₁
eggs and crisp bacon. I'll have to tackle the daily crossword
puzzle on my own, without Dad's carefully veiled hints.

Everything is gone. ☐22 Can anyone understand what I'm going
through?

As I lie crying into my pillow, hearing the door to the
₂₃
dorm suite open. It must be one of my two roommates. I
quickly stop crying—I couldn't stand the embarrassment

17. A. NO CHANGE
  B. new, cold
  C. new cold
  D. new cold,

18. F. NO CHANGE
  G. completely spectacle about
  H. completely spectacle of
  J. complete spectacle about

19. A. NO CHANGE
  B. whom have
  C. who has
  D. who have

20. F. NO CHANGE
  G. their own life.
  H. our own lives.
  J. your own life.

21. A. NO CHANGE
  B. milk, and fresh orange juice, fluffy,
  C. milk and fresh orange juice fluffy
  D. milk and fresh orange juice, fluffy

22. The writer is considering revising the sentence "Everything is gone" in the preceding sentence to read:

  "It feels like everything I have ever loved is being
  ripped away from me."

Should the writer make this change, or keep the sentence
as it is?

  F. Make the revision, because it conveys more vividly the
  type of emotions felt by the writer.
  G. Make the revision, because it describes the stages of
  emotion the writer faces as she mourns.
  H. Keep the sentence as it is, because it is already specific
  and does not need to be changed.
  J. Keep the sentence as it is, because it's short and more
  concise than the proposed revision.

23. A. NO CHANGE
  B. I was hearing
  C. I hear
  D. having heard

GO ON TO THE NEXT PAGE.

if she knew her new roommate was an emotional wreck! [24]

24. If the writer were to delete the phrase "—I couldn't stand the embarrassment if she knew her new roommate was an emotional wreck!" from the preceding sentence, the passage would primarily lose:

    F. a description of the uneasy relationship between the roommates.
    G. an insight into the reasons the writer stopped crying.
    H. a justification for her dissatisfaction with college.
    J. nothing at all, since the writer has already expressed her sadness.

Being full of surprise, I hear *her* crying as she runs to her room.
25

25. **A.** NO CHANGE
    B. Since I was surprised,
    C. Being surprised,
    D. Much to my surprise,

Curiosity overwhelming me and I tiptoe through the common
26
room to her still-open door.

26. **F.** NO CHANGE
    G. me, and I
    H. me, I
    J. me. I

    I stand in the doorway for merely a second before she reacts. Slowly, her face jolts up, and her sudden shock at my
27
appearance is clearly written on her face. "Are you okay?" I

27. Given that all the choices are true, which one provides the best transition by illustrating how quickly the roommate responded to the writer's presence?

    A. NO CHANGE
    B. Abruptly,
    C. After several moments,
    D. Sluggishly,

quietly ask. "I'm sorry," she stammers. "I thought I was alone.
28
I know this must seem very childish to you. I'm just very close to my younger sister, and saying goodbye to her just now...." Her sentence trails off as she turns her face away from me. "I remember when she was born."
29

28. **F.** NO CHANGE
    G. asserts.
    H. quotes.
    J. screams.

    "I completely understand," I say, and I really do. "Maybe we can help each other get used to this new college life."

29. Given that all the choices are true, which conclusion to this paragraph is most consistent with the writer's subsequent response?

    A. NO CHANGE
    B. "My sister has always been so fun to live with."
    C. "I wish that they would have left sooner."
    D. "It's going to be hard to adjust, that's all."

GO ON TO THE NEXT PAGE.

Question 30 asks about the preceding passage as a whole.

30. Suppose the writer's goal was to describe personal hardships first-time college students may experience. Does this essay successfully accomplish that goal?

F. Yes, because it gives an anecdotal account of separation anxiety experienced by the writer and her roommate.
G. Yes, because it focuses on the initial awkwardness between roommates who don't know each other.
H. No, because it focuses on the emotions of only one person instead of the experiences of many students.
J. No, because it fails to provide enough background information on the narrator's mental state before college.

PASSAGE III

The following paragraphs may or may not be in the most logical order. Each paragraph is numbered in brackets, and question 45 will ask you to choose where Paragraph 2 should most logically be placed.

Thrill Seekers Wanted

[1]

Like Indiana Jones, the staid college professor who undertakes daring adventures in his spare time, my father is a businessman by day and a thrill-seeking adrenaline fanatic by night. [31] His enthusiasm rubbed off on me, and I have been lucky to be his sidekick on many an adventure. We started out small by conquering America's fastest, most twisted rollercoasters. After that, a whitewater rafting excursion through

31. The writer is considering deleting the phrase "Like Indiana Jones, the staid college professor who undertakes daring adventures in his spare time," from the preceding sentence (and capitalizing the word *my*). Should the phrase be kept or deleted?

A. Kept, because it clarifies that the writer's father is also named Indiana.
B. Kept, because it adds a descriptive detail that heightens the thrill of the adventures described later in the passage.
C. Deleted, because it draws attention from the paragraph's focus on the father and places it on movies.
D. Deleted, because the information fails to specify if the writer's father is interested in archaeology.

GO ON TO THE NEXT PAGE.

the Grand Canyon on the <u>majestic, if murky</u> Colorado River
₃₂
jumpstarted our search for other extreme thrills across the globe.

[2]

Anyone who loves a challenging thrill should try

canyoning. [33] Our adventure began with a 90-foot rappel

down a canyon wall into a rushing, ice-cold <u>river, and without</u>
₃₄
wetsuits we surely would have become popsicles! Intrepidly, we

traversed the bone-chilling water toward the mouth of the river,

our final destination, where the reward for the journey would be

a panoramic <u>view of the natural wonder</u> of the lush Interlaken
₃₅
basin.

[3]

Spectacular thrills awaited us at every corner of the world.

A remarkable activity in its own right, <u>like skydiving was</u>
₃₆
especially momentous when performed from a helicopter over

the breathtaking Swiss Alps. We have gone spelunking in damp

and ominous Peruvian caves. [37] We have traveled to New

Zealand for *Zorb*, a strange activity in which participants enter

a giant, inflatable ball and roll down steep, grassy hills. Most

32. F. NO CHANGE
G. majestic if murky
H. majestic; if murky,
J. majestic, if murky,

33. The writer is considering deleting the phrase "who loves a challenging thrill" from the preceding sentence. Should the phrase be kept or deleted?

A. Kept, because it clarifies the term *anyone* and contributes to the logic of the paragraph.
B. Kept, because it indicates the paragraph's focus on people who love challenges.
C. Deleted, because the term *anyone* describes all people and does not need clarification.
D. Deleted, because the phrase is too long and confuses the focus of the sentence.

34. F. NO CHANGE
G. river, without
H. river without
J. river and without

35. A. NO CHANGE
B. view naturally of the wonder
C. viewing of the wonderful nature
D. view

36. F. NO CHANGE
G. skydiving was
H. skydiving,
J. like skydiving

37. At this point, the writer is considering adding the following true statement:

> We have bungee jumped from the world's highest platform, Bloukrans Bridge in South Africa.

Should the writer make this addition here?

A. Yes, because it is an additional detail consistent with the main point of this paragraph.
B. Yes, because it helps establish the main idea that Africa has the most exciting thrills in the world.
C. No, because its focus is on a location and activity different than those in the rest of the paragraph.
D. No, because the other activities in this paragraph do not involve the use of a bungee cord.

GO ON TO THE NEXT PAGE.

recently, in Interlaken, Switzerland, we attempted "canyoning,"

because of which was our most exhilarating adventure yet!
         _____
         38

                    [4]

    We had to navigate both the flowing river and the canyon

walls we became amphibious, moving seamlessly between
_____
    39

land and water. We slid over slick rocks at one moment,

leapt and descended from waterfalls and swam through
_____
       40

underwater tunnels the next. Back and forth we alternated,

scaling rope ladders before zooming down zip lines back into

the fresh mountain water. Certainly, danger from possible

miscalculations were lurking in each of these activities, but that
_____
         41

very danger provided the rush. Canyoning was indeed one thrill

after another, from beginning to end.
              _____
                      42

                    [5]

    While canyoning is possible only in certain locales, thrills

and adventure can be found anywhere. Our humble beginnings

in the U.S. showed us just that. We continue to seek the big

thrills, but in doing so, we have learned to seek lesser forms of
        ___
        43

excitement in daily life as well. After all, we can't go canyoning

every day, and small thrills are better than none for us thrill
          _____
                              44

seekers.
_____
  44

38. F. NO CHANGE
  G. and which was
  H. which was
  J. in which was

39. A. NO CHANGE
  B. walls, we
  C. walls so we
  D. walls, so we

40. F. NO CHANGE
  G. leapt
  H. leapt in the air and descended down
  J. leapt to descend

41. A. NO CHANGE
  B. miscalculations will be lurking
  C. miscalculations was lurking
  D. miscalculations lurking

42. Given that all the choices are true, which one best clarifies the distinction between the two types of activities mentioned in this paragraph?

  F. NO CHANGE
  G. both on rocky surfaces and in the chilly water.
  H. adventure after adventure.
  J. long after the waterfalls.

43. A. NO CHANGE
  B. and
  C. moreover,
  D. furthermore,

44. Given that all the choices are true, which one concludes the paragraph with a phrase that relates to the main topic of the essay?

  F. NO CHANGE
  G. and that's a shame.
  H. because we don't live near any canyons.
  J. but it's the last thrill I'll ever need!

GO ON TO THE NEXT PAGE.

Question 45 asks about the preceding passage as a whole.

45. For the sake of the logic and coherence of this essay, the best placement for Paragraph 2 would be:

A. where it is now.
B. before Paragraph 1.
C. before Paragraph 4.
D. before Paragraph 5.

PASSAGE IV

Enriching the American Tradition

The Mexican-American War, with its many conflicts and compromises, <u>represent</u> a largely overlooked part of the history of the United States, but its importance in the current shape and culture of the United States cannot be overstated. Certainly, it is difficult to imagine the present-day United States without the list of former Mexican territories, which <u>includes</u> Texas, Arizona, California, and others, but it is equally difficult to imagine America's vibrant multicultural society without the influence of Mexican-Americans.

But despite the obvious richness that Mexican-Americans have brought to American culture, one aspect of <u>their contributions, to American arts</u> is often overlooked: literature. Although the names of many famous Mexican-Americans are identifiable in film and music, many Americans are at a loss to name even a single Mexican-American author. <u>Carlos Santana, a musician born and raised in Mexico, has achieved widespread popularity in the United States.</u>

46. F. NO CHANGE
 G. represents
 H. have represented
 J. representing

47. A. NO CHANGE
 B. includes:
 C. included,
 D. included:

48. F. NO CHANGE
 G. their contributions, to American arts,
 H. their contributions to American arts,
 J. their contributions to American arts

49. A. NO CHANGE
 B. A musician who has achieved popularity in the United States is Carlos Santana, who was born and raised in Mexico.
 C. However, many Americans can easily identify Carlos Santana, a popular musician born and raised in Mexico.
 D. DELETE the underlined portion.

GO ON TO THE NEXT PAGE.

A major landmark in early Mexican-American literature came in 1885, when author, María Amparo Ruiz de Burton, published her second novel, *The Squatter and the Don*. In addition to being the first major novel written in English by an author of Mexican descent, *The Squatter and the Don* was also noteworthy for its revolutionary perspective. [51] María

Amparo Ruiz de Burton helped to acquaint American readers with and introduce them to an as yet unfamiliar group through her fictional family, the Alamars. A family of landed gentry

living in San Diego, nearly all is lost to the Alamars after

the American annexation of California during the Mexican-American War. As a result of the lopsided Treaty of Guadalupe Hidalgo, Mexico lost nearly forty percent of its previous territories and many, like Ruiz de Burton and her creations the Alamars, were uprooted from their previous comfort and made citizens of a new nation. Ruiz de Burton's wish that her works would speak for the many Mexican-Americans who felt

50. F. NO CHANGE
   G. author María Amparo Ruiz de Burton
   H. author, María Amparo Ruiz de Burton
   J. author María Amparo Ruiz de Burton,

51. If the writer were to delete the phrase "In addition to being the first major novel written in English by an author of Mexican descent," from the preceding sentence, the essay would primarily lose:

   A. an indication of Ruiz de Burton's command of the English language.
   B. a fact that reveals that the novel was the first by a Mexican author to be read in the United States.
   C. information that helps to strengthen the sense of the novel's historical importance.
   D. a suggestion that María Amparo Ruiz de Burton considered writing the novel in her native Spanish.

52. F. NO CHANGE
   G. give American readers a glimpse at
   H. introduce American readers unacquainted with Mexican-American literature to
   J. introduce American readers to

53. A. NO CHANGE
   B. the Alamars lose nearly all that they own
   C. losing all that they own
   D. Ruiz de Burton describes a family that loses all that they own

54. F. NO CHANGE
   G. within
   H. throughout
   J. through

55. A. NO CHANGE
   B. being that
   C. was that
   D. being

GO ON TO THE NEXT PAGE.

the same concerns. |56| *The Squatter and the Don* marked an early and important exploration of many themes that Mexican-

American authors continue to explore, including themes of personal integrity, identity, and the relationships between individuals and collective history.

[1] Poet Ana Castillo has been publishing well-received novels and volumes of poetry prolifically since 1977, and her work has been essential in bringing issues of Mexican-American women, particularly those living in urban places such as Castillo's hometown of Chicago, to a larger audience. [2] Sandra Cisneros is the author of *The House on Mango Street*, which has sold over two million copies since its original publication in 1984, and her work, including the novel *Caramelo*, published in 2002, has helped give voice to the often difficult position of living between two cultures that Mexican-Americans face. [3] Ruiz de Burton's writings and that of other

authors remain important parts of American literature today. |59|

56. At this point, the writer is considering adding the following true statement:

> After the Louisiana Purchase in 1803, many people of French descent living in the United States felt displaced as well.

Should the writer make the addition here?

F. Yes, because it provides historical information about another group that deepens the reader's understanding of the difficulties faced by Mexican-Americans.

G. Yes, because it links those with French descent with the characters in *The Squatter and the Don*.

H. No, because it does not provide a direct connection between the work of María Amparo Ruiz de Burton and the work of later Mexican-American authors.

J. No, because it is clear from the essay that the Louisiana Purchase had no importance to the Mexican-American authors discussed.

57. Which of the following alternatives to the underlined portion would be LEAST acceptable?

A. investigate
B. examine
C. look into
D. solve

58. **F.** NO CHANGE
G. by
H. those of
J. with

59. For the sake of the logic and coherence of this paragraph, Sentence 3 should be placed:

A. where it is now.
B. before Sentence 1.
C. before Sentence 2.
D. after Sentence 4.

GO ON TO THE NEXT PAGE.

[4] Along with many others, <u>these authors</u> continue to expand
₆₀
the boundaries of American literature, just as Mexican-
Americans all over the country continue to enrich and challenge
accepted notions of what we call "American culture."

60. F. NO CHANGE
G. the writers Ana Castillo and Sandra Cisneros and many other Mexican-American authors
H. the Mexican-American authors being published today
J. the many Mexican-American authors whose work as a whole represents them

---

PASSAGE V

A Simple but Complex Modern Vision

Ludwig Mies van der Rohe, typically cited alongside
Walter Gropius and Le Corbusier as a pioneer of modern
<u>architecture. Was</u> integral to the founding and proliferation of
₆₁
the "modern style" in architecture. Van der Rohe felt the design
of a building should be reflective of its age, as the Gothic and
Classical masterpieces surely were. Van der Rohe, called Mies
by friends and students, found many architects' attitudes toward
architectural design problematic, particularly these architects'
reliance on older, outdated architectural styles.

Van der Rohe, instead, sought to express through his
buildings what he <u>feels</u> to be the core tenets of modern
₆₂

existence. The <u>buildings based on van der Rohe's designs,</u>
₆₃

were primarily constructed <u>with</u> industrial steel and plate
₆₄

glass—<u>that is,</u> only the materials of modern, twentieth-century
₆₅
life and industry. By using only the bare minimum materials
produced from American and German factories, Mies sought
to cast off what he found to be one of the main problems

61. A. NO CHANGE
B. architecture. Being
C. architecture, being
D. architecture, was

62. F. NO CHANGE
G. is feeling
H. felt
J. who felt

63. A. NO CHANGE
B. buildings based on van der Rohe's designs
C. buildings, based on van der Rohe's designs
D. buildings based on van der Rohe's designs;

64. Which of the following alternatives to the underlined portion would NOT be acceptable?
F. from
G. using
H. out of
J. into

65. A. NO CHANGE
B. that is
C. this is,
D. this is

GO ON TO THE NEXT PAGE.

with contemporary <u>architecture, and</u> overly decorative and
₆₆
ornamental structures with no "function" were wasteful uses of

space and material. Through steel and plate glass, van der Rohe

felt that he could better practice the idea of "efficiency" that he

had pulled from his earlier readings of Russian Constructivism,

and using these materials as he did to create simple, planar,

rectilinear designs, Mies invested his buildings with a strange

intensity that conveyed at once the simplicity of design and

<u>many of the buildings have been named National Historic</u>
₆₇
<u>Landmarks.</u>
₆₇

    Van der Rohe's architectural education was unique, and

many describe the architect as largely self-taught. From

1908 to 1912, under <u>teacher Peter Behrens's guidance,</u> Mies
₆₈
became a proponent of many modern and avant-garde ideas in

architecture in Germany. From Behrens, van der Rohe began

to see the potential of developing an architecture of ideas, and

indeed, he was a "self-taught" expert in many ancient and

modern philosophical concepts. <u>This</u> helped him to understand
₆₉
the character of the modern world, and with his maturing ideas

of this character, van der Rohe set out to create a style truly

of the twentieth century. <u>While</u> van der Rohe was committed
₇₀
to creating a philosophical, theoretical basis for his works, he

helped to create a new vocabulary for the creation and study of

architecture.

    [1] In order to escape the oppressive Nazi regime, van der

Rohe <u>who left</u> Germany for the United States in 1937. [2] Mies
₇₁
was originally invited to become head of the school and to

contribute designs for the school's growing campus (which, as

the Illinois Institute of Technology, continues to grow today).

66. F. NO CHANGE
   G. architecture that
   H. architecture, which
   J. architecture: that

67. Given that all the choices are true, which one would add
the most effective detail to the description of the visual
appeal of the buildings mentioned in the first part of the
sentence?

   A. NO CHANGE
   B. the structure that had taken months, even years, to
build.
   C. the complex beauty of the free-flowing structures
inside.
   D. the buildings on display in many American and European cities.

68. F. NO CHANGE
   G. teacher, Peter Behrens's guidance,
   H. teacher Peter Behrens's guidance;
   J. teacher, Peter Behrens's guidance

69. A. NO CHANGE
   B. Studying philosophy
   C. Something
   D. This thing

70. F. NO CHANGE
   G. Even though
   H. Moreover
   J. Because

71. A. NO CHANGE
   B. left
   C. leaves
   D. leaving

GO ON TO THE NEXT PAGE.

[3] He had two commissions waiting for him there—one in Wyoming and <u>another</u> at the Armour Institute of Technology in
₇₂

Chicago. [4] <u>Pupils learning</u> his new method and architectural
₇₃
vocabulary, van der Rohe worked tirelessly as an educator, with only limited success. [5] While many students were initially

<u>enthusiastic,</u> Mies van der Rohe's influence was eventually
₇₄
eclipsed by the rise of Postmodern Architecture in the early

1980s. ☐₇₅

There can be no doubt, though, that van der Rohe has left a huge mark on the look of the North American city. Not only do his buildings help to create the skylines of Chicago, New York, and Toronto, but van der Rohe also gave architects from all over the world a new vocabulary and set of materials with which to create spaces for living and working, and he helped to make architecture one of the great arts of the twentieth century.

72. Which of the following alternatives to the underlined portion would NOT be acceptable?

    F. the other
    G. one
    H. this one
    J. the other one

73. A. NO CHANGE
    B. While pupils learn
    C. To teach pupils
    D. Pupils being taught

74. F. NO CHANGE
    G. enthusiastic and extremely excited,
    H. enthusiastic, overwhelmed with excitement,
    J. enthusiastic, thrilled,

75. For the sake of the logic and coherence of this paragraph, Sentence 3 should be placed:

    A. where it is now.
    B. after Sentence 1.
    C. after Sentence 4.
    D. after Sentence 5.

END OF TEST 1
STOP! DO NOT TURN THE PAGE UNTIL TOLD TO DO SO.

MATHEMATICS TEST
60 Minutes—60 Questions

DIRECTIONS: Solve each problem, choose the correct answer, and then darken the corresponding oval on your answer sheet.

Do not linger over problems that take too much time. Solve as many as you can; then return to the others in the time you have left for this test.

You are permitted to use a calculator on this test. You may use your calculator for any problems you choose, but some of the problems may best be done without using a calculator.

Note: Unless otherwise stated, all of the following should be assumed:

1. Illustrative figures are NOT necessarily drawn to scale.
2. Geometric figures lie in a plane.
3. The word *line* indicates a straight line.
4. The word *average* indicates arithmetic mean.

---

1. Violet is baking a mixed berry pie that contains blueberries, cherries, blackberries, and raspberries. She uses three times as many blackberries as cherries, twice as many blueberries as raspberries, and the same number of blackberries and raspberries. If Violet has 10 cherries, how many of each of the other berries must she use?

	Raspberries	Blueberries	Blackberries
A.	3	2	3
B.	30	2	3
C.	30	2	30
D.	30	60	10
E.	30	60	30

2. The expression $(3x - 5)(x + 2)$ is equivalent to:

F. $3x^2 - 10$
G. $3x^2 + x + 10$
H. $3x^2 + x - 10$
J. $3x^2 + 11x - 10$
K. $3x^2 - 11x - 10$

3. A function f is defined by $f(x,y) = x - (xy - y)$. What is the value of $f(8,6)$?

A. -46
B. -34
C. 46
D. 50
E. 62

4. What is $\frac{1}{7}$ of 28% of 8,000 ?

F. 32
G. 320
H. 1,568
J. 3,200
K. 15,680

DO YOUR FIGURING HERE.

GO ON TO THE NEXT PAGE.

5. If $6x + 3 = 12 + 3x$, then $x = ?$

   A.   6

   B.   5

   C.   3

   D. $\dfrac{5}{3}$

   E.   1

DO YOUR FIGURING HERE.

6. The second term of an arithmetic sequence is –2, and the third term is 8. What is the first term?

(Note: An arithmetic sequence has a common difference between consecutive terms.)

   F.   –12

   G.   –10

   H. $\dfrac{1}{2}$

   J.   3

   K.   10

7. Stacie has a bag of solid colored jellybeans. Each jellybean is orange, purple, or pink. If she randomly selects a jellybean from the bag, the probability that the jellybean is orange is $\dfrac{2}{9}$, and the probability that it is purple is $\dfrac{1}{3}$. If there are 72 jellybeans in the bag, how many pink jellybeans are in the bag?

   A. 16
   B. 24
   C. 32
   D. 40
   E. 48

8. A cellular phone company unveiled a new plan for new customers. It will charge a flat rate of $100 for initial connection and service for the first two months, and $60 for service each subsequent month. If Bob subscribes to this plan for one year, how much does he pay in total for the year?

   F. $600
   G. $700
   H. $720
   J. $800
   K. $820

GO ON TO THE NEXT PAGE.

9. A square and a regular pentagon (a 5-sided polygon with congruent sides and interior angles) have the same perimeter. One side of the pentagon measures 20 inches. How many inches long is one side of the square?

   A.   4
   B.   16
   C.   25
   D.   36
   E.   100

DO YOUR FIGURING HERE.

10. Two contractors bid on a job to build a brick wall in a yard. Contractor A charges a flat fee of $1,600 plus $2 per brick. Contractor B charges a flat fee of $400 plus $8 per brick. If x represents the number of bricks in the wall, which of the following equations could be solved to determine the number of bricks which would make B's charge to build the wall equal to A's charge?

   F. $1600 + 2x = 400 + 8x$
   G. $1600 + 8x = 400 + 2x$
   H. $2x + 8x = x$
   J. $2x + 8x = 1600$
   K. $2x + 8x = 400$

11. Given that $E = ABCD$, which of the following is an expression of B in terms of E, A, C, and D ?

   A. $\dfrac{ACD}{E}$

   B. $E + ACD$

   C. $E - ACD$

   D. $\dfrac{E}{ACD}$

   E. $EACD$

GO ON TO THE NEXT PAGE.

DO YOUR FIGURING HERE.

12. Lines $\overline{XV}$ and $\overline{YV}$ intersect at point V on line $\overline{WZ}$, as shown in the figure below. The measures of 2 angles are given in terms of a, in degrees. What is the measure of $\angle XVZ$ in degrees?

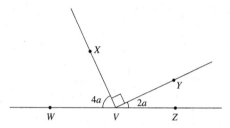

F.   30
G.   90
H.   120
J.   150
K.   180

13. An outdoor thermometer in Hanover, NH reads 70°F. The temperature in Hanover is 25°F cooler than in New Orleans, LA. What is the temperature, C, in degrees Celsius, in New Orleans?

(Note: $F = \dfrac{9}{5}C + 32$)

A.   21°C
B.   35°C
C.   68°C
D.   95°C
E.   113°C

14. If $3x + 2y = 5$, what is the value of the expression $6x + 4y - 7$?

F.   –2
G.   3
H.   8
J.   10
K.   19

GO ON TO THE NEXT PAGE.

15. Mike sold $3\frac{2}{7}$ pounds of beef at his deli on Wednesday and $2\frac{1}{3}$ pounds of beef on Saturday. Which of the following ranges includes the total amount of beef, in pounds, Mike sold during these two days?

   DO YOUR FIGURING HERE.

   A. At least 5 and less than $5\frac{1}{2}$

   B. At least $5\frac{1}{2}$ and less than $5\frac{2}{3}$

   C. At least $5\frac{2}{3}$ and less than 6

   D. At least 6 and less than $6\frac{1}{2}$

   E. At least $6\frac{1}{2}$ and less than $6\frac{2}{3}$

16. Dave leaves his house and bikes directly east for 3 miles. He then turns and bikes directly south for 4 miles. How many miles is Dave from his house?

   F. 3
   G. 4
   H. 5
   J. 6
   K. 7

17. A sensor records a piece of data every .0000000038 seconds. The sensor will record 100,000,000,000 pieces of data in how many seconds?

   A. 3,800
   B. 380
   C. 38
   D. 3.8
   E. 0.0038

18. Alan has a rectangular photograph that is 20 centimeters wide by 30 centimeters long. Alan wants to reduce the area of the photograph by 264 square centimeters by decreasing the width and length by the same amount. What will be the new dimensions (width by length), in centimeters?

   F. 11 by 24
   G. 12 by 22
   H. 12 by 28
   J. 14 by 24
   K. 16 by 21

GO ON TO THE NEXT PAGE.

19. A quadrilateral has a perimeter of 36 inches. If the lengths of the sides are 4 consecutive, even integers, what is the length, in inches, of the shortest side?

    A. 2
    B. 4
    C. 6
    D. 7
    E. 8

DO YOUR FIGURING HERE.

20. In the standard (x,y) coordinate plane, what is the slope of the line with equation $7y - 3x = 21$?

    F. $-\dfrac{3}{7}$

    G. $\dfrac{3}{7}$

    H. $\dfrac{7}{3}$

    J. 3

    K. 7

21. In the figure shown below, points A, B, C, and D are collinear, and distances marked are in feet. Rectangle $ADEG$ has an area of 48 square feet. What is the area, in square feet, of the trapezoid $BCEF$?

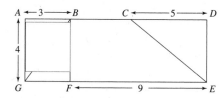

    A. 16
    B. 20
    C. 26
    D. 36
    E. 58

GO ON TO THE NEXT PAGE.

DO YOUR FIGURING HERE.

Use the following information to answer questions 22–24.

Quadrilateral *FGHJ* is shown below in the standard (x,y) coordinate plane. For this quadrilateral, $\overline{FG} = 10$, $\overline{FJ} = 6$, $\overline{HJ} = \sqrt{136}$, and $\overline{GH} = 12$.

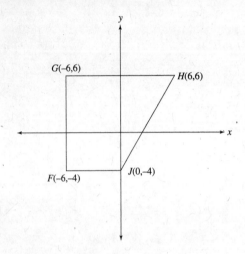

22. Which of the following is closest to the perimeter of quadrilateral *FGHJ*, in coordinate units?

    F.   28.0
    G.   39.7
    H.   60.0
    J.   108.0
    K.   120.0

23. What is the length of $\overline{GJ}$, in coordinate units?

    A.   4
    B.   8
    C.   16
    D. $\sqrt{108}$
    E. $\sqrt{136}$

GO ON TO THE NEXT PAGE.

24. Which of the following are the coordinates of the image of *J* under a 90° clockwise rotation about the origin?

   F. (–4,0)
   G. (0,–4)
   H.   (0,0)
   J.   (0,4)
   K.   (4,0)

DO YOUR FIGURING HERE.

---

25. Which of the following geometric figures has at least 1 rotational symmetry and at least 1 reflectional symmetry?

(Note: The angle of rotation for the rotational symmetry must be less than 360°.)

   A.

   B.

   C.

   D.

   E.

26. What is the coefficient of x^8 in the product of the polynomials below?

$$(-x^4 + 3x^3 - 5x^2 + x - 5)(5x^4 - 2x^3 + x^2 - 5x + 2)$$

   F.   0
   G.   5
   H.   4
   J. –2
   K. –5

GO ON TO THE NEXT PAGE.

DO YOUR FIGURING HERE.

Use the following information to answer questions 27–28.

The stem-and-leaf plot below shows the scores for each golfer in a recent tournament at the Lehigh Valley Golf Club. There were 13 golfers participating in the tournament.

Stem	Leaf
6	6, 7
7	1, 2, 2, 3, 5, 7, 9
8	2, 3, 3, 7

(Note: For example, a score of 72 would have a stem value of 7 and a leaf value of 2.)

27. Which of the following is closest to the mean score of all the golfers in the tournament?

  A. 72.0
  B. 74.4
  C. 75.0
  D. 75.9
  E. 83.0

28. If a score represented in the stem-and-leaf plot is selected randomly, what is the probability that the score selected is exactly 83 ?

  F. $\dfrac{2}{13}$

  G. $\dfrac{4}{13}$

  H. $\dfrac{83}{87}$

  J. $\dfrac{83}{987}$

  K. $\dfrac{166}{987}$

29. What is the least common multiple of 8, 2, 3*a*, 6*b*, and 4*ab* ?

  A. 16*ab*
  B. 24*ab*
  C. 24*a*²*b*
  D. 54*ab*
  E. 60*a*²*b*

GO ON TO THE NEXT PAGE.

DO YOUR FIGURING HERE.

30. Aleksandra began collecting model airplanes in May of 2008. The number of model airplanes that she owns in each month can be modeled by the function $A(m) = 2m + 2$, where $m = 0$ corresponds to May. Using this model, how many model airplanes would you expect Aleksandra to own in December of 2008 ?

F. 2
G. 12
H. 14
J. 16
K. 18

31. In the standard (x,y) coordinate plane, line segment $\overline{CD}$ has end points $C(-3,5)$ and $D(11,-7)$. What is the midpoint of $\overline{CD}$?

A. (14,−12)
B. (8, 2)
C. (7, 1)
D. (7, −6)
E. (4, −1)

32. Given $x \neq \pm 4$, which of the following is equivalent to the expression $\dfrac{x^2 - 8x + 16}{x^2 - 16}$?

F. $\dfrac{1}{2}x - 1$

G. $-8x$

H. $\dfrac{x-2}{2}$

J. $\dfrac{1}{x+4}$

K. $\dfrac{x-4}{x+4}$

33. Evan purchased 6 boxes of sugar cookies, each box containing 10 snack bags and each bag containing 12 cookies. Evan could have purchased the same amount of cookies by buying how many family-sized packs of 30 cookies each?

A. 12
B. 24
C. 48
D. 72
E. 180

GO ON TO THE NEXT PAGE.

34. When $\dfrac{r}{s} = -\dfrac{1}{2}$, $16r^4 - s^4 = ?$

F.   0
G.   16
H.   32
J.   −16
K.   −32

35. Emilia is going to bake cookies. She rolls out a square of dough that is 12 inches wide by 12 inches long and cuts 9 identical circular cookies from the dough, as shown in the figure below. Each circular cut-out is tangent to the circular cut-outs next to it and tangent to the edge or edges of the square piece of dough it touches. Approximately, what is the area, in square inches, of the remaining dough, as shown in the figure?

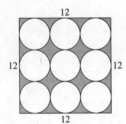

A.   30.9
B.   42.3
C.   50.24
D.   87.5
E.   113.04

36. Which of the following lists contains only prime numbers?

F.   63, 73, and 97
G.   71, 87, and 91
H.   73, 89, and 91
J.   79, 89, and 97
K.   81, 87, and 97

GO ON TO THE NEXT PAGE.

37. The costs of tutoring packages of different lengths, given in quarter hours, are shown in the table below.

DO YOUR FIGURING HERE.

Number of quarter hours	8	10	12	20
Cost	$200	$230	$260	$380

Each cost consists of a fixed charge and a charge per quarter hour. What is the fixed charge?

A. $15
B. $23
C. $80
D. $120
E. $380

38. At 3 p.m., the afternoon sun shines over a building and its rays hit the ground at a 34° angle. The building is 100 meters tall and is perpendicular to the ground. How long, to the nearest meter, is the building's shadow that is cast by the sun?

(Note: sin 34° ≈ 0.56, cos 34° ≈ 0.83, tan 34° ≈ 0.67)

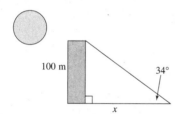

F. 56
G. 67
H. 83
J. 120
K. 148

39. In the standard (x,y) coordinate system, circle O has its center at $(4,-3)$ and a radius of 12 units. Which of the following is an equation of the circle?

A. $(x - 4)^2 + (y + 3)^2 = 12$
B. $(x + 4)^2 + (y + 3)^2 = 12$
C. $(x + 4)^2 - (y + 3)^2 = 12$
D. $(x - 4)^2 + (y - 3)^2 = 144$
E. $(x - 4)^2 + (y + 3)^2 = 144$

GO ON TO THE NEXT PAGE.

40. What is the least integer value of x that makes the inequality $\dfrac{14}{21} < \dfrac{x}{12}$ true?

   F.   7
   G. 8
   H. 9
   J.   10
   K. 11

DO YOUR FIGURING HERE.

41. When $f(a) = a^2 + 2a + 5$, what is the value of $f(a + b)$?

   A. $a^2 + b^2 + 2ab + 5$
   B. $a^2 + b^2 + 2a + 2b + 10$
   C. $a^2 + b^2 + 2a + 2b + 5$
   D. $(a + b)^2 + a + b + 5$
   E. $(a + b)^2 + 2a + 2b + 5$

42. In the figure below, M is on $\overline{LN}$ and O is on $\overline{NP}$. $\overline{LP}$ and $\overline{MO}$ are parallel. The dimensions given are in feet. What is the length, in feet, of $\overline{NO}$?

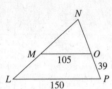

   F.   39
   G.   91
   H. 105
   J.   273
   K. 294

43. Gina watched as a plane took off from the runway and climbed to 30,000 feet. She calculated the plane's height, h feet, t seconds after takeoff to be given by $h = 1{,}200 + 32t$. To the nearest second, how many seconds did it take the plane to climb to a height of 2 miles? (Note: 1 mile = 5,280 feet)

   A.   37
   B.   128
   C.   293
   D.   900
   E. 1,264

GO ON TO THE NEXT PAGE.

44. In $\triangle ABC$, the measures of $\angle A$, $\angle B$, and $\angle C$ are $2x°$, $3x°$, and $5x°$, respectively. What is the measure of $\angle C$?

    F.   18°
    G.   36°
    H.   54°
    J.   90°
    K. 180°

45. A basketball player has attempted 30 free throws and made 12 of them. Starting now, if he makes every free throw attempted, what is the *least* number of additional free throws he must attempt to raise his free-throw percentage to at least 55% ?

(Note: Free-throw percentage =

$$\frac{number\ of\ free\ throws\ made}{number\ of\ free\ throws\ attempted} \times 100.)$$

    A.   5
    B. 10
    C. 16
    D. 17
    E. 29

46. If y is a negative integer, which of the following has the least value?

    F. $\sqrt[3]{y^2}$

    G. 100^y

    H. $\dfrac{\pi}{y}$

    J. $\dfrac{1}{y^2}$

    K. $\dfrac{1}{y^3}$

47. Jonathan, Ellery, and 3 other groomsmen are rehearsing for a wedding by walking down an aisle one at a time, one groomsman in front of the other. Each time all 5 walk down the aisle, the groom tells them to walk in a different order from first to last. What is the greatest number of times the groomsmen can walk down the aisle without walking in the same order twice?

    A. 3,125
    B.   720
    C.   120
    D.   100
    E.   25

DO YOUR FIGURING HERE.

GO ON TO THE NEXT PAGE.

48. In the circle below, O is the center and measures 5 inches from chord $\overline{MN}$. The area of the circle is 169π square inches. What is the length of $\overline{MN}$, in inches?

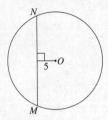

- **F.** 12
- **G.** 13
- **H.** 18
- **J.** 24
- **K.** 26

49. What is the x-intercept of the line that passes through points $(-3,7)$ and $(6,4)$ in the standard (x,y) coordinate plane?

- **A.** $(18,0)$
- **B.** $(0,\frac{1}{3})$
- **C.** $(0,6)$
- **D.** $(0,18)$
- **E.** $(\frac{1}{3},0)$

50. Which of the following equations represent a graph that intersects the x-axis at $x = 7$?

- **F.** $y = (x + 7)^2$
- **G.** $y = (x - 7)^2$
- **H.** $y = (-x - 7)^2$
- **J.** $y - 7 = x^2$
- **K.** $y + 7 = x^2$

GO ON TO THE NEXT PAGE.

51. If $0° < \theta < 90°$ and $\tan \theta = \dfrac{2}{9}$, what is $\sin \theta + \cos \theta$?

DO YOUR FIGURING HERE.

A. $\dfrac{11}{\sqrt{85}}$

B. $\dfrac{-7}{\sqrt{170}}$

C. $\dfrac{11}{\sqrt{170}}$

D. $\dfrac{9}{\sqrt{85}}$

E. $\dfrac{2}{\sqrt{85}}$

52. In the figure below, $\overline{OA} = \overline{AB}$, and $\overline{OB}$ is a radius of the circle, having a length of 8 inches. What is the area of $\triangle OAB$, in square inches?

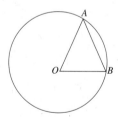

F. $8\sqrt{3}$

G. $16\sqrt{3}$

H. 32

J. $32\sqrt{3}$

K. 64

GO ON TO THE NEXT PAGE.

53. In $\triangle XYZ$, shown below, $\overline{YZ} = 30$. Which of the following represents the length of $\overline{XY}$?

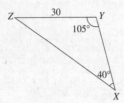

DO YOUR FIGURING HERE.

(Note: For a triangle with sides of lengths x, y, and z, and respective opposite angles measuring X, Y, and Z, it will be true that: $\dfrac{\sin X}{x} = \dfrac{\sin Y}{y} = \dfrac{\sin Z}{z}$, according to the law of sines.)

A. $\dfrac{30\sin 105°}{\sin 35°}$

B. $\dfrac{30\sin 105°}{\sin 40°}$

C. $\dfrac{30\sin 35°}{\sin 40°}$

D. $\dfrac{30\sin 40°}{\sin 105°}$

E. $\dfrac{30\sin 35°}{\sin 105°}$

54. Points P and Q lie on circle O with radius of 9 feet. The measure of $\angle POQ$ is 120°. What is the length, in feet, of minor arc $\overset{\frown}{PQ}$?

F. 3π
G. 6π
H. 9π
J. 18π
K. 27π

GO ON TO THE NEXT PAGE.

DO YOUR FIGURING HERE.

55. $\begin{bmatrix} w & x \\ y & z \end{bmatrix} - \begin{bmatrix} x & y \\ z & w \end{bmatrix} - \begin{vmatrix} \dfrac{1}{w+x} & \dfrac{1}{x+y} \\ \dfrac{1}{y+z} & \dfrac{1}{z+w} \end{vmatrix} = ?$

A. $\begin{vmatrix} 1 & 1 \\ 1 & 1 \end{vmatrix}$

B. $\begin{vmatrix} \dfrac{w-x}{w+x} & \dfrac{x-y}{x+y} \\ \dfrac{y-z}{y+z} & \dfrac{d-a}{d+a} \end{vmatrix}$

C. $\begin{bmatrix} w-x-\dfrac{1}{w+x} & x-y-\dfrac{1}{x+y} \\ y-z-\dfrac{1}{y+z} & z-w-\dfrac{1}{z+w} \end{bmatrix}$

D. $\begin{bmatrix} \dfrac{wx}{w+x} & \dfrac{xy}{x+y} \\ \dfrac{yz}{y+z} & \dfrac{zw}{z+w} \end{bmatrix}$

E. $\begin{bmatrix} \dfrac{1}{2w-2x} & \dfrac{1}{2x-2y} \\ \dfrac{1}{2y-2z} & \dfrac{1}{2z-2w} \end{bmatrix}$

56. If function f is defined by $f(x) = -2x^3$, then what is the value of $f(f(1))$?

F. -16
G. -8
H. 4
J. 8
K. 16

GO ON TO THE NEXT PAGE.

57. The function y varies directly as x for all real numbers in the (x,y) coordinate plane. Which of the following could be the graph of y ?

DO YOUR FIGURING HERE.

A.

D.

B.

E.

C.

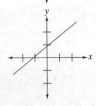

58. Gopi took 5 quizzes for which the scores are integer values ranging from 0 to 10. The median of her scores is 9. The mean of her scores is 8. The only mode of her scores is 10. Which of the following *must* be true about her quiz scores?

F. Her lowest score is 4.
G. Her lowest score is 5.
H. The median of the 3 lowest scores is 6.
J. The sum of the 5 scores is 50.
K. The sum of the 2 lowest scores is 11.

59. To make a cardboard table for her dollhouse, Ouisie uses a rectangular piece of cardboard measuring 40 inches wide and 60 inches long. She cuts out four equal-sized squares from each corner and folds down the sides at a 90° angle. If the top of the table measures 800 square inches, how tall, in inches, is the table?

A. 40
B. 30
C. 25
D. 20
E. 10

GO ON TO THE NEXT PAGE.

60. Which of the following expressions gives the area, in square feet, of $\triangle ABC$, shown below with the given side lengths in feet?

DO YOUR FIGURING HERE.

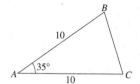

- **F.** 50 tan 35°
- **G.** 50 cos 35°
- **H.** 50 sin 35°
- **J.** 100 cos 35°
- **K.** 100 sin 35°

READING TEST
35 Minutes—40 Questions

DIRECTIONS: There are four passages in this test. Each passage is followed by several questions. After reading each passage, choose the best answer to each question and blacken the corresponding oval on your answer document. You may refer to the passages as often as necessary.

Passage I

PROSE FICTION: This passage is adapted from the novel *Shipwreck* by Adam C. Thomas (© 2005 by Adam Thomas).

"Let the dead bury their dead."

The words rang in the boy's ears as he trudged through the inhospitable jungle, vines snarling around his ankles. Over and over again, he heard the captain shout, "Full speed ahead,
5   let the dead bury their dead."

Now the captain was gone and the boy felt alone despite his companions, now leading him through the alien jungle. He wondered what the words meant. How can the dead do anything? How can the dead have dead of their own?

10   These thoughts circled the boy's head, intermingled with the events of the last days. Again he heard the roar of the storm, felt the ship bucking and braying beneath his feet. The typhoon had come out of nowhere, it had seemed; even the captain, who surely knew everything, was taken aback by
15   its sudden appearance.

"Avast and hold the mainsail!" he shouted to the crew. "Stay fast and let the dead bury their dead!"

The boy had held fast, even as the ship had come apart. Even as the lightning lit up the sky like the fireworks the boy
20   had heard about, but never seen. Even as the thunder filled the air, shaking the very timbers of the ship with its bellowing ferocity. The walls of water rose up, crashing over the deck, then receded for an instant of calm before rising up as a dark mountain to once again besiege the small ship.

25   These memories would come to the boy in a split-second, filling his brain before he had a chance to consciously remember what had happened. Then they would recede, just as the storm had eventually receded, and the jungle would return, the monotonous trudging, day after day amid the vines and
30   trees that were nothing like his second home on the ocean.

Sometimes, the boy would think back to before the storm, and even before the ship, to his life on land—the stultifying life on the farm where he felt landlocked before he even understood what that word signified. He thought of his mother

35   and father, frail and worn-looking. He believed his parents did all they could to create a home for him, but his mother's sad, creased face and his father's cracked hands crowded out all other childhood memories. They filled the boy's sky, just as the thunder had, and were just as devastating, in their own
40   way, as the storm.

For the boy, his birthplace's rocky ground yielded only a life he could not live and a place he could not love. But the sea was softer, a malleable place in which an enterprising lad could reinvent himself. So the boy had run off to sea. He
45   vowed to leave the land forever to live atop the ocean. Now he had learned the hardness of the sea, he thought, as he jerked his mind back to the jungle.

Soon, his thoughts drifted back to his blissful days upon the ship. Although he had come aboard as a stowaway, the
50   captain took him in and gave him daily lessons in reading the stars and plotting the ship's course. "Ignorance is dangerous, not only aboard ship but also in life," the captain warned. The eager boy soon grew familiar with the night's sky and knew the maps in the captain's quarters as well as he knew his own
55   reflection. He had felt so secure in the captain's knowledge and in his own growing understanding.

But if the captain could be caught unawares, how could the boy ever feel safe again? How could he trust that everything the captain had said wouldn't lead to the same disastrous end?

60   "Let the dead bury their dead." Well, he had seen the dead after the storm. As the remaining crew members had urged him away from the wreckage, finally having to pull him by his arms to force his legs to move, the words "Let the dead bury their dead" appeared unbidden in his mind. But what
65   did those words mean? Searching his memory, the boy was shocked to find that after the shipwreck, his mind's eye could no longer distinguish the captain from any other man—the cook, the lowest deckhand, or even the boy's father. Was that what the captain meant by "their dead"—that all the dead
70   belonged to one another?

He walked mechanically, pace after pace, leading him away from the remains of his home and the only man he had ever loved. Toward what? He had no knowledge of what lay ahead. But still his legs moved, seemingly of their own

GO ON TO THE NEXT PAGE.

75 accord, his heart continued to beat, his lungs continued
to fill with air. His mind continued to retrace his life, and
with the beating of his heart and the filling of his lungs,
still he walked.

1. As it is used in line 32, the word *stultifying* most nearly
means:

  A. stifling.
  B. strengthening.
  C. welcoming.
  D. productive.

2. The first seven paragraphs (lines 1–30) establish all of the
following about the boy EXCEPT that he:

  F. had companions on the walk through the jungle.
  G. had often watched fireworks light up the sky.
  H. respected the captain.
  J. often had his thoughts filled with memories of the
storm.

3. The passage states that the boy saw himself as:

  A. contented with life in the jungle.
  B. afraid of his mother.
  C. toughened by farm labor.
  D. at home on the sea.

4. The time sequence of the passage indicates that the shipwreck takes place:

  F. after the boy leaves the farm.
  G. after the boy walks through the jungle.
  H. before the boy meets the captain.
  J. before his mother tries to protect him.

5. How does the twelfth paragraph (lines 60–70) offer one
way to interpret the phrase "let the dead bury their dead,"
as implied by the passage?

  A. The boy remembers the captain's explanation of this
phrase.
  B. The dead cannot do anything, so one should trust only
the living.
  C. Death erases the distinctions that make the living
unique individuals.
  D. Without his experiences, the boy cannot expect to lead
a better life.

6. Compared to the captain's ideas, the boy's are:

  F. opposing; the captain is uncertain about the meaning
of the phrase, "let the dead bury their dead."
  G. opposing; the captain understood why the boy's father
was worn down.
  H. similar; the captain disliked the harsh life of the sea.
  J. similar; the captain valued learning and knowledge.

7. It is most reasonable to infer from the passage that the
ship's remaining crewmates accompanying the boy on his
walk through the jungle would agree with which of the
following statements about the boy?

  A. The boy's grief over the captain's death made him
unwilling to leave the scene of the shipwreck.
  B. The boy's grief over the captain's death made him run
away from his companions.
  C. The boy was constantly startled by loud noises.
  D. The boy hated his life on land and had escaped to the
sea to find freedom.

8. Which of the following statements best describes the
actions taken by the captain on finding the boy stowed
away on the ship?

  F. He scolds the boy because he did not pay the fare for
passage on the ship.
  G. He teaches the boy the meaning of the phrase "let the
dead bury their dead."
  H. He teaches the boy how to navigate using maps and
the stars.
  J. He ignores the boy, leaving him to fend for himself.

9. According to the passage, the storm features all of the
following EXCEPT:

  A. loud thunder.
  B. huge walls of water.
  C. bright lightning.
  D. ferocious hail.

10. Which of the following statements about the storm is supported by the passage?

  F. It blew up without warning, taking the captain by
surprise.
  G. It happened in the middle of the night.
  H. It was the most violent storm any of the crew had ever
seen.
  J. It was the storm the boy's father had warned him about.

GO ON TO THE NEXT PAGE.

Passage II

SOCIAL SCIENCE: This passage is adapted from the article "Slang: Why It's Totally Sweet" by Patrick Tyrrell (© 2008 by Patrick Tyrrell).

Tony Thorne's email inbox is bloated with messages from teenagers and college students around the world explicating the meaning behind local terms such as "toop," "tonk," and "chung." Why would the Director of the Language Center at
5 King's College of London concern himself with seemingly nonsensical linguistic inventions?

Thorne is busy compiling a current dictionary of slang from around the English-speaking world. Although *neologisms*, new adaptations or inventions of words, are normally
10 born out of a specific geographic and cultural context, the ease of worldwide communication ushered in by the technological age has made slang an instantly exportable commodity. College students in Iowa are just as likely to use British slang like "bum" (one's posterior) as British homemakers are to employ
15 American slang like "dust bunny," since both groups are exposed to each other's movies, TV, music, and other media.

In the world of linguistics, slang is often viewed condescendingly as an affliction of vulgar speech, its users condemned for their intellectual laziness. Early 20th century
20 linguist Oliver Wendell Holmes described slang as "at once a sign and a cause of mental atrophy." Meanwhile, Thorne points out, some legendary authors such as Walt Whitman elevated the status of slang, referring to it as "an attempt by common humanity to escape from bald literalism, and express
25 itself illimitably."

What are the origins of most slang words? Many philologists, those who attempt to study and determine the meaning of historical texts, believe that slang is created as a response to the status quo, that its usage represents a defiant opposition
30 of authority. For example, many Americans use the phrase *a cup of joe* to refer to a cup of coffee; however, few know that it originated from one Admiral Joe Daniels who in 1914 denied his sailors wine. As a result, they decided their strict leader was a fitting namesake for the terribly acidic black
35 coffee they were forced to drink instead.

Thorne, however, would point out that most slang is derived for much more innocent purposes. For example, terms like "ankle-biters" (infants), "ramping up" (on the job training), and "Googling" (searching on the internet) do not involve
40 opposition to authority. Usually, slang evolves out of very insular groups with specific needs for informative or vibrant expressions that normal language does not encapsulate. It is the marriage of jargon, nuance, and effective imagery. While traditional hotbeds of slang have been the military, industrial
45 factories, and street markets, most modern slang comes from such arenas as corporate offices, college campuses, and users/designers of computers.

In determining the sources of slang terms, Thorne and his contemporaries repeatedly refine their definition of "slang"
50 as distinctive from "idioms," "euphemisms," "hyperbole," and other instances of conventional figurative language. Many linguists consider slang the polar opposite of formal speech, with other figurative language devices falling somewhere in between. Whereas a "colloquialism" still indicates a mea-
55 sure of respect owed to the expression's regional usefulness, "slang" brands a word as having fallen into a state of overused emptiness.

How do we know when a word has become overused or empty? Much slang is attached to some sense of style or fad
60 and therefore risks being as short-lived in nature as the trend upon which it is based. However, some terms such as "punk" and "cool" have been in common use for a century or more and have completely assimilated into the acceptable mainstream dialect. Clearly, then, some words fall into a gray area
65 between slang and proper language. Although lexicologists like Thorne attempt to define and apply standard principles in their classification of slang, there is definitely some subjectivity involved in determining whether a term deserves the maligning moniker.

70 Furthermore, intellectuals who would categorically denounce slang struggle with the fact that slang, when first conceived, involves as much inherent creativity and word play as the figurative language revered in poetry. It is ultimately how the word survives, or rather who continues to use it, that
75 determines its stature as artful rhetoric or the dreaded slang. If "respectable" people continue to use an expression for its conceptual vivacity, then the word was a clever invention worth enriching a nation's lexicon. If the "common man" uses a term and uses it too liberally, the word is deemed slang,
80 and an eloquent speaker will have the tastefulness to avoid it.

Whatever slang's level of social esteem, Thorne believes that it is an essential project to compile accurate modern dictionaries of its usage. When one considers the large amount of written artifacts our present world creates on a daily basis,
85 it is reasonable to also consider providing future generations (or civilizations) of humans with an effective way of decoding our meaning, which could easily be confused by our prevalent use of slang. Imagine how much less debate there would be over the meaning of some Shakespearean verses if we had a
90 detailed description of his contemporary slang. Because of this need to inform future scholars, Thorne's dictionary of slang attempts to not only define each term but also to explain its origins, connotations, and typical conversational uses.

GO ON TO THE NEXT PAGE.

11. Based on the passage, Thorne most likely describes some slang as *innocent* (line 37) to indicate his belief that not all slang is created to be:

    A. rebellious.
    B. informative.
    C. nuanced.
    D. accusatory.

12. The author includes the information in the last paragraph primarily to:

    F. criticize Thorne for being too subjective with which words he chooses to include in his dictionary.
    G. illustrate how a future scholar might be able to use Thorne's dictionary as a resource.
    H. identify the ways Thorne uses Shakespearean slang to describe modern terms.
    J. argue that Thorne's dictionary should be the primary focus of modern linguistics.

13. All of the following groups are mentioned in the passage as related to the academic study of slang EXCEPT:

    A. philologists.
    B. college professors.
    C. linguists.
    D. lexicologists.

14. The quotation marks around the phrase "common man" in line 78 primarily serve to:

    F. emphasize the subjective and somewhat derogatory process of categorizing people and the words they use.
    G. reveal the author's suspicion that the man in question is not common at all.
    H. introduce a demeaning term the author believes is appropriate to describe users of slang.
    J. show how an inventive term may enjoy popularity briefly but ultimately does not have the proper usage to survive.

15. As it is used in line 18, the word *vulgar* most nearly means:

    A. sickening.
    B. malicious.
    C. unsophisticated.
    D. profane.

16. The passage indicates that the efforts to compile current dictionaries of slang are viewed by some as essential because these dictionaries:

    F. could possibly provide future scholars with a way of deciphering the meaning of today's writings.
    G. are the only way that speakers of other languages can decode the subtle meaning of English texts.
    H. currently do not exist except for those chronicling Shakepeare's era.
    J. will provide modern English speakers with the correct conversational uses of each slang term.

17. According to the passage, Walt Whitman seems to view the use of slang as an attempt to:

    A. show civility.
    B. conform to traditions.
    C. broaden expression.
    D. defy authority.

18. The main purpose of the first paragraph in relation to the passage is to:

    F. acquaint the reader with some examples of slang.
    G. establish that British scholars are the leaders in slang research.
    H. introduce slang as a possibly surprising topic of academic study.
    J. outline Tony Thorne's problems with managing his email inbox.

19. The author's reference to groups like the military as being *hotbeds* of slang (line 44) most nearly means that such groups are:

    A. prophetic.
    B. old-fashioned.
    C. innovative.
    D. strict.

20. The passage suggests that of the following, which one encapsulates the greatest obstacle for intellectuals who would categorically denounce slang?

    F. Their own invention of some slang terms
    G. Disagreement on how certain slang terms are used
    H. Respect for Thorne's academic interest and tireless determination.
    J. Appreciation for the creativity involved in the origination of slang

GO ON TO THE NEXT PAGE.

Passage III

HUMANITIES: This passage is excerpted from the entry "Antonio Gaudi" in *Great Spanish Architects* (© 2006 by Teshigahara Press).

Most of the world's great cathedrals are impressive in their size and beauty, but the Sagrada Familia stands apart even from these architectural masterpieces because of its unique and startling design. This stunning cathedral tow-
5 ers above Barcelona like a strange, ornate sandcastle. With bright carvings of fruit baskets, a central nave that mirrors a forest of trees, bizarre spires, and beautiful spiral staircases, the iconic Sagrada Familia has become as well-known as the Eiffel Tower or Statue of Liberty. Moreover, the Sagrada
10 Familia captures the "freakish genius" of its designer Antoni Gaudi better than any of his other creations.

Today, crowds flock to Barcelona to witness Gaudi's great works, including Casa Mila, Casa Battlo, Palau Güell, Park Güell, and, of course, the Sagrada Familia. However,
15 the current popularity of Gaudi's work would not have been foreseen when he first unveiled his creations. Critics of his time described his work as hideous and compared his buildings to monsters or dungeons; as recently as 50 years ago, the so-called genius of Gaudi was not well-recognized.

20 Antoni Gaudi I Cornet was born in 1852 to a family of artisans in a small town in northern Spain. When he was 16, he moved to Barcelona to finish his secondary education and study architecture. Even at this early age, he engendered controversy: often truant from class, he criticized the standard
25 architectural education of the day and complained that his classes were devoid of creativity. Ultimately, he was granted a degree, but just barely. His school director insightfully commented that Gaudi was either "a genius or a madman."

After graduation, Gaudi remained in Barcelona. The city
30 was growing, and rich benefactors were looking for artists to design modern, trendy buildings. In his mid-twenties, Gaudi met his lifelong patron Eusebi Guell, a wealthy industrialist and politician. For almost four decades, Güell would fund Gaudi's work for a wide array of venues, from Güell's private
35 mansion (the Palau Güell) to a massive public park (Park Güell) to the Guells' own crypt.

Nature was Gaudi's muse; many artists find inspiration in nature as he did, but few actually carved shapes found in nature such as trees, fruit baskets, lizards, and bones into
40 the physical architecture of his buildings. For example, the Sagrada Familia has huge carvings of fruit baskets amid its spires. Gaudi said that nature was "the Great Book, always open, that we should force ourselves to read." For Gaudi, nature was inspiration for the forms and motifs of his buildings
45 and for the colors he used liberally. In order to represent the limitless diversity of colors found in nature, he even forged a new architectural practice known as *trencadis*, in which tiles, bottles, and pottery were smashed into small tiles to create abstract mosaics.

50 In 1883, Gaudi began work on his masterpiece, the Sagrada Familia. However, when the initial and substantial financial contributions for the church's construction fizzled out completely around the turn of the century, Gaudi had to sell his own home and even beg on street corners to raise funds.
55 As his health declined in later years, Gaudi moved into the Sagrada Familia to be closer to "his temple" and remained there for the rest of his life. At the time of his death, forty-three years after construction began, the church was only 15 percent complete.

60 Conflicting artistic vision and pesky finances have been the source of much grief for those who have hoped to finish Gaudi's vision for the Sagrada Familia. After his death, politicians and architects clashed over whether other architects would be able to do his design justice. Eventually, the major
65 players agreed that the blueprints and plans Gaudi left behind would be sufficient to achieve his vision; unfortunately, bombing during the Spanish Civil War destroyed Gaudi's crypt, workroom, and all the remaining designs. Construction on the church slowly resumed in the mid-1950s, in part due to
70 a lot more funding than in the past, but little progress was made until the 1980s, when steady donations began funding significant progress. However, the church will still take at least another three decades to realize Gaudi's complete design. It is likely, moreover, that there will always be grumblings that
75 modern architects ruined the purity of Gaudi's design.

In recent decades, the art world has experienced a renewed appreciation of the style known as Art Nuevo. As the most famous of all Art Nuevo architects, Gaudi has been showered with acclaim. In fact, Barcelona declared 2002 the Year of
80 Gaudi and held over 30 exhibitions and events in his honor. Buildings that had previously been closed to the public were opened for the first time, and over 90,000 people gathered in front of the Sagrada Familia to celebrate the 150th anniversary of Gaudi's birth.

85 Gaudi would most likely approve of such recognition. He never doubted his creative genius, did not allow his assistants to question him, and persevered with his fanciful designs despite harsh reviews by critics of his day. Current critics, however, see the gift of Gaudi as clearly as he did at the
90 time. After decades of functional designs in the architectural world, Gaudi's architecture-as-art is once more popular. As modern architect Norman Foster asserts, "Gaudi's methods, one century on, continue to be revolutionary." His genius is and will continue to be undisputed.

GO ON TO THE NEXT PAGE.

21. It can be most reasonably inferred from the passage that the author views the description of Gaudi as a "freakish genius" in line 10 as:

A. an overstatement of Gaudi's skill and contributions to modern architecture.

B. an inadequate explanation of a complex man and his controversial contributions to architecture.

C. a reasonable suggestion for how first-time viewers should explore Gaudi's work.

D. an accurate representation of the view of Gaudi's skill and artistic vision many current critics hold.

22. Based on information in the passage, when were donors LEAST likely to fund construction of the Sagrada Familia?

F. 1880s
G. 1900s
H. 1950s
J. 1980s

23. The passage's author indicates that compared to the world's other great cathedrals, the Sagrada Familia is:

A. more remarkable in terms of appearance and design.

B. less remarkable in terms of size and beauty.

C. more likely to be a part of the ongoing debate about how to construct a building after the original designer has died.

D. less likely to influence future architectural designs by new artists in Europe.

24. The main purpose of the third paragraph (lines 20–28) is to make clear that from a young age, and throughout his childhood, Gaudi:

F. was a controversial figure who caused a stir within traditional artist circles.

G. came from a family of artists and therefore was a natural artist, destined for great success.

H. was a mediocre and uninspired student who disliked learning about architecture, despite the later success he achieved.

J. was just one of many students who found the education of his day boring, unsatisfying, and unrelated to real artistic skill.

25. The word *array*, as it is used in line 34, could reasonably mean any of the following EXCEPT:

A. arrangement.
B. range.
C. selection.
D. variety.

26. As used in line 74, the word *grumblings* most nearly means:

F. churnings.
G. criticisms.
H. theories.
J. growling.

27. The passage suggests that in the late 19th century, compared to Gaudi, other contemporary artists were:

A. more reserved when trying new artistic forms and techniques.

B. less inhibited when trying new artistic forms and techniques.

C. more focused on perfecting architectural techniques.

D. less focused on perfecting architectural techniques.

28. According to the passage, one reason that politicians and architects agreed to continue construction of the Sagrada Familia after Gaudi's death was:

F. the survival of Gaudi's original designs to effectively guide ongoing work.

G. they witnessed the stunning design of the cathedral in person.

H. they wished to complete as much as possible before the impending Civil War.

J. the popularity of Gaudi's design inspired the public to demand its construction.

29. It can most reasonably be inferred from the passage that throughout his lifetime, from his schoolboy days to his years as a well-established artist, Gaudi:

A. successfully overcame harsh and damaging criticisms of his work to complete his lifetime dreams.

B. created both excitement and controversy over his non-traditional designs and techniques.

C. blurred the distinction between art and nature, using natural plants and animals as motifs.

D. adjusted a building's design to conform to its location, his patron's vision, and the environmental conditions.

30. It can most reasonably be inferred from the discussion of architecture-as-art's renewed popularity that in previous generations, some architects:

F. were never open to creative and unconventional designs.

G. preferred classic designs inspired by historical architecture.

H. created practical designs that were not necessarily aesthetically pleasing.

J. do not have one single design that they preferred and identified with.

GO ON TO THE NEXT PAGE.

Passage IV

NATURAL SCIENCE: This passage is excerpted from the article "Frank Drake and Project Ozma" by Arnold C. Topton (© 2004 by Crackpot Press).

On a cool April night in 1960, in Green Bank, West Virginia, Frank Drake became a scientific pioneer. Careful research had given him reason to believe that, if he tuned his radio to the correct frequency and aimed it at the correct
5 stars, he might pick up interstellar transmissions from another planet. Hoping for a breakthrough, he tuned the radio and began to listen.

So began Project Ozma, widely considered the first organized attempt to detect alien life by way of radio. Al-
10 though it was ultimately unsuccessful in its goal of finding other intelligent life in the universe, Project Ozma was hugely influential, inspiring the creation of many similar programs. The following fifty years would see a steady increase in both the sophistication and the scope of similar programs, ranging
15 from a wide-ranging but short-term program funded by NASA to the meticulously orchestrated Project Phoenix, designed to monitor carefully selected regions of space over a period of ten years. Today, many such programs are ongoing, in locations as august as the University of California at Berkeley and the
20 University of Western Sydney, both of which have reputations that draw respected scientists from around the world.

The scientists involved in the Search for Extraterrestrial Intelligence, or SETI, are far from the wide-eyed dreamers that many people associate with the field. The SETI scientists
25 are, in fact, esteemed academics, typically specializing in the areas of physics, astronomy, and engineering. Indeed, they have to be able to complete such complex tasks as calculating where to position the radios so as to achieve the best effect, deciding what messages are most likely to be understood
30 by an alien culture, and determining which stars to monitor.

Although these scientists' understanding of the origins of life on Earth is still imperfect, those involved in SETI do have some idea of what combinations of size, location, and chemical composition make a planet more likely to harbor
35 intelligent life. The general understanding is that there are two main factors that determine whether or not a planet is habitable (able to sustain life): temperature and mass. There are other factors that are often considered, such as the presence of certain chemicals, the proximity of other planets, and
40 planetary age, but temperature and mass are the initial, and most crucial, tests.

Liquid water is widely believed to be critical to the development of life, and this belief has led scientists to hypothesize that, in order to support life, a planet must experience tem-
45 peratures that fall within a range that allows for the presence of liquid water. This, in turn, suggests that hospitable planets must be located within a certain distance of their respective suns. If a planet is too far from the sun, its temperatures will fall below that range, as in the case of Saturn. If a planet is
50 too close to the sun, as in the case of Venus, its temperatures will be too high. Planets that fall within the range of appropriate temperatures are often called "Goldilocks Planets," since they are neither too hot nor too cold but instead "just right" to provide environments hospitable to life. However, even
55 when a planet is found that is within this range, there is still no guarantee that all of the related factors will be suitable. It is also necessary that the planet have an orbit that allows the planet to rotate at a speed and angle that prevents either side from freezing or boiling, ruling out most binary systems due
60 to their unstable orbits.

The other key to habitability is the mass of a planet. In order to sustain life, a planet must have sufficient mass to hold a gravitational field, while not having so much as to create an excessively heavy atmosphere. Truly massive planets also
65 tend to retain hydrogen gases and become "gas giants" with no solid surface. How large a planet can be, while retaining the ability to host living organisms, depends in part on that planet's distance from the sun. Larger planets have heavier atmospheres, so they also tend to retain more heat, creat-
70 ing a greenhouse effect, wherein atmospheric gases absorb radiation, causing an increase in temperature. Therefore, a planet on the outer edge of the Goldilocks zone might be able to sustain life if its mass were great enough to hold in enough heat to bring the temperature back into the habitable
75 zone, while a smaller planet might be able to do the same on the inner edge.

The search for extraterrestrial life, and perhaps intelligence, that started in West Virginia back in 1960 continues today. The more knowledge scientists are able to gather
80 about our own galaxy, the better equipped they will be when it comes to seeking out similar planets outside our solar system. Perhaps someday Frank Drake's dream of a message from outer space will come true—once we know where to look for it.

31. According to the passage, Frank Drake:

   A. was one of the first scientists to use radio technology to look for alien life.
   B. successfully found signs of extraterrestrial life.
   C. ran Project Phoenix from his radio telescope in West Virginia.
   D. is a highly esteemed astronomer and physicist.

GO ON TO THE NEXT PAGE.

32. Which of the following would be the most appropriate characterization of Project Ozma, as portrayed by the author of the passage?

   F. Its unexpected success took the scientific community by surprise, altering the face of the field.
   G. Although it was a failure in one sense, it helped usher in a new era of interstellar research.
   H. Drake's goals were unrealistic, given his limited knowledge and resources.
   J. Without the financial support of institutions such as NASA, the Project was doomed to failure.

33. As it is used in line 19, the word *august* most nearly means:

   A. summery.
   B. elusive.
   C. esteemed.
   D. antique.

34. As conveyed in the passage, the author's attitude toward the search for life on other planets is:

   F. ironic yet sympathetic.
   G. scornful and angry.
   H. hopeful yet pragmatic.
   J. uncertain and fearful.

35. According to the passage, scientists involved in the search for life on other planets are likely to be:

   A. trained in scientific disciplines such as physics, astronomy, and engineering.
   B. wide-eyed dreamers prone to unrealistic expectations about space.
   C. employed at institutions such as universities or NASA.
   D. skilled radio mechanics, due to their work with radio telescopes.

36. The primary point of the fourth paragraph (lines 31–41) is that:

   F. even today scientists do not understand why life developed on our planet.
   G. liquid water is crucial to the evolution of intelligent life on any planet.
   H. only planets within a "Goldilocks Zone" are able to sustain life.
   J. there appear to be two crucial components in determining whether a planet may be habitable.

37. It can reasonably be inferred that, as it is used in line 46, the term *hospitable planets* is intended to mean:

   A. planets with cultures that are similar to those found on our planet.
   B. locations outside of our solar system that are in close proximity to the sun.
   C. binary planets with generally stable orbits and moderate temperatures.
   D. places with temperatures and masses that fall within the range able to support life.

38. Based on the information in the passage, Saturn is most likely unable to sustain life because:

   F. its close proximity to the sun causes a greenhouse effect.
   G. the atmosphere is too heavy to allow for liquid water to exist.
   H. its distance from the sun is too great for it to contain liquid water.
   J. it is an unstable gas giant, due to the chemical combinations present.

39. The passage indicates that any new planet discovered in a location that is comparable to Venus' location, relative to the sun, would most likely be:

   A. an overheated gas giant, due to its heavy atmosphere.
   B. incapable of supporting life due to its lack of a gravitational field.
   C. prone to the development of an unstable orbit.
   D. unable to sustain life unless it were small enough not to retain too much heat.

40. According to the passage, Goldilocks Planets are characterized by:

   F. temperatures that are moderate enough to allow for the existence of liquid water.
   G. heavy atmospheres that retain hydrogen gases, creating a greenhouse effect.
   H. either extremely hot or extremely cold temperatures, depending on proximity to the sun.
   J. the presence of both liquid water and a high concentration of hydrogen gases.

END OF TEST 3
STOP! DO NOT TURN THE PAGE UNTIL TOLD TO DO SO.
DO NOT RETURN TO A PREVIOUS TEST.

SCIENCE REASONING TEST

35 Minutes—40 Questions

DIRECTIONS: There are seven passages in the following section. Each passage is followed by several questions. After reading a passage, choose the best answer to each question and blacken the corresponding oval on your answer document. You may refer to the passages as often as necessary.

You are NOT permitted to use a calculator on this test.

Passage I

In recent years, the technology of magnetic levitation ("maglev") has been investigated to provide an alternative rapid transportation option. Using repulsion of magnetic fields, maglev trains can be pushed forward at speeds of up to 300 miles per hour. One specific type of magnetic levitation currently being investigated is electrodynamic suspension (EDS).

In EDS, magnetic rods are located at the bottom of the maglev train and within the track underneath the train. An electric current can induce a magnetic field in the magnets of the track. If this magnetic field can be induced to repel constantly the magnet in the maglev train, then the train will maintain a distance above the track known as an "air gap" and move forward. Theoretically, the maglev train in EDS should travel at least 4 inches above the track, so there would be virtually no energy lost to friction. If the system does lose energy, it will be in the form of thermal energy.

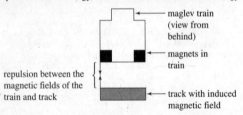

maglev train
(view from
behind)

magnets in
train

repulsion between the
magnetic fields of the
train and track

track with induced
magnetic field

Figure 1

Under controlled conditions, scientists conducted tests on an experimental maglev track oriented in an east-to-west direction.

Study 1

A maglev train with magnetic rods of fixed length was moved along the experimental track from east to west at various velocities v. The current I in the track required to induce these velocities was measured in amperes (A).

Table 1		
Trial	v (m/s)	I (A)
1	40	50
2	80	100
3	120	150
4	160	200
5	200	250

Study 2

The maglev train was run in five trials with varying lengths, L, of the magnetic rods, and run at a constant velocity of 40 m/s. The current I in the track required to induce this velocity given the different lengths of the rods was recorded.

Table 2		
Trial	L (m)	I (A)
6	0.6	50
7	0.8	67
8	1.0	84
9	1.2	100
10	1.4	116

Study 3

The magnetic field, B, measured in tesla (T), was varied in the maglev track. The current running through the maglev track was then measured in five new trials. Throughout these trials, the lengths of the magnetic rods and the maglev train velocities were kept constant.

GO ON TO THE NEXT PAGE.

Table 3

Trial	B (T)	I (A)
11	5.90×10^{-4}	300
12	7.87×10^{-4}	400
13	9.84×10^{-4}	500
14	1.05×10^{-3}	600
15	1.20×10^{-3}	700

Study 4

The maglev train with magnetic rods of fixed length was moved along the experimental track from west to east at various velocities, and the current in the track required to induce these velocities was measured. The magnetic field was kept constant for each of these trials.

Table 4

Trial	v (m/s)	I (A)
16	40	−50
17	80	−100
18	120	−150
19	160	−200
20	200	−250

1. In Study 1, I would most likely have equaled 500 A if v had been:

A. 40 m/s.
B. 125 m/s.
C. 200 m/s.
D. 400 m/s.

2. In Study 2, as the length of the magnetic rods in the maglev train increased, the amount of the current required to induce the train's velocity:

F. increased only.
G. decreased only.
H. remained constant.
J. varied, but with no consistent trend.

3. In Study 3, I would most likely have equaled 570 A if B had equaled which of the following?

A. 6.00×10^{-4} T
B. 8.00×10^{-4} T
C. 1.00×10^{-3} T
D. 1.50×10^{-3} T

4. During each trial, an electrical current moves through the magnetic track because a nonzero voltage was produced in the track. During which of the following trials in Study 3 was the voltage greatest?

F. Trial 11
G. Trial 12
H. Trial 13
J. Trial 14

5. In which of the studies, if any, did the electrical current flow in the opposite direction as compared with the other studies?

A. Study 1 only
B. Study 4 only
C. Studies 1, 2, and 3 only
D. None of these studies

6. The results of Study 3 are best represented by which of the following graphs?

F.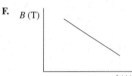

G.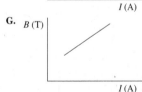

H.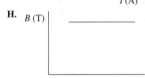

J.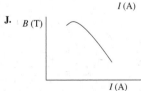

GO ON TO THE NEXT PAGE.

Passage II

Bats of the family *Vespertilionidae* (Vesper bats) are commonly found in North America. A guide for identifying Vesper bats found in Utah is presented in Table 1.

Step	Trait	Appearance	Result
			Table 1
1	If the ears are:	longer than 25 mm	go to Step 2
		shorter than 25 mm	go to Step 5
2	If the dorsum (back) has:	3 white spots	*Euderma maculotum*
		no spots	go to Step 3
3	If the ears are:	separated at the base	*Antrozous pallidus*
		not separated at the base	go to Step 4
4	If the muzzle has:	well-defined skin glands	*Idionycteris phyllotis*
		ill-defined skin glands	*Corynorhinus townsendii*
5	If the uropatagium* is:	heavily furred	go to Step 6
		not heavily furred	go to Step 7
6	If the fur color is:	pale yellow at the base	*Lasiurus cinereus*
		dark with silver tips	*Lasionyceris noctivagans*
		brick red to rust	*Lasiurus blossevillii*
7	If the tragus** is:	< 6 mm and curved	go to Step 8
		> 6 mm and straight	go to Step 9
8	If the forearm length is:	> 40 mm	*Eptesicus fuscus*
		< 40 mm	*Pipistrellus hesperus*
9	If there is an obvious fringe of fur:	on the edge of the uropatagium	*Myotis thysanodes*
		between the elbows and knees	*Myotis volans*

*Wing-like tissue between hind legs
**Cartilage structure in the ear

Students observed Vesper bats in a Utah nature reserve and recorded descriptions of them in Table 2.

Bat	Ears	Dorsum	Muzzle	Uropatagium	Fur	Tragus	Forearm
				Table 2			
I	20 mm long, separate at base	no spots	ill-defined skin glands	not heavily furred	brown	4 mm, curved	50 mm long
II	18 mm long	no spots	ill-defined skin glands	not heavily furred; only an obvious fringe of fur on its edge	brown	7 mm, straight	25 mm long
III	30 mm long, joined at base	no spots	well-defined skin glands	not heavily furred	olive	9 mm, curved	30 mm long
IV	15 mm long	no spots	ill-defined skin glands	heavily furred	black with silver tips	4 mm, curved	20 mm long

GO ON TO THE NEXT PAGE.

7. Based on the given information, which of the following characteristics distinguishes Bat IV from a *Pipistrellus hesperus*?

   A. 4 mm and curved tragus
   B. 15 mm long ears
   C. 20 mm long forearm
   D. Heavily furred uropatagium

8. Based on Table 1, Bats I and II share the same results through step:

   F. 1.
   G. 5.
   H. 7.
   J. 9.

9. Which of the following best describes the family *Vespertilionidae*?

   A. Mammals
   B. Protists
   C. Lampreys
   D. Birds

10. According to Table 1, *Lasiurus cinereus* and *Lasiurus blossevillii* could have all of the following traits in common EXCEPT:

    F. ears not separated at the base.
    G. 35 mm long ears.
    H. a heavily furred uropatagium.
    J. 20 mm long ears.

11. Based on Table 1, which of the following is likely to be most genetically similar to Bat II ?

    A. *Lasiurus blossevillii*
    B. *Idionycteris phyllotis*
    C. *Lasionyceris noctivagans*
    D. *Myotis volans*

GO ON TO THE NEXT PAGE.

Passage III

A heater was placed in a room with a measured initial temperature of 0°C. The heater was set to heat the room to 25°C, and a mercury thermometer recorded the change of the air temperature in the room over time. This process was then repeated with the heater set to heat the room to 37°C and 50°C (see Figure 1).

Next, a cooling device was placed in a tank filled with 50°C saltwater. For three separate tests, the cooler was set to cool the water to 25°C, 10°C, and 0°C, respectively, while a mercury thermometer recorded the temperature of the saltwater over time (see Figure 2).

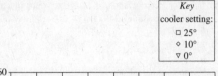

Key
heater setting:
□ 25°
◇ 37°
▽ 50°

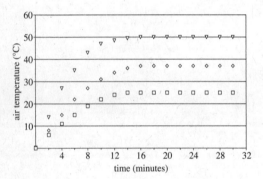

Figure 1

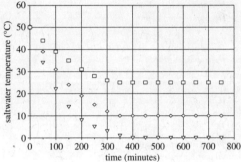

Figure 2

(Note: Assume that the temperature of the air was uniform throughout the room and that the temperature of the saltwater was uniform throughout the tank in all tests. Assume that at all times the heater and cooling device operated at full capacity.)

12. Based on the information presented in Figure 2, what was the most likely temperature of the saltwater in the 0°C setting at 220 minutes?

   F. 52°C
   G. 29°C
   H. 17°C
   J.   7°C

GO ON TO THE NEXT PAGE.

13. In the time interval from 8 minutes to 10 minutes, approximately how fast, in °C/min, was the temperature of the air changing when the heater was set to 37°C ?

   A.   0.5°C/min
   B.   2°C/min
   C.   27°C/min
   D.   31°C/min

14. When the cooling device was set to 0°C, for which of the following time periods represented in Figure 2 was the temperature of the water changing most rapidly?

   F.   0–100 min
   G.   100–200 min
   H.   200–300 min
   J.   300–400 min

15. According to Figure 2, when the cooling device was set to 25°C, at which of the following times was the average kinetic energy of the thermometer's mercury atoms the greatest?

   A.   150 min
   B.   350 min
   C.   550 min
   D.   750 min

16. Based on Figure 2, if another test were performed with the cooling device set to –10°C, approximately how long would it take for the saltwater to reach –10°C ?

   F.   Greater than 400 min
   G.   Between 100 and 350 min
   H.   Between 10 and 50 min
   J.   Less than 10 min

GO ON TO THE NEXT PAGE.

Passage IV

Pepsin is an enzyme in humans that catalyzes the digestion of proteins, like the milk protein *casein*, into smaller subunits called peptides. Pepsin is active only in acidic solutions.

The researchers prepared a solution of casein, a solution of *anserine* (a small peptide), a solution of pepsin, and various *buffer solutions* (solutions maintaining a constant pH). The following experiments were conducted using these solutions.

Experiment 1

Seven solutions were prepared in test tubes using a 5 mL solution buffered to pH 3.0. Different amounts of casein, anserine, and pepsin solutions were added to each tube, and then diluted to 10 mL with the buffer solution, so that the final pH in each test tube would be 3.0. Each tube was incubated at a constant temperature for 15 minutes, and then was monitored to determine whether there was any activity by pepsin (see Table 1).

			Table 1		
Trial	Casein (mL)	Anserine (mL)	Pepsin (mL)	Temperature (°C)	Pepsin Activity
1	1	1	1	30	No
2	1	1	1	35	Low
3	1	1	1	40	High
4	1	0	1	40	High
5	0	1	1	40	No
6	0	0	1	40	No
7	1	1	1	45	No

Experiment 2

Seven solutions were prepared in test tubes according to the same procedure as in Trial 3 of Experiment 1, and each test tube was diluted with different buffer solutions of varying pH (see Table 2).

	Table 2	
Trial	pH	Pepsin Activity
8	2.5	High Activity
9	3.0	High Activity
10	3.5	High Activity
11	4.0	Low Activity
12	4.5	Low Activity
13	5.0	Low Activity
14	5.5	No Activity

17. Pepsin is most likely to be found in which of the following organs?

   A. Kidney
   B. Heart
   C. Stomach
   D. Spinal cord

GO ON TO THE NEXT PAGE.

18. Suppose another trial had been performed in Experiment 2, and the results showed a high level of pepsin activity. Which of the following would be the most likely pH of the buffer solution used in this new trial?

    F. 2.0
    G. 4.0
    H. 6.0
    J. 8.0

19. Which of the following is the most likely reason that Trials 3 and 4 show high levels of pepsin activity while Trial 5 shows no pepsin activity?

    A. Pepsin activity is dependent on both casein and anserine.
    B. Pepsin activity is blocked by anserine.
    C. Pepsin is able to digest casein, but not anserine.
    D. Pepsin is able to digest anserine, but not casein.

20. According to the results from Experiment 1, which of the following trials are most likely to contain undigested casein?

    F. Trials 1, 3, 4, and 7 only
    G. Trials 1, 5, 6, and 7 only
    H. Trials 1 and 7 only
    J. Trials 5, 6, and 7 only

21. The experimental conditions for Trial 3 are most similar to those for which of the following trials?

    A. Trial 9
    B. Trial 11
    C. Trial 13
    D. Trial 14

22. According to the results from Experiments 1 and 2, which of the following best explains the relationship between pepsin activity, pH, and temperature?

    F. Pepsin digests proteins at a fast rate when the pH is greater than 4.0 and the temperature is about 40°C.
    G. Pepsin digests proteins at a fast rate when the pH is less than 4.0 and the temperature is about 40°C.
    H. Pepsin digests proteins at a fast rate when the pH is greater than 3.0 and the temperature is about 30°C.
    J. Pepsin digests proteins at a fast rate when the pH is less than 3.0 and the temperature is about 30°C.

GO ON TO THE NEXT PAGE.

Passage V

Chemical researchers studied the *viscosity* (a fluid's resistance to flow) for several liquids. Highly viscous fluids take more time to flow through a vessel than do low viscous fluids. They measured the viscosity in *centipoise* (cP) (.01 grams per centimeter per second). Some solutions were treated with chemical additives before the fluids were heated. The results are shown in Figures 1–3.

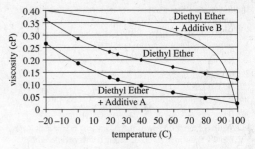

Figure 3

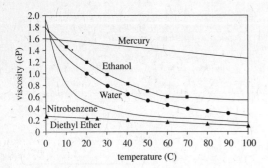

Figure 1

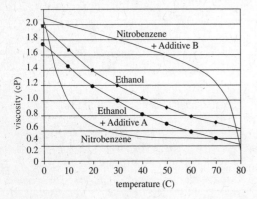

Figure 2

23. For which of the 3 figures did at least one sample fluid have a viscosity greater than 1.0 cP at a temperature of 0°C ?

   A. Figure 1 only
   B. Figure 3 only
   C. Figures 1 and 2 only
   D. Figures 1, 2, and 3

24. According to Figure 2, for the sample that contained nitrobenzene without Additive B, the greatest decrease in fluid viscosity occurred over which of the following intervals of temperature change?

   F. From 0°C to 10°C
   G. From 10°C to 20°C
   H. From 30°C to 40°C
   J. From 40°C to 50°C

GO ON TO THE NEXT PAGE.

25. According to Figure 1, after water was heated to reach a temperature of 70°C, the viscosity was closest to which of the following?

   A. 1.0 cP
   B. 0.7 cP
   C. 0.4 cP
   D. 0.2 cP

26. Based on the information given, which of the following best describes and explains the experimental results presented in Figure 2? As the temperature increased, the time required for the sample fluids to flow out of their containers:

   F. decreased, because heating the fluids increased each fluid's viscosity.
   G. decreased, because heating the fluids decreased each fluid's viscosity.
   H. increased, because heating the fluids increased each fluid's viscosity.
   J. increased, because heating the fluids decreased each fluid's viscosity.

27. A researcher hypothesized that a solution of nitrobenzene treated with Additive A would have a lower viscosity at 60°C than would untreated diethyl ether at that same temperature. Do the results in the figures confirm this hypothesis?

   A. Yes; according to Figure 2, at 60°C, nitrobenzene had a higher viscosity than did nitrobenzene treated with Additive B.
   B. Yes; according to Figure 3, at 60°C, diethyl ether had a higher viscosity than did diethyl ether treated with Additive A.
   C. No; according to Figure 2, at 60°C, nitrobenzene had a higher viscosity than did nitrobenzene treated with Additive B.
   D. No; according to Figures 1–3, samples of nitrobenzene treated with Additive A were not tested for viscosity.

GO ON TO THE NEXT PAGE.

Passage VI

Earthquakes disrupt the infrastructure of buildings and dwellings by displacing the ground beneath them as a result of surface waves. The origin of an earthquake is known as the *epicenter*. Surface waves propagate from the epicenter outward and are directly affected by the density of the ground through which they propagate. As seen in Figure 1, the strength of the wave may be characterized into three distinct types: strong, moderate, and weak.

Strong

Moderate

Weak

Figure 1

In order to study the effect of ground density on wave propagation, a seismologist has assembled a circular small-scale model with varying densities. Ground density and propagation duration were controlled in the experiment. In each study, earth and clay were laid down in a circular pattern with increasing density. Seismometers were positioned to detect the type of waves propagating at specific locations. A large speaker was placed 2 m below the surface of the epicenter to mimic an earthquake and each study was conducted over a period of 2 min with a fixed frequency of 10 Hz.

Study 1

The sound source was adjusted to 60 dB to mimic the impact of a magnitude 5 earthquake. The resulting *waveform plot* (exhibits wave type as a result of varying densities and distances from the epicenter) is shown in Figure 2.

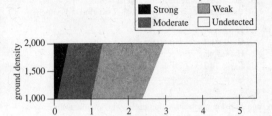

Figure 2

Study 2

Study 1 was repeated with the sound source adjusted to 80 dB to mimic the impact of a magnitude 7 earthquake. The resulting waveform plot is shown in Figure 3.

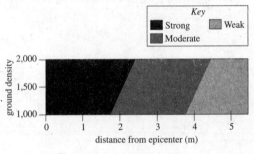

Figure 3

Study 3

The study was repeated with the sound source adjusted to 100 dB to mimic the impact of a magnitude 9 earthquake. The resulting waveform plot is shown in Figure 4.

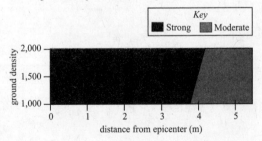

Figure 4

GO ON TO THE NEXT PAGE.

28. According to the results of Study 2, as the distance from the epicenter increases, the type of wave observed:

    F. remained strong.
    G. changed from strong to moderate.
    H. changed from moderate to strong.
    J. remained moderate.

29. According to the results of Studies 2 and 3, which of the following statements comparing the maximum distance from the epicenter for strong wave propagation and maximum distance for moderate wave propagation is true?

    A. At all ground densities studied, the maximum distance from the epicenter at which strong waves may propagate was greater than the corresponding maximum distance from the epicenter at which moderate waves propagated.
    B. At all ground densities studied, the maximum distance from the epicenter at which strong waves may propagate was less than the corresponding maximum distance from the epicenter at which moderate waves propagated.
    C. For some of the ground densities studied, the maximum distance from the epicenter at which strong waves may propagate was greater than the corresponding maximum distance from the epicenter at which moderate waves propagated.
    D. For some of the ground densities studied, the maximum distance from the epicenter at which strong waves may propagate was less than the corresponding maximum distance from the epicenter at which moderate waves propagated.

30. Which of the following factors in the seismologist's studies was NOT directly controlled?

    F. Sound intensity (in dB)
    G. Ground density
    H. Propagation duration
    J. Wave type

31. Consider the relative wavelengths of a moderate wave and a weak wave, as shown in Figure 1. Which, if either, is less than 100 cm ?

    A. The wavelength of a moderate wave only.
    B. The wavelength of a weak wave only.
    C. Both the wavelength of the moderate wave and the wavelength of the weak wave.
    D. Neither the wavelength of the moderate wave nor the wavelength of the weak wave.

32. Suppose Study 1 were repeated using a sound intensity of 70 dB. The resulting waveform plot would include which of the wave types referred to in the passage?

    F. Strong only
    G. Strong and weak waves only
    H. Strong and moderate waves only
    J. Strong, moderate, and weak waves

33. A study was conducted using a sound intensity between 75 dB and 85 dB. The minimum ground density where strong waves began propagating ranged from 1,000 kg/m^3 to 2,000 kg/m^3. Based on the information presented, the distance from the epicenter was most likely:

    A. less than 2.5 m.
    B. between 2.5 and 3.5 m.
    C. between 3.5 and 4.5 m.
    D. greater than 4.5 m.

GO ON TO THE NEXT PAGE.

Passage VII

A *solution* results from dissolving a *solute* into a *solvent*. The van 't Hoff factor (*i*) is the number of moles (1 mole = 6.02 $\times 10^{23}$ entities such as molecules, ions, or atoms) of particles produced in solution for every 1 mole of solute dissolved.

The temperature at which a solution changes state from liquid to solid is the *freezing point*. Two scientists observed that the freezing point of H_2O decreased after adding KCl to it. To explore this further, they conducted an experiment and each scientist provided separate explanations of the results.

Experiment

One mole each of fructose, KCl, and $MgCl_2$ were separately dissolved in 1 kg of pure water. The concentration of each solution was thus 1.0 mole/kg. In addition, 1 kg of pure water only was placed in a fourth container. The containers were placed in a cooling device. The temperature was gradually decreased and the freezing point of each solution was recorded. The results are shown in Table 1.

			Table 1	
Solution	Solute	*i*	Solution properties	Freezing point
1	—	—	Pure water only	0 °C
2	fructose	1	1 dissolved neutral particle	−1.9 °C
3	KCl	2	2 dissolved charged particles (K^+ and Cl^-)	−3.8 °C
4	$MgCl_2$	3	3 dissolved charged particles (Mg^{2+} and 2 Cl^-)	−5.7 °C

Scientist 1

For a solvent to freeze, its molecules must arrange in an orderly fashion relative to each other. When a solute is added, the dissolved solute molecules are attracted to the solvent molecules by the intermolecular force of charge. The attraction of the solute particles to the solvent particles interferes with the orderly arrangement of solvent molecules, and the net effect is that the freezing point is lowered. This decrease in freezing point is related only to the charge of the solute particles and occurs with solutes that form charged particles in solution.

Scientist 2

The freezing point of a solvent is the temperature at which the liquid and solid states of that solvent have equivalent energetic potentials. Below the freezing point, the solvent has a lower energetic potential in the solid state. When a solute is dissolved in a solvent, the energetic potential of the liquid phase is decreased more than the energetic potential of the solid phase. Because of the different energetic potentials, it takes a larger drop in temperature for the liquid to freeze. Thus, the size of the decrease in freezing point is in direct proportion with the van 't Hoff factor. This decrease in freezing point is related only to the concentration of particles, not to the identity or properties of each individual particle.

34. Based on the results in Table 1, how did the concentration of dissolved particles in Solution 4 compare with the concentration of dissolved particles in Solution 2? Solution 4 contained:

F. fewer particles in solution than did Solution 2, resulting in a lower freezing point.
G. more particles in solution than did Solution 2, resulting in a lower freezing point.
H. fewer particles in solution than did Solution 2, resulting in a higher freezing point.
J. more particles in solution than did Solution 2, resulting in a higher freezing point.

GO ON TO THE NEXT PAGE.

35. The freezing point of benzene is lowered with the addition of the solute naphthalene ($C_{10}H_8$), which has no charge. According to the information in the passage, this observation *disagrees* with the explanation provided by:

A. Scientist 1, who argued that only charged particles can have an effect on the freezing point of a solution.
B. Scientist 1, who argued that any solute is capable of increasing the stability of the liquid phase of a solvent.
C. Scientist 2, who argued that only charged particles can have an effect on the freezing point of a solution.
D. Scientist 2, who argued that any solute is capable of increasing the stability of the liquid phase of a solvent.

36. With which of the following statements about solutes would both scientists agree? Adding to a liquid a substance that has:

F. a positive or negative charge will decrease the liquid's freezing point.
G. a positive or negative charge will increase the liquid's freezing point.
H. no charge will decrease the liquid's freezing point.
J. no charge will increase the liquid's freezing point.

37. Suppose an experiment showed that adding the positively-charged solute $NaClO_4$ to the solvent H_2O but holding the concentration of the solution constant, the freezing point was significantly lower than an equally concentrated uncharged solution of $NaClO_4$ in pure H_2O. This finding would support the explanation(s) of which of the scientists, if either?

A. Scientist 1 only
B. Scientist 2 only
C. Both Scientists 1 and 2
D. Neither Scientist

38. Of the following diagrams, which best illustrates how Scientist 1 would describe the results after a charged solute (•) has been added to H_2O (×)?

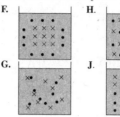

39. Do the scientists offer different explanations for the impact of a solute's physical properties, such as solute charge, on the decrease in freezing point of a solution?

A. Yes, Scientist 1 states that solute physical properties have an impact but Scientist 2 states they do not.
B. Yes, Scientist 2 states that solute physical properties have an impact but Scientist 1 states they do not.
C. No, both scientists state that solute physical properties have an impact on solution freezing point.
D. No, neither Scientist discusses the impact of solute physical properties on solution freezing point.

40. Assume the following for the addition of a substance to a pure liquid: k is a constant, ΔT is the decrease in freezing point, and i is the van 't Hoff factor. Which of the following equations is most consistent with Scientist 2's explanation?

F. $\Delta T = k/i$
G. $\Delta T = ki^2$
H. $\Delta T = k/i^2$
J. $\Delta T = ki$

END OF TEST 4
STOP! DO NOT RETURN TO ANY OTHER TEST.

Directions

This is a test of your writing skills. You will have thirty (30) minutes to write an essay. Before you begin planning and writing your essay, read the writing prompt carefully to understand exactly what you are being asked to do. Your essay will be evaluated on the evidence it provides of your ability to express judgments by taking a position on the issue in the writing prompt; to maintain a focus on the topic throughout your essay; to develop a position by using logical reasoning and by supporting your ideas; to organize ideas in a logical way; and to use language clearly and effectively according to the conventions of standard written English.

You may use the unlined pages in this test booklet to plan your essay. These pages will not be scored. *You must write your essay on the lined pages in the answer folder.* Your writing on those lined pages will be scored. You may not need all the lined pages, but to ensure you have enough room to finish, do NOT skip lines. You may write corrections or additions neatly between the lines of your essay, but do NOT write in the margins of the lined pages. *Illegible essays cannot be scored, so you must write (or print) clearly.*

If you finish before time is called, you may review your work. Lay your pencil down immediately when time is called.

DO NOT OPEN THIS BOOK UNTIL YOU ARE TOLD TO DO SO.

ACT Assessment Writing Test Prompt

Many schools have removed soda and unhealthy snack machines from school property. Some think this is a good way to combat the rising rates of childhood obesity because these machines feature high-calorie snacks with low nutritional value. Others argue that the machines are necessary sources of food and drink outside the hours the cafeteria is open. In your opinion, should schools ban soda and vending machines on school property?

In your essay, take a position on this question. You may write about either one of the two points of view given, or you may present a different point of view on this question. Use specific reasons and examples to support your position.

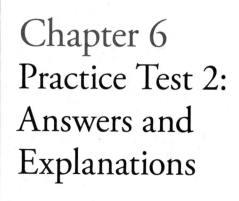

Chapter 6
Practice Test 2:
Answers and
Explanations

TEST 2 ENGLISH ANSWERS

1.	A	36.	G
2.	J	37.	A
3.	D	38.	H
4.	F	39.	D
5.	C	40.	G
6.	H	41.	C
7.	B	42.	G
8.	J	43.	A
9.	B	44.	F
10.	J	45.	C
11.	B	46.	G
12.	J	47.	A
13.	A	48.	J
14.	J	49.	D
15.	B	50.	G
16.	H	51.	C
17.	B	52.	J
18.	F	53.	B
19.	C	54.	F
20.	H	55.	C
21.	D	56.	H
22.	F	57.	D
23.	C	58.	H
24.	G	59.	B
25.	D	60.	F
26.	H	61.	D
27.	B	62.	H
28.	F	63.	B
29.	D	64.	J
30.	F	65.	A
31.	B	66.	J
32.	J	67.	C
33.	A	68.	F
34.	F	69.	B
35.	D	70.	J

71. B
72. H
73. C
74. F
75. B

TEST 2 MATH ANSWERS

1. E
2. H
3. B
4. G
5. C
6. F
7. C
8. G
9. C
10. F
11. D
12. H
13. B
14. G
15. B
16. H
17. B
18. J
19. C
20. G
21. C
22. G
23. E
24. F
25. C

26. K
27. D
28. F
29. B
30. J
31. E
32. K
33. B
34. F
35. A
36. J
37. C
38. K
39. E
40. H
41. E
42. G
43. C
44. J
45. B
46. H
47. C
48. J
49. A
50. G
51. A
52. G
53. C
54. G
55. C
56. K
57. A
58. K
59. E
60. H

TEST 2 READING ANSWERS

1.	A		21.	D
2.	G		22.	G
3.	D		23.	A
4.	F		24.	F
5.	C		25.	A
6.	J		26.	G
7.	A		27.	A
8.	H		28.	F
9.	D		29.	B
10.	F		30.	H
11.	A		31.	A
12.	G		32.	G
13.	B		33.	C
14.	F		34.	H
15.	C		35.	A
16.	F		36.	J
17.	C		37.	D
18.	H		38.	H
19.	C		39.	D
20.	J		40.	F

TEST 2 SCIENCE ANSWERS

1.	D		21.	A	
2.	F		22.	G	
3.	C		23.	C	
4.	J		24.	F	
5.	B		25.	C	
6.	G		26.	G	
7.	D		27.	D	
8.	G		28.	G	
9.	A		29.	B	
10.	G		30.	J	
11.	D		31.	D	
12.	J		32.	J	
13.	B		33.	A	
14.	F		34.	G	
15.	A		35.	A	
16.	F		36.	F	
17.	C		37.	A	
18.	F		38.	G	
19.	C		39.	A	
20.	H		40.	J	

TEST 2 ENGLISH EXPLANATIONS

1. **A** The mother says that the author will be surprised to find that *family histories can be very interesting*, which implies that the author currently believes the opposite. Choice (A) is the best answer, expressing boredom and disinterest. Choices (B) and (C) are too optimistic, and choice (D) is irrelevant in this paragraph.

2. **J** Choice (F) creates a fragment because *hoping* begins an incomplete thought. Choice (G) creates a fragment because there is no subject for the verb *hope*. Choice (J) is the best answer because it corrects the sentence fragment error by connecting the incomplete thought to the complete one before it with a comma. Choice (H) confuses the meaning of the sentence.

3. **D** *Pictures and letters* is a list of only two items, so no commas are needed before the *and*, eliminating choices (A) and (B). Choice (C) also has an unnecessary comma after *letters*, interrupting the flow of the sentence.

4. **F** In EXCEPT/LEAST/NOT questions, the underlined portion of the sentence is correct. Choice (G) has the same structure and meaning as the original, since *yet* and *but* are both coordinating conjunctions, which, with a comma, can join two complete ideas. Choice (H) is acceptable because a semicolon is an appropriate punctuation to separate two complete thoughts. Choices (F) and (J) eliminate the need for punctuation by deleting he and making the second half of the sentence incomplete. However, choice (F) uses an incorrect tense and is NOT acceptable.

5. **C** Choice (C) correctly uses the apostrophe to show possession. An apostrophe after *relatives* is necessary to indicate more than one relative has the memories, eliminating choices (A) and (B). *Memory* does not possess *into;* thus choice (D) is incorrect.

6. H   Sentences 1 and 2 continue the narrative by providing a setting and the scanner's activity. Sentence 4 shows an important shift in the author's attitude from reluctance to happiness. Sentence 3 offers information that can be figured out from the context and is therefore the least relevant to the telling of the story.

7. B   The word *belongings* refers to the relatives, which is plural, so you can eliminate choices (A) and (C). The correct answer is choice (B), not choice (D); *there* refers to a place and *their* is the plural possessive pronoun.

8. J   Choice (J) gives the past perfect form of the verb *to send*; this form is needed because the letters were sent in the distant past. Choices (G) and (H) are in the wrong tense, and choice (F) does not use the proper past participle form of the verb *send*.

9. B   A pause is necessary between *kitchen* and *penning* to clarify that the great-grandmother, not the kitchen, was *penning* the entries, which makes choice (B) better than choice (A). Choices (C) and (D) can also be eliminated because *which* and *that* refer to the closest preceding noun, which is *kitchen*, and create the same error in meaning.

10. J   This sentence continues the same attitude about stories that is expressed in the previous sentence, so you can eliminate choice (F) for incorrect direction. *Because* makes the phrase after incomplete, so choice (G) is incorrect because it creates a sentence fragment. *Therefore* indicates the correct direction but doesn't link the ideas in a logical way. The best answer is choice (J).

11. B   A comma should precede the last *and* in a list of 3 or more things, eliminating choices (C) and (D). Choice (A) has an unnecessary comma after the *and*, so the correct answer is choice (B).

12. J   The best answer is (J) because it clearly introduces the paragraph's focus on the author's growing interest in her family. Choices (F) and (H) mention the relatives; however, the focus is not on how many names and relatives the writer needs to keep track of. Choice (G)

revisits the idea of using the computer to preserve family memories but does not match this paragraph's main idea.

13. **A** Paragraph 6 discusses what the writer gained from her experience, and the conclusion should continue that idea. Choice (A) is the best choice because it discusses what the writer plans to do with what she gained and emphasizes the important relationship between grandfather and grandchild seen in this narrative. Choices (B), (C), and (D) digress from the main point of the essay about the significance of the experience.

14. **J** Paragraph 5 discusses the writer's positive view of her grandfather's stories. Her change in attitude is first introduced at the end of Paragraph 3. Paragraph 5 then concludes by introducing the chest of stuff, which explains what the *belongings* are in the beginning of Paragraph 4. Therefore, the best placement of Paragraph 5 should be between Paragraphs 3 and 4.

15. **B** The writer concludes the essay by stating how much she appreciates family memories and mementoes after helping her grandfather research their family lineage; thus her purpose has been achieved, eliminating choices (C) and (D). Choice (A) is not true because the computer skills are not the benefit the writer gained from her experience.

16. **H** The writer is trying to state that she is standing alone; thus the correct pronoun is *myself* not *me*, eliminating choices (F) and (G). The phrase after *myself* is incomplete and cannot be separated by a period, eliminating choice (J). A comma can be used to connect a complete thought to an incomplete thought.

17. **B** The words *new* and *cold* are both adjectives describing *bedroom* and should be separated by a comma, eliminating choices (C) and (D). A comma after *cold* is unnecessary and disruptive to the flow of the sentence, eliminating choice (A).

18. **F** The writer is trying to describe *spectacle,* which is a noun, so *complete* should be an adjective, eliminating choices (G) and (H). The correct idiomatic expression is *to make a spectacle of,* so choice (F) is better than choice (J).

19. C Since the action *has never been more than 30 minutes away...* refers to *only child*, the pronoun should be in subject case *who*, eliminating choices (A) and (B). Choice (D) incorrectly uses the plural verb form, rather than the singular.

20. H The pronoun *one's* does not agree with the subject *we* earlier in the sentence. Only choice (H) uses the correct possessive pronoun of *we*, which is *our*.

21. D The sentence is listing two different pairs of breakfast items—milk and juice, eggs and bacon. There should not be a comma after *milk* because the *and* is used to connect two nouns, *milk* and *juice*, not to list 3 or more items. You can eliminate choices (A) and (B). The comma is necessary between *juice* and *fluffy* in order to separate the two different pairs of items.

22. F Choice (F) clearly articulates the angst she feels and clarifies that she misses her old way of life. Choice (G) is incorrect because the different stages of mourning are not described. Although the original sentence is short and concise, it is too literal and does not accurately describe her emotional state. Eliminate Choices (H) and (J).

23. C Because the first half of the sentence is an incomplete thought, the underlined portion must include a subject to make the second half a complete thought, eliminating choices (A) and (D). Choice (C) uses the present tense of the verb, which fits better in the context of the story than the present perfect tense in choice (B).

24. G Choice (G) is correct, because the phrase does clarify why the writer stops crying in the first half of the sentence. There is no evidence to support a strained roommate relationship, so choice (F) is incorrect. Choice (H) is incorrect because the phrase does not show that the writer is right to feel sad. The phrase does give new understanding into what the author is thinking and feeling, so choice (J) is incorrect.

25. D Choices (A), (B), and (C) imply that the writer hears her roommate crying because she is surprised, which is not the intended meaning.

The writer is surprised to hear her roommate cry, making choice (D) correct.

26. **H** The conjunction *and* is not the correct link between the incomplete thought *Curiosity overwhelming me* and the complete second half the sentence, eliminating choices (F) and (G). Choice (J) is incorrect because a period cannot come after an incomplete thought.

27. **B** Choice (B) is the only transition listed that suggests a quick, unexpected reaction from the roommate. Choices (A), (C), and (D) all indicate that some time passes before the roommate responds.

28. **F** Choice (F) is the only appropriate verb that is consistent in meaning with the description of the roommate as shaken up and surprised by the presence of the writer. Choice (G) means to state confidently, choice (H) means to use another person's words, and choice (J) means to yell loudly.

29. **D** Choice (D) both captures the roommate's emotion and explains why the writer responds by suggesting they adjust to college life together. Choices (A) and (B) are not consistent with the writer's response. Choice (C) completely disagrees with the emotions of both the writer and the roommate.

30. **F** The passage is a personal account of the writer, a first-time college student who is worried after moving away from home, and of the writer's roommate, who feels similar emotions. Thus, choice (F) is the best answer.

31. **B** Choice (B) is the best answer here because the analogy provides vivid detail. The reasons provided in choices (A), (C), and (D) are not compelling.

32. **J** The phrase *if murky* is unnecessary information, so it should be off-set by commas. Thus choice (J) is correct. Choice (G) has no pauses to offset this information, which confuses the flow of the sentence. Choices (F) and (H) create sentence fragments.

33. **A** The phrase clarifies the term *anyone* by describing the kind of people who should try canyoning, so choice (A) is correct. Choice (B) is incorrect because the paragraph focuses on canyoning, not people. Choice (C) is extreme and not logical. Choice (D) is incorrect because the phrase does not confuse the focus of the sentence in any way.

34. **F** The word *river* ends a complete thought, and the word *without* begins a second complete thought. Choice (F) correctly uses a comma with a coordinating conjunction to link two complete thoughts. Choices (G), (H), and (J) create run-on sentences and do not provide proper punctuation to link two complete thoughts.

35. **D** Choice (D) is the most concise answer that conveys the correct meaning. Choices (A), (B), and (C) are wordy and unclear.

36. **G** Because *A remarkable activity in its own right* is a modifier, the *activity*—skydiving—must be named immediately after the modifier. Thus, choices (F) and (J) are wrong. Choice (H) omits the sentence's verb and also treats skydiving as unnecessary information by setting it off with commas. Choice (G) is the answer.

37. **A** Choice (A) is correct because the statement describes an additional thrilling activity in an exotic location, which is the focus of this paragraph. Choice (B) does not correctly describe the main idea of the paragraph. Choice (C) is incorrect because the locations and activities are different in each scenario, not just this one. Choice (D) is too narrowly focused and strays from the main idea.

38. **H** The phrase *because of which was our most exhilarating adventure yet* is intended to describe (modify) *canyoning.* Thus, the phrase should begin with the word *which,* as in choice (H). The remaining answer choices are unclear and create fragments.

39. **D** The word *walls* ends a complete thought, and the word *we* begins a second complete thought. Choice (D) correctly uses a comma with a coordinating conjunction to link two complete thoughts. Choices (A), (B), and (C) create run-on sentences and do not provide proper punctuation to link two complete thoughts.

40. **G** Choice (G) is the most concise answer that conveys the correct meaning, since *leaping* naturally implies a following descent. Choices (F), (H), and (J) are redundant.

41. **C** The subject of the sentence is the word *danger*, so its verb must be singular to agree with it, as with choice (C). Choice (A) contains a plural form of the verb, so it does not agree with the subject. Choice (B) contains a future tense, so it does not agree with the past tense of this sentence and of the passage. Choice (D) uses a gerund form incorrectly.

42. **G** A clear distinction between water and land activities is made in this paragraph, so choice (G) best clarifies this distinction with its mention of *rocky surfaces* and *chilly water*. Choices (F), (H), and (J) do not address the distinction at all.

43. **A** The word *thrills* begins a complete thought that switches the direction of the sentence, so an opposite direction conjunction is necessary at the beginning of the thought preceding it. Choice (A) provides the correct conjunction. Choices (C) and (D) are adverbs that indicate the ideas are going in the same direction, so you can eliminate those choices.

44. **F** The essay focuses on the enjoyment of thrills, so choice (F) is correct. Choices (G) and (H) do not mention thrills at all. Choice (J) mentions thrills but with a tone opposite to that of the entire essay.

45. **C** The best location for Paragraph 2 is before Paragraph 4, choice (C), because Paragraph 3 introduces the activity of *canyoning* discussed in the first sentence of Paragraph 2. There is also a logical sequence from the introduction and description of the river in Paragraph 2 to its navigation in the beginning of Paragraph 5.

46. **G** Note that the subject of this sentence—*Mexican-American War*—is singular. Don't be thrown off by the words *conflicts* and *compromises*, which, although closer to the verb, are not the main subjects of the sentence. Since *Mexican-American War* is singular, you can eliminate choices (F) and (H), and (J) creates a sentence fragment. Only choice (G) works.

47. **A** Two main things are changing in the answer choices here. First, the verb in the sentence changes from the present *include* to the past *included*, but this sentence discusses the Mexican-American War as being *overlooked* in the present (and note the mention of the *current shape and culture* in the following sentence), so you'll want to keep *include*. Moreover, if you're going to use a colon (:), you must have, at the very least, a complete idea before it, which you do not in this case.

48. **J** Choices (F) and (H) break the flow of the sentence unnecessarily, so they can be eliminated easily, but to determine whether you need the commas around the phrase *to American arts,* determine whether the sentence makes sense without this piece of information. As you can see, without this phrase, the word *contributions* is not clearly defined in the text. Accordingly, *to American arts* is an essential part of the sentence and should not be set off by commas.

49. **D** Choices (A), (B), and (C) are all rewriting the same sentence—only choice (D) gives a completely different option. If you check (D) first, you can save yourself a lot of work. In this case, you can DELETE this sentence because it is inappropriately placed in the paragraph. While Mexican-American musicians are mentioned earlier in the paragraph, the previous sentence represents an important transition to the following paragraphs discussing Mexican-American authors.

50. **G** To determine whether or not a selection should be set off by commas as *María Amparo Ruiz de Burton* is in this sentence, see if the sentence makes sense without that selection. In this case, it does not make sense to say, *A major landmark in early Mexican-American literature came in 1885, when author published her first novel...*The author's name is an essential part of this sentence and so cannot be set off by commas.

51. **C** Choices (A) and (D) are out, because neither is indicated elsewhere in the passage. (B) is deceptive—the paragraph says this novel was

the first to be written in English by an author of Mexican descent, not that it was the first by a Mexican author to be read in the United States. Only choice (C) captures the historical importance of the novel having been the first written in English by an author of Mexican descent.

52. **J** Since all of these answer choices ultimately say the same thing, pick the most concise answer that preserves the meaning of the original sentence. This definitely eliminates choices (F) and (H), and while choice (G) seems similar in length to choice (J), choice (G) is unclear and awkward in its construction, not least because *give a glimpse at* is idiomatically incorrect.

53. **B** Because *A family of landed gentry living in San Diego* is a modifier, the *family*—the Alamars—must be named immediately after the modifier. Thus, choices (A), (C), and (D) are wrong, and choice (B) is the answer.

54. **F** The sentence discusses a single event that took place during the Mexican-American War, so choice (H), which implies that the event was continuous, must be eliminated. Choices (G) and (J) alter the meaning of the sentence and are idiomatically incorrect. Only choice (F) works appropriately.

55. **C** Choices (A), (B), and (D) all create sentence fragments. Only choice (C) contains a verb, *was*, that can make this sentence complete.

56. **H** You need to determine here whether the sentence should be added to or kept out of the paragraph. If you're not sure whether to answer Yes or No, look at the reasons in each answer choice. Choice (F) can't work because the sentence discusses individuals of French descent, and there is no indication that the writer is drawing any kind of parallel between individuals of French descent and those of Mexican descent. Choice (G) can't work because the sentence does not give any indication that it is meant to be connected to *The Squatter and the Don*. Choice (J) can't work because the reaction of Mexican-Americans to the Louisiana Purchase is never discussed. Only choice (H)

indicates that the sentence does not provide information relevant to this paragraph.

57. **D** In EXCEPT/LEAST/NOT questions, the underlined portion of the sentence is correct. In this case, the words in choices (A), (B), and (C)—*investigate*, *examine*, and *look into*—are all roughly synonyms for *explore*. Choice (D), *solve*, has a meaning different than *explore* and its synonyms and changes the meaning of the sentence. Thus, choice (D) is the LEAST acceptable solution and the correct answer to this question.

58. **H** Choices (G) and (J) are both idiomatically incorrect and change the meaning of the sentence, so all you really need to decide is whether to use the relative pronoun *that* or *those*. To determine this, find which word or words the pronoun will be replacing. In this case, the word replaced is *writings*, a plural noun, which can be replaced only by the plural pronoun *those*.

59. **B** Sentence 3 introduces *other authors* for the first time in the passage. Sentences 1 and 2 provide examples of two other authors who are important. Therefore, Sentence 3 must come before Sentence 1. Choice (B) is correct.

60. **F** Because all four answer choices have the same meaning, select the most clear and concise. Choice (F) is the most clear and concise.

61. **D** Note the context of this sentence. The underlined portion ends a portion of the sentence that should be set off by commas—*typically cited alongside Walter Gropius and Le Corbusier as a pioneer of modern architecture*, so you can eliminate choices (A) and (B). The word *being*, as in choice (C), creates a sentence fragment, so the best answer is choice (D).

62. **H** Note the other verb in this sentence, *sought*. Since this is in the past tense, the other verbs in this sentence must be in the past tense. For the underlined portion, only choices (H) and (J) are written in the past tense, and choice (J) creates a sentence fragment with its use of the relative pronoun *who*.

63. **B** The easiest answer to eliminate is choice (D), as the semicolon would improperly separate two incomplete ideas. The phrase *based on van der Rohe's designs* is a necessary part of the sentence, so it should not be set off by commas. Likewise, it is not part of an introductory clause, so it should not be followed by a comma. Choice (B) correctly omits any commas.

64. **J** In EXCEPT/LEAST/NOT questions, the underlined portion of the sentence is correct. Choice (J) is NOT acceptable, because it changes the meaning of the sentence by suggesting that something is being made *into* steel and glass, when in fact the buildings are constructed *out of* steel and glass.

65. **A** The phrase *that is* is an introductory clause and therefore is properly followed by a comma. The part of the sentence after the dash serves to elaborate upon the sentence's earlier mention of the materials, and *that is* (an idiomatically shortened form of *that is to say*) functions in the same way that expressions like *for example* or *in this case* might in another sentence.

66. **J** Of the choices available here, only the colon is appropriate. The latter part of the sentence gives an example of *one of the problems* mentioned earlier in the passage. Accordingly, only choice (J) can be appropriate. Also note, when using a colon, make sure there is a complete sentence before it as there is in choice (J).

67. **C** Choices (A) and (B) don't directly discuss the visual elements of the buildings, merely how long they took to construct or their historical importance. Choice (D) gets closer by mentioning that the buildings are *on display* in various cities, but only choice (C) really discusses the buildings' *visual appeal* in its description of the buildings' *complex beauty*.

68. **F** The easiest answer to eliminate is choice (H), as the semicolon would improperly separate two incomplete ideas. Because the phrase *under teacher Peter Behrens's guidance* is unnecessary to the sentence as a

whole, it should be set off by commas. Therefore, choice (F) is correct. Choice (J) is wrong because it eliminates the comma needed at the end of an unnecessary phrase and it incorrectly inserts a comma after *teacher*. Choice (G) is wrong because, while the entire phrase as a whole may be unnecessary, *Peter Behrens's guidance* is a necessary part of the phrase, so the comma following *teacher* is inappropriate.

69. **B** In the sentence as written, it is unclear what the pronoun *This* refers to, so to fix this pronoun ambiguity, you'll need a substitute that is more specific. Choices (C) and (D) are no more specific than is (A); only choice (B) fixes the problem by giving a specific subject.

70. **J** First, consider whether the last sentence of the paragraph provides a contrast to or a continuation of the prior sentence. Both sentences concern van der Rohe's development of a new style, so contrasting choices (F) and (G) are wrong. Choice (H) is wrong because it would transform an incomplete sentence followed by a comma and a complete sentence into two complete sentences separated by a comma. Choice (J) is grammatically correct and clear.

71. **B** Since this sentence refers to an event that occurred in 1937, the sentence must be in the past tense (note, also, that the other sentences in the paragraph are in the past tense). Only choices (A) and (B) satisfy this condition, but (A) creates a sentence fragment by introducing the relative pronoun *who*.

72. **H** In EXCEPT/LEAST/NOT questions, the underlined portion of the sentence is correct. Choices (F), (G), and (J) all preserve the meaning of the original sentence. Choice (H) changes the meaning of the sentence and, moreover, contains a pronoun, *this*, that does not refer to any noun. Choice (H) is thus NOT an acceptable substitution.

73. **C** Choices (A) and (D) create a misplaced modifier—since *van der Rohe* comes directly after the introductory phrase, the introductory phrase must properly refer to *van der Rohe*, and must be modifying this subject in some way. The word *while* in choice (B) suggests that a contradiction will come later in the sentence, but none does. Only choice (C) functions properly to modify the actions of van der Rohe.

74. **F** Since all the answer choices are roughly synonymous, choose the most concise that preserves the meaning. Choices (G), (H), and (J) all contain some redundancy and do not contain any essential information beyond the word *enthusiastic*.

75. **B** Look for clues in Sentence 3 that might give you some hints as to its proper placement. The main clue is the word *there*, which suggests that a previous sentence will contain some mention of a place. Sentence 2 discusses the Illinois Institute of Technology, but look closely, the end of Sentence 3 indicates that this is one of the commissions awaiting him there, so we still don't have a clear idea of what *there* is. In Sentence 1, however, you see that the architect is discussed as moving from Germany to the United States, so Sentence 3 should clearly be placed after Sentence 1 because the *there* in this situation clearly refers to the United States.

TEST 2 MATH EXPLANATIONS

1.   **E**   Use Process of Elimination aggressively. Since Violet has 10 cherries, she uses *three times* 10 = 30 blackberries, eliminating choices (A), (B), and (D). Thus, she also uses 30 raspberries and *twice* 30 = 60 blueberries. Choice (C) lists 2 rather than 2 × 30 for the number of blueberries.

2.   **H**   Expand the equation with FOIL (first, outside, inside, last): $(3x)(x) + (3x)(2) + (-5)(x) + (-5)(2) = 3x^2 + 6x + (-5x) + (-10)$. Combine the middle terms to get the simplified expression $3x^2 + x - 10$. Choices (G), (J), and (K) are the results of confusing the signs. Choice (F) only multiplies the first terms and the last terms, which is not the correct way to multiply binomials.

3.   **B**   Substitute 8 and 6 for x and y, respectively, into the equation $f(x,y)$, to get $f(8,6) = 8 - [(8 \times 6) - 6] = 8 - 42 = -34$. Choices (A), (C), (D), and (E) are wrong because they do not distribute the negative correctly.

4.   **G**   Use the words in the problem to create an equation: *percent* means "divide by 100," *of* means "multiply," and *what number* means "use a variable." The equation is $x = \dfrac{1}{7} \times \dfrac{28}{100} \times 8{,}000$. So, $x = 320$. Choice (H) is $7 \times \dfrac{28}{100} \times 8{,}000$, a common fraction mistake.

5.   **C**   When you have numbers in the answer choices and variables in the question, you can plug the answer choices into the variables in the question to find out which answer choice makes the equation true. Start with answer choice (C) when plugging in the answer choices because it is the middle value and will sometimes tell you whether you need a bigger or smaller number if answer choice (C) is not the correct answer. Does $6(3) + 3 = 12 + 3(3)$, or, 21 = 21? Yes, and you're done!

6. **F** First, calculate the difference of the third and second terms: $8 - (-2) = 10$. The first term, therefore, is the second term minus the difference: $(-2) - 10 = -12$. Choices (G) and (K) are variations of the actual common difference, rather than the value of the first term. Choice (H) calculates the first term in a geometric, rather than arithmetic, sequence. Choice (J) incorrectly calculates −2 as the first term, rather than the second.

7. **C** Probability is equal to $\dfrac{number\ of\ favorable\ outcomes}{number\ of\ total\ possible\ outcomes}$. If you find a common denominator between the two probabilities, you can determine the number of unfavorable outcomes. The least common denominator between $\dfrac{2}{9}$ and $\dfrac{1}{3}$ is 9. The probability that the jellybean is NOT pink is $\dfrac{5}{9}$, so the probability that the jellybean is pink is $\dfrac{4}{9}$. Now, multiply $\dfrac{4}{9}$ by the total number of jellybeans, 72, to find the bag contains 32 pink jellybeans, choice (C).

8. **G** Because the flat rate of $100 includes the first two months, Bob will be billed $60/month for only 10 months out of the year. The total cost is $100 + $60 (10) = $700, so choice (G) is correct. Choice (F) results if you incorrectly charge $100 for every two-month period. The flat rate applies only for the first two months. Choice (H) calculates the total without the flat rate. Choice (J) incorrectly charges the flat rate twice for the first two months. Choice (K) adds 12, rather than 10, months of service charges to the flat rate.

9. **C** If one side of the pentagon measures 20 inches, the perimeter of the pentagon is 100 inches (20 × 5). Because the pentagon and the square have the same perimeter, the square also has a perimeter of 100 inches. Each side of the square is then 25 inches (100 ÷ 4). Choice (E) is wrong because it is equal to the perimeter of both the square and the pentagon, which is not what the question asks for. Choices (A), (B), and (D) give a perimeter that is not equal to our target of 100 inches.

10. **F** Translate the words into an equation, making x the number of bricks. Contractor A charges $1,600 *plus* $2 *times* the number of bricks, 1,600 + 2x. Contractor B charges $400 plus $8 times the number of bricks, 400 + 8x. Set the expressions equal to each other to get 1,600 + 2x = 400 + 8x. Choice (G) sets each contractor's flat rate plus the other contractor's per brick charge equal. Choice (H) sets the sum of each contractor's per brick charges and the number of bricks equal. Choices (J) and (K) set the per brick charges equal to Contractor A's and B's flat rates, respectively.

11. **D** Solve for B. Divide both sides of the equation by ACD to get $B = \dfrac{E}{ACD}$.

12. **H** You need to remember some things about angles and lines: A straight line, in this case $\angle WVZ$, measures 180°, and $\angle XVY$ measures 90° because it is marked as a right angle. The sum of the measures of $\angle WVX$ and $\angle YVZ$ = 180°− 90° = 90°. Since $\angle WVX$ and $\angle YVZ$ measure 4a and 2a respectively, 6a = 90° so a = 15°. Therefore, $\angle YVZ$ = 30° and $\angle XVY$ = 90° + 30° = 120°. Choice (F) is the value of $\angle YVZ$. Choice (J) is the sum of $\angle WVX$ and $\angle WVY$. Choice (K) is too big because we know that $\angle VVZ$ is not a straight line.

13. **B** First find the temperature of New Orleans in °F by adding 25°F to 70°F to get 95°F. Your answer choices give you different values of °C. You can start with the middle answer choice, 68°C, and substitute this

value for C in the equation to see if you get 95°F. Choice (C) gives $\frac{9}{5}(68) + 32 = 154\,°F$. Since this value is too large, you can eliminate choices (C), (D), and (E). Choice (B) gives $\frac{9}{5}(35) + 32 = 95\,°F$.

14. **G** The factored form of the expression is $2(3x + 2y) - 7$, so you can substitute 5 for $3x + 2y$ to get $2(5) - 7 = 3$. Choice (F) results if you forget to multiply $3x + 2y$ by 2, and choice (J) forgets to subtract 7. Choices (H) and (K) incorrectly use the coefficients of x and y to determine the value.

15. **B** The total amount of beef in pounds would be $3\frac{2}{7} + 2\frac{1}{3} = 5\frac{13}{21}$. This number falls in the range "At least $5\frac{1}{2}$ and less than $5\frac{2}{3}$." Choices (A), (C), (D), and (E) are incorrect because $5\frac{13}{21}$ does not fall within those ranges.

16. **H** Draw a picture. Since Dave went directly east and then directly south, the distance to his house can be found using a right triangle. The distance is $d = \sqrt{3^2 + 4^2} = 5$. Careful not to select choice (K), which is the sum of the two legs of the triangle!

17. **B** The rate at which the sensor records—1 piece of data every .0000000038 seconds, or $\dfrac{1}{.0000000038}$—is constant, and therefore the ratio of pieces of data recorded per second will be equal for any given number of pieces of data or seconds. Set $\dfrac{1}{.0000000038}$

equal to the ratio 100,000,000,000 pieces of data every x seconds:

$$\frac{1}{.0000000038} = \frac{100,000,000,000}{x}$$. Solve for x by multiplying diago-

nally across the equation: $x \times 1 = 100,000,000,000 \times .0000000038$.

$x = 380$.

18. **J** Use the answers: Since the width and length are reduced by the same amount, you can eliminate any that do not use the same difference between original and new dimensions, choices (F), (H), and (K). Then, calculate the original area of the photograph: $A = l \times w = 20 \times 30 = 600$ cm². The final area of the photo, therefore, equals $600 - 264 = 336$ cm². Choice (G) gives you $12 \times 22 = 264$ cm². The correct answer is choice (J), $14 \times 24 = 336$.

19. **C** The perimeter is the sum of all 4 side lengths of the quadrilateral. The answer choices give you the length of the shortest side, so you can work backwards by adding the three larger consecutive even numbers to each answer choice. You can immediately eliminate choice (D) because 7 is not an even number. Choice (C) correctly gives you $6 + 8 + 10 + 12 = 36$. Choices (A), (B), and (E) do not give you a sum of 36.

20. **G** Rearrange the equation into the slope-intercept form, $y = mx + b$. The resulting equation is $y = \frac{3}{7}x + 3$, with slope m of $\frac{3}{7}$. Choice (F) confuses the signs. Choice (H) results if you rearrange the equation into "$x =$" form, which does not indicate slope. Choice (J) is the y-intercept of the line.

21. **C** To find the area of the trapezoid *BCEF*, subtract the area of triangle *CDE* from rectangle *BDEF*. The area of rectangle *BDEF* is 36 square

feet (9 × 4), and the area of triangle *CDE* is 10 square feet [(5 × 4) ÷ 2]; therefore, the area of the trapezoid *BCEF* is 26 square feet (36 − 10). Choice (A) is incorrect because it finds the area of the square with sides *BC* and *BF*. Choice (D) is incorrect because it is only solving for the area of the rectangle *BDEF*.

22. **G** Make sure you read the given information carefully. You don't have to do any figuring aside from approximating $\sqrt{136}$ because all the other values are given to you. Because $\sqrt{136} \approx 11.7$, to find the perimeter, simply add the sides: 11.7 + 10 + 6 + 12 = 39.7. If you chose (F), you may have forgotten to include the diagonal in your calculation. If you chose (J), you did too much work—this is the area!

23. **E** Use the Pythagorean theorem $a^2 + b^2 = c^2$. Since $\overline{FG}$ = 10 and $\overline{FJ}$ = 6, $(10)^2 + (6)^2 = \overline{GJ}^2$, and $\overline{GJ} = \sqrt{136}$. If you chose (B), you may have confused this with a 6:8:10 triangle, but be careful—$\overline{FG}$ and $\overline{FJ}$ are just the legs in this triangle. If this were a 6:8:10 triangle, the longest side would have to be 10. Also note, that because point *J* shares a *y*-coordinate with the midpoint of $\overline{GH}$, $\overline{GJ} = \overline{HJ}$.

24. **F** Since the graph is rotating clockwise, the point will be moving 90° and will have a new point on the *x*-axis. Any point on the *x*-axis must have a *y*-coordinate of 0, so you can eliminate choices (G) and (J) immediately. If you chose choice (K), be careful—you may have rotated the graph in a *counter*clockwise direction rather than a clockwise direction.

25. **C** A geometric figure has rotational symmetry if it looks the same after a certain amount of rotation. A geometric figure has reflectional symmetry when one half is the reflection of the other half. Choice (C) is the only figure that has rotational and reflectional symmetry.

26. K Expand the equation with FOIL (first, inside, outside, last) and you will see that only the first term in each polynomial has exponents that add together to become x^8: $-x^4 \cdot 5x^4 = -5x^8$. Choice (F) wrongly assumes the absence of a x^8 term. Choice (G) confuses the sign; choice (H) incorrectly adds the coefficients; choice (J) multiplies the wrong terms.

27. D To find the mean, add up all the scores: $66 + 67 + 71 + 72 + 72 + 73 + 75 + 77 + 79 + 82 + 83 + 83 + 87 = 987$. Divide this number by the total number of scores, 13, to find $\frac{987}{13} \approx 75.9$. If you selected choice (C), be careful—this is the median. If you chose (B), you may have taken the means of the stems and leaves separately and added them together.

28. F To find the probability, determine the number of desirable outcomes divided by the number of total possible outcomes. Since you want a score of exactly 83, go to the stem-and-leaf plot to see that two of the golfers had a score of 83. Since there were 13 total golfers, the probability that an 83 would be selected out of the whole group is $\frac{2}{13}$. If you chose either choices (J) or (K), be careful—this question is asking about the probability of selecting a certain score; the actual numerical value of that score is not relevant.

29. **B** First, factor each number. In this problem, the given numbers are all products of 2, 3, *a*, and *b*. To find the lowest common multiple of the given values, you need to figure out the maximum number of times each component (2, 3, *a*, and *b*) appears in any one of our given values. $8 = 2 \times 2 \times 2$, so the lowest common multiple must have $2 \times 2 \times 2$ as a factor. No value has more than one factor of 3, so our number is only required to have one factor of 3. Finally, our least common multiple must have one *a* and one *b*. Multiply the mandatory factors together, $2 \times 2 \times 2 \times 3 \times a \times b$, to get $24ab$.

30. **J** To solve for the function, you need to determine the value of *m* in December. Since December is 7 months after May and $m = 0$ in May, $m = 7$ in December. Substitute 7 for *m* in the function to get $A(7) = 2(7) + 2$, so Aleksandra will have 16 model airplanes. Choice (F) is the number of airplanes she had in May. Choices (G), (H), and (K) result if you use the wrong value of *m* for December.

31. **E** The midpoint of a line is $(\frac{x_1 + x_2}{2})$, $(\frac{y_1 + y_2}{2})$. Thus, the *x*-coordinate of the midpoint $= \frac{-3+11}{2} = 4$, eliminating choices (A), (B), (C), and (D). The only remaining choice is (E), which also has the correct *y*-coordinate $= \frac{5-7}{2} = -1$. Be careful not to subtract x_2 from x_1, which would give you an *x*-coordinate of 7. Choices (A) and (B) merely add or subtract the *x*- and *y*-coordinates, rather than finding their averages.

32. **K** Factor the numerator and denominator separately: $\frac{(x-4)(x-4)}{(x+4)(x-4)}$. The factor $(x - 4)$ on both the top and the bottom of the fraction cancel each other out, so you're left with choice (K). Choices (F), (G), and

(H) are all the result of incorrectly canceling out terms without factoring. Choice (J) cancels both factors from the numerator, which is not possible with only one $(x - 4)$ in the denominator.

33. B   If Evan purchased 6 boxes, with 10 bags in each box, and 12 cookies in each bag, he will have purchased 720 cookies ($6 \times 10 \times 12$). Dividing 720 by 30 will give us the number of family packs with 30 cookies that he could have purchased instead. $720 \div 30 = 24$. Choices (A), (B), (C), and (E) are wrong because they do not result in the target amount of total cookies.

34. F   If $\dfrac{r}{s} = -\dfrac{1}{2}$, then $s = -2r$. Substitute $-2r$ for s in the given expression: $16r^4 - (-2r)^4 = 16r^4 - 16r^4 = 0$. If you selected choice (H) you may have made a sign error.

35. A   Because the nine circles fit into the square "as shown," quickly estimate the area that remains to eliminate any answer choices that couldn't possibly be correct. Roughly, it appears that $\dfrac{1}{4}$ of the square remains. Since the total area of the square is 144 square inches, and $144 \div 4 = 36$, choices (C), (D), and (E) are out because they are too big. Choice (A) is slightly closer to our estimate than answer choice (B), but if you have time, do the math. Since the circles are identical and are tangent to all adjacent circles and to the edges, the diameter of any circle must be $\dfrac{1}{3}$ of a 12-inch side, or 4 inches, and the radius of any circle must

be 2 . The area of each circle is π × the radius squared, or 3.14 × 4, or 12.56. Multiply 12.56 square inches by 9 cookie cut-outs to get 113.04 square inches cut out, and 30.96 square inches remaining. You can also make this problem fast if you know that the area of a circle inscribed in a square is always equal to $\dfrac{\pi}{4}$ × the area of the square, and can see that the area remaining in each of the small squares is proportional to the area remaining in the big square. $144 - (\dfrac{\pi}{4} \times 144) = 30.9$.

36. **J**   Use the answer choices and Process of Elimination. Remember that a prime number has only two distinct factors, itself and 1. 63 is divisible by 3, 7, 9, and 21, eliminating choice (F). 91 is divisible by 7 and 13, eliminating choices (G) and (H). 81 is divisible by 3, 9, and 27, eliminating choice (K).

37. **C**   First determine the cost per quarter hour using the rate formula:

$rate = \dfrac{change\ in\ cost}{change\ in\ quarter - hours}$.   Pick   two   different   packages: $\dfrac{\$230 - \$200}{10 - 8} = \dfrac{\$30}{2}$ to find the rate that is \$15 per quarter-hour. Now use the 8 quarter-hour package: fixed cost + \$15×8 = \$200 to find that the fixed cost is \$80. Choice (B) finds the rate for the 10-quarter-hour package without a fixed cost. Choice (D) is a partial answer.

38. **K** Because you know the height of the building *opposite* the angle and want to find the shadow length *adjacent* the angle, use SOHCAH-TOA: $tan(45°) = 1 = \dfrac{Opposite}{Adjacent} = \dfrac{100}{x}$, thus $x = 100/\tan 34° \approx 100/0.67 \approx 148$. Choices (F), (H), and (J) are the result if you use the wrong trigonometric function. Choice (G) is the result if you incorrectly set up $\tan \theta = \dfrac{adjacent}{opposite}$.

39. **E** The general equation for a circle with center (h,k) and radius r, is $(x - h)^2 + (y - k)^2 = r^2$. Because $h = 4$, $k = -3$, and $r = 12$, the equation for this circle is $(x - 4)^2 + (y + 3)^2 = 144$. Choices (A), (B), and (C) are incorrect because they do not square r. Choice (D) is incorrect because it does not distribute the negative in the $(y - k)^2$ term.

40. **H** Use your calculator to make the comparisons easier: $\dfrac{14}{21} = 0.\overline{66}$. Now, test the answers. Choice (F) is $\dfrac{7}{12} = 0.58\overline{3}$, which is less than $0.\overline{66}$, and choice (G) is $\dfrac{8}{12} = 0.\overline{66}$, which makes the two fractions equal. Choice (H) is $\dfrac{9}{12} = 0.75$, which makes the inequality true. Choices (J) and (K) also make the inequality true but neither is the *least* integer that makes the inequality true.

41. **E** Substitute $(a + b)$ for a. Square the quantity $(a + b)$, distribute the 2 within $(a + b)$ by multiplying a and b both by 2, and add 5.

42. G Since lines $\overline{MO}$ and $\overline{LP}$ are parallel, $\angle NMO \cong \angle NLP$ and $\angle NOM \cong \angle NPL$. Thus, $\triangle MNO$ and $\triangle LNP$ are similar triangles with congruent angles and proportional sides. To find the length of $\overline{NO}$, set up a proportion: $\dfrac{\overline{MO}}{\overline{LP}} = \dfrac{\overline{NO}}{\overline{NP}}$. Using x for $\overline{NO}$, solve for x: $\dfrac{105}{150} = \dfrac{x}{x+39}$. $\overline{NO}$ = 91 feet. Choice (F) gives the length of $\overline{OP}$. Choice (K) is the sum of the three side lengths.

43. C First, convert 2 miles to feet, $2\ miles \times \dfrac{5{,}280\ feet}{1\ mile} = 10{,}560\ feet$, because height, h, is given in feet in the equation. Now, substitute the answer choices for the value of t to see which choice equals 10,560 feet. Choice (C) gives you: $1{,}200 + 32(293) = 10{,}576$. The precise answer is 292.5 seconds, but the question asked for the nearest second.

44. J The three angles of a triangle will always equal 180°, so $2x + 3x + 5x = 180$. Since $\angle C = 5x$ and $x = 18°$, $\angle C = 5(18°) = 90$. Choices (F) and (K) are partial answers. Choices (G) and (H) give the measures for the wrong angles.

45. B If the basketball player made 12 out of his 30 shots, he currently has a free-throw percentage of 40%. Use the answers to calculate the least number of additional free throws he must make. Make sure you add the number to both the numerator and denomination, since any addition free throws are both attempted and made. Choice (B) gives you $\dfrac{12+10}{30+10} \times 100 = 55\%$. Choice (A) is the result of adding 5 only to the numerator. Choices (C) and (D) approximate 55% to 56% of 30 free throws. Choice (E) incorrectly raises the percentage *by* 55% rather than *to* 55%.

46. **H** Pick a number in the provided range and try out the answers. If $y = -2$, choices (F), (G), and (J) yield positive results. Choice (H) is approximately $-\frac{3}{2}$, which is less than the result of choice (K), $-\frac{1}{8}$.

47. **C** Draw five placeholders for the positions of each of the 5 groomsmen: _____. How many groomsmen could possibly walk in the first position? Five. Write a 5 in the 1st position. Next, if one groomsman takes the first position, how many possible groomsmen are left to take the second position? Four. Write a 4 in the second position, and multiply the 5 possibilities for the first position by the 4 possibilities for the second position (each of the 5 possible groomsmen in the 1st position could be with 4 different other groomsmen in the 2nd position). After another of the groomsmen is chosen for the 2nd position, there are 3 possible groomsmen for the 3rd position, then 2 possible groomsmen for the 4th position, and finally only 1 possible groomsman for the 5th position. _5_ × _4_ × _3_ × _2_ × _1_ = 120 total possible orderings.

48. **J** As with all circle problems, it is helpful to first calculate and draw the radius. Given the area of the circle is 169π square inches, use the area formula: $A = 169\pi = \pi r^2$, so $r = 13$. Radii $\overline{MO}$ and $\overline{NO}$ form two right triangles with chord $\overline{MN}$, so you can use the Pythagorean theorem to find the length of the two missing legs: $5^2 + b^2 = 13^2$, so $b = 12$. The length of the chord is $2 \times 12 = 24$ inches. Choice (F) gives only half the length of the chord. Choices (G) and (K) give the radius and diameter of the circle, rather than the chord. Choice (H) is the sum of 5 and 13, which is not the correct operation to calculate lengths of a right triangle.

49. **A** The x-intercept occurs where $y = 0$, eliminating choices (B), (C), and (D).

Next, find the slope of the line: $\dfrac{rise}{run} = \dfrac{4-7}{6+3} = -\dfrac{3}{9}$, or $-\dfrac{1}{3}$. The line to

the x-intercept must have the same slope. The slope between choice (A)

and $(-3,7)$ is $\dfrac{7-0}{-3-18} = -\dfrac{1}{3}$. Careful not to select choice (C), which is the

y-intercept.

50. **G** Intercepting the x axis at $x = 7$ means the equation must satisfy the coordinate $(7,0)$. The only equation that does this is choice (G). Choices (F) and (H) incorrectly give x-intercepts at $(-7,0)$. Choice (J) gives the y-intercept at $y = 7$, and choice (K) gives the y-intercept at $(0,-7)$.

51. **A** If the $\tan \theta = \dfrac{2}{9}$, the side opposite to θ is 2, and the side adjacent is 9.

Therefore the hypotenuse is $\sqrt{85}$ (h $= \sqrt{2^2 + 9^2}$), so $\cos \theta = \dfrac{9}{\sqrt{85}}$ and

$\sin \theta = \dfrac{2}{\sqrt{85}}$. $\cos \theta + \sin \theta = \dfrac{11}{\sqrt{85}}$.

52. G Triangle *OAB* is equilateral since *OA* and *OB* are both radii of the circle and *OA* = *AB*. The formula for the area of a triangle is $A = \frac{1}{2}bh$. The base of $\triangle OAB$ is 8. To find the height of $\triangle OAB$, draw a line from *A* that is perpendicular to *OB*, creating two 30°-60°-90° triangles. Using the relationship $a : a\sqrt{3} : 2a$, the height of $\triangle OAB$ is $4\sqrt{3}$. So, $A = \frac{1}{2}(8)(4\sqrt{3}) = 16\sqrt{3}$. Choice (F) uses 4 for the base. If you choose (J), you probably forgot the $\frac{1}{2}$ in the area formula. Choice (H) uses 8 for both the base and the height of the triangle.

53. C Use the formula given and replace variables with values from the diagram. You will also need to find the degree measure of angle *Z*, since the problem asks for the length of the side opposite *Z*. Given that there are 180° in a triangle, subtract 105° and 40° from 180° to get 35° for angle *Z*. Now Plug In all of the information in the equation: $\frac{\sin 40°}{30} = \frac{\sin 35°}{z}$. Solve for *z* by multiplying both sides by *z* and by 30 to get: $z \sin 40° = 30 \sin 35°$. Divide both sides by sin 40°.

54. G To find arc length, use a ratio of $\frac{sector}{circle} : \frac{central\ angle}{360°} = \frac{arc\ length}{circumference}$. Since the radius is 9 ft., the circumference is $C = 2\pi(9) = 18\pi$. Now, fill

known values into the ratio: $\dfrac{120°}{360°} = \dfrac{\text{arc } PQ}{18\pi}$. Cross-multiply and solve

to find the length of the arc is 6π. Choice (J) is a partial answer that

gives the circumference rather than arc length. Choice (K) is the sec-

tor's area, rather than arc length.

55.　C　In order to subtract these matrices, you must combine the corre-

sponding elements from each matrix. That is, you subtract the first

row, first column numbers in the second and third matrices from

the first row, first column number in the first matrix. Thus, the ma-

trix $\begin{bmatrix} w - x - \dfrac{1}{w+x} & x - y - \dfrac{1}{x+y} \\ y - z - \dfrac{1}{y+z} & z - w - \dfrac{1}{z+w} \end{bmatrix}$, choice (C), is the best answer.

Choices (A), (B), and (E) all improperly subtract fractions and integers.

Choice (D) uses multiplication rather than subtraction.

56. **K** To deal with compound functions, the trick is to work inside out. First, determine the value of the inside $f(1) = -2(1)^3 = -2$. The value of $f(1)$ becomes the new x-value for the outside f function, so determine $f(-2) = -2(-2)^3 = -2(-8) = 16$. Remember that a negative number raised to an odd integer stays negative; thus choices (F) and (G) are wrong because they confuse the signs. Choice (H) is the value of $-x^3$, rather than $-2x^3$. Choice (H) is the result of multiplying $f(x)$ by $f(x)$, which is not the same operation as compound functions.

57. **A** If a function y varies directly with x, this means that as x increases, y increases proportionally, eliminating choices (B) and (D). This proportionality means that the function must be a straight line, eliminating choice (E), with the equation $y = kx$, where k is a constant. This line must then pass through the origin, because if $x = 0$, then $y = 0$. Choices (C) is incorrect because it does not pass through the origin.

58. **K** If the quiz scores are listed from lowest to highest, the middle score, the median, is 9. The two highest scores are both 10. Since the only mode of the quiz scores is 10, the remaining two scores must be distinct integers. The mean of the 5 scores is 8, so the sum of the five scores is $8 \times 5 = 40$. The sum of the two lowest scores must be $40 - (9 + 10 + 10) = 11$. Choices (F), (G) and (H) *could* be true because the quiz scores could be (3, 8, 9, 10, 10), (4, 7, 9, 10, 10), or (5, 6, 9, 10, 10). Choice (J) is the number of scores multiplied by the mode.

59. **E** First, draw a picture and fill in as much information as you can from the problem. Two opposite sides of the cardboard are 60 inches, and two opposite sides are 40 inches. Since you're looking for the height of the table and the answer choices are numbers, not variables, representing the height of the table, use the answer choices to fill in the diagram further. Try labeling the height of the table starting with choice (C), the middle value. Given that the width of the cardboard is 40 inches, a height of 25 inches on either side of the tabletop is not possible—50 inches is greater than the size of the paper. Try the next smallest

number, 20 inches, in choice (D). 20 inches is too big: If the paper table were 20 inches tall on either side, the top of the table would be a line. Choice (E), 10 inches, must be the correct answer.

60.   H   To find the area of a triangle, use the formula $A = \frac{1}{2} base \times height$. You already know the base is 10, but you need to find the height. Draw a line from point B that is perpendicular to line $\overline{AC}$. Use SOHCAH-TOA: $\sin 35° = \frac{height}{AB}$, so the height of this triangle is $10 \sin 35°$. The area is $A = \frac{1}{2}(10)(10 \sin 35°) = 50 \sin 35°$. Choices (F), (G), and (H) use the wrong trigonometric functions. Choice (K) does not take $\frac{1}{2}$ the product of $\overline{AB}$ and $\overline{AC}$.

TEST 2 READING EXPLANATIONS

1. **A** The use of the word *stultifying* refers to the boy's experience of life on his family's farm; later in the sentence, the passage tells us that the boy felt *landlocked* by this life, so something like trapped would fit well. Therefore, you can eliminate choices (B) and (C), because *strengthening* and *welcoming* don't match this description. Choice (D) is incorrect because nothing in the passage implies productivity.

2. **G** Line 20 shows that the boy had only heard about but never seen fireworks. Line 7 shows that the boy has companions who lead him through the jungle, so choice (F) is incorrect; line 55 implies that the boy respects the captain's knowledge, so Choice (H) can be eliminated. Line 25 shows that memories of the storm often intruded in the boy's thoughts, so choice (J) doesn't work.

3. **D** Line 30 refers to the boy's second home on the ocean, the idea presented in choice (D). Line 3 refers to the jungle as *inhospitable* and mentions the *snarling* vines in the jungle, making choice (A) incorrect; choice (B) is incorrect because the passage portrays the boy's mother only as *frail and worn-looking* (line 35), not frightening; and choice (C) is incorrect because the passage doesn't note that the boy feels positive about any aspect of farm life.

4. **F** This choice is correct because the passage about the boy leaving the farm is a flashback, as shown in line 44. Choice (G) is incorrect because the boy is remembering his past life while he continues to walk through the jungle; choice (H) doesn't work because the boy meets the captain and sets sail before the captain is killed and the ship is destroyed in the wreck; choice (J) is incorrect because his parents *create a home for him* (line 36) on the farm, before he goes off to sea.

5. **C** This choice is correct because the boy follows his question about what the phrase means with an acknowledgment that he can't distinguish the captain from the other men in his mind (lines 63–67). Choice (A)

is incorrect because the passage up to this point has shown the boy wondering about the meaning behind the captain's words, implying that the captain hadn't explained the phrase previously; choice (B) is incorrect because, although the boy wonders what the dead can do earlier in the passage, his thoughts here are focused on the captain; choice (D) is incorrect because there is no indication that the boy's experiences will lead him to a better life.

6. **J** Choice (J) is correct because the boy was eager to learn about navigation from the captain, as seen in lines 52–55, and the passage shows us the captain's dislike of ignorance, which he sees as *dangerous* (line 51). Choice (F) is incorrect because the boy wonders what the words mean at the beginning and end of the passage (lines 60–70); choice (G) is incorrect because the passage contains no evidence that the captain even knew the boy's father was worn down; choice (H) is incorrect because the passage contains no evidence about the captain's view of life at sea.

7. **A** Choice (A) is correct because lines 61–63 show the crewmates urging the boy (and finally pulling him) away from the scene of the wreck, showing his reluctance to leave. Choice (B) is incorrect because lines 6–7 shows the boy continuing to walk with his companions—no running away here; choice (C) is incorrect because, although lines 10–12 say that unpleasant memories of the storm often filled his thoughts, there is nothing in the passage that describes his reaction to loud noises; choice (D) is incorrect because the passage contains no evidence that the crewmates know about the boy's feelings about life on the farm.

8. **H** This choice is correct because the passage shows the captain teaching the boy about navigation (lines 49–51). Choice (F) is incorrect because the passage never describes the captain scolding the boy for stowing away; choice (G) is incorrect because the boy wonders what the phrase means even at the end of the story, as shown in lines 68–70; choice (J)

is incorrect because lines 48–56 show the captain paying attention to the boy by teaching him navigation.

9. **D** This choice is correct because the passage does not mention hail. Thunder is described in lines 20–22, the *walls of water* are mentioned in line 22, and lightning is described in lines 19–20, making choices (A), (B), and (C) incorrect.

10. **F** This choice is correct because lines 13–15 shows the unexpectedness of the storm. Choice (G) is incorrect because the passage does not mention the time at which the storm arrived; choice (H) is incorrect because the passage does not mention how the crew responded to the storm; choice (J) is incorrect because the passage does not contain any reference to the boy's father mentioning a storm.

11. **A** The *however* at the beginning of this sentence tells you that Thorne's comment is in direct contrast to the paragraph that came before, which identified the typical understanding of slang as something that is said in *defiant opposition of authority*. Choice (A) is most relevant to undermining that generalization. Choices (B) and (C) do not relate to defying authority, and rather they represent Thorne's attempts to provide counterexamples to the claim that all slang is intended to be against the status quo. Choice (D) is unsupportable anywhere in the passage; it is a trap answer based on the normal association of the contrast between *accusing* someone of guilt and his/her *innocence*.

12. **G** The final paragraph establishes the need to compile a slang dictionary so that people of future eras will have a way to understand our current forms of communication. The details regarding how Thorne's dictionary will explain each term and the analogy to modern attempts to decipher Shakespearean slang support choice (G). There is nothing critical in tone in this paragraph to support choice (F). The passage does not say that Thorne uses Shakespearean slang in his dictionary as choice (H) states. While the author does agree that a dictionary of slang would be useful to future generations, he does not argue that the

project of compiling such a dictionary is the *primary* goal of modern linguistics as choice (J) states.

13. **B** Choice (B) is correct because college professors, while possibly involved in the study of slang, are never mentioned in the passage. Choices (A), (C), and (D) are all mentioned in the passage.

14. **F** The quotation marks around *common man* highlight the fact that this is a questionable term that is being applied by someone else's point of view. This paragraph discusses how a word becomes viewed as slang based on a very subjective assessment of the people who use that word. The parallelism of the two sentences tells you that *common man* must be the opposite of the *respectable* people mentioned in the previous sentence. Choice (F) correctly relates the derogatory classification of slang to its less respected users. Choice (G) is not supported anywhere in the passage. Choice (H) incorrectly identifies a point of view held by *intellectuals who would categorically denounce slang* as the author's own. Choice (J), while related to this paragraph, is too extreme in wording and does not answer the question of the intended effect of adding quotation marks around a certain term.

15. **C** The context of this sentence tells you that slang is viewed *condescendingly* and as a signal of *intellectual laziness*. Choice (C) reinforces these ideas by identifying vulgar speech as containing something (slang) that sophisticated speech would not include. Choices (A), (B), and (D) are all correctly negative in tone but to an unfairly severe and specific degree. Certain uses of slang may be *sickening, malicious,* or *profane,* but this sentence is concerned with the way linguists view ALL slang as being uneducated in tone.

16. **F** According to the final paragraph, Thorne believes that in order for *future generations* or *civilization* to be able to decode the meaning contained in all our written artifacts, we need to provide them with a way of understanding our usage of slang. Choice (F) correctly identifies this purpose. Choice (G) suggests the purpose is for foreign language

learners, choice (H) suggests the purpose is to write the first-ever slang dictionary, and choice (J) suggests the purpose is to provide a current how-to-use manual of slang. All three are unsupported and do not address the stated need for this sort of resource.

17. **C** The quote from Whitman describes slang as an attempt to escape from *bald literalism*, meaning an attempt to find more colorful ways of saying what one means, and as humanity's attempt to *express itself illimitably*, meaning to have limitless expression. Choice (C) is a fair paraphrase of those ideas. Choice (A) is irrelevant and unsupportable. Choices (B) and (D) are stated elsewhere in the passage as reasons for slang but not attributable to Whitman or related to his quote.

18. **H** The first paragraph attempts to make a contrast between unscholarly sounding words and a man of great academic distinction. The rhetorical question at the end of the paragraph attempts to invite the reader's curiosity as to why these two things would go together. Choice (H) effectively ties the first paragraph's anecdote to the purpose of the passage as a whole, discussing the academic treatment of slang. Choices (F) and (J) are too narrow in scope, failing to explain the first paragraph's relation to the passage as a whole. Choice (G) has an extreme claim that British scholars are the *leaders*, which is unsupported by the passage.

19. **C** The parallelism of this sentence indicates that while *most modern slang comes from* groups like corporate office workers, students, and computer users, previously most slang came from groups like the military. In describing groups such as the military as *hotbeds of slang*, the author is saying that such groups are likely inventors of slang. Choice (C) correctly matches this concept. Choice (A) means to predict the future, which is not supported by the passage. Choices (B) and (D) are unsupportable and make use of the trap language association between *traditionally* and *old-fashioned* as well as *the military* and *strict*.

20. J The passage indicates that most intellectuals do not completely reject slang because they *realize almost all slang* initially *involves as much inherent creativity* as the admired word play of poetry. Choice (J) addresses this detail. Choices (F), (G), and (H) are not supported anywhere in the passage.

21. D The author says *his genius is and will continue to be undisputed* (lines 93–94), so she does not think it is an *overstatement* or inadequate to suggest Gaudi's work is *genius,* eliminating choices (A) and (B). It is reasonable to assume that the author views the description of Gaudi's work as *freakish genius* as a correct interpretation of how current critics and viewers understand his contributions to architecture (choice (D)). Choice (C) is wrong because it is directed only at first-time viewers and is only a suggestion.

22. G The harsh images of Gaudi begging on the street suggest that the 1900s (choice (G)) were a time of great need, and when funders were least likely to fund construction. The passage also says, *financial contributions for the church's construction fizzled out completely around the turn of the century.* Choice (F) is incorrect because Gaudi began construction in the 1880s and there was "significant funding." The progress of the 1950s, choice (H) is due to increases in funding and construction picked up in the 1980s because of steady donations to fund that work, choice (J).

23. A The passage says that the Sagrada Familia stands apart from the rest of the world's cathedrals because of its *unique and startling design* (line 4), supporting the claim that it is more remarkable because of its unique appearance and design, choice (A). Choice (B) is incorrect because the passage does not indicate that the Sagrada Familia compares unfavorably to other cathedrals. There is no information in the passage to support choices (C) or (D), and neither is mentioned in comparison to other great cathedrals.

24. **F** The primary objective of the third paragraph is to tell the reader about Gaudi's childhood and show that he caused controversy from an early age choice (F). The reference to his family is not the primary point of the paragraph, choice (G). The education of the day was boring and unsatisfying because he was looking for more creativity, so choice (H) and choice (J) take excerpts of the paragraph out of context.

25. **A** The passage says that Guell funded a wide *array* of structures, including a mansion, park, and crypt, meaning a wide range choice (B), a broad selection choice (C) or large variety choice (D). *Arrangement* choice (A) does not capture a similar idea.

26. **G** In context of the sentence, *grumblings* refers to the reasons the finished Sagrada Familia may receive criticism, thus choice (G) is the best answer. Choices (F) and (J) are more literal, common usages of the word.

27. **A** When compared to his contemporaries and artists since his time, Gaudi used controversial methods, developed unique designs, and pioneered his own techniques like *trencadis* (line 47). Therefore Gaudi was less inhibited, eliminating choice (B), and other contemporaries were more reserved, making choice (A) the best answer. The passage never compares Gaudi's focus on architectural techniques to that of his peers. Eliminate choices (C) and (D).

28. **F** The passage says that politicians and architects *agreed that the plans Gaudi had left behind were sufficient to achieve his vision* and that, therefore, they would continue with the construction (choice (F)). There is no evidence to suggest that viewing the Sagrada Familia in person (choice (G)), the impending civil war (choice (H)), or the popularity of Gaudi's design (choice (J)) influenced their decision.

29. **B** The passage says that *even at this early age, he engendered controversy* (lines 23–24), which supports choice (B). While it is true that Gaudi was able to withstand harsh criticisms (choice (A)), he was unable to complete the Sagrada Familia. His inspiration from Nature also influenced his work (choice (C)), but it not clear when he started using

natural inspiration. Moreover, there is no support in the passage that his creations ever *blurred* the distinction between art and nature—no one mistook his buildings for nature itself. There is also no evidence in the passage to suggest that Gaudi changed his building's design (choice (D)) according to surroundings or other people's desires.

30. H   In the passage, the discussion of the architecture-as-art includes the statement that *functional designs dominated the architectural world* for years, suggesting that the most recent generations preferred pragmatic designs, supporting choice (H). There is no mention of historical architecture or modern unconventional designs in the passage, eliminating choices (F) and (G). Choice (J) is also weaker than choice (H), since the passage mentioned functional designs.

31. A   Frank Drake is primarily discussed in the first paragraph and briefly mentioned during the conclusion. He is described as the person in charge of Project Ozma, which is in turn called *the first organized attempt to detect alien life by way of radio.* The correct answer, choice (A), correctly summarizes this information. The project was unsuccessful in its search for alien life, making choice (B) incorrect. Choice (C) confuses Project Ozma with Project Phoenix, which is not mentioned in connection with Drake. The passage does not explicitly state Drake's education or position, as in choice (D).

32. G   Project Ozma is discussed in the second paragraph, immediately after the description of Frank Drake's experiment. The passage tells us that the project was a failure in the sense that it failed to find signs of intelligent life but a success in terms of leading to other similar programs. Therefore, choice (G) is the best answer. Choice (F) is incorrect because the project was not a success. The passage does not call Drake's goals unrealistic, as in choice (H), nor does it discuss NASA at this time, as in choice (J).

33. **C** The word *august* is used to describe two colleges, the University of California at Berkeley and the University of Western Sydney. Those programs are then described as having *reputations that draw respected scientists from around the world.* Therefore, a good word to replace *august* would be respected. Choice (C), *esteemed*, is a good synonym for respected. Choice (A), *summery*, might sound like it's related to *august*, but it doesn't mean respected.

34. **H** The author concludes the passage by stating that *Perhaps someday Frank Drake's dream of a message from outer space will come true once we know where to look for it.* This implies a certain hopefulness about the search while acknowledging that there are difficulties yet to be over-come. Therefore, the best answer is choice (H). There is no evidence that the author is *ironic*, as in choice (F), or *angry*, as in choice (G). Choice (J) goes too far, since the author is inclined to be hopeful, not fearful.

35. **A** The passage describes scientists in this field in the third paragraph. They are described as *esteemed academics, typically specializing in the areas of physics, astronomy, and engineering.* Choice (A), the best answer, is a good paraphrase of this information. Choice (B) includes words from the passage, but goes against the information given. Choice (C) mentions specific places of employment. Although the passage does mention such institutions, it does not discuss these researchers as specifically employed there. Choice (D) incorrectly focuses on radio mechanics, instead of interstellar research.

36. J The fourth paragraph serves as a bridge between the introductory paragraphs, which discuss the search for extraterrestrial life in general terms, and the rest of the passage, which goes into greater detail about two of the relevant factors in determining various planets' habitability. Choice (J) is the best answer because it correctly identifies the shift to the two factors as the primary point of the paragraph. Choice (F) incorrectly identifies a minor point in the first sentence as the main idea. Liquid water is not discussed until paragraph five, ruling out choice (G). *Goldilocks Zones* are not mentioned until paragraph six, ruling out choice (H).

37. D The term *hospitable planets* is used in the fifth paragraph, during the discussion of temperature and liquid water. The sentence states that *hospitable planets must be located within a certain distance of their respective suns.* This sentence falls in the middle of the discussion of what conditions will allow for life, so a good phrase to replace *hospitable planets* with would be *life-supporting* or, to use another term introduced in the passage, *life-sustaining.* Choice (D) is the best answer, since it is the best match for *life-supporting.* Choice (A) refers to cultures, which are not within the scope of this passage. Choice (B) incorrectly focuses on distance from the sun, which does not necessarily mean *life-supporting.* Choice (C) goes against the information in the passage.

38. H Saturn is mentioned in paragraph five, as an example of a planet that is too far from the sun to have temperatures conducive to life. Choice (H) correctly connects this statement to the earlier statement that planets too far away from the sun cannot sustain liquid water, making it the best answer. Choice (F) incorrectly states that Saturn is too close to the sun. Choice (G) incorrectly associates distance from the sun with a heavy atmosphere, a link not discussed in this passage. Choice (J) mentions *gas giants,* which the passage does not discuss until the following paragraph, and not in connection with Saturn.

39. **D** This question asks you to find a situation analogous to that of Venus. The passage mentions Venus in the fifth paragraph, as an example of a planet that is too close to the sun, and thus too hot, to support life. Later in the passage, the author also notes that the size of a planet may alter this rule, since smaller planets retain less heat and can thus be closer to the sun. The correct answer, choice (D), correctly connects these facts. The passage never describes Venus as a *gas giant*, as in choice (A), nor does it state that Venus lacks a gravitational field, as in choice (B). Choice (C) incorrectly identifies Venus as having an unstable orbit.

40. **F** Goldilocks Planets are discussed in the fifth paragraph and are described as *planets that fall within the range of appropriate temperatures.* Therefore, choice (F) is the best answer. Choice (G) incorrectly discusses atmospheres, while choice (H) has the opposite information as the passage. Choice (J) incorrectly mentions hydrogen gases, which are not mentioned in this part of the passage.

TEST 2 SCIENCE EXPLANATIONS

1. **D** In Table 1, when the current doubles, the velocity of the train also doubles. Therefore, a current of 500 A must be associated with a train velocity of 2 × 200 m/s = 400 m/s.

2. **F** Table 2 shows that the current consistently increases as the length of the magnetic rods increases, so choice (F) is the best answer.

3. **C** When $B = 9.84 \times 10^{-4}$ T, $I = 500$ A, and when $B = 1.05 \times 10^{-3}$ T, $I = 600$ A. Therefore, $I = 570$ A would be produced by a magnetic field with a values in between these two B values. Choice (C) is the only option that fits.

4. **J** The question suggests that an increasing electrical current results from an increasing voltage. Of the options listed, Trial 14 has the greatest electrical current, so it must also have the greatest voltage.

5. **B** Study 4 stands out because all of the values for electrical current are negative. Therefore, choice (B) is the correct answer.

6. **G** In Study 3, both current (I) and magnetic field (B) increase with a direct relationship. Choice (G) shows this direct increasing linear relationship.

7. **D** Using Figure 1, determine the features of a *Pipistrellus hesperus* starting at Step 8 and work backwards. Step 8 describes it to have a *forearm length < 40 mm*. Step 7 describes it to have a *tragus < 6 mm and curved*. Step 5 describes it to have a *uropatagium not heavily furred*, and Step 1 describes it to have *ears shorter than 25 mm*. Only choice (D) refers to a feature of Bat IV, *uropatagium heavily furred*, that differs from those of *Pipistrellus hesperus* found using the above method. Alternatively, you could use the features of bat IV from Table 1 and find the point on Figure 1 where the result differs from the path necessary to get to *Pipistrellus hesperus*.

8. **G** Follow Figure 1 step by step using the descriptions for bats I and II from Table 1 until you find the last step with the same result. Starting

at Step 1, both bats have ears *shorter than 25 mm* making Step 5 next. Therefore, choice (F) must be wrong. Both bats have a uropatagium that is *not heavily furred*, making Step 7 next. Bat I has a *4 mm, curved* tragus, and Bat II has a *7 mm, straight* tragus. Therefore, the results of Step 7 differ making choices (H) and (J) wrong. This leaves choice (G), Step 5, as the last point where the bats had similar traits. Note that the *obvious fringe of fur* on the uropatagium of Bat II does not come into play until Step 9 of Figure 1.

9.   A   All of the choices are in the kingdom Animalia and phylum Chordata. Vesper bats, like all bats, belong to the class Mammalia. Mammals are vertebrates with sweat glands, hair, and similar middle ear structures that give birth to live young (except monotremes which lay eggs).

10.   G   Both species are found at Step 6 in Figure 1. Step 6 can only be reached from having *heavily furred* uropatagium in Step 5, eliminating choice (H). Step 5 can only be reached from having *shorter than 25 mm* ears in Step 1, eliminating choice (J). Choice (F) refers to Step 3 which is not part of the path for either species, meaning it may or may not be a common trait. Choice (G) is more definitive because it refers to the only feature that neither species can have according to Figure 1. It is not possible to get to Step 6 if the ears are greater than 25 mm long.

11.   D   Using the features listed in Table 1 for Bat II, follow the steps in Figure 1. Bat II's *18 mm long* ears lead from Step 1 to Step 5 in Figure 1. The uropatagium overall is *not heavily furred*, which then leads to Step 7. The tragus is *7 mm* and *straight*, leading next to Step 9. Since there is an *obvious fringe of fur* on the edge of the uropatgium, bat II is *Myotis thysanodes*. Choice (D), *Myotis volans*, is most likely the closest genetic relative because it is in the same genus, has very similar features, and is adjacent on Figure 1.

12.   J   Looking at Figure 2, the 0°C setting is the lowest curve, represented by triangles. At 200 min. the saltwater temperature is about 8°C, and

at 250 min. the temperature is about 5°C. Therefore, at 220 min., you should expect the temperature to be between 5°C and 8°C.

13. B Since we are asked about a heater and a 37°C trial, Figure 1 will be the relevant chart. At 8 min. the air temperature is about 27°C, and at 10 min. the temperature is about 31°C. If the air changes 4°C in 2 minutes, divide 4 by 2 to get the answer: 2°C/min.

14. F For every temperature setting in each figure, the temperature changes fastest in the beginning and slower as time progresses. The 0°C cooling trial is no different: from 0–100 min. the saltwater temperature goes from 50°C to about 22°C, a change of 28°C, a much greater change than those recorded in any of the other 100-minute intervals listed in the answer choices.

15. A Average kinetic energy is directly proportional to temperature. That is, when temperature is high, average kinetic energy is high, and when temperature is low, average kinetic energy is low. Choice (A) corresponds to the highest temperature. However, you don't need to know what kinetic energy is to answer the question. Choices (B), (C), and (D) all yield the same temperature (25°C), and since there is no other variable in either figure to which average kinetic energy could be related, if one of them were correct, they would all have to be correct. Therefore, by process of elimination, choice (A) is the only possibility.

16. F The lower the cooling device's temperature setting, the longer it takes for the saltwater to reach that temperature. It takes the cooling device about 300 min. to reach the 25°C setting; about 350 min. to reach the 10°C setting, and about 400 min. to reach the 0°C. Therefore, you should expect the cooler to take more than 400 min. to reach an even lower setting, such as –10°C.

17. C Pepsin is described as an enzyme that is involved with protein breakdown, and that is active in an acidic environment. Of the choices listed, only choice (C) is a component of the digestive system, which is responsible for the breakdown of nutrients. Also, the stomach is an organ with a highly acidic environment.

18. **F** Note where the Pepsin Activity in Table 2 is High. There is no evidence on the table that Pepsin activity is high at any pH higher than 3.5, so you can only be sure of choice (F).

19. **C** Pepsin is capable of high activity in the absence of anserine in Trial 4, thus choice (A) cannot be correct. Pepsin activity is also high in the presence of anserine in Trial 3, thus choice (B) cannot be correct. Casein is described as a protein that can be digested by pepsin, so choice (D) cannot be correct. This leaves choice (C) as the only possible answer. Another way to approach this problem is to notice that what makes Trial 5 different from Trials 3 and 4 is that it does not contain casein. If no pepsin activity is seen when casein is absent, it would follow that casein is a substance that can be digested by pepsin, supporting choice (C).

20. **H** In order for casein to remain undigested, casein must first be present in the solution. Trials 5 and 6 do not contain casein, so choices (G) and (J) can be eliminated. Choice (H) is a better choice than choice (F) because the high pepsin activity in Trials 3 and 4 would break casein down into the smaller peptides.

21. **A** Trial 3 in Experiment 1 is conducted at a pH of 3.0 and at a temperature of 40°C. While all of answer choices feature Experiment 2 trials conducted at a temperature of 40°C, only Trial 9 is conducted at a similar pH of 3.0. Therefore, choice (A) is the best answer.

22. **G** The results from Experiment 1 show high activity of pepsin, meaning a fast rate of protein digestion by pepsin, at a temperature of 40°C, which excludes choices (C) and (D). The results from Experiment 2 show high activity of pepsin at pH values that are less than 4.0, so choice (B) is the best answer.

23. **C** Read the vertical axes in all 3 figures when $T = 0$°C. The only fluid whose viscosity is less than 1.0 cP is diethyl ether, eliminating choices (B) and (D). Ethanol, water, mercury, and nitrobenzene are all found in both Figures 1 and 2, so the correct answer is choice (C).

24. **F** The nitrobenzene line in Figure 2 has a sharp initial decrease and then plateaus. Thus, choice (F) has the greatest decrease in viscosity of approximately 1.1 cP. Choice (G) has only a decrease of approximately 0.25 cP. Choices (H) and (J) both decreases less than 0.1 cP.

25. **C** Figure 1 shows that the viscosity of water at 70°C is approximately 0.4 cP. Although choices (A), (B), and (D) provide values that are represented in the figure, they are all values for temperatures other than the specified 70°C.

26. **G** Figure 2 demonstrates that viscosity decreased with an increase in temperature, eliminating choices (F) and (H). The introduction states that the greater the viscosity, the greater the resistance to flow, thus the greater time it would take for a fluid to move out of its container. Given Figure 2 shows decreasing viscosity, the time for the fluids to leave their containers would also decrease. Thus, choice (G) is the correct answer.

27. **D** To assess the hypothesis, you would require values for viscosity at 60°C for nitrobenzene with Additive A and untreated diethyl ether. Although Figure 2 provides the viscosity for nitrobenzene treated with Additive B, no figure shows the viscosity value for nitrobenzene blended with chemical additive A. Figure 1 shows that nitrobenzene has a viscosity higher than that of diethyl ether, and Figures 2 and 3 show that Additive A lowers the viscosity of both ethanol and diethyl ether; however, you cannot assume that treatment of nitrobenzene with Additive A would lower its viscosity below 0.07cP. Thus, choice (D) is the best option.

28. **G** Examine Figure 3 along the x-axis. Notice how the farther you go to the right along the x-axis, the weaker the wave type becomes. Only choice (G) accurately describes this phenomenon.

29. **B** First, examine Figures 3 and 4 closely. In both figures, the transition lines show that at densities between 1,000 and 2,000 kg/m³, strong waves appear always to begin to propagate at shorter distances from

the epicenter than moderate waves. Thus, choices (C) and (D) may be eliminated. Since the maximum distance from the epicenter is less for strong waves than moderate waves, choice (A) may also be eliminated.

30. **J** Look at the passage closely, the passage states that *ground density and propagation duration were controlled in the experiment.* Thus, answer choices (G) and (H) may be eliminated. Choice (F) may be eliminated because in each experiment, the sound intensity was controlled. The wave type formed in the experiments was not controlled as it varied with distance and density.

31. **D** Examine Figure 1 closely. A wavelength constitutes the distance from one hump to the next. The moderate wave is approximately 150 cm, and the weak wave is approximately 500 cm. Subsequently, neither wave type exhibits a wave length of less than 100 cm.

32. **J** From the passage, Studies 1 and 2 were conducted using sound intensities of 60 and 80 dB, respectively. Accordingly, the resulting waveform plot of study using 70 dB should exhibit wave types reminiscent of Figures 2 and 3. Both figures exhibit all three types of waves; therefore choice (J) is the best answer. The waveform plot of Study 3 does not include weak waves, but its sound intensity was set to 100 dB, well above the sound intensity of 70 dB given in this question.

33. **A** Use the range of sound intensities given in the passage to determine which waveform plot you need to use. Since this range is 75 dB to 85 dB, you can confidently use the waveform plot from Study 2, which has as its sound intensity 80 dB. Using Figure 3 (Study 2), therefore, note the range of distances from the epicenter for strong waves: roughly 0 m to 2.3 m. Accordingly, any distance from the epicenter for strong waves between sound intensities of 75 dB and 85 dB can be reasonably expected to have a distance shorter than 2.5 m.

34. **G** The information in Table 1 indicates that Solution 4 contained three dissolved particles, where Solution 2 contained only one dissolved particle. Solution 4 thus had more dissolved particles, enabling you to

eliminate choices (F) and (H). Now compare the respective freezing point of each solution. The freezing point of Solution 2 was −1.9°C while the freezing point of Solution 4 was lower at −5.7°C. Be careful here—a large negative number is smaller than a small one!

35. A Scientist 2 states that the change in freezing point is NOT related *to the identity or properties* of the solute dissolved. The observation that a solute with no charge such as naphthalene can still lower the freezing point of a solvent does not contradict Scientist 2's viewpoint, so choices (C) and (D) are incorrect. Scientist 1 specifically states that a change in freezing point *only occurs with solutes that form charged particles in solution*. Therefore, the fact that naphthalene causes a change in the freezing point of benzene directly contradicts Scientist 1's viewpoint as stated in choice (A).

36. F Use process of elimination. Scientist 2 argues that any increase in the concentration of a solution will lower its freezing point, so you can eliminate choices (G) and (J). Scientist 1 argues that only charged solvents can have an influence on the freezing point, so you can eliminate choice (H) as well. This leaves you only with choice (F), which agrees with the hypotheses of both scientists.

37. A Scientist 2 states that only the concentration of a solution can change its freezing point, and since the concentration here is held constant, choices (B) and (C) are not the best answers. Scientist 1 states that *the decrease in freezing point is related only to the charge of the solute particles*, a hypothesis which is supported by the observations in the question.

38. **G** Scientist 1 states that *solute molecules are attracted to the solvent molecules by intermolecular forces* and interfere *with the orderly arrangement of solvent molecules.* Choices (F) and (J) are eliminated because they do not depict attraction between solute and solvent molecules, and both show a very orderly arrangement of solvent molecules. Choice (G) and choice (H) demonstrate attraction between solute and solvent, but only choice (G) illustrates interference with non-orderly arrangement of solvent molecules.

39. **A** Only Scientist 1 states that the physical properties (charge) of the solute have an impact on changing the freezing point of a solvent. This eliminates choices (B) and (D). Scientist 2 states that the physical properties of the solute do not have an effect on freezing point depression. Therefore, choice (C) is eliminated and choice (A) is correct.

40. **J** Scientist 2 states that the decrease in temperature *is in direct proportion with the van 't Hoff factor.* Choices (F) and (H) show the decrease in temperature and the van 't Hoff factor in an inverse proportion, so they can be eliminated. Choice (G) can also be eliminated because there is no indication that the van 't Hoff factor should be squared in the proportion. Only choice (J) shows decrease in temperature (ΔT) and the van 't Hoff factor (i) in direction proportion with one another.

WRITING TEST

Essay Checklist

1. The Introduction
   Did you
   o start with a topic sentence that paraphrases or restates the prompt?
   o clearly state your position on the issue?

2. Body Paragraph 1
   Did you
   o start with a transition/topic sentence that discusses the opposing side of the argument?
   o give an example of a reason that one might agree with the opposing side of the argument?
   o clearly state that the opposing side of the argument is wrong or flawed?
   o show what is wrong with the opposing side's example or position?

3. Body Paragraphs 2 and 3
   Did you
   o start with a transition/topic sentence that discusses your position on the prompt?
   o give one example or reason to support your position?
   o show the grader how your example supports your position?
   o end the paragraph by restating your thesis?

4. Conclusion
   Did you
   o restate your position on the issue?
   o end with a flourish?

5. Overall
   Did you
   o write neatly?
   o avoid multiple spelling and grammar mistakes?
   o try to vary your sentence structure?
   o use a few impressive-sounding words?

SCORING YOUR PRACTICE EXAM

Step A
Count the number of correct answers for each section and record the number in the space provided for your raw score on the Score Conversion Worksheet below.

Step B
Using the Score Conversion Chart on the next page, convert your raw scores on each section to scaled scores. Then compute your composite ACT score by averaging the four subject scores. Add them up and divide by four. Don't worry about the essay score; it is not included in your composite score.

Score Conversion Worksheet		
Section	Raw Score	Scaled Score
1	_____/75	_____
2	_____/60	_____
3	_____/40	_____
4	_____/40	_____

SCORE CONVERSION CHART

Scaled Score	Raw Score			
	English	Mathematics	Reading	Science Reasoning
36	75	60	39–40	40
35	74	59	38	39
34	72–73	58	37	38
33	71	57	36	—
32	70	55–56	35	37
31	69	53–54	34	36
30	67–68	52	33	—
29	65–66	50–51	32	35
28	62–64	46–49	30–31	33–34
27	59–61	43–45	28–29	31–32
26	57–58	41–42	27	30
25	55–56	39–40	26	29
24	52–54	37–38	25	28
23	50–51	35–36	24	27–26
22	49	33–34	23	25
21	48	31–32	21–22	24
20	45–47	29–30	20	23
19	43–44	27–28	19	22
18	40–42	24–26	18	20–21
17	38–39	21–23	17	18–19
16	35–37	18–20	16	16–17
15	32–34	16–17	15	15
14	29–31	13–15	14	13–14
13	27–28	11–12	12–13	12
12	24–26	9–10	11	11
11	21–23	7–8	9–10	10
10	18–20	6	8	9
9	15–17	5	7	7–8
8	13–14	4	—	6
7	11–12	—	6	5
6	9–10	3	5	—
5	7–8	2	4	4
4	5–6	—	3	3
3	3–4	1	2	2
2	2	—	1	1
1	0	0	0	0

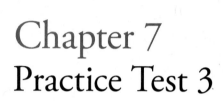

Chapter 7
Practice Test 3

ACT Diagnostic Test Form

Use a No. 2 pencil only. Be sure each mark is dark and completely fills the intended oval. Completely erase any errors or stray marks.

1. YOUR NAME: _____
   (Print)   Last   First   M.I.

SIGNATURE: _____ DATE: _____ / _____ / _____

HOME ADDRESS: _____
   (Print)   Number and Street

_____
   City   State   Zip

E-MAIL: _____

PHONE NO.: _____
   (Print)

SCHOOL: _____

CLASS OF: _____

IMPORTANT: Please fill in these boxes exactly as shown on the back cover of your tests book.

2. TEST FORM

_____

3. TEST CODE

⓪	⓪	⓪	⓪
①	①	①	①
②	②	②	②
③	③	③	③
④	④	④	④
⑤	⑤	⑤	⑤
⑥	⑥	⑥	⑥
⑦	⑦	⑦	⑦
⑧	⑧	⑧	⑧
⑨	⑨	⑨	⑨

4. PHONE NUMBER

⓪	⓪	⓪	⓪	⓪	⓪	⓪
①	①	①	①	①	①	①
②	②	②	②	②	②	②
③	③	③	③	③	③	③
④	④	④	④	④	④	④
⑤	⑤	⑤	⑤	⑤	⑤	⑤
⑥	⑥	⑥	⑥	⑥	⑥	⑥
⑦	⑦	⑦	⑦	⑦	⑦	⑦
⑧	⑧	⑧	⑧	⑧	⑧	⑧
⑨	⑨	⑨	⑨	⑨	⑨	⑨

5. YOUR NAME

First 4 letters of last name				FIRST INIT	MID INIT
Ⓐ	Ⓐ	Ⓐ	Ⓐ	Ⓐ	Ⓐ
Ⓑ	Ⓑ	Ⓑ	Ⓑ	Ⓑ	Ⓑ
Ⓒ	Ⓒ	Ⓒ	Ⓒ	Ⓒ	Ⓒ
Ⓓ	Ⓓ	Ⓓ	Ⓓ	Ⓓ	Ⓓ
Ⓔ	Ⓔ	Ⓔ	Ⓔ	Ⓔ	Ⓔ
Ⓕ	Ⓕ	Ⓕ	Ⓕ	Ⓕ	Ⓕ
Ⓖ	Ⓖ	Ⓖ	Ⓖ	Ⓖ	Ⓖ
Ⓗ	Ⓗ	Ⓗ	Ⓗ	Ⓗ	Ⓗ
Ⓘ	Ⓘ	Ⓘ	Ⓘ	Ⓘ	Ⓘ
Ⓙ	Ⓙ	Ⓙ	Ⓙ	Ⓙ	Ⓙ
Ⓚ	Ⓚ	Ⓚ	Ⓚ	Ⓚ	Ⓚ
Ⓛ	Ⓛ	Ⓛ	Ⓛ	Ⓛ	Ⓛ
Ⓜ	Ⓜ	Ⓜ	Ⓜ	Ⓜ	Ⓜ
Ⓝ	Ⓝ	Ⓝ	Ⓝ	Ⓝ	Ⓝ
Ⓞ	Ⓞ	Ⓞ	Ⓞ	Ⓞ	Ⓞ
Ⓟ	Ⓟ	Ⓟ	Ⓟ	Ⓟ	Ⓟ
Ⓠ	Ⓠ	Ⓠ	Ⓠ	Ⓠ	Ⓠ
Ⓡ	Ⓡ	Ⓡ	Ⓡ	Ⓡ	Ⓡ
Ⓢ	Ⓢ	Ⓢ	Ⓢ	Ⓢ	Ⓢ
Ⓣ	Ⓣ	Ⓣ	Ⓣ	Ⓣ	Ⓣ
Ⓤ	Ⓤ	Ⓤ	Ⓤ	Ⓤ	Ⓤ
Ⓥ	Ⓥ	Ⓥ	Ⓥ	Ⓥ	Ⓥ
Ⓦ	Ⓦ	Ⓦ	Ⓦ	Ⓦ	Ⓦ
Ⓧ	Ⓧ	Ⓧ	Ⓧ	Ⓧ	Ⓧ
Ⓨ	Ⓨ	Ⓨ	Ⓨ	Ⓨ	Ⓨ
Ⓩ	Ⓩ	Ⓩ	Ⓩ	Ⓩ	Ⓩ

6. DATE OF BIRTH

MONTH	DAY		YEAR	
○ JAN				
○ FEB				
○ MAR	⓪	⓪	⓪	⓪
○ APR	①	①	①	①
○ MAY	②	②	②	②
○ JUN	③	③	③	③
○ JUL		④	④	④
○ AUG		⑤	⑤	⑤
○ SEP		⑥	⑥	⑥
○ OCT		⑦	⑦	⑦
○ NOV		⑧	⑧	⑧
○ DEC		⑨	⑨	⑨

7. SEX

○ MALE
○ FEMALE

8. OTHER

1 Ⓐ Ⓑ Ⓒ Ⓓ Ⓔ
2 Ⓐ Ⓑ Ⓒ Ⓓ Ⓔ
3 Ⓐ Ⓑ Ⓒ Ⓓ Ⓔ

OpScan iNSIGHT™ forms by Pearson NCS EM-255315-1:654321   Printed in U.S.A.

THIS PAGE INTENTIONALLY LEFT BLANK

The Princeton Review
Diagnostic ACT Form

ENGLISH

1	Ⓐ Ⓑ Ⓒ Ⓓ		21	Ⓐ Ⓑ Ⓒ Ⓓ		41	Ⓐ Ⓑ Ⓒ Ⓓ		61	Ⓐ Ⓑ Ⓒ Ⓓ
2	Ⓕ Ⓖ Ⓗ Ⓙ		22	Ⓕ Ⓖ Ⓗ Ⓙ		42	Ⓕ Ⓖ Ⓗ Ⓙ		62	Ⓕ Ⓖ Ⓗ Ⓙ
3	Ⓐ Ⓑ Ⓒ Ⓓ		23	Ⓐ Ⓑ Ⓒ Ⓓ		43	Ⓐ Ⓑ Ⓒ Ⓓ		63	Ⓐ Ⓑ Ⓒ Ⓓ
4	Ⓕ Ⓖ Ⓗ Ⓙ		24	Ⓕ Ⓖ Ⓗ Ⓙ		44	Ⓕ Ⓖ Ⓗ Ⓙ		64	Ⓕ Ⓖ Ⓗ Ⓙ
5	Ⓐ Ⓑ Ⓒ Ⓓ		25	Ⓐ Ⓑ Ⓒ Ⓓ		45	Ⓐ Ⓑ Ⓒ Ⓓ		65	Ⓐ Ⓑ Ⓒ Ⓓ
6	Ⓕ Ⓖ Ⓗ Ⓙ		26	Ⓕ Ⓖ Ⓗ Ⓙ		46	Ⓕ Ⓖ Ⓗ Ⓙ		66	Ⓕ Ⓖ Ⓗ Ⓙ
7	Ⓐ Ⓑ Ⓒ Ⓓ		27	Ⓐ Ⓑ Ⓒ Ⓓ		47	Ⓐ Ⓑ Ⓒ Ⓓ		67	Ⓐ Ⓑ Ⓒ Ⓓ
8	Ⓕ Ⓖ Ⓗ Ⓙ		28	Ⓕ Ⓖ Ⓗ Ⓙ		48	Ⓕ Ⓖ Ⓗ Ⓙ		68	Ⓕ Ⓖ Ⓗ Ⓙ
9	Ⓐ Ⓑ Ⓒ Ⓓ		29	Ⓐ Ⓑ Ⓒ Ⓓ		49	Ⓐ Ⓑ Ⓒ Ⓓ		69	Ⓐ Ⓑ Ⓒ Ⓓ
10	Ⓕ Ⓖ Ⓗ Ⓙ		30	Ⓕ Ⓖ Ⓗ Ⓙ		50	Ⓕ Ⓖ Ⓗ Ⓙ		70	Ⓕ Ⓖ Ⓗ Ⓙ
11	Ⓐ Ⓑ Ⓒ Ⓓ		31	Ⓐ Ⓑ Ⓒ Ⓓ		51	Ⓐ Ⓑ Ⓒ Ⓓ		71	Ⓐ Ⓑ Ⓒ Ⓓ
12	Ⓕ Ⓖ Ⓗ Ⓙ		32	Ⓕ Ⓖ Ⓗ Ⓙ		52	Ⓕ Ⓖ Ⓗ Ⓙ		72	Ⓕ Ⓖ Ⓗ Ⓙ
13	Ⓐ Ⓑ Ⓒ Ⓓ		33	Ⓐ Ⓑ Ⓒ Ⓓ		53	Ⓐ Ⓑ Ⓒ Ⓓ		73	Ⓐ Ⓑ Ⓒ Ⓓ
14	Ⓕ Ⓖ Ⓗ Ⓙ		34	Ⓕ Ⓖ Ⓗ Ⓙ		54	Ⓕ Ⓖ Ⓗ Ⓙ		74	Ⓕ Ⓖ Ⓗ Ⓙ
15	Ⓐ Ⓑ Ⓒ Ⓓ		35	Ⓐ Ⓑ Ⓒ Ⓓ		55	Ⓐ Ⓑ Ⓒ Ⓓ		75	Ⓐ Ⓑ Ⓒ Ⓓ
16	Ⓕ Ⓖ Ⓗ Ⓙ		36	Ⓕ Ⓖ Ⓗ Ⓙ		56	Ⓕ Ⓖ Ⓗ Ⓙ		
17	Ⓐ Ⓑ Ⓒ Ⓓ		37	Ⓐ Ⓑ Ⓒ Ⓓ		57	Ⓐ Ⓑ Ⓒ Ⓓ		
18	Ⓕ Ⓖ Ⓗ Ⓙ		38	Ⓕ Ⓖ Ⓗ Ⓙ		58	Ⓕ Ⓖ Ⓗ Ⓙ		
19	Ⓐ Ⓑ Ⓒ Ⓓ		39	Ⓐ Ⓑ Ⓒ Ⓓ		59	Ⓐ Ⓑ Ⓒ Ⓓ		
20	Ⓕ Ⓖ Ⓗ Ⓙ		40	Ⓕ Ⓖ Ⓗ Ⓙ		60	Ⓕ Ⓖ Ⓗ Ⓙ		

MATHEMATICS

1	Ⓐ Ⓑ Ⓒ Ⓓ Ⓔ	16	Ⓕ Ⓖ Ⓗ Ⓙ Ⓚ	31	Ⓐ Ⓑ Ⓒ Ⓓ Ⓔ	46	Ⓕ Ⓖ Ⓗ Ⓙ Ⓚ
2	Ⓕ Ⓖ Ⓗ Ⓙ Ⓚ	17	Ⓐ Ⓑ Ⓒ Ⓓ Ⓔ	32	Ⓕ Ⓖ Ⓗ Ⓙ Ⓚ	47	Ⓐ Ⓑ Ⓒ Ⓓ Ⓔ
3	Ⓐ Ⓑ Ⓒ Ⓓ Ⓔ	18	Ⓕ Ⓖ Ⓗ Ⓙ Ⓚ	33	Ⓐ Ⓑ Ⓒ Ⓓ Ⓔ	48	Ⓕ Ⓖ Ⓗ Ⓙ Ⓚ
4	Ⓕ Ⓖ Ⓗ Ⓙ Ⓚ	19	Ⓐ Ⓑ Ⓒ Ⓓ Ⓔ	34	Ⓕ Ⓖ Ⓗ Ⓙ Ⓚ	49	Ⓐ Ⓑ Ⓒ Ⓓ Ⓔ
5	Ⓐ Ⓑ Ⓒ Ⓓ Ⓔ	20	Ⓕ Ⓖ Ⓗ Ⓙ Ⓚ	35	Ⓐ Ⓑ Ⓒ Ⓓ Ⓔ	50	Ⓕ Ⓖ Ⓗ Ⓙ Ⓚ
6	Ⓕ Ⓖ Ⓗ Ⓙ Ⓚ	21	Ⓐ Ⓑ Ⓒ Ⓓ Ⓔ	36	Ⓕ Ⓖ Ⓗ Ⓙ Ⓚ	51	Ⓐ Ⓑ Ⓒ Ⓓ Ⓔ
7	Ⓐ Ⓑ Ⓒ Ⓓ Ⓔ	22	Ⓕ Ⓖ Ⓗ Ⓙ Ⓚ	37	Ⓐ Ⓑ Ⓒ Ⓓ Ⓔ	52	Ⓕ Ⓖ Ⓗ Ⓙ Ⓚ
8	Ⓕ Ⓖ Ⓗ Ⓙ Ⓚ	23	Ⓐ Ⓑ Ⓒ Ⓓ Ⓔ	38	Ⓕ Ⓖ Ⓗ Ⓙ Ⓚ	53	Ⓐ Ⓑ Ⓒ Ⓓ Ⓔ
9	Ⓐ Ⓑ Ⓒ Ⓓ Ⓔ	24	Ⓕ Ⓖ Ⓗ Ⓙ Ⓚ	39	Ⓐ Ⓑ Ⓒ Ⓓ Ⓔ	54	Ⓕ Ⓖ Ⓗ Ⓙ Ⓚ
10	Ⓕ Ⓖ Ⓗ Ⓙ Ⓚ	25	Ⓐ Ⓑ Ⓒ Ⓓ Ⓔ	40	Ⓕ Ⓖ Ⓗ Ⓙ Ⓚ	55	Ⓐ Ⓑ Ⓒ Ⓓ Ⓔ
11	Ⓐ Ⓑ Ⓒ Ⓓ Ⓔ	26	Ⓕ Ⓖ Ⓗ Ⓙ Ⓚ	41	Ⓐ Ⓑ Ⓒ Ⓓ Ⓔ	56	Ⓕ Ⓖ Ⓗ Ⓙ Ⓚ
12	Ⓕ Ⓖ Ⓗ Ⓙ Ⓚ	27	Ⓐ Ⓑ Ⓒ Ⓓ Ⓔ	42	Ⓕ Ⓖ Ⓗ Ⓙ Ⓚ	57	Ⓐ Ⓑ Ⓒ Ⓓ Ⓔ
13	Ⓐ Ⓑ Ⓒ Ⓓ Ⓔ	28	Ⓕ Ⓖ Ⓗ Ⓙ Ⓚ	43	Ⓐ Ⓑ Ⓒ Ⓓ Ⓔ	58	Ⓕ Ⓖ Ⓗ Ⓙ Ⓚ
14	Ⓕ Ⓖ Ⓗ Ⓙ Ⓚ	29	Ⓐ Ⓑ Ⓒ Ⓓ Ⓔ	44	Ⓕ Ⓖ Ⓗ Ⓙ Ⓚ	59	Ⓐ Ⓑ Ⓒ Ⓓ Ⓔ
15	Ⓐ Ⓑ Ⓒ Ⓓ Ⓔ	30	Ⓕ Ⓖ Ⓗ Ⓙ Ⓚ	45	Ⓐ Ⓑ Ⓒ Ⓓ Ⓔ	60	Ⓕ Ⓖ Ⓗ Ⓙ Ⓚ

The Princeton Review
Diagnostic ACT Form

READING

1 (A) (B) (C) (D)	11 (A) (B) (C) (D)	21 (A) (B) (C) (D)	31 (A) (B) (C) (D)
2 (F) (G) (H) (J)	12 (F) (G) (H) (J)	22 (F) (G) (H) (J)	32 (F) (G) (H) (J)
3 (A) (B) (C) (D)	13 (A) (B) (C) (D)	23 (A) (B) (C) (D)	33 (A) (B) (C) (D)
4 (F) (G) (H) (J)	14 (F) (G) (H) (J)	24 (F) (G) (H) (J)	34 (F) (G) (H) (J)
5 (A) (B) (C) (D)	15 (A) (B) (C) (D)	25 (A) (B) (C) (D)	35 (A) (B) (C) (D)
6 (F) (G) (H) (J)	16 (F) (G) (H) (J)	26 (F) (G) (H) (J)	36 (F) (G) (H) (J)
7 (A) (B) (C) (D)	17 (A) (B) (C) (D)	27 (A) (B) (C) (D)	37 (A) (B) (C) (D)
8 (F) (G) (H) (J)	18 (F) (G) (H) (J)	28 (F) (G) (H) (J)	38 (F) (G) (H) (J)
9 (A) (B) (C) (D)	19 (A) (B) (C) (D)	29 (A) (B) (C) (D)	39 (A) (B) (C) (D)
10 (F) (G) (H) (J)	20 (F) (G) (H) (J)	30 (F) (G) (H) (J)	40 (F) (G) (H) (J)

SCIENCE REASONING

1 (A) (B) (C) (D)	11 (A) (B) (C) (D)	21 (A) (B) (C) (D)	31 (A) (B) (C) (D)
2 (F) (G) (H) (J)	12 (F) (G) (H) (J)	22 (F) (G) (H) (J)	32 (F) (G) (H) (J)
3 (A) (B) (C) (D)	13 (A) (B) (C) (D)	23 (A) (B) (C) (D)	33 (A) (B) (C) (D)
4 (F) (G) (H) (J)	14 (F) (G) (H) (J)	24 (F) (G) (H) (J)	34 (F) (G) (H) (J)
5 (A) (B) (C) (D)	15 (A) (B) (C) (D)	25 (A) (B) (C) (D)	35 (A) (B) (C) (D)
6 (F) (G) (H) (J)	16 (F) (G) (H) (J)	26 (F) (G) (H) (J)	36 (F) (G) (H) (J)
7 (A) (B) (C) (D)	17 (A) (B) (C) (D)	27 (A) (B) (C) (D)	37 (A) (B) (C) (D)
8 (F) (G) (H) (J)	18 (F) (G) (H) (J)	28 (F) (G) (H) (J)	38 (F) (G) (H) (J)
9 (A) (B) (C) (D)	19 (A) (B) (C) (D)	29 (A) (B) (C) (D)	39 (A) (B) (C) (D)
10 (F) (G) (H) (J)	20 (F) (G) (H) (J)	30 (F) (G) (H) (J)	40 (F) (G) (H) (J)

I hereby certify that I have truthfully identified myself on this form. I accept the consequences of falsifying my identity.

Your signature

Today's date

The Princeton Review
Diagnostic ACT Form

ESSAY

Begin your essay on this side. If necessary, continue on the opposite side.

Continue on the opposite side if necessary.

The Princeton Review
Diagnostic ACT Form

Continued from previous page.

The Princeton Review
Diagnostic ACT Form

Continued from previous page.

_____

The Princeton Review
Diagnostic ACT Form

Continued from previous page.

THIS PAGE INTENTIONALLY LEFT BLANK

ACT ENGLISH TEST
45 Minutes—75 Questions

DIRECTIONS: In the five passages that follow, certain words and phrases are underlined and numbered. In the right-hand column, you will find alternatives for each underlined part. In most cases, you are to choose the one that best expresses the idea, makes the statement appropriate for standard written English, or is worded most consistently with the style and tone of the passage as a whole. If you think the original version is best, choose "NO CHANGE." In some cases, you will find in the right-hand column a question about the underlined part. You are to choose the best answer to the question.

You will also find questions about a section of the passage or the passage as a whole. These questions do not refer to an underlined portion of the passage but rather are identified by a number or numbers in a box.

For each question, choose the alternative you consider best and blacken the corresponding oval on your answer document. Read each passage through once before you begin to answer the questions that accompany it. For many of the questions, you must read several sentences beyond the question to determine the answer. Be sure that you have read far enough ahead each time you choose an alternative.

PASSAGE I

Roast Done Right

Just like being the artist sculpting the Venus de Milo or
                    ‾‾‾‾‾‾‾‾‾‾‾‾‾
                          1
painting the Sistine Chapel, preparing a delicious meal is an art.

Even the seemingly mundane pot roast can be a true master-

piece. Nothing can be more rewarding to a cook than the sign of
                                                    ‾‾‾‾‾‾‾‾
                                                        2
a roast done right.

Cooking a delicious roast with vegetables require three
                                            ‾‾‾‾‾‾‾
                                               3
things: the freshest ingredients, a slow-cooker, and good

timing. My friend Eric goes to the butcher shop just after its
                            ‾‾‾‾‾‾‾‾‾‾‾‾‾‾‾‾‾‾‾‾‾‾‾‾‾‾
                                        4
5 a.m. delivery to snatch up the best cuts of meat, then heads

to the local farmer's market. He fills his canvas shopping bag

with ripe red tomatoes, crisp yellow onions, and thick russet

potatoes. The tastiest vegetables are the results of natural

sunshine and of a farmer's careful tending.
‾‾‾‾‾‾‾‾‾‾‾‾‾‾‾‾‾‾‾‾‾‾‾‾‾
            5

With supplies in tote, Eric heads to the kitchen. While

the beef marinates in garlic and spices, he chops the colorful

1. **A.** NO CHANGE
  B. the artist
  C. one
  D. DELETE the underlined portion.

2. The writer would like to convey the distinct scent of a properly cooked roast. Given that all the choices are true, which best accomplishes the writer's goal?

  F. NO CHANGE
  G. the swirling rush of robust aromas
  H. the fine textures of vegetables and meats
  J. the diners' eager expectation

3. **A.** NO CHANGE
  B. has the requirements of
  C. requiring
  D. requires

4. Which of the following would be the LEAST acceptable alternative for the underlined portion?

  F. out to the butcher shop right before
  G. into the butcher shop just around
  H. at the butcher shop right after
  J. to the butcher shop close to

5. **A.** NO CHANGE
  B. sunshine, of which a farmer is
  C. sunshine, and a farmer is
  D. sunshine, which is a farmer's

GO ON TO THE NEXT PAGE.

array of fresh vegetables. Eric slowly places the vegetables
₆

around the meat in the slow-cooker's pot, he alternates rings of
₇
bright orange carrots and chunks of red potatoes. He sprinkles

in sliced onions and herbs until the ingredients nearly spill

over the top. Like with many cooks, Eric has a secret, final
₈
ingredient: a splash of red wine for flavor.

At this point, it's time to cram the lid onto the heaping
₉
potful of ingredients and turn on the cooker. The temperature

inside the pot rises slowly as the contents stew in their natural
₁₀
juices. The roast will take six to eight hours to cook, but after

an hour or two, the first spicy scents start wafting through the
₁₁
kitchen. A few hours later, the rich, juicy smell of beef begins

to escape. Every half hour, using a long, meat thermometer
₁₂
Eric reads the temperature of the roast and carefully examines

the stewing contents. He doesn't want it overcooked or

6. The writer wishes to emphasize Eric's attention to detail
in making his pot roast. Given that all the choices are true,
which one best accomplishes the writer's goal?

   F. NO CHANGE
   G. is very careful when pouring the vegetables
   H. meticulously layers the finely cut vegetables
   J. arranges the vegetables in a kind of order

7. **A.** NO CHANGE
   B. he has alternated
   C. alternates
   D. alternating

8. **F.** NO CHANGE
   G. Like many
   H. As most
   J. As many do

9. Which of the following alternatives to the underlined portion would be LEAST acceptable?

   A. Next,
   B. After that,
   C. Now,
   D. At least,

10. Given that all the choices are true, which one provides the
most specific sensory detail and maintains the style and
tone of the essay?

   F. NO CHANGE
   G. rises slowly but surely, stewing
   H. rises slowly to a lazy, bubbling boil, stewing the savory
contents
   J. increases to about 200 degrees Fahrenheit to stew the
contents

11. **A.** NO CHANGE
   B. drifting through the air to make the whole kitchen
smell.
   C. wafting and floating through the whole kitchen.
   D. wafting through the air of the kitchen.

12. **F.** NO CHANGE
   G. half hour, using a long meat thermometer,
   H. half hour using a long meat thermometer
   J. half hour, using a long, meat thermometer;

GO ON TO THE NEXT PAGE.

undercooked, but "just right." [13]

<u>Lift the finished roast</u> out of the pot to serve, the tender
14
meat plops juicily onto our plates in generous servings. He tops

it off with zesty, steaming vegetables. Eric is obviously proud

to share his work of art, and his friends are more than willing to

eat it, <u>this masterpiece of his.</u>
15

13. The writer is considering deleting the preceding sentence. Should it be kept or deleted?

    A. Kept, because it provides a reason for Eric's diligent attention to the temperature.

    B. Kept, because it reinforces that roasts are typically done cooking after 8 hours.

    C. Deleted, because it puts the focus on Eric and his cooking, rather than the roast.

    D. Deleted, because it doesn't provide enough information about temperature's effects on the roast.

14. F. NO CHANGE

    G. As he lifts the finished roast

    H. When you lift the finished roast

    J. Lifting the finished roast

15. A. NO CHANGE

    B. ready for us to eat.

    C. a masterpiece.

    D. DELETE the underlined portion, replacing the comma with a period after "it."

PASSAGE II

Growing Up On a Farm

    Back in middle school, I went to live with my mother for

two years on her farm. Whenever people hear that I lived on a

farm, they immediately conjure up an image <u>visualized in their</u>
16
<u>minds</u> of dairy cows, tractors, hay, and overalls. Nothing could
16
be further from the truth.

    <u>To start,</u> I wasn't on the kind of farm everyone imagines. I
17

didn't feed cows <u>or pigs;</u> I didn't grow corn or wheat. I helped
18
my mother breed llamas.

    [1] It is odd that such non-traditional livestock should

be raised on a long-established farm such as ours, which has

16. F. NO CHANGE

    G. assuming that they know what it was like

    H. of my life on the farm that consists

    J. DELETE the underlined portion.

17. Which of the following alternatives to the underlined portion would NOT be acceptable?

    A. First of all,

    B. To begin,

    C. For start,

    D. Firstly,

18. F. NO CHANGE

    G. or, pigs

    H. or pigs,

    J. or pigs

GO ON TO THE NEXT PAGE.

been in the family for generations. [19] [2] Our family did indeed grow field crops, harvest orchards, and raise traditional

19. The writer is considering deleting the phrase "which has been in the family for generations" (and ending the sentence with a period) from the preceding sentence. If the writer were to make this change, the essay would primarily lose:

   A. evidence of a broken relationship between the narrator and his mother.

   B. a transition into the discussion of traditional farm practices.

   C. a detail that reinforces the longevity of the family farm.

   D. an indication of what will eventually happen to the narrator.

livestock for many decades. [3] He must of learned that wool from llamas was more profitable than wool from sheep. [4] The

20. **F.** NO CHANGE
   G. of learned of
   H. have learned that
   J. have learned about

llama wool business turned out to be so successful in fact, that my great-grandfather converted the family business to a full-

21. **A.** NO CHANGE
   B. successful, in fact, that
   C. successful, in fact that
   D. successful in fact that

fledged llama farm. [22]

22. Upon reviewing this paragraph and realizing that some information has been left out, the writer composes the following sentence:

> Then, fifty years ago, my great-grandfather decided to buy a llama.

This sentence should most logically be placed after Sentence:

   F. 1.
   G. 2.
   H. 3.
   J. 4.

Before I began to live on the farm, I had held naive illusions of rural life. What could possibly be easier than

23. Which of the following alternatives to the underlined portion would NOT be acceptable?

   A. started to live
   B. began living
   C. went to live
   D. begun to live

feeding and grooming some animals? After I had settled into my new home, however, I realized that farm work was much more

24. Which of the following alternatives to the underlined portion would NOT be acceptable?

   F. As soon as I
   G. When I
   H. Once I
   J. I

GO ON TO THE NEXT PAGE.

involved than I had expected. Collecting manure, for example,
doesn't seem so bad when someone else does it on TV, but I
had to get up before dawn every day to finish that chore before
catching the bus to school.

    School in the country was also not what I had expected.
The school I attended had twenty students total: that's from
first to twelfth grade, and I was the only student in my grade.

We had one teacher who would occasionally educate us on a
specific academic study and methods of learning, but most of

my learning came from studying textbooks on my own.

    I don't mean to say that my life on the farm was a bad
experience. I learned a lot about myself: for example, I'm not

a morning person. I also learned about llama's habits, such as
spitting when they are unhappy. Most importantly, my mother
and I got to spend a lot of time together during those years, for

which I'm so grateful. Although I doubt I'll pursue a career as
farming, I look forward to returning to the family farm for short
visits.

25. **A.** NO CHANGE
    B. would expect.
    C. would be expecting.
    D. have expected.

26. Given that all the choices are true, which one most
effectively introduces the information that follows in this
paragraph?
    F. NO CHANGE
    G. Farming is a full-time job, taking up your entire day.
    H. Llamas can grow to be six feet tall.
    J. Life on the farm was tough but worthwhile.

27. **A.** NO CHANGE
    B. verbally acknowledge how well the class was working
for us,
    C. tell us how to learn about a specific academic study,
    D. lecture about a specific topic,

28. Which choice provides the most specific and precise information?
    F. NO CHANGE
    G. studying.
    H. other things.
    J. reading by myself.

29. **A.** NO CHANGE
    B. llamas' habits,
    C. llamas habits
    D. llamas habits,

30. **F.** NO CHANGE
    G. career of
    H. career in
    J. careers of

GO ON TO THE NEXT PAGE.

PASSAGE III

> The following paragraphs may or may not be in the most logical order. Each paragraph is numbered in brackets, and question 45 will ask you to choose where Paragraph 2 should most logically be placed.

Conjuring a Prophetic Literary Career

[1]

Born in Ohio in 1858, Charles W. Chesnutt was an author and essayist whom, during the Reconstruction era, spent much
₃₁
of his youth in North Carolina. Though his parents were free African-Americans, Chesnutt felt intensely the struggles of African-Americans in the United States in the period directly after the Civil War. [32] Amid all the turmoil of the South of his

31. A. NO CHANGE
  B. who,
  C. which,
  D. DELETE the underlined portion.

32. If the writer were to delete the last part of the preceding sentence (ending the sentence with a period after the word *States*), the paragraph would primarily lose:

  F. a direct link to the following paragraph.
  G. an unnecessary digression into historical details.
  H. an important detail about the period of Chesnutt's youth.
  J. a fact suggesting the extent of Chesnutt's historical writing.

boyhood, Chesnutt took solace in literature, and he had already
₃₃
decided, in his teens, that he would become a writer.

33. Which of the following alternatives to the underlined portion would NOT be acceptable?

  A. literature; he
  B. literature, and he consequently
  C. literature, he
  D. literature. He

[2]

Although Chesnutt continues to write until his death in
₃₄

34. F. NO CHANGE
  G. has continued
  H. still continues
  J. continued

1932, it had become as clear as day that the work he completed
₃₅
after *The House Behind the Cedars* and *The Marrow of Tradition* (1901) had become too inflammatory to a society ever uneasy about the topic of race relations in the United States, particularly when authors had brought these problems as close to the surface as Chesnutt had. In recent years, however, Chesnutt's reputation has been restored and he has been treated as the pioneer that he most certainly was. Today as much as in the late nineteenth century, Chesnutt's works provide us with a

35. A. NO CHANGE
  B. so extremely clear
  C. clear
  D. clear to an incredible degree

GO ON TO THE NEXT PAGE.

number of literary masterpieces and a powerful and prophetic
vision of race relations in the United States.

[3]

"The Goophered Grapevine," published in 1887 in *The
Atlantic*, was Chesnutt's first major literary success, and
this success encouraged Chesnutt to publish additional tales,
which were eventually collected in *The Conjure Woman*
(1899). *The Conjure Woman* was written in the tradition of
earlier folklorists from a previous era Joel Chandler Harris
                              36

36. F. NO CHANGE
G. from a previous time
H. from the years before
J. DELETE the underlined portion.

and Thomas Nelson Page. However, it presented a much
                          37
more frank treatment of race relations in the South during

37. A. NO CHANGE
B. Page, however,
C. Page. Consequently,
D. Page, consequently,

slavery and Reconstruction. [38] *The Conjure Woman* and

38. At this point, the writer is considering adding the following true statement:

> The slaves were freed with the Emancipation Procla-
> mation in 1862, but many conditions like those under
> slavery resurfaced after the collapse of Reconstruction
> efforts in 1877.

Should the writer add the sentence here?

F. Yes, because it shows how many of the gains made by
ex-slaves were later taken away.
G. Yes, because it is necessary to understand Chestnutt's
motivation.
H. No, because it provides information that is detailed
later in this essay.
J. No, because it would distract readers from the essay's
main focus.

it's narrator, Uncle Julius McAdoo, were clearly written in
 39
response to the immensely popular Uncle Remus of Harris's
tales, but the similarities between the two authors' works ended

39. A. NO CHANGE
B. their
C. its
D. its'

GO ON TO THE NEXT PAGE.

there. While Harris's tales used mostly animals and not voodoo,
conjure, and the injustices of slavery, which *The Conjure*
Woman did, also incorporating human characters instead of Brer
Rabbit and animals.

[4]

Chesnutt's true masterpiece, however, is *The House Behind*
the Cedars. The novel details the lives of an African-American

familys children who have chosen to "pass" as white, making
The House Behind the Cedars one of the first novels to talk

about racial passing. Chesnutt uses his characters' divided
status to travel back and forth between the black and white
worlds of the South, and in the process, Chesnutt manages to
show both the shocking disparity between the two worlds and
the insurmountable difficulties his characters, and those who
"pass" in real life, face. From the moment it was published in
1900, the novel was a sensation in American letters, garnering
the respect and admiration of such prominent white literary
critics as William Dean Howells and black intellectuals such as
W.E.B. Dubois.

40. Which choice provides the most logical arrangement of the
parts of this sentence?

F. NO CHANGE

G. Humans were used as characters by *The Conjure Wom-*
an and participated in tales relating to conjure, and the
injustice of slavery and voodoo, which was different
from Brer Rabbit and the animals from Harris's tales.

H. Conjure, voodoo, and the injustices of slavery and others were used by *The Conjure Woman*, along with real
human characters instead of animals and Brer Rabbit
from Harris's tales.

J. In the place of Brer Rabbit and the animals from Harris's tales, *The Conjure Woman* used human characters
in stories that incorporated conjure, voodoo, and the
injustices of slavery.

41. A. NO CHANGE
B. families
C. family's
D. families's

42. F. NO CHANGE
G. it.
H. them.
J. its topics.

43. Which of the following alternatives to the underlined portion would NOT be acceptable?

A. From the moment of its publication in 1900,
B. Having been first published in 1900,
C. Publishing it first in 1900,
D. In 1900, the year of its initial publication,

GO ON TO THE NEXT PAGE.

[5]

Author and essayist, Charles W. Chesnutt published two
books, *The Conjure Woman* and *The House Behind the Cedars*,
that were widely appreciated in his own time.
⁴⁴

44. Given that all the choices are true, which one most effectively concludes and summarizes this essay?

F. NO CHANGE
G. Both author and essayist, Charles W. Chesnutt was a
pioneer in African-American literature whose novels
and tales are as meaningful today as they were when
first published.
H. Author of *The House Behind the Cedars*, Charles W.
Chesnutt already knew he wanted to be a writer in his
teens during the era of Reconstruction in the history of
the United States.
J. Author of *The Conjure Woman*, Charles W. Chesnutt
succeeded where earlier writers Joel Chandler Harris
and Thomas Nelson Page had failed in representing
the characters in their stories as people.

> **Question 45 asks about the preceding passage as a
> whole.**

45. For the sake of the logic and coherence of this essay, Paragraph
2 should be placed:

A. where it is now.
B. before Paragraph 1.
C. after Paragraph 3.
D. after Paragraph 4.

PASSAGE IV

Jackie Robinson: More Than a Ballplayer

When baseball resumes in America every spring, one April
day is always reserved to honor Jackie Robinson, the man who
broke the color barrier of America's national pastime. While
his accomplishments on the baseball field was numerous and
⁴⁶

46. **F.** NO CHANGE
G. is
H. will be
J. were

impressive, his civil rights activism was according to his widow
⁴⁷
Rachel Robinson, equally important and often overlooked

47. **A.** NO CHANGE
B. was, according,
C. was, according
D. was—according

without being noticed.
⁴⁸

48. **F.** NO CHANGE
G. while not being noticed.
H. as no one notices.
J. DELETE the underlined portion and end the sentence
with a period.

GO ON TO THE NEXT PAGE.

The tenacious and spirited way for the Brooklyn Dodgers
Jackie Robinson played baseball was a reflection of his focus
on civil rights. From the outset of the "Great Experiment"

of having African-Americans in baseball; he knew that his
performance on the field would be a determining factor in
sports segregation. Jackie gradually converted jeers and

harassment into cheers and acceptance because white spectators
could see his immense talent from any seat in the stadium.
Jackie became a highly respected figure by continually
succeeding on and off the field, all the while displaying stoic

restraint in the face of initial prejudice. 52

[1] The vast amount of energy Jackie expended avoiding
a myriad of potential pitfalls could have caused an ordinary

man to wilt; for example, Jackie instinctively and relentlessly
increased his efforts for positive civil rights changes, both in his
sport and in the African-American community at large.

[2] While many athletes today use their status to garner endorse-
ments and live as celebrities, Jackie constantly utilized his

49. The best placement for the underlined portion would be:
   A. where it is now.
   B. after the word *baseball.*
   C. after the word *focus.*
   D. after the word *rights.*

50. F. NO CHANGE
   G. baseball, and he
   H. baseball. He
   J. baseball, he

51. Which choice fits most specifically with the information at
   the end of this sentence?
   A. NO CHANGE
   B. people
   C. popcorn vendors
   D. pitchers

52. If the writer were to delete this paragraph from the essay,
   which of the following would be lost?
   F. A scientific explanation of the "Great Experiment"
   G. A description of the way Jackie influenced society's
      outlook on segregation in baseball
   H. A passionate plea to end prejudice around the world
   J. A comment on why the Brooklyn Dodgers were the
      best team in baseball

53. A. NO CHANGE
   B. as a result,
   C. rather,
   D. therefore,

54. F. NO CHANGE
   G. his
   H. its
   J. theirs

GO ON TO THE NEXT PAGE.

status to stimulate civil rights advancements. [55] [3] He often used his baseball travels as opportunities to speak publicly to blacks in U.S. cities about ending segregation and vigilantly defending their rights. [4] Post-baseball, Jackie became an

entrepreneur, but his focus did not stray as he found time to
56
write impassioned letters and telegrams to various U.S. presidents during the civil rights movement. [5] He had the status to demand that they too remain firmly focused on civil rights measures. [57]

Though Jackie Robinson's baseball exploits may be most widely known than his tireless efforts in the civil rights
58

movement his astonishing courage on the baseball field was it-
59
self a resounding stance against segregation and inequality. His numerous detractors consistently found that not only was Jackie undeterred, but he was excelling in his efforts. As a result, the
60
spark of positive change was ignited. Jackie turned that spark for civil rights into a torch and carried it his entire life.

55. The writer is considering deleting the preceding sentence. Should this sentence be kept or deleted?
   A. Kept, because it describes important information about Jackie Robinson's endorsement deals.
   B. Kept, because it helps the reader understand how Jackie Robinson sacrificed personal advancement in favor of civil rights work.
   C. Deleted, because it doesn't provide exact details about the civil rights laws that Jackie Robinson enacted.
   D. Deleted, because it draws focus toward other athletes and away from Jackie Robinson.

56. F. NO CHANGE
   G. entrepreneur,
   H. entrepreneur
   J. entrepreneur; and

57. If the writer were to divide the preceding paragraph into two shorter paragraphs in order to differentiate between Jackie's civil rights activism during and after his baseball career, the new paragraph should begin with Sentence:
   A. 2.
   B. 3.
   C. 4.
   D. 5.

58. F. NO CHANGE
   G. very widely known
   H. more widely known
   J. widelier known

59. A. NO CHANGE
   B. movement. His
   C. movement; his
   D. movement, his

60. Which of the following alternatives to the underlined portion would be LEAST acceptable?
   F. Consequently,
   G. Instead,
   H. Thus,
   J. Therefore,

GO ON TO THE NEXT PAGE.

PASSAGE V

Antarctica's Adaptable Survivors

Many inhabit sporadic green <u>patches of moss;</u> fertilized
₆₁
by excrement from migrating birds and sheltered by the

rocky mountainsides. Some hibernate in the winter, frozen

in ice under rocks and <u>stones, becoming active</u> again when
₆₂

the climate warms and the ice <u>is melting.</u> Extreme cold
₆₃

and wind are <u>all good to go for survival;</u> indeed, some
₆₄
species are able to endure temperatures as low as –30

degrees Celsius. These adaptable <u>invertebrates classified as</u>
₆₅
<u>arthropods;</u> are able to survive on a continent once thought
₆₅

<u>to arctic, to windy, and to icy,</u> to maintain any permanent
₆₆
land animals. The coldest place on earth, Antarctica is home

to great quantities of life that don't simply tolerate the lower

<u>temperatures; they</u> flourish in them.
₆₇

Microscopic mites, springtails, and wingless midges

<u>accompanied</u> lice and ticks as the most prevalent permanent
₆₈
land fauna on Antarctica. The tiny midges and mites tolerate

the cold due to the antifreeze liquid they carry in their bodies.

Parasitic lice and ticks seek shelter from the harsh climate in the

61. A. NO CHANGE
   B. patches, of moss
   C. patches, of moss,
   D. patches of moss

62. Which of the following options to the underlined portion
would NOT be acceptable?

   F. stones, only to become active
   G. stones. Becoming active
   H. stones. Then they become active
   J. stones and then become active

63. A. NO CHANGE
   B. melting.
   C. melts.
   D. to melt.

64. F. NO CHANGE
   G. cool for survival;
   H. all right for survival;
   J. suitable for survival;

65. A. NO CHANGE
   B. invertebrates, classified as arthropods
   C. invertebrates, classified as arthropods,
   D. invertebrates classified as arthropods,

66. F. NO CHANGE
   G. to arctic, to windy, and to icy
   H. too arctic, too windy, and too icy
   J. too, arctic, too windy, and too icy,

67. Which of the following options to the underlined portion
would NOT be acceptable?

   A. temperatures they
   B. temperatures; in fact, they
   C. temperatures. They
   D. temperatures—they

68. F. NO CHANGE
   G. accompany
   H. had accompanied
   J. were accompanying

GO ON TO THE NEXT PAGE.

warm fur of seals, the waters of Antarctica teeming with marine
life, and the feathers of sea birds and penguins.

    In the Dry Valleys located on the western coast of McMurdo
Sound in Antarctica, nematode worms feed on bacteria, algae,
and tiny organisms known as rotifers and tardigrades. ☐70 Here,

ice-covered land is not as abundant. Beneath the
moss-covered polar rock, nematodes thrive, coping ingeniously

by dehydrating themselves in the winter with the low
temperatures and coming back to life with the summer and
increasing moisture.

69. A. NO CHANGE
B. seals, who return to land to breed,
C. seals, six different types in all,
D. seals

70. The writer is considering deleting the following phrase from the previous sentence (and adjusting the capitalization accordingly):

    In the Dry Valleys located on the western coast of McMurdo Sound in Antarctica,

Should this phrase be kept or deleted?

F. Deleted, because this fact is presented later in this paragraph.
G. Deleted, because it negates the preceding paragraph, which makes it clear that only insects live in Antarctica.
H. Kept, because it clarifies that nematodes live both in Antarctica and McMurdo Sound.
J. Kept, because it gives specific details about the "Here" mentioned in the subsequent sentence.

71. Given that all the choices are true, which one most explicitly and vividly describes the terrain of McMurdo Sound?

A. NO CHANGE
B. rocky land is colored vibrantly by green, yellow, and orange lichen, algae, and moss.
C. there are signs that this is a place with extremely low humidity and no snow cover.
D. the effects of low humidity are apparent in the presence of flora and orange lichen.

72. The best place for the underlined portion would be:

F. where it is now.
G. after the word *thrive*.
H. after the word *coping*.
J. after the word *moisture*.

GO ON TO THE NEXT PAGE.

Algae are another resilient life form of the Dry Valleys
[73]
of Antarctica. In an effort to adjust to the strong winds and icy
[73]
temperatures, some algae live inside the rocks as opposed to on
top of them. Phytoplankton, the most common of Antarctica's
algae, is an important food resource within Antarctica's
ecosystem. These tiny free-floating plants are preyed upon
by copepods and krill, which then provide food for fish, seals,

whales, and penguins. [74]

73. Given that all the choices are true, which one would
LEAST effectively introduce the subject of this paragraph?

  A. NO CHANGE
  B. Algae lack the various structures that characterize land
plants, such as the moss and lichen that inhabit Antarctica, which is why algae are most prominent in bodies
of water.
  C. Algae are typically autotrophic organisms whose adaptive qualities enable them to live successfully in the
Dry McMurdo Valleys.
  D. Although most often found in water, algae also inhabit
terrestrial environments such as the Dry Valleys of
Antarctica.

74. The writer is considering deleting the following phrase
from the preceding sentence:

    which then provide food for fish, seals, whales, and
    penguins.

Should this clause be kept or deleted?

  F. Kept, because it clarifies how phytoplankton support
Antarctica's ecosystem.
  G. Kept, because it addresses the most important life
forms in Antarctica's waters: seals, penguins, and
whales.
  H. Deleted, because it is irrelevant to the passage as a
whole, which addresses the smaller life forms living
on Antarctica.
  J. Deleted, because it misleads the reader into thinking
that penguins, seals, and whales are among the permanent land dwelling life forms of Antarctica.

Excluding its aquatic life, Antarctica has a lower species diversity than any other place on earth. Nevertheless, Antarctica is
[75]
a haven for 67 documented species of insects and 350 species of
flora, proof that life persists in the most dramatic of conditions.

75. A. NO CHANGE
  B. Indeed,
  C. Consequently,
  D. Therefore,

END OF TEST 1
STOP! DO NOT TURN THE PAGE UNTIL TOLD TO DO SO.

MATHEMATICS TEST
60 Minutes—60 Questions

DIRECTIONS: Solve each problem, choose the correct answer, and then darken the corresponding oval on your answer document.

Do not linger over problems that take too much time. Solve as many as you can; then return to the others in the time you have left for this test.

You are permitted to use a calculator on this test. You may use your calculator for any problems you choose, but some of the problems may best be done without using a calculator.

Note: Unless otherwise stated, all of the following should be assumed:

1. Illustrative figures are NOT necessarily drawn to scale.
2. Geometric figures lie in a plane.
3. The word *line* indicates a straight line.
4. The word *average* indicates arithmetic mean.

DO YOUR FIGURING HERE.

1. $|8-5|-|5-8| = ?$

   A. -6
   B. -5
   C. -3
   D. 0
   E. 6

2. A science tutor charges $60 an hour to help students with biology homework. She also charges a flat fee of $40 to cover her transportation costs. How many hours of tutoring are included in a session that costs $220 ?

   F. $2\frac{1}{5}$
   G. 3
   H. $3\frac{2}{3}$
   J. 4
   K. $5\frac{1}{2}$

3. Train A averages 16 miles per hour, and Train B averages 24 miles per hour. At these rates, how many more hours does it take Train A than Train B to go 1,152 miles?

   A. 20
   B. 24
   C. 40
   D. 48
   E. 72

4. $33r^2 - 24r + 75 - 41r^2 + r$ is equivalent to:

   F. $44r^2$
   G. $44r^6$
   H. $-8r^2 - 24r + 75$
   J. $-8r^4 - 23r^2 + 75$
   K. $-8r^2 - 23r + 75$

GO ON TO THE NEXT PAGE.

5. Six equilateral triangles form the figure below. If the perimeter of each individual triangle is 15 inches, what is the perimeter of *ABCDEF*, in inches?

A. 18

B. 30

C. 60

D. $54\sqrt{3}$

E. 90

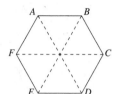

DO YOUR FIGURING HERE.

6. The expression $(5x + 2)(x - 3)$ is equivalent to:

F. $5x^2 + 13x - 6$
G. $5x^2 - 13x - 6$
H. $5x^2 - 4x + 5$
J. $5x^2 - 6$
K. $5x^2 - 5$

7. If 35% of a given number is 14, then what is 20% of the given number?

A. 2.8
B. 4.9
C. 7.0
D. 7.7
E. 8.0

8. The 7 consecutive integers below add up to 511,
$x - 2, x - 1, x, x + 1, x + 2, x + 3$, and $x + 4$.
What is the value of x ?

F. 71
G. 72
H. 73
J. 74
K. 75

9. In the standard (x,y) coordinate plane, point B with coordinates of (5,6) is the midpoint of line $\overline{AC}$, and point A has coordinates at (9,4).What are the coordinates of C ?

A. (13, 2)
B. (7, 5)
C. (1, 8)
D. (14,10)
E. (−1,−8)

GO ON TO THE NEXT PAGE.

10. Isosceles trapezoid *ABCD*, with equal sides $\overline{AB}$ and $\overline{CD}$, has vertices *A* (3,0), *B* (6,6), and *D* (15,0). These vertices are graphed below in the standard (*x,y*) coordinate plane below. What are the coordinates of one possible vertex *C* ?

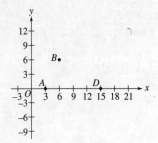

F. (11,7)
G. (13,6)
H. (12,6)
J. (13,5)
K. (12,7)

11. The town of Ashville has three bus stations (A, B, and C) that offer round-trip fares to its business district at both peak and off-peak rates. The matrices below show the average weekly sales for each station at each rate and the costs for both rates. In an average week, what are the combined peak and off-peak sales for Ashville's three bus stations?

	Peak	Off-peak
A	180	60
B	200	120
C	150	70

	Cost
Peak	$3
Off-peak	$2

A. $ 780
B. $1,590
C. $1,950
D. $2,090
E. $2,340

GO ON TO THE NEXT PAGE.

12. The triangle shown below has exterior angles a, b, and c.
What is the sum of those angles?

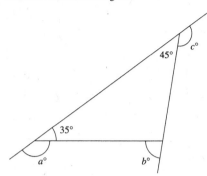

F. 360°
G. 315°
H. 225°
J. 180°
K. Cannot be determined from the information given

Use the following information to answer questions
13–15.

A sample of 300 jellybeans was removed from a barrel of jellybeans. All of the jellybeans in the barrel are one of four colors:
red, orange, green, and purple. For the sample, the number of
jellybeans of each color is shown in the table below.

Color	Number of jellybeans
red	75
orange	120
green	60
purple	45

13. What percent of the jellybeans in the sample are green?

A. 15%
B. 20%
C. 25%
D. 40%
E. 60%

GO ON TO THE NEXT PAGE.

DO YOUR FIGURING HERE.

14. The sample of jellybeans was removed from a barrel containing 25,000 jellybeans. If the sample is indicative of the color distribution in the barrel, which of the following is the best estimate of the number of red jellybeans in the barrel?

F. 3,750
G. 5,000
H. 6,250
J. 10,000
K. 18,750

15. If the information in the table were converted into a circle graph (pie chart), then the central angle of the sector for orange jellybeans would measure how many degrees?

A. 54°
B. 72°
C. 90°
D. 120°
E. 144°

16. In rectangle *ABCD* shown below, *E* is the midpoint of $\overline{BC}$, and *F* is the midpoint of $\overline{AD}$. Which of the following is the ratio of the area of quadrilateral *AECF* to the area of the entire rectangle?

F. 1:1
G. 1:2
H. 1:3
J. 1:4
K. 2:5

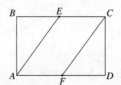

17. In the standard (*x,y*) coordinate plane, what is the slope of the line parallel to the line $y = \frac{1}{2}x - 3$?

A. −3

B. −2

C. $-\frac{1}{2}$

D. $\frac{1}{2}$

E. 2

GO ON TO THE NEXT PAGE.

18. Aru watches a movie that is 120 minutes long in 2 sittings. The ratio of the 2 sitting times is 3:5. What is the length, in minutes, of the longer sitting?

    F.   8
    G. 15
    H. 45
    J.   60
    K. 75

DO YOUR FIGURING HERE.

19. Which of the following could be a value of x if $11 < x < 12$?

    A. $\sqrt{23}$
    B. $\sqrt{121}$
    C. $\sqrt{140}$
    D. $\sqrt{145}$
    E. $\sqrt{529}$

20. Susan is planning the layout of her garden. She wants to plant tomatoes in 3 plots, each 10 feet by 16 feet. Within the total area, she will leave a 4-foot-by-6-foot rectangular plot for beans, and a $2\frac{1}{2}$-foot-by-5-foot rectangular plot for lettuce. If each packet of tomato seeds will cover between 150 and 200 square feet of soil, which of the following is the minimum number of packets of seeds Susan needs to buy to plant tomatoes?

    F. 5
    G. 4
    H. 3
    J. 2
    K. 1

21. What values of x are solutions in the equation $x^2 + 4x = 12$?

    A.   8 and 12
    B.   0 and 4
    C. −2 and 6
    D. −4 and 0
    E. −6 and 2

GO ON TO THE NEXT PAGE.

22. For all $xy \neq 0$, and when both x and y are greater than 1, the expression $\dfrac{x^4 y^2}{x^2 y^4}$ equals which of the following?

DO YOUR FIGURING HERE.

F. $-\dfrac{x^2}{y^2}$

G. $-\dfrac{y^2}{x^2}$

H. 1

J. $\dfrac{x^2}{y^2}$

K. $\dfrac{y^2}{x^2}$

23. If point A has a non-zero x-coordinate and a non-zero y-coordinate and at least one of these coordinate values is positive, then point A *must* be located in which of the 4 quadrants labeled below?

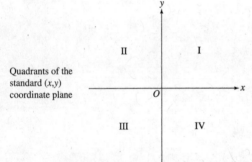

Quadrants of the standard (x,y) coordinate plane

A. I only
B. I or II only
C. II or IV only
D. II, III, or IV only
E. I, II, or IV only

24. The variable cost to produce a box of paper is $4.75. The fixed cost for the paper production machinery is $1,600.00 each day. Which of the following expressions correctly models the cost of producing b boxes of paper each day?

F. $1,600b + 4.75$
G. $1,600b - 4.75$
H. $1,600 + 4.75b$
J. $4.75b - 1600$
K. $1,600b$

GO ON TO THE NEXT PAGE.

25. In the figure below, where $\triangle ABC \sim \triangle XYZ$, lengths are given in inches and the perimeter of $\triangle ABC$ is 576 inches. What is the length, in inches, of $\overline{AC}$?

(Note: The symbol ~ means "is similar to.")

DO YOUR FIGURING HERE.

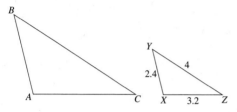

A. $126\dfrac{2}{5}$

B. 144

C. $168\dfrac{1}{5}$

D. 192

E. 240

26. Given that $\dfrac{\sqrt{11}}{x} \times \dfrac{6}{\sqrt{11}} = \dfrac{3\sqrt{11}}{11}$, what is the value of x ?

F. 6

G. 11

H. 121

J. $\sqrt{11}$

K. $2\sqrt{11}$

27. Natalie starts at the finish line of a straight 1,300-foot track and runs to the left toward the starting line at a constant rate of 12 feet per second. Jonathon starts 150 feet to the right of the starting line and runs to the right toward the finish line at a constant rate of 9 feet per second. To the nearest tenth of a second, after how many seconds will Natalie and Jonathon be at the same point on the track?

A. 483.3
B. 383.3
C. 63.7
D. 54.8
E. 10.9

GO ON TO THE NEXT PAGE.

28. Steve is going to buy an ice-cream sundae. He first must choose 1 of 3 possible ice-cream flavors. Next, he must choose 1 of 2 types of syrup. Finally, he must choose 1 of 6 kinds of candy toppings. Given these conditions, how many different kinds of sundaes could Steve possibly order?

    F.   162
    G.   36
    H.   18
    J.   9
    K.   6

DO YOUR FIGURING HERE.

29. The width of a rectangular cardboard box is half its length and twice its height. If the box is 12 cm long, what is the volume of the box in cubic centimeters?

    A.   72
    B.   216
    C.   252
    D.   1,296
    E.   1,728

30. At the end of each month, a credit card company uses the formula $D = B(1 + r) + 10m^2$ to calculate debt owed, where D is the cardholder's total debt; B is the amount charged to the card; r is the rate of interest; and m is the number of payments the cardholder has previously missed. If Daniel has charged $2,155 to his credit card with a 13% interest rate and has missed 2 payments, which value is closest to Daniel's total credit card debt?

    F. $2,195
    G. $2,435
    H. $2,455
    J. $2,475
    K. $2,495

GO ON TO THE NEXT PAGE.

31. In the figure below, a cone is shown, with dimensions given in centimeters. What is the total surface area of this cone, in square centimeters? (Note: The total surface area of a cone is given by the expression $\pi r^2 + \pi rs$, where r is the radius and s is the slant height.)

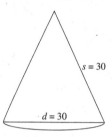

$s = 30$

$d = 30$

- **A.** 225π
- **B.** 450π
- **C.** 465π
- **D.** 675π
- **E.** $18{,}000\pi$

32. Given the functions f and g are defined as $f(a) = 3a - 4$ and $g(a) = 2a^2 + 1$, what is the value of $f(g(a))$?

- **F.** $6a^2 - 1$
- **G.** $6a^2 - 3$
- **H.** $2a^2 + 3a - 3$
- **J.** $-2a^2 + 3a + 3$
- **K.** $18a^2 - 48a + 33$

33. The table below shows the results of a recent poll in which 262 high school students were asked to rank a recent movie on a scale from 1 to 5 stars. To the nearest hundredth, what was the average star-rating given to this movie?

Stars given	Number of students who gave this rating
1	51
2	18
3	82
4	49
5	62

- **A.** 0.31
- **B.** 2.02
- **C.** 3.06
- **D.** 3.20
- **E.** 18.8

GO ON TO THE NEXT PAGE.

34. Lines p, q, r, and s are shown in the figure below and the set of all angles that are supplementary to $\angle x$ is $\{1,3,8,11\}$. Which of the following is the set of all lines that *must* be parallel?

DO YOUR FIGURING HERE.

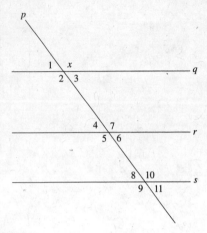

    F. $\{q,r\}$
    G. $\{q,s\}$
    H. $\{r,s\}$
    J. $\{p,q\}$
    K. $\{q,r,s\}$

35. $(4x^4 y^4)^4$ is equivalent to:

    A. xy
    B. $16x^8 y^8$
    C. $16x^{16} y^{16}$
    D. $256x^8 y^8$
    E. $256x^{16} y^{16}$

36. Which of the following expressions is equivalent to the inequality $6x - 8 > 8x + 14$?

    F. $x < -11$
    G. $x > -11$
    H. $x < -3$
    J. $x > -3$
    K. $x < 11$

GO ON TO THE NEXT PAGE.

37. As shown in the standard (x,y) coordinate plane below, A (2,4) lies on the circle with center L (10,–2) and radius 10 coordinate units. What are the coordinates of the image of A after the circle is rotated 90° counterclockwise (↺) about the center of the circle?

DO YOUR FIGURING HERE.

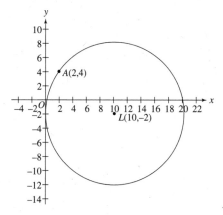

- **A.** (10, 2)
- **B.** (–2, 10)
- **C.** (2, –8)
- **D.** (0, –2)
- **E.** (4,–10)

38. The length of the hypotenuse of the right triangle figured below is 16, and the length of one of its legs is 12. What is the cosine of angle θ ?

F. $\dfrac{\sqrt{112}}{16}$

G. $\dfrac{16}{\sqrt{112}}$

H. $\dfrac{\sqrt{112}}{12}$

J. $\dfrac{12}{16}$

K. $\dfrac{16}{12}$

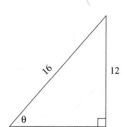

GO ON TO THE NEXT PAGE.

39. In the figure shown below, $\overline{CA}$ bisects $\angle BAD$, and $\overline{DA}$ bisects $\angle CAE$. What is the measure of $\angle CAD$?

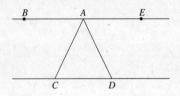

DO YOUR FIGURING HERE.

- **A.** 30°
- **B.** 45°
- **C.** 60°
- **D.** 90°
- **E.** Cannot be determined from the given information

40. If the average number of carbon dioxide molecules per cubic inch in a container is 3×10^4 and there are 6×10^8 molecules of carbon dioxide in the container, what is the volume of the container in cubic inches?

- **F.** 5×10^5
- **G.** 2×10^2
- **H.** 2×10^4
- **J.** 18×10^{12}
- **K.** 18×10^{32}

GO ON TO THE NEXT PAGE.

41. The figure below shows the screen of an automobile navigation map. Point A represents the car's starting point, point B represents the driver's intended destination, and point C, the center of the circle, is the car's current position. Currently, point A is 15 miles from point C and 250° clockwise from due north, and point B is 20 miles from point C and 30° clockwise from due north. Which of the following represents the shortest distance (a straight line) between the car's starting point and the driver's desired destination?

(Note: For any $\triangle ABC$ in which side a is opposite $\angle A$, side b is opposite $\angle B$, and side c is opposite $\angle C$, the law of cosines applies: $c^2 = a^2 + b^2 - 2ab \cos \angle C$.)

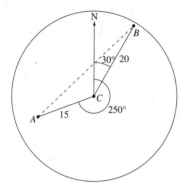

A. $\sqrt{15^2 + 20^2 - 2(15)(20)\cos 30°}$

B. $\sqrt{15^2 + 20^2 - 2(15)(20)\cos 140°}$

C. $\sqrt{15^2 + 20^2 - 2(15)(20)\cos 220°}$

D. $\sqrt{15^2 + 20^2 - 2(15)(20)\cos 250°}$

E. $\sqrt{15^2 + 20^2 - 2(15)(20)\cos 280°}$

42. What real number is halfway between $\frac{1}{4}$ and $\frac{1}{6}$?

F. $\frac{1}{6}$

G. $\frac{1}{5}$

H. $\frac{1}{2}$

J. $\frac{5}{24}$

K. $\frac{7}{24}$

GO ON TO THE NEXT PAGE.

43. In isosceles triangle △ACE, shown below, B and D are the midpoints of congruent sides $\overline{AC}$ and $\overline{CE}$, respectively. ∠ABE measures 95°, and ∠DAE measures 35°. What is the measure of ∠DEB ?

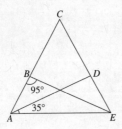

DO YOUR FIGURING HERE.

- A. 50°
- B. 30°
- C. 25°
- D. 15°
- E. 10°

44. A small square table and an L-shaped table fit together with no space between them to create a large square table. The area of the large square table is 108 square feet and is nine times the area of the small square. What is x, the edge of the L-shaped table labeled in the figure below in square feet?

- F. $2\sqrt{3}$
- G. 4
- H. $4\sqrt{3}$
- J. $4\sqrt{6}$
- K. 12

45. Which of the following is NOT an irrational number?

- A. $\sqrt{\pi}$
- B. $\sqrt{5}$
- C. $\sqrt{8}$
- D. $\sqrt{\dfrac{7}{49}}$
- E. $\sqrt{\dfrac{81}{25}}$

GO ON TO THE NEXT PAGE.

46. If $x < 0$ and $y < 0$, then $|x + y|$ is equivalent to which of the following?

  F. $x + y$

  G. $-(x + y)$

  H. $x - y$

  J. $|x - y|$

  K. $\sqrt{x^2 + y^2}$

DO YOUR FIGURING HERE.

47. Jane wants to bring her bowling average up to an 85 with her performance on her next game. So far she has bowled 5 out of 7 equally weighted games, and she has an average score of 83. What must her score on her next game be in order to reach her goal?

  A.   83
  B.   85
  C.   90
  D.   93
  E.   95

48. In a complex plane, the vertical axis is the *imaginary axis* and the horizontal axis is the *real axis*. Within the complex plane, a complex number $a + bi$ is comparable to the point (a,b) in the standard (x,y) coordinate plane. $\sqrt{a^2 + b^2}$ is the modulus of the complex point $a + bi$. Which of the complex numbers F, G, H, J, and K below has the smallest modulus?

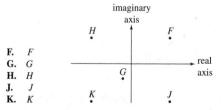

  F. F
  G. G
  H. H
  J. J
  K. K

GO ON TO THE NEXT PAGE.

DO YOUR FIGURING HERE.

49. In the real numbers, what is the solution of the equation

$9^{x-4} = 27^{3x+2}$?

A. $-\dfrac{6}{7}$

B. -2

C. -3

D. $-\dfrac{7}{2}$

E. -4

50. The graph of the trigonometric function $f(x) = 2 \sin \dfrac{1}{2} x$ is represented below. Which of the following is true of this function?

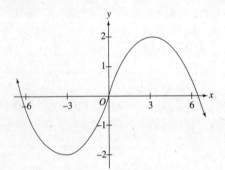

F. $f(x)$ is a 1:1 function (that is, x is unique for all $f(x)$ and $f(x)$ is unique for all x).
G. $f(x)$ is undefined at $x = 0$.
H. $f(x)$ is even (that is, $f(x) = f(-x)$ for all x).
J. $f(x)$ is odd (that is, $f(-x) = -f(x)$ for all x).
K. $f(x)$ falls entirely within the domain $-6 \le x \le 6$.

51. An integer from 299 through 1,000, inclusive, will be chosen randomly. What is the probability that the number chosen will have 1 as at least 1 of its digits?

A. $\dfrac{234}{1,000}$

B. $\dfrac{134}{702}$

C. $\dfrac{70}{702}$

D. $\dfrac{63}{702}$

E. $\dfrac{17}{702}$

GO ON TO THE NEXT PAGE.

52. In the figure below, side $\overline{MN}$ of isosceles triangle $\triangle NLM$
lies on the line $y + \dfrac{2}{3}x = 2$ in the standard (x,y) coordinate
plane, and side $\overline{NL}$ is parallel to the x-axis. What is the
slope of $\overline{LM}$?

F. $\dfrac{3}{2}$

G. $\dfrac{2}{3}$

H. $\dfrac{1}{3}$

J. $-\dfrac{2}{3}$

K. $-\dfrac{3}{2}$

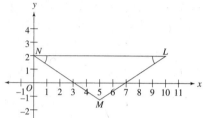

53. In the figure below, $0 < y < x$. One of the angle mea-
sures in the triangle is $\sin^{-1}\left(\dfrac{x}{\sqrt{x^2+y^2}}\right)$. What is
$\tan\left[\sin^{-1}\left(\dfrac{x}{\sqrt{x^2+y^2}}\right)\right]$?

A. $\dfrac{x}{y}$

B. $\dfrac{y}{x}$

C. $\dfrac{x}{\sqrt{x^2+y^2}}$

D. $\dfrac{y}{\sqrt{x^2+y^2}}$

E. $\dfrac{\sqrt{x^2+y^2}}{x}$

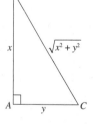

GO ON TO THE NEXT PAGE.

Use the following information to answer questions 54–56.

DO YOUR FIGURING HERE.

Melissa attaches her dog's leash to a metal anchor in the grass so that the dog can roam only within a radius of 12 feet in any direction from the anchor. A map of the area accessible to the dog is shown below in the standard (x,y) coordinate plane, with the anchor at the origin and 1 coordinate unit representing 1 foot.

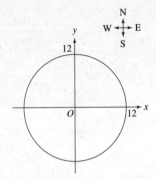

54. Which of the following is closest to the area, in square feet, the dog can roam?

F.   75
G.   144
H.   452
J.   904
K. 1,420

55. Which of the following is an equation of the circle shown on the map?

A. $(x - y)^2 = 12$
B. $(x + y)^2 = 12$
C. $(x + y)^2 = 12^2$
D. $x^2 + y^2 = 12$
E. $x^2 + y^2 = 12^2$

GO ON TO THE NEXT PAGE.

56. Joy brings her dog to the same park and anchors her dog 30 feet away from Melissa's anchor along a walking trail. Joy's dog can roam only within a radius of 20 feet in all directions from its anchor. For how many feet along the walking trail can *both* dogs roam?

(Note: Assume the leashes can't stretch.)

F.   2
G.   8
H.   10
J.   18
K.   42

DO YOUR FIGURING HERE.

57. The graphs of the equations $y = -(x) + 1$ and $y = -(x+1)^2 + 4$ are shown in the standard (x,y) coordinate plane below. What real values of x, if any, satisfy the following inequality: $-(x + 1)^2 + 4 > -(x) + 1$?

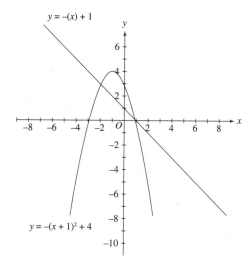

A. $x < -3$ and $x > 1$
B. $x < -2$ and $x > 1$
C. $-3 < x < 1$
D. $-2 < x < 1$
E.   No real values

GO ON TO THE NEXT PAGE.

DO YOUR FIGURING HERE.

58. For any positive two-digit integer x with tens digit t, units digit u, and $t \neq u$, y is the two-digit integer formed when the digits of x are reversed. What is the greatest possible value of $(y - x)$ when t is less than u ?

   F. $u - t$
   G. $ut - tu$
   H. $t^2 - 10tu + u^2$
   J. $9|u - t|$
   K.   Cannot be determined from the given information

59. In the figure below, the vertices of parallelogram $ABCD$ are A (2,–4), B (8,–4), C (10,–2), and D (4,–2). What is the area of the parallelogram?

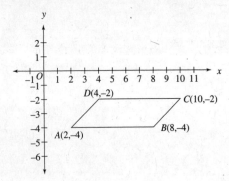

   A.   6
   B. $6\sqrt{2}$
   C.   12
   D. $12\sqrt{2}$
   E.   16

60. The sum, S, of an arithmetic sequence with first term x_1 is given by $S = n\left(\dfrac{x_1 + x_n}{2}\right)$, where n is the number of terms in the sequence. The sum of 5 consecutive terms in a given arithmetic sequence is 145, and x_5 is 48. What is the sixth term of this sequence?

   F.   49
   G.   57.5
   H.   77
   J.   154.5
   K.   174

END OF TEST 2
STOP! DO NOT TURN THE PAGE UNTIL TOLD TO DO SO.
DO NOT RETURN TO THE PREVIOUS TEST.

NO TEST MATERIAL ON THIS PAGE.

READING TEST
35 Minutes—40 Questions

DIRECTIONS: There are four passages in this test. Each passage is followed by several questions. After reading each passage, choose the best answer to each question and blacken the corresponding oval on your answer document. You may refer to the passages as often as necessary.

Passage I

PROSE FICTION: This passage is adapted from the short story "A Prisoner in His Castle" by Curtis Longweather (© 2008 by Curtis Longweather).

Since he returned from the hospital, he has been unable to reclaim his speaking voice. That is not to say that he can't make sounds, but that he often can't make his thoughts into sounds like words and sentences. Something is polluting the
5 chemistry that distills mental language into vocal output. His mind lights up with ideas just like mine does, but his ideas cannot escape. His thoughts are dispatched like knights to battle only to find they are unable to cross the moat that surrounds their castle. They are held prisoner in their own home,
10 quarantined in frustrated isolation from the outside world.

"I fear that I will eventually choke on my own thoughts," he worries aloud to me in one of his desperate letters.

"Then expel them all on to the page," I remind him. He is a volcano with no air vents to relieve the pressure of the heat
15 churning in his belly. His insides roil with fire, occasionally bubbling to the surface. His core vibrates with tightly coiled anticipation, the roof of his head eventually shedding off all shingles as a prelude to its propelling explosively into the atmosphere.

20 I tell him that his speaking voice may be like the oceanic cloud of dust and debris that the volcano spews into the air, but his writing can flow like omni-directional lava, indiscriminately absorbing everything in its path. Eventually, the continents that form as this lava cools will be fertile grounds
25 for his readers. Each of his letters stands proudly as an island within the sloshing seas of his mind, and his clarity of prose allows us explorers to navigate him.

"There is plenty of solace in writing," he acknowledges, but maintains, "never explain to someone who can't run that
30 at least he can drive a car."

He will always hear his thoughts as an echo, either reverberating within his own skull or as a crude imitation when transferred by pen.

I concede that the Page's shortcoming is a lack of dy-
35 namic human ears, but I optimistically point to the fact that written language has the potential to be seen by *countless*

human eyes. It has the potential to be richly revered classical music, not just catchy pop expressions that inspire bystanders to twitch in accordance. It has the advantage of being me-
40 thodically composed and purposefully orchestrated. However, it can be spontaneous and stream-of-consciousness as well.

"A verbal speech can be a symphony of thought just as an essay can be an improvisational blunder." He responds. "You are wrongly contrasting two styles of music when the more
45 appropriate comparison is two very different instruments."

His distinction is a valid one, but I continue to stubbornly assert the superiority of literary communication. When we *speak* to convey meaning, I argue, we can too easily get away with lazy word choice by using context, body language, tone,
50 and other non-verbal devices to supplement our stated words. In a piece of writing, the words exist in isolation from their author. They belong only to each other, like pirates who share a common destiny but no longer pledge allegiance to any sovereign entity. Judge them by your own standards
55 if you wish to be confused, but realize that the only telling diagnosis rests in the internal consistency of their ways. Do the various tensions created by the professed actions, ideas, and feelings of the writing allow the reader to vicariously behold the mental state of the author? If so, then the reader
60 has the satisfying experience of being simultaneously in the audience and backstage as well.

He enjoys coming to watch me during my trials. Sometimes I look over at him while I am delivering my closing arguments to a jury, and I see the mix of pride and pain in
65 his eyes as he listens to me express myself more lucidly than he may ever be able to again. If my profession would allow it, I would gladly yield my voice to him and become a mere puppet for his ideas, just so he could again experience the instant gratification of vocal persuasion. (I frequently wonder
70 if my friendship with him will ultimately venture into the territory of Cyrano de Bergerac, who so wished to woo the heart of a woman that he enlisted the help of a friend to speak his thoughts aloud to her.)

It is not the organization of thought that he treasures in
75 listening to my courtroom orations. It is the expressiveness that a human voice can add to the meaning of words that he deeply misses. He will occasionally have me rehearse my

GO ON TO THE NEXT PAGE.

speeches to him and never permits me to begin reciting my words too mechanically. The moment I begin *reading* and not
80 *speaking*, he will clap his hands and signal me to return back to the beginning of the idea.

In this way, just as I continue to remind him of the un-speakable value of written language, he continues to remind me of the irreplaceable value of the human voice.

1. As it relates to his friend's fear as described in the second paragraph, the narrator's description of a volcano (lines 13–19) most serves to:

  A. elaborate the friend's inner torment.
  B. speculate that his friend's thoughts will be unleashed.
  C. explain why the friend is unable to speak.
  D. imply the friend needs to be more patient.

2. Which of the following best describes the structure of the passage?

  F. A detailed character study of two close friends by means of describing one extended argument between them.
  G. A debate about a topic during which the two main characters take equal turns discussing their positions and reasons.
  H. An exploration of the author's experience of his friend's speech impairment using their verbal and written exchanges as a primary source.
  J. The depiction of a unique friendship that allows the narrator to explain his successes and struggles as a lawyer.

3. The erupting volcano simile refers to a dust cloud and a lava flow to portray:

  A. intuition and logic.
  B. simplicity and complexity.
  C. instinct and deliberation.
  D. vocal and non-vocal expression.

4. Based on the passage, which of the following statements most clearly portrays the respective attitudes of the narrator and his friend?

  F. The friend is argumentative and cynical; the narrator is jaded and indifferent.
  G. The friend is scornful and depressed; the narrator is apologetic and idealistic.
  H. The friend is anxious and despondent; the narrator is sympathetic and encouraging.
  J. The friend is shy and reclusive; the narrator is outgoing and nonchalant.

5. In the passage, the narrator most nearly describes Cyrano de Bergerac as:

  A. someone who was afraid of losing the love of his life.
  B. unable to produce any sound of his own due to a physical condition.
  C. someone who had reason to communicate indirectly with a woman.
  D. too caught up in the emotions of love to be able to describe them.

6. Which of the following statements about pirates is best supported by the narrator's characterization of them?

  F. They have no rules of conduct that they must follow.
  G. They succeed by means of confusing their enemies.
  H. They are not accountable to anyone other than themselves.
  J. They recognize the superior value of written language.

7. It can be most strongly inferred from the passage that the friend values which of the following in vocal speech?

  A. Meaningful expression
  B. Proper mechanics
  C. Rich vocabulary
  D. Clever humor

8. According to the passage, the friend is worried he may:

  F. say something embarrassing if he speaks.
  G. grow exasperated from his inability to vocalize thoughts.
  H. be damaging the narrator's chances of courtroom success.
  J. not be clever enough to compose a symphony of thought.

9. As it is used in (line 68), the word *puppet* most nearly means:

  A. entertainer.
  B. conversationalist.
  C. toy.
  D. mouthpiece.

10. Based on the narrator's account, the friend's reaction to watching the narrator during legal proceedings is:

  F. appreciative and yearning.
  G. confused and hopeless.
  H. awestruck and overbearing.
  J. bitter and resentful.

GO ON TO THE NEXT PAGE.

Passage II

SOCIAL SCIENCE: This passage is adapted from the entry "Larsen B" in *Down Off the Shelf: Recent Antarctic Natural Disasters* (© 2009 Subzero Publications).

Most people associate Antarctica with frigid temperatures, glaciers, and massive sheets of ice; however, recent geological events highlight not the cold, but issues of warming. Further, such events emphasize the ways in which human behavior

5　influences climactic and geological changes. Though scientists may disagree as to the extent of human influence, there is no doubt that our behavior does have significant and lasting outcomes. One of the most dramatic environmental events in recent years is the loss of ice shelves that float around much

10　of Antarctica; in particular, the collapse of the Larsen B ice shelf. This long, fringing mass was assumed to be the latest in a long line of victims of Antarctic summer heat waves linked to global warming; new research, however, calls this assumption into question.

15　In 2002, the northern section of the Larsen B ice shelf (a thick floating sheet of freshwater ice fed by glaciers) shattered and separated from the continent in the largest single event in a 30-year series of ice-shelf retreats in the peninsula. The Larsen B was about 220 meters thick and is thought to

20　have existed for at least 400 years prior to its collapse. The shattered ice from Larsen B set thousands of icebergs adrift in the Weddell Sea, east of the Antarctic Peninsula. A total of about 1,250 square miles of shelf area disintegrated in a 35-day period beginning on January 31 of 2002. The collapse

25　was perhaps foreshadowed when standing water appeared on the ice. (Scientists theorize that once melt-water appears on the surface of an ice shelf, the rate of ice disintegration increases; pooling water puts weight on the ice, filling small cracks that expand, eventually causing breakage.) The appear-

30　ance of standing water on ice shelves is generally attributed to global warming; thus, the collapse of the Larsen B ice shelf seemed to be one of the most obvious and stunning signs of worldwide climate change.

In support of this postulation, the *Journal of Climate*

35　published a 2006 study by Dr. Gareth Marshall of the British Antarctic Survey, providing the first direct evidence linking human activity to the collapse of Antarctic ice shelves. Scientists revealed that stronger westerly winds in the northern Antarctic Peninsula, driven principally by human-induced

40　climate change, are responsible for the significant increase in summer temperatures that led to the retreat and collapse of the Larsen B. They argue that global warming and the ozone hole have changed Antarctic weather patterns such that strengthened westerly winds force warm air eastward

45　over the natural barrier created by the Antarctic Peninsula's mountain chain. Elevated temperatures in the summer warm the area by approximately five degrees Celsius, creating the conditions that allowed melt-water to drain into crevasses on the Larsen ice shelf, a key process that led to its 2002

50　break-up. Dr. Marshall asserts that this is the first time anyone has demonstrated a process directly linking the collapse to human activity, and that climate change does not impact our planet evenly, as evidenced by the significant increase in temperatures in certain geographical areas, particularly the

55　western Antarctic Peninsula. According to his research, this icy region has shown the largest increase in temperatures observed anywhere on Earth over the past half-century.

Marshall's breakthrough research was followed, two years later, by new and somewhat contradictory information. In a

60　paper published in the Journal of Glaciology, Professor Neil Glasser and Dr. Ted Scambos assert that despite the dramatic nature of the break-up in 2002, observations by glaciologists and computer modeling by scientists at NASA pointed to an ice shelf in distress for decades. Glasser and Scambos contend

65　that the shelf was already teetering on the brink of collapse before the final summer, and though they acknowledge that global warming had a major role in the collapse, they empha-size that it is only one of a number of atmospheric, oceanic and glaciological factors. The amount of melt-water on the

70　Larsen B shelf just before the collapse caused many to assume that air temperature increases were primarily to blame, but Scambos and Glasser's research shows that ice-shelf breakup is not controlled simply by climate, citing, for example, that the location and spacing of crevasses and rifts on the ice do

75　much to determine its strength. Scientists in the field consider this study imperative, as the collapse of ice shelves contributes (albeit indirectly) to global sea-level rise.

Scientists agree that the break-up of Larsen B alone will not change sea level, but other glaciers previously restricted

80　by the ice shelf have surged forward, lowering their surfaces. Since lower elevations have warmer temperatures, these glaciers melt more quickly, causing more ice to flow into the sea, and levels to rise. If more and more ice shelves are lost in subsequent years, the concern is that the rise in sea

85　levels could affect ecosystems worldwide, generating such problems as widespread flooding, loss of coastal cities and island countries, decreased crop yields, and the possible ex-tinction of millions of species. Determining the cause of ice shelf collapse, and the ways in which humans can contribute

90　to both the problem and the solution, may help to prevent such catastrophes in the future; it becomes clear, then, why researchers are compelled to continue their studies of ice shelves in the Antarctic.

GO ON TO THE NEXT PAGE.

11. The author most nearly characterizes the role of human activity in regard to the collapse of ice shelves as:

   A. a significant though previously unproven contributing factor.
   B. insignificant in comparison to glaciological influences.
   C. less of a contributor than initial evidence predicted.
   D. the primary and irreversible cause of all detrimental effects.

12. The author lists all of the following as possible effects of sea level rise EXCEPT:

   F. loss of island countries.
   G. extinction of millions of species.
   H. decreased crop yields.
   J. surging glaciers.

13. The author indicates that the common factor in Dr. Marshall's study (lines 34–57) and that of Doctors Scambos and Glasser (lines 58–77) is that both studies:

   A. cite global warming as a reason for the Larsen B ice-shelf collapse
   B. discredit climate change as a reason for the Larsen B ice-shelf collapse.
   C. found little compelling evidence to explain the Larsen B ice-shelf collapse.
   D. agree that structural weaknesses caused the Larsen B ice-shelf collapse.

14. In his statement in lines 50–55, the author most nearly means that human activity:

   F. is inconsequential compared to other factors influencing climate change.
   G. could eventually affect weather patterns worldwide, doing great harm.
   H. makes certain areas of the world much warmer than they would otherwise be.
   J. will cause sea level to rise, wiping out entire countries and species of animals.

15. The author calls which of the following a stunning sign of worldwide climate change?

   A. Worldwide sea-level rise
   B. Melt-water on the Larsen B ice shelf prior to its collapse
   C. The collapse of the Larsen B ice shelf
   D. Increased temperatures in the western Antarctic Peninsula

16. The author includes the findings in lines (64–75) primarily in order to:

   F. support the prevailing theory that global warming causes glacier break-up.
   G. encourage people to make environmentally-friendly choices in their daily lives.
   H. imply that ice shelf break-up is simpler than scientists originally thought.
   J. highlight the interaction between factors in a major environmental event.

17. The main idea of the third paragraph is that the Larsen B ice-shelf collapse:

   A. was not caused by global warming.
   B. was foreshadowed for years prior to the event.
   C. was caused by the uneven impact of climate change on the earth.
   D. was caused in part by direct human activity.

18. Which of the following is NOT listed in the passage as a cause of ice-shelf collapse?

   F. Global warming
   G. Human activity
   H. Spacing and location of crevasses and rifts
   J. Deep ocean currents

19. The author calls the increased westerly winds in the northern Antarctic Peninsula:

   A. irrelevant to the problem of ice-shelf collapse.
   B. responsible for an increase in summer temperatures.
   C. a common weather pattern in certain times of year.
   D. an unmistakable warning of sea-level rise.

20. The author uses the remark "largest increase in temperatures observed anywhere on Earth" lines (56–57) to:

   F. demonstrate how scientists are prone to exaggeration when talking about ice shelves.
   G. give a strong incentive for people to change their behavior.
   H. explain that global warming doesn't occur at the same rate in all regions.
   J. clarify a common misconception about weather patterns in cold areas.

GO ON TO THE NEXT PAGE.

Passage III

HUMANITIES: This passage is excerpted from the essay "Salman Rushdie: A Man of Multiple Worlds" by Paul Lopez (© 2010 by Paul Lopez). In this selection, the term *partition* refers to the British Empire's official relinquishment of its claim on India, at which point the area was divided into two self-governing countries: India and Pakistan. Also, the contemporary city of Mumbai was known as Bombay during the time this passage discusses.

As well-known for his life story as for his writing, Salman Rushdie is nonetheless a virtuosic author of the first degree. His books are filled with lyrical passages capable of transporting the reader to a kitchen in India, a mountain in Pakistan, or a street corner in London. Although his plots often involve metaphysical or even magical elements, somehow they seem reasonable. He has the art of drawing the reader in, explaining each bizarre incident in such a way that, suddenly, it becomes plausible, if only for the moment.

Born in Bombay, on the Western coast of India, to Muslim parents during the year of the partition, Rushdie grew up amidst the India-Pakistan and Hindi-Muslim struggle. Each group strove to create a new identity and independence, apart from the colonial past, and Rushdie paid close attention to each group's stories. Later, he immigrated to England to attend school, and there too he listened. As an author, he began to integrate these stories, and his books show the complex interplay that exists between these three cultures.

In his books, it is clear that each area has, for him, its own unique beauty. Rushdie's India is a world of food; in one book, he spends pages discussing chutneys—their flavor, their coloring, and their preparation. His Bombay is described as a raucous place, filled with colors, scents that assault the nostrils, and people thronging the streets everywhere you look. It is a place teeming with life and all that life entails. His Pakistan, on the other hand, is a place of stark beauty, and of dry, desert landscapes with communities centered on lakes scattered throughout the countryside. A people that has fought for its independence, filled with a ferocious pride of place, but quiet, withdrawn. A private people, in stark contrast to the overflowing life of India. In Rushdie's Pakistan, it seems, they have room for quiet and have chosen that for themselves. It is also a world of hospitality, but on a personal scale. Instead of describing markets or streets, Rushdie dwells on families and individuals, describing their appearances and behaviors minutely. And finally, there is Rushdie's England. Often, his characters in India and Pakistan long to be in England, causing the reader to wonder if Rushdie himself felt that longing at one time. Once they arrive, however, they often find England disconcerting, its orderly chaos overwhelming to someone unaccustomed to the Western world. The colors too are missing, along with the pungent spices in the air. Even when his characters are describing how happy they are to have made it to their promised land, they cannot seem to leave their homelands completely behind.

It is this merging of three disparate cultures that makes Rushdie's writing stand out. Each culture is made to come alive for the reader, allowing his Western readers a chance to peer into a culture very different from their own. One of his earlier books, written in 1981 and called *Midnight's Children*, takes as its focal point the partition of India. The main character is born at the stroke of midnight, drawing his first breath just as the partition becomes a reality. The book follows the many ways in which this coincidence affects the character throughout his life, tying the events in his personal life to those in the larger life of the country and community, showing that neither one exists separate of the other. While Rushdie was not quite born at the stroke of midnight, he was born a mere month before the partition took place, and he too would have grown up watching the people of India and Pakistan work to create new worlds for themselves. This experience permeates not only *Midnight's Children* but also all of his other works, as he describes characters striving to find a place for themselves in a world that doesn't always make sense. He wants, it seems, for his readers to get a sense of the struggle to merge yet stay distinct.

In the end, many writers have discussed colonialism, independence, and migration, but none perhaps as engagingly as Rushdie. As interesting as his subjects are, certainly the way his prose draws readers into his world has been the essential factor in making his work so enduring. His books may not be the first, but they are some of the most prominent books to deal with these subjects and, as such, have had a profound influence on the works of other writers, as well as on the reading public. No matter what the future holds, the portraits of India and Pakistan drawn by Rushdie will continue to influence the literary world for years to come.

21. The first paragraph establishes all of the following about Rushdie EXCEPT:

   A. his intention to make Western readers more aware of what life in India and Pakistan is like.
   B. the kinds of elements that might be included in Rushdie's writing.
   C. whether or not he is well-known in his chosen profession.
   D. some of the locations he tends to use in his writing.

GO ON TO THE NEXT PAGE.

22. The primary function of the second paragraph (lines 10–18) is to:

   F. discuss Rushdie's religious upbringing and personal faith.
   G. give some background information on Rushdie's childhood.
   H. contrast the Hindi and Muslim belief systems.
   J. list all the factors that led to Rushdie's emigration from India.

23. Which of the following statements most correctly identifies the main idea of the passage?

   A. Rushdie is a highly talented writer but his personal failings prevent readers from empathizing with his characters.
   B. The partition of India was a traumatic experience for the many people who were compelled to move in the years following the division.
   C. Rushdie uses his personal life experiences to describe for readers what life is like in the part of the world where he grew up.
   D. The book *Midnight's Children* is an insightful book about the events surrounding the official partition of India.

24. All of the following details are used in the passage to describe Rushdie's vision of Bombay EXCEPT that it:

   F. is filled with scents, some of which can be very pungent.
   G. is a place filled with many colors.
   H. is typically very hot and humid, with temperatures reaching uncomfortable levels.
   J. is overwhelmed with people and life.

25. One of the main points in the fourth paragraph is that, in his writing, Rushdie is trying to convey a sense of:

   A. futility.
   B. sadness.
   C. struggle.
   D. longing.

26. Which of the following questions is NOT answered in the passage?

   F. In general terms, which parts of the world tend to be prominently featured in Rushdie's works?
   G. How do Rushdie's descriptions of the Pakistani people differ from his descriptions of the Indian people?
   H. In which part of the world was Rushdie himself born?
   J. How many books had Rushdie, at the time of this essay's publication, written?

27. According to the passage, in which of the following countries did Rushdie attend school?

   A. Pakistan
   B. England
   C. India
   D. America

28. Which of the following words is the best characterization of Rushdie's Bombay, according to this passage?

   F. Frustrating
   G. Chaotic
   H. Vibrant
   J. Stark

29. The information in lines 69–71 is most likely included by the author in order to suggest:

   A. that it is Rushdie's skill as a writer, rather than his subjects alone, that has brought him lasting fame.
   B. Rushdie's tendency to rely too heavily on historical events for the plots of his novels.
   C. Rushdie's likelihood of remaining a literary icon well into the future is very uncertain.
   D. that the subjects that Rushdie writes about aren't actually very interesting to most people.

30. The passage suggests that Rushdie's most important contribution to literature is his:

   F. description of Pakistan's landscapes.
   G. portrayal of India's partition.
   H. ability to draw readers into his world.
   J. beautifully crafted prose.

GO ON TO THE NEXT PAGE.

Passage IV

NATURAL SCIENCE: This passage is excerpted from the article "Alternative Medicines: A New Perspective" by Audrey C. Tristan (© 2004 by Audrey Tristan).

The view of health as a holistic and integrative state of physical, spiritual, and emotional well-being is deeply rooted in mind-body philosophies that have survived thousands of years. Traditional *mindful movement* therapies found in
5   *yoga, tai chi,* and *qigong,* for example, couple aerobic and anaerobic exercise with mental focus. These practices, which originated in Eastern medicine, guide participants through a series of specialized movements synchronized to the breath and mental images. Involving more than cardiovascular activ-
10 ity, these exercise routines are said to improve overall health by bringing deeper awareness to the body and promoting strength, flexibility, and balance.

Modern Western biomedicine, on the other hand, has advanced largely by splitting the mind and body to allow for
15 the objective study of health and disease mechanisms, and thus has been slow to embrace the implications of mind-body health. However, as alternative and traditional therapies have become increasingly more popular and available in the West, researchers have begun to delve deeper into mind-body therapy
20 efficacy, that is, the ability to consistently produce a desired, therapeutic effect.

There is particularly solid research to support the use of mind-body therapy to counteract the debilitating effects of stress. Certain mind-body therapies may alter the way
25 we experience pain and manage stress through the use of conscious strategies to avert automatic responses. Stress, as defined in biomedical terms, is the physiological response to a perceived threat. It is not to be confused with the common usage of the term, which generally equates stress with those
30 activities that provoke a stress response (these are deemed *stressors*). When the central nervous system perceives a threat, the sympathetic division of the autonomic nervous system is engaged, signaling the release of stress hormones such as epinephrine and cortisol into the bloodstream that in
35 turn activate particular physiological responses: heart and respiratory rate acceleration, muscles tension, perspiration, indigestion, and pupil dilation.

This "fight-or-flight" response alludes to the conditions of ancestral humans and the presumed adaptive function of
40 such a response in evolutionary history. The response, how-ever, does not occur only in reaction to isolated incidences. Indeed, most stressors today, related to work, family, school, and interpersonal relationships, are prolonged, and the fight-or-flight responses are thus sustained. This continual state
45 of arousal results in deleterious effects on health over time, such as high blood pressure, cardiovascular disease, diabetes, digestive disorders, and suppressed immune response.

Mind-body therapies, such as guided imagery and medita-tion, essentially work by altering responses to stressors. The
50 simple act of breathing deeply and focusing on the breath will, in contrast to a stress response, engage the parasympathetic division of the autonomic nervous system, which lowers blood pressure, heart, and respiratory rates, and decreases muscle tension, thus counteracting the negative consequences of
55 fight-or-flight response.

Other mind-body therapies alter the experience of pain itself. Pain is a multidimensional experience that traverses four physiological pathways. *Transduction* occurs first, as sensory neurons, the *nociceptors*, detect potentially damaging stimuli
60 and transmit signals from affected tissue to neural activity. The next step is *transmission*, in which the pain messages are exchanged between the nociceptors and the spinal cord. *Central representation* follows as the information is relayed from the spinal cord through the thalamus to the limbic and cortical
65 structures of the brain, which identify the sensations relayed. *Modulation,* the last step, is a descending pathway in which the brain sends signals back to the spinal cord to moderate the sensation of pain, basically "numbing" the pain. Since the limbic system is also the brain center for emotion, memory,
70 and autonomic nervous system integration, the experience of pain is ultimately mediated by emotions, an individual's own past experiences, and present external environment.

In clinical hypnosis, or *hypnotic analgesia,* patients are taught alternative skills to alter the experience of pain.
75 Hypnotic analgesia produces psychophysiological effects as patients are taught to consciously re-evaluate and manage a painful stimulus, using visual imagery and positive emotional reinforcement. A recent review of controlled studies of hyp-notic analgesia suggests that the treatment can reduce pain
80 in chronic conditions resulting from osteoarthritis, cancer, fibromyalgia, and disability. The authors cautioned, however, that a number of questions remain unanswered.

Mind-body research has provided important insights into both the efficacy of such therapies and our understanding of
85 the cognitive and physiological perception of pain. More investigation is needed, however, to ascertain if outcome expectations influence the success of particular therapies, if response rates differ as a result of pain type or pain diagnosis, and to what degree variation in individual response, and if
90 research design should preclude broader inferences.

GO ON TO THE NEXT PAGE.

31. The studies reviewed in the seventh paragraph (lines 73–82) have shown that hypnotic analgesia may be effective in:

A. restructuring the brain non-invasively.
B. fighting cancer and fibromyalgia.
C. decreasing depression in patients.
D. altering the experience of pain.

32. According to the sixth paragraph, (lines 56–72), when a door slams on a person's hand, the detection of pain results from:

F. the transmission of nerve signals from damaged tissue to the spinal cord and sympathetic nervous system.
G. the transmission of nerve signals from damaged tissue to the spinal cord and brain.
H. the sympathetic nervous system releasing chemical hormones, which reach the heart via the bloodstream.
J. the sympathetic nervous system releasing chemical hormones, which reach the brain via the spinal cord.

33. According to the passage, overall health may be improved in part through any of the following EXCEPT:

A. exercise combined with mental focus.
B. cardiovascular activity combined with nutritious diet.
C. awareness of the body.
D. movement synchronized with breath and mental imagery.

34. As it is used in line 33, the word *engaged* most nearly means:

F. stimulated.
G. taken.
H. obligated.
J. destined.

35. According to the passage, the limbic system would be directly involved in all of the following EXCEPT:

A. pain modulation.
B. stress management.
C. muscle movement.
D. memory.

36. Information in the second paragraph indicates that mind-body therapies in Western medicine have been:

F. increasingly used in place of biomedicine.
G. rejected because there has not been enough clinical studies.
H. an emerging field of scientific investigation.
J. successful in curing many conditions and diseases.

37. The mind-body therapies mentioned in the fifth paragraph (lines 48–55) function by:

A. preventing stress hormones from activating negative physiological responses.
B. engaging the sympathetic nervous system to reduce stress responses.
C. effectively eliminating emotional stressors.
D. counterbalancing the effects of flight or fight responses.

38. According to the passage, stress responses with adaptive functions, as would have evolved in ancestral conditions, can be expected to:

F. increase cortisol levels in the blood.
G. suppress immune activity.
H. perceive threats.
J. decrease muscle tension.

39. In the last paragraph, the author expresses the belief that mind-body therapy should be further investigated because results from research are:

A. carefully controlled to yield results consistent with expectations.
B. valid only when analyzing Western-originating therapies.
C. susceptible to external variables, the effects of which are yet to be determined.
D. proof of the effectiveness in fighting stress and eliminating pain.

40. According to the passage, healthy mind-body therapies would have been deemed ineffective if which of the following effects occurred after patients engaged in positive meditation to manage work-related stress?

F. Nociceptive signals were transmitted.
G. Parasympathetic nervous system was engaged.
H. Fight-or-flight response was prolonged.
J. Spinal cord activity diminished.

END OF TEST 3
STOP! DO NOT TURN THE PAGE UNTIL TOLD TO DO SO.
DO NOT RETURN TO A PREVIOUS TEST.

SCIENCE REASONING TEST
35 Minutes—40 Questions

DIRECTIONS: There are seven passages in the following section. Each passage is followed by several questions. After reading a passage, choose the best answer to each question and blacken the corresponding oval on your answer document. You may refer to the passages as often as necessary.

You are NOT permitted to use a calculator on this test.

Passage I

In the solar system, solid planets and moons are made up of different layers, which have different compositions. The Earth's moon is surrounded by an outer crust, which is visible to observers on Earth. Beneath this crust is a solid *lithosphere*. Beneath the lithosphere is another layer called the *asthenosphere*. This layer is thought to have high temperatures, so the structure of this layer is said to be *plastic*, or easily changed. The innermost region of the moon is called the *core*, and it is thought to contain iron.

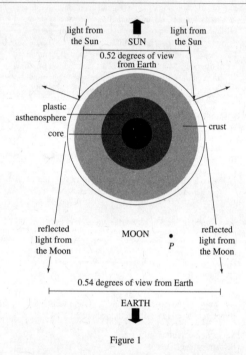

Figure 1

A solar eclipse occurs when the moon travels directly between the Earth and the Sun, temporarily blocking the transmission of sunlight to the Earth and creating a shadow. Most solar eclipses are partial, because the moon does not always travel entirely within the path of the sunlight. However, complete solar eclipses are possible because the moon and the Sun have approximately the same diameter from the perspective of a viewer on the Earth. An observer on the Earth would view the sky as occupying 180 degrees. Of this entire distance, the moon takes up 0.54 degrees while the Sun takes up 0.52 degrees. Since the Sun appears to take up a smaller section of the sky, the Sun's rays can be blocked from traveling to the Earth during a complete solar eclipse (see Figure 1).

The gravitational force exerted on the Earth by the moon, and by the Sun to a lesser extent, results in water *tides*, which are the changes in the level of the Earth's ocean surface. Figure 2 shows data collected by a tidal station on the western coast of the United States, showing the change in the ocean water level over a 60-hour period. During this period, the highest water level was 6 feet above mean sea level, while the lowest water level was 1 foot below mean sea level (represented by "–1" feet).

GO ON TO THE NEXT PAGE.

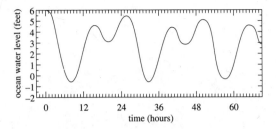

Figure 2

The highest and lowest ocean surface levels change over the course of a year. Figure 3 shows the change in the highest and lowest water levels measured by the same tidal station over a year.

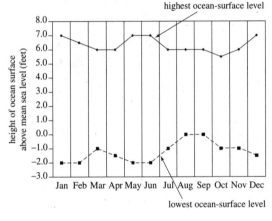

highest ocean-surface level

lowest ocean-surface level

Figure 3

1. Figure 1 shows that a lunar orbiter at point *P* would be able to view which of the following?

A. The moon only
B. The Sun only
C. The moon and the Earth only
D. The moon, the Sun, and the Earth

2. According to Figure 1, when the Sun's rays encounter the surface of the moon during a solar eclipse, the rays most likely:

F. stop transmitting forward and do not continue to the Earth's surface.
G. enter the plastic asthenosphere and are absorbed.
H. reflect off the surface of the moon, and then continue to the Earth.
J. transmit unobstructed to the Earth's surface.

3. Based on Figure 2, for a given set of consecutive days, the time elapsed between the maximum values of the highest ocean-surface levels would most nearly be:

A. 12 hours.
B. 24 hours.
C. 48 hours.
D. 60 hours.

4. Based on the information provided in Figure 3, during what month was the data in Figure 2 most likely collected?

F. January
G. March
H. June
J. December

5. According to Figure 2, which of the following statements best describes the ocean surface level between *t* = 0 hours and *t* = 12 hours?

A. The ocean surface level rises continuously during that entire time.
B. The ocean surface level falls continuously during that entire time.
C. The ocean surface level rises and then falls during that time.
D. The ocean surface level falls and then rises during that time.

GO ON TO THE NEXT PAGE.

Passage II

Approximately 45,000 to 35,000 years ago, Lake Brussia straddled the boundary between modern Smith and Union counties. The lake was believed to have been formed as a result of seismic activity in the region. As seen in Figure 1, the cities of Middleton, West Union, and Basalt Valley rest over the sediment of the ancient lake. In order to test this hypothesis, a study examining the strata of the region was conducted using radioactive dating. Inconsistencies in the age of the rock layers indicate the presence of a fault in the region.

Radioactive dating is a technique which utilizes the amount of radiation exhibited by a distinct isotope within a sample to approximate its age. Uranium-235 is an isotope commonly found in varying types of strata with a half-life of approximately 700 million years. The half-life of an isotope is the time it takes for half of the isotope to decompose. 1,000-m core samples were acquired from three sites between the modern cities of Middleton and West Union as seen in Figure 2. Figure 3 shows the results of the Uranium-235 assays for each of the three sites. The age of the rock is determined using a ratio of the Uranium content in the sample to that of newly formed rock.

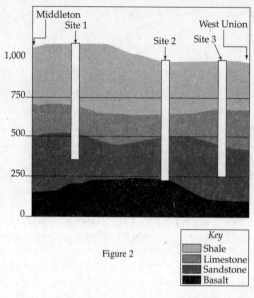

Figure 2

Key
■ Shale
■ Limestone
■ Sandstone
■ Basalt

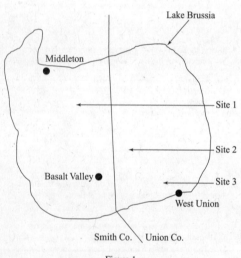

Figure 1

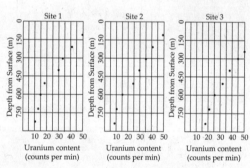

Figure 3

Note: $\dfrac{64}{\text{Counts per minute of Uranium -235 in Sample}} \times 700 =$ approx. age of rock in millions of years

GO ON TO THE NEXT PAGE.

6. According to Figure 2, the shale layer was thickest at which of the following cities or sites?

   F. Middleton
   G. Site 1
   H. Site 3
   J. West Union

7. According to Figure 2, as the thickness of shale decreases between Sites 2 and 3, the thickness of limestone residing below:

   A. increases.
   B. decreases.
   C. first decreases then increases.
   D. remains constant.

8. Based on Figure 2, which of the following graphs best displays the thickness of the shale layer at Sites 1, 2, and 3 ?

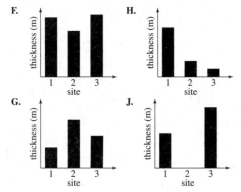

9. According to Figure 3, at Sites 1, 2, and 3 the highest number of counts of Uranium-235 detected were recorded at a depth of:

   A. less than 300 m below the surface.
   B. between 300 and 450 m below the surface.
   C. between 450 and 600 m below the surface.
   D. greater than 600 m below the surface.

10. The uranium recorded in Sites 1, 2, and 3 is reduced by ½ roughly every 0.7 billion years. Based on Figure 3, and assuming no alteration of this uranium decay, the age of the rock with the greatest depth surveyed at Site 2 is closest to:

   F. 2.8 billion years old.
   G. 5.6 billion years old.
   H. 280 million years old.
   J. 560 million years old.

GO ON TO THE NEXT PAGE.

Passage III

For a science fair, a middle school student tested the hypothesis that bubbles in liquids would affect how far a water gun could shoot. To do this, she set up a holding device so that the water gun would always shoot at the same angle (the angle of inclination) and from the same place. She then measured the horizontal distance from the holding device to the furthest observable trace of liquid (see Figure 1).

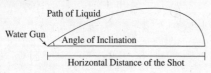

Path of Liquid

Water Gun — Angle of Inclination

Horizontal Distance of the Shot

Figure 1

The angle of inclination was 30° in all experiments. The same metal water gun was used in Experiments 1 and 2.

Experiment 1

The student filled the metallic water canister of a water gun to 80% of its capacity with water from her tap (water with no bubbles in it) and measured how far from the holding device the water gun shot. Then, she again filled the canister to 80% of its capacity with tap water, shook the water gun, and immediately measured how far it shot. She repeated these tests with water mixed with laundry detergent, which contained many bubbles, and a flat-tasting cola beverage that showed no visible bubbles. Table 1 shows the results of these trials.

Table 1			
		Distance Shot	
Trial	Liquid	before shaking (meters)	after shaking (meters)
1	water	6.42	6.42
2	water with detergent	5.36	4.79
3	flat-tasting cola	6.42	5.49

Experiment 2

Next, the student filled the water gun canister to 80% of its capacity with the flat-tasting cola, shook it to create bubbles and then let it sit, undisturbed. When 10 minutes had elapsed, she tested how far the water gun shot the cola, before and after shaking it (Trial 4). She then let it sit undisturbed for an hour before again testing how far it shot before and after shaking it (Trial 5). Table 2 shows the results of these trials.

Table 2		
	Distance shot	
Trial	before shaking (meters)	after shaking (meters)
4	5.98	5.49
5	6.42	5.61

Experiment 3

For the third experiment, the student used an old-fashioned, plastic water gun, with transparent walls and the water container in the handle of the water gun. The student added the flat-tasting cola to fill the water container to 80% of its capacity, shot the water gun, and observed that no bubbles formed upon shooting. She then shook the water gun, which caused bubbles to form. After 10 minutes, there were still some visible bubbles in the cola; however, after an hour had passed, there were no visible bubbles.

11. In Experiment 3, what is the most likely reason the student chose to use an old-fashioned plastic water gun rather than a metal water gun? Compared to the metal water gun, the plastic water gun:

   A. exhibited different effects of bubbles on shooting distance.
   B. did not shoot as far as the metal gun.
   C. allowed the student to view the bubbles in the liquid.
   D. was easier to fit into the holding device.

12. Based on the results of Experiments 1 and 2, in which of the following two trials, before shaking the water gun, were the distances shot the same?

   F. Trials 1 and 4
   G. Trials 2 and 3
   H. Trials 3 and 4
   J. Trials 3 and 5

GO ON TO THE NEXT PAGE.

13. In Experiment 2, a result of shaking the water gun containing the flat-tasting cola was that the:

A. density of the liquid increased.
B. bubbles in the liquid disappeared.
C. distance the liquid was shot increased.
D. distance the liquid was shot decreased.

14. In Trial 5, is it likely that bubbles were present in large numbers in the cola immediately before the can was shaken?

F. Yes; based on the results of Experiment 1, the bubbles generated in Trial 4 probably lasted for less than 10 minutes.
G. Yes; based on the results of Experiment 1, the bubbles generated in Trial 4 probably lasted for more than 1 hour.
H. No; based on the results of Experiment 3, the bubbles generated in Trial 4 probably lasted for less than 1 hour.
J. No; based on the results of Experiment 3, the bubbles generated in Trial 4 probably lasted for more than 2 hours.

15. Suppose that in Experiment 2, the student had decided to measure the distance the water gun shot the cola one hour after finishing Trial 5 without shaking the water gun again. Based on the observations made in Trials 4 and 5, the horizontal distance the cola was shot would most likely have been:

A. less than 5.49 meters.
B. between 5.49 and 5.51 meters.
C. between 5.52 and 5.98 meters.
D. greater than 5.98 meters.

16. Based on the results of Trials 3–5, if the student filled the metal water gun to 80% of its capacity with the flat-tasting cola and shook it, the time it would take for the bubbles in the cola to disappear to the point that they would have no effect on the distance of the shot would most likely have been:

F. greater than 1 hour.
G. between 10 minutes and 1 hour.
H. between 3 minutes and 9 minutes.
J. less than 3 minutes.

GO ON TO THE NEXT PAGE.

Passage IV

An ecological study measured the reflection of light by different algae types and water samples. The study found that a water sample's reflectance of light is determined by the density of algae in it. As the density of algae in a water sample increases, the water sample's reflectance of light became more similar to the pure algae's reflectance of light.

Table 1 lists the wavelength range of the visible spectrum and the wavelength ranges of the colors of the visible spectrum.

Table 1	
Color	Wavelength (nm)
Violet	380–430
Blue	430–500
Green	500–565
Yellow	565–585
Orange	585–630
Red	630–750

Figure 1 shows the relative reflectance of light by pure samples of water and three types of algae versus the wavelength of light from 350 nm to 750 nm.

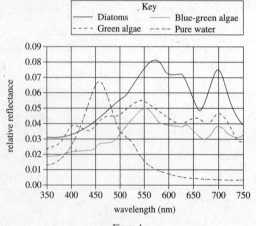

Figure 1

Figure 2 shows the relative reflectance light of a sample of lake water versus the wavelength of light from 350 nm to 750 nm.

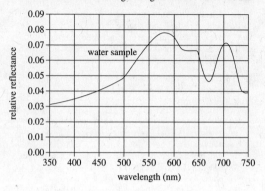

Figure 2

17. Based on Table 1 and Figure 1, which color of light is most reflected by blue-green algae?

A. Violet
B. Yellow
C. Red
D. Green

GO ON TO THE NEXT PAGE.

18. Autotrophic organisms, such as blue-green algae, absorb wavelengths using the molecule chlorophyll. Chlorophyll is typically associated with which of the following chemical reactions?

    F. Binary fission
    G. Condensation
    H. Photosynthesis
    J. Respiration

19. According to Figure 1, at which of the following wavelengths does the amount of light reflected by green algae exceed the amount of light reflected by diatoms?

    A. 400 nm
    B. 520 nm
    C. 670 nm
    D. 710 nm

20. Green algae is classified in which kingdom of organisms?

    F. Animalia
    G. Plantae
    H. Fungi
    J. Protista

21. Based on Figures 1 and 2, what type of algae has the greatest density in the lake water sample?

    A. Blue-green algae
    B. Diatoms
    C. Green algae
    D. No algae are in the water sample.

GO ON TO THE NEXT PAGE.

Passage V

Oceanographers conducted a series of experiments with water to explore the relationship between temperature, salinity (% salt by mass), and density (mass per unit volume).

Experiment 1

In a beaker, 35 g of NaCl and 965 g of distilled H_2O were mixed, and the solution was brought to a specific temperature. A graduated cylinder was then used to measure 150 mL of the solution. The mass of this 150-mL sample was measured with an electronic balance and the density (g/mL) was calculated. This procedure was repeated for 5 different temperatures with the results recorded in Table 1.

	Table 1		
Sample	Solution mass (g)	Temperature (°C)	Density (g/mL)
I	154.2	0	1.028
II	154.1	10	1.027
III	153.9	15	1.026
IV	153.8	20	1.025
V	153.3	30	1.022

Experiment 2

A graduated cylinder was placed on an electronic balance and a certain mass of NaCl was added. Distilled water at 10°C was added to make a 150 mL solution, and the total mass of this was noted. The density (g/mL) and salinity (%) of the solution were calculated. This procedure was repeated for 5 different quantities of NaCl with the results recorded in Table 2.

	Table 2		
Sample	Solution mass (g)	Salinity (%)	Density (g/mL)
VI	153.0	2.60	1.020
VII	152.7	2.35	1.018
VIII	152.4	2.10	1.016
IX	152.1	1.83	1.014
X	151.8	1.58	1.012

Experiment 3

Water samples from Experiments 1 and 2 were used individually to fill a test pool. For each sample, multiple prototypes of a newly designed instrument were placed in the pool. If a prototype stayed afloat, it was marked with a (+). If a protoype sank, it was marked with a (–). These data were then collected and recorded in Table 3.

Water Sample	Table 3					
	Prototype					
	R5	R6	U3	U4	X1	X2
I	+	+	+	+	+	+
II	+	+	+	+	+	+
III	–	+	+	+	+	+
IV	–	+	+	+	+	+
V	–	–	+	+	+	+
VI	–	–	–	+	+	+
VII	–	–	–	–	+	+
VIII	–	–	–	–	–	+
IX	–	–	–	–	–	–
X	–	–	–	–	–	–

22. In Experiment 1, if an additional sample were brought to 40°C and a density of 1.018 g/mL, what would its expected mass be in the graduated cylinder?

F. 150.9 g
G. 151.8 g
H. 152.7 g
J. 153.6 g

GO ON TO THE NEXT PAGE.

23. Based on Table 2, what is the most likely density of water at 10°C and 2.50% salinity?

   A. 1.019
   B. 1.017
   C. 1.013
   D. 1.010

24. An engineer states that prototype U3 is better suited than X2 for water surface data collection in a 10°C and 2.35% salinity environment. Do the results of the experiments support this claim?

   F. Yes, because prototype U3 will sink and X2 will float in these water conditions.
   G. Yes, because prototype U3 will float and X2 will sink in these water conditions.
   H. No, because prototype U3 will sink and X2 will float in these water conditions.
   J. No, because prototype U3 will float and X2 will sink in these water conditions.

25. A new prototype is tested in water samples IV through VII in a manner similar to Experiment 3. Which of the following results would NOT be possible?

	Water Sample			
	IV	V	VI	VII
A.	–	–	–	–
B.	+	+	+	+
C.	+	+	–	–
D.	–	–	+	+

26. In Experiment 1, samples were transferred to a graduated cylinder to obtain a more accurate and precise measurement of the:

   F. mass of the NaCl added to the H_2O.
   G. salinity after it reached the designated temperature.
   H. volume used to calculate the density.
   J. temperature used to determine the final salinity.

27. In a later analysis, the density of prototype U3 is manually determined. Which of the following values would be consistent with the results of Experiments 1 through 3 ?

   A. 1.021 g/mL
   B. 1.023 g/mL
   C. 1.026 g/mL
   D. 1.028 g/mL

GO ON TO THE NEXT PAGE.

Passage VI

Haloarchaea are single-celled microorganisms that can use light to generate energy, through a unique form of *photosynthesis*. To compare haloarchaeal photosynthesis with plant photosynthesis and bacterial fermentation, researchers performed two experiments in which they exposed plant haloarchaeal and bacterial cells to either red or green light. The researchers measured the growth of these cells by measuring how much acid and CO_2 were produced; more production of these indicated more growth.

Experiment 1

Water containing salt and sucrose was added to eight large test tubes. Next, *phenolphthalein* (a pH indicator that is colorless in the presence of acid and has a pink color in its absence) was added to each large test tube. A smaller test tube was then added, inverted, into each large test tube to collect CO_2; if CO_2 had been produced, a gas bubble would appear in this smaller tube (see Figure 1).

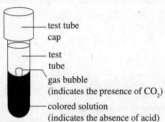

test tube cap

test tube

gas bubble (indicates the presence of CO_2)

colored solution (indicates the absence of acid)

Figure 1

The large test tubes were capped, heated until the solutions were sterile, and then cooled. Nothing was added to the first test tube (T1). Cells of the plant *Rosa carolina* were added to the second test tube (T2), cells of the haloarchaea *NRC-1* were added to the third test tube (T3), and cells of the bacterium *Bacillus anthracis* were added to the fourth test tube (T4). These four test tubes were exposed to red light, and incubated at 37°C for 48 hr. Then, the procedure was repeated with exposure to green light, using the four remaining test tubes: T5 (no cells), T6 (plant cells), T7 (haloarchaeal cells), and T8 (bacterial cells). In Table 1, + means presence and – means absence.

Table 1					
Red light			Green light		
	Acid	CO_2		Acid	CO_2
T1: Control	–	–	T5: Control	–	–
T2: Plant	–	+	T6: Plant	–	–
T3: Haloarchaea	–	–	T7: Haloarchaea	+	–
T4: Bacterium	+	+	T8: Bacterium	+	+

Experiment 2

Some of the cells tested in Experiment 1 are thought to contain pigments that help them absorb light. To determine whether these cells absorbed light to generate energy, cells of the same species are exposed to red and green light in new test tubes. The researchers measure the *transmittance*, or the amount of light that transmits through the test tube. If the transmittance is low, then the cells in the test tube are assumed to contain pigments that absorb most of the light to generate energy. If the transmittance is high, then the cells are assumed to contain no pigment that could absorb light and generate energy. Instead, most of the light passes through the test tube.

Table 2			
Red light		Green light	
	Transmittance		Transmittance
T9: Plant	Low	T12: Plant	High
T10: Haloarchaea	High	T13: Haloarchaea	Low
T11: Bacterium	High	T14: Bacterium	High

28. In Experiment 1, which cell types grew in the presence of green light?

F. Plant cells only
G. Plant and bacterial cells only
H. Plant and haloarchaeal cells only
J. Haloarchaeal and bacterial cells only

GO ON TO THE NEXT PAGE.

29. Suppose that plant cells and haloarchaeal cells that are situated close to each other do not interfere with each other's absorption of light and generation of energy. If a new test tube containing both plant and haloarchaeal cells were prepared, what would be the most likely results for Experiments 1 and 2 ?

	Red light			Green light		
	Acid	CO_2	Transmittance	Acid	CO_2	Transmittance
A.	−	−	High	−	−	High
B.	−	+	Low	+	−	Low
C.	+	−	Low	−	+	High
D.	+	+	High	+	+	Low

30. Suppose that a scientist isolates a cell type that is one of the four cell types used in Experiment 1. She finds that this cell type produces CO_2 in the presence of red light. She then tests the cell type in the presence of green light and finds that neither CO_2 nor acid is produced. Based on the results of Experiment 1, the cell type is most likely the:

F. control with nothing added.
G. plant *Rosa carolina*.
H. haloarchea *NRC-1*.
J. bacterium *Bacillus anthracis*.

31. What is the evidence from Experiments 1 and 2 that haloarchaea require green light to generate energy?

A. In the presence of red light, haloarchaea show low transmittance of light and produce acid.
B. In the presence of red light, haloarchaea show high transmittance of light and produce no acid.
C. In the presence of green light, haloarchaea show low transmittance of light and produce acid.
D. In the presence of green light, haloarchaea show high transmittance of light and produce no acid.

32. Which of the following best illustrates the results of Experiment 1 for the plant *Rosa carolina* in red light?

F.

H.

G.

J.

33. Do the results of Experiment 1 support the hypothesis that haloarchaea and bacteria use similar processes to generate energy?

A. Yes, because both haloarchaea and bacteria produce CO_2 in the presence of green light.
B. Yes, because both haloarchaea and bacteria produce CO_2 in the presence of red light.
C. No, because haloarchaea produce only acid in the presence of green light, while bacteria produce acid and CO_2 in both red and green light.
D. No, because neither haloarchaea nor bacteria produce CO_2 in the presence of either red or green light.

GO ON TO THE NEXT PAGE.

Passage VII

For most of the 20th century, scientists recognized two basic domains of living organisms, *prokaryotes* and *eukaryotes*. The presence of nuclei and other membrane-bound organelles within the cell primarily distinguished eukaryotes from prokaryotes. The possibility of revising this dichotomy resulted from the discovery of the *Archaea*, organisms with unique cell membrane and *ribosomal RNA (rRNA)* structure. Cell membranes are composed of *phospholipids* that have both water-insoluble and water-soluble subunits. *Ribosomes* are made of protein and rRNA and build new proteins within the cell.

Two scientists in the 1990s debate whether organisms should be classified into two or three domains.

2-Domain Hypothesis

The Archaea are prokaryotes because they lack intracellular membrane-bound organelles. Although they are found in extreme and unusual environments, the gross structure and life cycle of the Archaea are similar to prokaryotic bacteria. Like bacteria, their cells are usually surrounded by a cell wall, and they reproduce asexually through binary fission.

The structural and metabolic characteristics that are unique to the Archaea are not significantly different from other prokaryotes to warrant their separation into a third domain. Although the Archaea were distinguished very early on in the diversification of life, today they remain appropriately defined by the original definition of prokaryote.

3-Domain Hypothesis

The Archaea are a distinct form of life requiring a revision of the previously held dichotomy of prokaryote and eukaryote. Eukaryota should remain the same, but prokaryotes should be split into Archaea and Bacteria because of significant differences in genetics, structure, and metabolism.

Archaea as a domain is justified by detailed analysis. The genetic sequence of rRNA in the Archaea is so distinct from prokaryotes and eukaryotes that these groups of organisms likely diverged over 3 billion years ago. Archaea cell membranes contain more rigid *ether linkages* instead of the *ester linkages* found in eukaryotes and bacteria. This contributes to their survival in harsh environments. Finally, the Archaea are capable of exploiting a wider range of energy sources compared to eukaryotes and bacteria.

34. Which of the following statements is most consistent with the *3-Domain Hypothesis*? The time, in millions of years ago, when two groups of organisms diverge on the evolutionary tree increases as the:

   F. similarities between rRNA gene sequences increases.
   G. differences between rRNA gene sequences increases.
   H. number of ester linkages in the cell membrane increases.
   J. number of ether linkages in the cell membrane decreases.

35. By referring to the observation that the newly discovered organisms do not have membrane-bound organelles, the scientist supporting the 2-Domain Hypothesis implies that these new organisms do not have which of the following structures?

   A. Phospholipids
   B. Ribosomes
   C. rRNA
   D. Nuclei

36. According to the passage, a similarity between eukaryotes and prokaryotes is that both groups of organisms:

   F. have ester linkages in their membranes.
   G. contain membrane-bound organelles.
   H. reproduce sexually.
   J. are composed of cells.

37. According to the scientist who supports the 2-Domain Hypothesis, which of the following is the strongest argument *against* using a 3-Domain classification?

   A. rRNA does not exist in prokaryotes.
   B. Ether linkages are found in the cell membranes of the Archaea.
   C. The Archaea meet the primary definition of prokaryotic.
   D. The Archaea synthesize proteins in the cell cytoplasm.

GO ON TO THE NEXT PAGE.

38. It is shown that the Archaea have protein synthesis structures and mechanisms more like eukaryotes than prokaryotes. This observation contradicts arguments stated in which hypothesis?

   F. The 2-Domain Hypothesis, because the discovery would show that the new organisms and bacteria fundamentally differ in cellular metabolism.

   G. The 2-Domain Hypothesis, because the discovery would show that the new organisms and eukaryotes fundamentally differ in cellular metabolism.

   H. The 3-Domain Hypothesis, because the discovery would show that the new organisms and bacteria fundamentally differ in cellular metabolism.

   J. The 3-Domain Hypothesis, because the discovery would show that the new organisms and eukaryotes fundamentally differ in cellular metabolism.

39. The scientist who supports the 3-Domain Hypothesis implies that the 2-Domain Hypothesis is *weakened* by which observation?

   A. The Archaea have membrane-bound organelles.
   B. Microscopes cannot accurately describe organisms.
   C. The Archaea lack ester linkages in their cell membranes.
   D. Eukaryotes are not related to the Archaea.

40. Which of the following illustrations of a portion of a phospholipid cell membrane is consistent with the description in the passage?

Key
◯ — water soluble
|| — water insoluble

F.

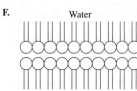

Water

Water

G.

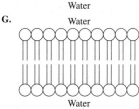

Water

Water

H.

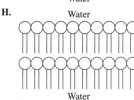

Water

Water

J.

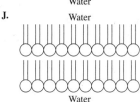

Water

Water

END OF TEST 4
STOP! DO NOT RETURN TO ANY OTHER TEST.

Directions

This is a test of your writing skills. You will have thirty (30) minutes to write an essay. Before you begin planning and writing your essay, read the writing prompt carefully to understand exactly what you are being asked to do. Your essay will be evaluated on the evidence it provides of your ability to express judgments by taking a position on the issue in the writing prompt; to maintain a focus on the topic throughout your essay; to develop a position by using logical reasoning and by supporting your ideas; to organize ideas in a logical way; and to use language clearly and effectively according to the conventions of standard written English.

You may use the unlined pages in this test booklet to plan your essay. These pages will not be scored. *You must write your essay on the lined pages in the answer folder.* Your writing on those lined pages will be scored. You may not need all the lined pages, but to ensure you have enough room to finish, do NOT skip lines. You may write corrections or additions neatly between the lines of your essay, but do NOT write in the margins of the lined pages. *Illegible essays cannot be scored, so you must write (or print) clearly.*

If you finish before time is called, you may review your work. Lay your pencil down immediately when time is called.

DO NOT OPEN THIS BOOK UNTIL YOU ARE TOLD TO DO SO.

ACT Assessment Writing Test Prompt

Recently, one state has passed legislation making it illegal for anyone under the age of 18 to use a cell phone—including hands-free models—or any other electronic communications device while driving. Supporters argue that such devices distract drivers' attention from the road, and thus this law will lower the number of accidents and save lives. Opponents argue the law is discriminatory, since adults may use hands-free cell phones while driving. In your opinion, should all states pass a law banning drivers 18 and younger from using communication devices while driving?

In your essay, take a position on this question. You may write about either one of the two points of view given, or you may present a different point of view on this question. Use specific reasons and examples to support your position.

Chapter 8
Practice Test 3:
Answers and
Explanations

TEST 3 ENGLISH ANSWERS

1.	D		36.	J
2.	G		37.	A
3.	D		38.	J
4.	H		39.	C
5.	A		40.	J
6.	H		41.	C
7.	D		42.	F
8.	G		43.	C
9.	D		44.	G
10.	H		45.	D
11.	A		46.	J
12.	G		47.	C
13.	A		48.	J
14.	G		49.	B
15.	D		50.	J
16.	J		51.	A
17.	C		52.	G
18.	F		53.	C
19.	C		54.	F
20.	H		55.	B
21.	B		56.	F
22.	G		57.	C
23.	D		58.	H
24.	J		59.	D
25.	A		60.	G
26.	F		61.	D
27.	D		62.	G
28.	F		63.	C
29.	B		64.	J
30.	H		65.	C
31.	B		66.	H
32.	H		67.	A
33.	C		68.	G
34.	J		69.	D
35.	C		70.	J

71.	B		26.	K
72.	H		27.	D
73.	B		28.	G
74.	F		29.	B
75.	A		30.	J
			31.	D
			32.	F
			33.	D
			34.	G

TEST 3 MATH ANSWERS

1.	D		35.	E
2.	G		36.	F
3.	B		37.	E
4.	K		38.	F
5.	B		39.	C
6.	G		40.	H
7.	E		41.	B
8.	G		42.	J
9.	C		43.	D
10.	H		44.	H
11.	D		45.	E
12.	F		46.	G
13.	B		47.	E
14.	H		48.	G
15.	E		49.	B
16.	G		50.	J
17.	D		51.	B
18.	K		52.	G
19.	C		53.	A
20.	H		54.	H
21.	E		55.	E
22.	J		56.	F
23.	E		57.	D
24.	H		58.	J
25.	D		59.	C
			60.	G

TEST 3 READING ANSWERS

1.	A	21.	A
2.	H	22.	G
3.	D	23.	C
4.	H	24.	H
5.	C	25.	C
6.	H	26.	J
7.	A	27.	B
8.	G	28.	H
9.	D	29.	A
10.	F	30.	H
11.	A	31.	D
12.	J	32.	G
13.	A	33.	B
14.	H	34.	F
15.	C	35.	C
16.	J	36.	H
17.	D	37.	D
18.	J	38.	F
19.	B	39.	C
20.	H	40.	H

TEST 3 SCIENCE ANSWERS

1.	C		21.	B
2.	F		22.	H
3.	B		23.	A
4.	G		24.	H
5.	D		25.	D
6.	G		26.	H
7.	A		27.	A
8.	H		28.	J
9.	A		29.	B
10.	G		30.	G
11.	C		31.	C
12.	J		32.	G
13.	D		33.	C
14.	H		34.	G
15.	D		35.	D
16.	G		36.	J
17.	D		37.	C
18.	H		38.	F
19.	A		39.	C
20.	J		40.	G

TEST 3 ENGLISH EXPLANATIONS

1. **D** The phrase *just like* introduces a comparison to *preparing a meal*, which means the correct answer must also start with an *-ing* word to compare two like items, eliminating choices (B) and (C). Choice (D) is a better answer than (A) because it is more concise.

2. **G** Choice (G) addresses the writer's goal by describing the robust aromas and provides sensory detail of *swirling rush*. Choices (F), (H), and (J) do not describe the richness of smell.

3. **D** Don't be fooled by the stuff in between! *Cooking,* one activity, is the subject of the underlined plural verb *require,* so you need the singular form of the verb. This means you can eliminate choices (A) and (C). Choice (D) is more concise than choice (B).

4. **H** In EXCEPT/LEAST/NOT questions, the underlined portion of the sentence is correct. All the choices use correct prepositions for going to the store, except choice (H) which implies that Eric is attacking the store.

5. **A** Two things caused the vegetables to be tasty: *natural sunshine and the farmers' careful tending,* which should be separated by *and,* eliminating choices (B) and (D). To be consistent, the two causes should both be introduced with the preposition *of* making choice (A) the best answer. The comma preceding *and* in choice (C) is not necessary because it doesn't separate two complete thoughts.

6. **H** Choice (H) describes how Eric precisely cuts his vegetables and arranges the vegetables in layers. Just because Eric *slowly* places the vegetables does not necessarily mean he is paying attention to detail, eliminating choice (F). Choices (G) and (J) are weaker descriptions, because *pours* is less meticulous than *layers* and *kind of order* is vague.

7. **D** Commas cannot join two complete ideas. Because the first half of the sentence is complete, the underlined phrase must begin an incomplete thought, eliminating choices (A) and (B). Choice (C) is the

wrong form of the verb for adding an incomplete, descriptive thought: *alternating* is the correct form, which is choice (D).

8. **G** Since you're comparing people, *Eric* to *many cooks*, the best answer is choice (G). Choice (F) confuses the phrases *like* and *as with*, creating an incorrect idiomatic expression. A verb needs to immediately follow *as* in order to compare Eric's actions to those of many cooks, eliminating choices (H), which doesn't have a verb, and (J), which has the verb *do* in the wrong place.

9. **D** In EXCEPT/LEAST/NOT questions, the underlined portion of the sentence is correct. In the original sentence, the phrase *At this point* introduces the next step in a sequence of actions. Choices (A), (B), and (C) all indicate what Eric is going to do after splashing red wine into the cooker. Choice (D) is the incorrect expression, confusing *at least* with *at last*.

10. **H** Choice (H) adds detail to help readers visualize what the roast looks like as the pot heats up. Choices (F), (G), and (J) describe the slow rise in temperature, but provides no sensory detail.

11. **A** Choice (A) is the most concise answer, as choices (B), (C), and (D) add words but not any additional information.

12. **G** The introductory phrase *Every half hour* must be followed by a comma, and the incomplete idea *using a long meat thermometer* must also be followed by a comma to link it to the complete idea, *Eric reads the temperature...* Choice (G) is the only option that provides a pair of commas around this phrase. Choice (F) offsets the wrong phrase *using a long,* confusing the meaning of the sentence. The lack of commas in choice (H) creates a run-on sentence. Choice (J) uses a semicolon instead of a comma, incorrectly separating an incomplete thought from a complete one.

13. **A** What choice (B) describes is redundancy, which would mean the sentence should be deleted, not kept, so cross this one off. The overall essay describes both Eric and the roast he cooks, so the reasoning

in choice (C) is incorrect. You can eliminate choice (D) because the previous paragraph already described the relationship between rising temperature and stewing vegetables. Choice (A) maintains consistent flow and focus within the paragraph and overall essay.

14. **G** Choice (F) incorrectly has a comma separating two complete ideas. You can also eliminate choice (H) because *you* is inconsistent with the third-person *he* the author has been using throughout the rest of the essay. Choice (J) has a misplaced modifier, suggesting that the *plump meat* is lifting itself. Choice (G) is the most clear and consistent answer, describing Eric lifting the meat.

15. **D** Choices (A), (B), and (C) all reiterate what has been already stated in the sentence: that the roast is a work of art. Choice (D) is the most concise answer.

16. **J** Choice (J) is the most concise and doesn't omit necessary information. Choices (F), (G), and (H) make the sentence wordy and redundant; they describe the speculation that the narrator already mentions (*people conjure up an image*).

17. **C** In EXCEPT/LEAST/NOT questions, the underlined portion of the sentence is correct. The writer uses *to start* to introduce his argument about people's misconceptions of the type of farm he was on. Choices (A), (B), and (D) are acceptable substitutions to achieve the same effect. Choice (C) is unacceptable because the correct expression is *For starters*, not *For start*.

18. **F** Choice (F) uses a semicolon to divide the sentence into two complete thoughts. Choices (G), (H), and (J) create run-on sentences.

19. **C** The writer is trying to illustrate the contrast between the unconventional livestock and the conventions expected of a farm that has existed as long as that of her family. Therefore, the phrase is used to emphasize the longevity of the farm. The sentence gives no indication of the narrator's relationship with her mother (A), nor does it indicate that anything bad is going to happen, (D). The following sentences

also discuss the untraditional practices of her family farm, eliminating choice (B).

20. **H** The correct expression to express a person's assumption is *must have* not *must of*, eliminating choices (F) and (G). Choice (J) uses *about*, which is idiomatically incorrect; therefore, (H) is the best answer.

21. **B** The phrase *in fact* is unnecessary and should be offset with commas, making choice (B) the best answer. The single comma in choices (A) and (C) creates a disruptive pause within the sentence.

22. **G** Sentences 1 and 2 describe the farm before the introduction of the llamas. Choice (F) interrupts this description. Choice (G) makes it clear that the *he* referred to in Sentence 3 is the narrator's great-grandfather. Choices (H) and (J) introduce the narrator's great-grandfather too late, leaving the reader to wonder who Sentence 3's *he* is.

23. **D** In EXCEPT/LEAST/NOT questions, the underlined portion of the sentence is correct. Choices (A) and (C) use appropriate synonyms for the past tense verb *began*. *Living* can replace *to live*, making choice (B) also acceptable. Choice (D) is incorrect because it uses the wrong verb form *begun*, which should always be preceded by a helping verb to indicate past perfect tense rather than past tense.

24. **J** In EXCEPT/LEAST/NOT questions, the underlined portion of the sentence is correct. Choices (F), (G), and (H) use appropriate synonyms for *after*. Without an introductory conjunction, choice (J) creates a run-on sentence.

25. **A** Choice (A) correctly puts the verb in the past perfect tense because the narrator's expectation came before his realization. Choices (B) and (C) make the action hypothetical by using *would*. Choice (D) puts the action in the present perfect tense, but the story takes place in the past tense.

26. **F** Choice (F) correctly introduces the topic of school, which is the focus of the remainder of the paragraph. Choices (G), (H), and (J) provide information that strays from the topic of this paragraph.

27. **D** Choice (D) is the most clear and concise answer. Choices (A), (B), and (C) are all too wordy and confusing.

28. **F** Choice (F) makes it clear that she learned from reading textbooks on her own, rather than the instruction from the teacher. Choices (G), (H), and (J) are vague in comparison.

29. **B** Because the habits describe all llamas, the apostrophe should show plural possessive, making choice (B) the best answer. Choice (A) uses the singular possessive. Choices (C) and (D) do not use the possessive form at all.

30. **H** The correct expression is to *make a career in farming*, making choice (H) the best answer. Choices (G) and (J) would be correct if the expression were *make a career out of farming*. Choice (F) would be correct if the expression were *make a career as a farmer*.

31. **B** This can't be *which* because it refers to a person, and the portion can't be omitted because the sentence doesn't make sense without the relative pronoun; eliminate choices (C) and (D). The question now is whether to use *who* or *whom*. Look at the other parts of the sentence, noticing what you need to connect it to: *who/whom spent much of his childhood*. You need the subjective *who* form here. Would you say *he spent much of his childhood*, or *him spent much of his childhood*? The best answer is choice (B).

32. **H** Choice (F) can't work because the following paragraph doesn't talk about the Civil War. Choice (G) can't work because the underlined portion is not an *unnecessary digression*; it's merely a mention of the Civil War. Choice (J) can't work because there is no mention in this essay that Chesnutt was a historical writer. Only choice (H) agrees with the main theme of this paragraph, which is a discussion of Chesnutt's childhood.

33. **C** In EXCEPT/LEAST/NOT questions, the underlined portion of the sentence is correct. Note the differences between what separates the words *literature* and *he* in each of the answer choices. Since *literature* ends a complete thought and *he* begins a new one, only choices (A), (B), and (D) can work—choice (A) because it has a semicolon separating the two complete thoughts, choice (B) because it has a comma and coordinating conjunction separating the thoughts (as in the original sentence), and choice (D) because it has a period separating the two complete thoughts. Choice (C), however, creates a comma splice, and without a coordinating conjunction (such as *and* or *but*), a comma cannot be used to separate two complete thoughts.

34. **J** Because the sentence indicates that action ended with the author's death in 1932, the underlined verb must be in the past tense, which only choice (J) is.

35. **C** Since all choices are roughly synonymous, choose the most concise answer that preserves the meaning of the sentence. Choice (C) is the most concise, and it preserves the meaning of the sentence.

36. **J** Note that in the part of the sentence before the underlined portion, the author refers to *earlier folklorists*. The word *earlier* makes choices (F), (G), and (H) redundant. Only choice (J) correctly opts to DELETE the underlined portion.

37. **A** Begin by determining whether the sentence beginning with *However* provides a continuation of the prior sentence or a contrast to the prior sentence. Because the author illustrates a difference between the work of earlier folklorists and that of Chesnutt, eliminate the continuation words, choices (C) and (D). Choice (B) is wrong because two complete sentences may not be separated by a comma. Choice (A) properly uses a period.

38. **J** The proposed addition does not relate to or flow from the paragraph, which is about Chesnutt's works. Eliminate choices (F) and (G). The

substance of choice (H) is incorrect. Choice (J) correctly observes that the addition is distracting.

39. **C** This pronoun refers to *The Conjure Woman*, a singular noun, so it cannot be *their* as in choice (B). Choice (D) is not a word, so that can be eliminated as well. Choice (A) gives the contraction *it is*, which is not used to show possession. Choice (C) shows the appropriate possession. Remember: possessive pronouns don't have an apostrophe (think of hers, yours, and ours).

40. **J** Because the underlined portion is difficult to follow, don't try to rewrite it on your own. Rather, read all four answer choices to determine which one is the clearest. Choice (J) clearly articulates the author's meaning and does so without wordiness.

41. **C** Since the sentence is referring to only a single *family*, eliminate choices (B) and (D). Between choices (A) and (C), remember that although a family includes many people, it is actually a singular noun, and its possessive should thus be punctuated as *family's*, as in choice (C).

42. **F** While choices (G), (H), and (J) all make the sentence shorter, each makes the meaning of the sentence unclear. Choice (G) gives an ambiguous pronoun with no clear antecedent. Choice (H) is also ambiguous, although it probably refers to the children, changing the meaning of the sentence. Choice (J) suggests that the novel was the first to talk about itself, which does not make logical sense. Only choice (F) gives a clear, unambiguous indication of what the novel was the first to talk about.

43. **C** In EXCEPT/LEAST/NOT questions, the underlined portion of the sentence is correct. The underlined portion is a modifier, properly followed by what the modifier describes: *the novel*. Choices (A), (B), and (D) are also modifiers describing *the novel*. Choice (C), however, is a modifier describing the person or company that published the novel. Thus, choice (C) would have to be followed by that person or company, not *the novel*.

44. **G**   Choices (F), (H), and (J) are all too narrow to be described as summarizing the essay. Choice (F) refers only to the two books discussed in the text, but the last paragraph indicates that Chesnutt's influence extends beyond these two books and beyond his lifetime. Choice (H) refers to only the first paragraph. Choice (J) refers only to the paragraph about *The Conjure Woman*. Only choice (G) is general enough to encapsulate the entire essay.

45. **D**   Notice the time periods in each paragraph. Paragraph 2 talks about the end of Chesnutt's life, his death in 1932, and his current reputation. Accordingly, it must come after discussions of earlier points in his biography but before Paragraph 5, which is meant to conclude and summarize the essay. Also note that *The House Behind the Cedars* is mentioned as if the reader already has some familiarity with it, so the paragraph must come after Paragraph 4, which discusses *The House Behind the Cedars*.

46. **J**   The subject of the sentence is *accomplishments*, so the verb must be plural to agree with it. Choice (J) provides a plural verb in the correct past tense. Choices (F) and (G) are singular. Choice (H) can be either singular or plural, but it uses a future tense, which does not agree with the tense of the passage.

47. **C**   The sentence makes sense if you remove the phrase *according to his widow Rachel Robinson*. Since the phrase is not essential to the meaning of the sentence, it should be offset by commas. Thus, choice (C) is correct. Choice (A) has no pauses to offset this information, and choice (B) has an additional and unnecessary comma. Both choices confuse the flow of the sentence. Choice (D) uses a long dash incorrectly because the non-underlined portion uses a comma instead of a second long dash to indicate that the phrase must be offset.

48. J   Choice (J) is the most concise answer that conveys the correct meaning, and it removes the redundancy of the original sentence. Choices (F), (G), and (H) are wordy and redundant. Note, when DELETE is offered as an answer choice, always give it serious consideration—omitting an unnecessary part of the sentence can often make it more clear and concise.

49. B   The underlined phrase describes the team for which Jackie Robinson played baseball, so choice (B) is correct. Choices (A), (C), and (D) confuse the meaning of the sentence or disrupt its flow.

50. J   The word *baseball* ends an incomplete thought, and the word *he* begins a complete thought. Choices (F), (G), and (H) all contain punctuation that can only be used to separate two complete thoughts. Choice (J) is the only answer choice that uses a comma to correctly link an incomplete thought to a complete one.

51. A   The end of the sentence details the seats in the stadium, so the most specific type of person to fill them is a spectator, choice (A). Choice (B) is not specific enough. Choices (C) and (D) describe types of people that would be at a baseball game but not occupying the seats in the stadium.

52. G   Choice (G) is correct because the paragraph describes how Jackie's excellent play changed the attitudes of whites toward having blacks in baseball. Choices (F), (H), and (J) do not accurately describe the point of the paragraph, so they are not things that would be lost with its deletion.

53. C   First, determine whether the sentence following *for example* provides a continuation of the prior sentence or a contrast to the prior sentence. Because the prior sentence explains that an ordinary man who did what Jackie did would wilt, and the sentence following *for example* describes Jackie's increased efforts, a contrasting term is needed. Thus, eliminate choices (A), (B), and (D). Choice (C) is correct.

54. **F** The noun being referred to is *athletes*, so the possessive pronoun relating to it must agree in person and number, as it does in choice (F). Choices (G) and (H) do not agree because the possessive pronouns in these choices are singular. Choice (J) contains the proper agreement, but it incorrectly acts as a noun instead of an adjective.

55. **B** The sentence should be kept because it provides important information about Jackie Robinson's personality, eliminating choices (C) and (D). Choice (B) is correct because the mention of other athletes using their status for personal gain emphasizes Jackie's personal sacrifice and dedication to civil rights advancement. Choice (A) is incorrect because there is no indication in the passage that Jackie had any endorsement deals.

56. **F** The word *entrepreneur* ends a complete thought, and the word *his* begins a second complete thought. Choices (G) and (H) contain punctuation that can not be used to connect complete thoughts. Choice (J) incorrectly uses a semicolon instead of a comma with the coordinating conjunction *and,* causing the second thought to become incomplete.

57. **C** Sentence 3 contains the description of Jackie's civil rights activism during his baseball career, and Sentence 4 describes his activism after his baseball career, so choice (C) is correct. Choices (A), (B), and (D) do not correctly separate the two periods of his activism.

58. **H** The word *than* indicates a comparison between two things, as with choice (H). Choice (F) contains a superlative, which is used for three or more things. Choice (G) does not contain any words of comparison. Choice (J) contains a word that is not proper English.

59. **D** The word *movement* ends an incomplete thought, and the word *his* begins a complete thought. Choice (D) correctly uses a comma to link an incomplete thought to a complete one. Choice (A) creates a run-on sentence. Choices (B) and (C) contain punctuation that can be used only to separate two complete thoughts.

60. **G** In EXCEPT/LEAST/NOT questions, the underlined portion of the sentence is correct. This sentence agrees in tone with the one preceding it. Therefore, a transition word that indicates that agreement is required, as with choices (F), (H), and (J). Choice (G) provides a transition word that indicates an opposing tone, so it is the LEAST acceptable alternative and thus the correct answer.

61. **D** Choice (D) corrects the punctuation error in the passage. A semicolon should not be used if it separates essential parts of a sentence (the verb *fertilized* should not be separated from its subject *patches of moss*). Choices (B) and (C) incorrectly insert a comma between a preposition and its object.

62. **G** In EXCEPT/LEAST/NOT questions, the underlined portion of the sentence is correct. Choice (G) inserts a period, incorrectly separating the dependent clause from the independent clause. The dependent clause *becoming active again when the climate warms and the ice is melting* cannot stand on its own as a complete sentence.

63. **C** Choice (C) provides a verb form that is parallel in structure to the preceding verb, *warms*. Choices (A), (B), and (D) are not parallel, and choice (B) also creates a sentence fragment.

64. **J** Choice (J) presents wording that is consistent with the style and tone of the rest of the essay. Choices (F), (G), and (H) are all too informal.

65. **C** Because the phrase *classified as arthropods* is not necessary to the sentence, it needs to be set off by commas, as in choice (C). Choices (B) and (D) are incorrect because each omits one of the required commas. Choice (A) is incorrect because a semicolon may be used only in between two complete ideas.

66. **H** Choice (H) provides the correct usage of the adverb *too*, which means to an excessive degree, and removes the improper comma after *icy*. Choices (F) and (G) incorrectly use the preposition *to*. Choice (J) improperly inserts a comma after *icy*.

67. **A** In EXCEPT/LEAST/NOT questions, the underlined portion of the sentence is correct. Choice (A) incorrectly omits a necessary comma, thereby creating a run-on sentence.

68. **G** Choice (G) correctly uses the present tense (*accompany*), which is in accordance with the use of the present tense in the rest of this paragraph. Choices (F) and (J) incorrectly use the past tense and choice (H) uses the past perfect tense.

69. **D** Choice (D) is the clearest, most concise answer. Choices (A), (B), and (C) all provide information that is not relevant to the passage.

70. **J** Choice (J) is correct because without the inclusion of the modifying phrase, the *Here* in the following sentence does not refer to anything. Choice (F) incorrectly suggests removing the phrase, and the modifying phrase does not include a fact that is provided later in the paragraph. Choice (G) incorrectly proposes removing the phrase and wrongly states that the above paragraph mentions insects as the only life forms in Antarctica. While it's true that the clause should be kept, choice (H) incorrectly assumes that Antarctica and McMurdo Sound are two different places; the phrase clearly specifies that McMurdo Sound is part of the continent of Antarctica.

71. **B** Choice (B) is the most descriptive and relevant of the answer choices. Choice (C) provides no visual detail besides snow cover, and choices (A) and (D) lack the vivid detail of choice (B), which adds description to the flora with the adjectives green, yellow, and orange. In addition, only choice (B) directly addresses the *terrain* in its description of the *rocky land*.

72. **H** Choice (H) is the most logical place to move this prepositional phrase. The nematode worms are not *thriving with the low temperatures*, or *dehydrating themselves with the low temperatures*, or *increasing moisture with the low temperatures*, they are *coping with the low temperatures*. In addition, note that Choices (F), (G), and (J) all match verbs with prepositions in idiomatically incorrect ways.

73.   **B**   Choice (B) does not effectively address the central point made in Paragraph 4: namely, that algae exist not only in the water, but also on land. Choices (A), (C), and (D) all effectively introduce the subject of Paragraph 4, signaling that the paragraph will discuss the ways in which algae adapt to the harsh climate of Antarctica, both on land and in the sea.

74.   **F**   Choice (F) correctly suggests keeping the phrase and ties it back into the point made in the preceding sentence: that phytoplankton help maintain the equilibrium of Antarctica's ecosystem. While Choice (G) is correct to propose keeping the clause, it incorrectly identifies seals, whales, and penguins as the most important creatures in Antarctica's seas, a debatable topic. Choices (H) and (J) incorrectly suggest removing the clause.

75.   **A**   Choice (A) correctly fits between the preceding sentence and the sentence that follows, because it indicates a contrasting relationship between the two ideas; while *Antarctica has the lowest species diversity of anywhere on earth,* the numbers of those species that do exist are staggering considering the harsh climatic conditions of the environment. Choice (B) wrongly inserts *indeed,* which is incorrect because the writer is presenting a contrasting relationship, not emphasizing a point made in the preceding sentence. Choices (C) and (D) each suggest a cause-effect relationship that is not indicated in the passage.

TEST 3 MATH EXPLANATIONS

1. **D** Treat absolute–value bars like parentheses and evaluate what's inside

   the absolute value bars first: $|8-5|-|5-8|=|3|-|-3|=3-3=0$. Re-

   member that absolute–value is a measure of distance, so the result is

   always nonnegative. Choice (E) is 3 – (–3) = 6.

2. **G** First, subtract the flat fee from the total cost to determine how much
   the tutor charged exclusively for tutoring: $220 – $40 = $180. $180 =
   $60/hr × 3 hours, so choice (G) is correct. Choice (F) incorrectly uses
   $40 + $60 = $100 as the hourly rate. Choices (H) and (K) divide
   $220 by $60 and $40, respectively, without subtracting the flat fee.
   Choice (J) calculates the session with a $60 flat fee and $40 hourly
   rate.

3. **B** The time it takes Train A can be found by dividing the number of

   miles it goes by the speed, $\frac{1152}{16}=72$. Train B then takes 48 hours,

   $\frac{1152}{24}=48$. To find how many more hours it takes, subtract the hours

   it takes Train B to go from the hours it takes Train A, 72 – 48 = 24,

   choice (B). Choice (A) is the result of averaging the miles per hour

   values, and choice (C) from adding them. Choice (D) and (E) are the

   hours that each train takes, not the difference.

4. **K** The question is asking you to simplify the expression by combining like terms. $33r^2-41r^2=-8r^2$, $-24r+r=-23r$. The simplified
   expression is $-8r^2-23r+75$. Choices (F) and (G) combine all
   coefficients between unlike terms. Choice (H) forgets that r is actually
   $1r$. Choice (J) incorrectly multiplies variables rather than just adding
   the coefficients.

5. **B** Since the triangles are equilateral and each one's perimeter is 15, each side is 5. Figure *ABCDEF* has six sides, so its perimeter is 6(5) = 30. Choice (D) finds the area of the figure rather than its perimeter. Choice (E) treats the sides of each triangle, rather than the perimeter of each triangle, as 15. Choice (A) miscalculates the side of the triangle as 3 inches, and choice (C) includes the dotted interior lines in calculating the perimeter.

6. **G** Use the FOIL method. Multiply the First, Outside, Inside, and Last terms together, and then add the results. $(5x + 2)(x - 3) = 5x^2 - 15x + 2x - 6 = 5x^2 - 13x - 6$.

7. **E** Use the words in the problem to create an equation: *percent* means "divide by 100," *of* means "multiply," and *what number* means "use a variable." The first equation is $\frac{35}{100}x = 14$ and $x = 40$. The second equation is $y = \frac{20}{100}(40) = 8$. Choice (A) is 20% of 14. Choice (B) is 35% of 14. Choice (D) is (20% + 35%) of 14.

8. **G** The list of integers adds up to 7x + 7. Set that equal to 511 then solve, and you'll get choice (G), 72. Choice (H) divides 511 by 7 without first subtracting 7, and choice (J) mistakenly adds 7 to the sum. Choices (F) and (K) are both incorrect estimates.

9. **C** The easiest approach to this problem is to test all the answer choices. If point B is the midpoint of line A, you can use the midpoint formula $(\frac{x_1 + x_2}{2}, \frac{y_1 + y_2}{2})$ by plugging in the answer choices into the equation along with the values given for point A. When plugging in answer choice (C), the equation is $(\frac{1+9}{2}, \frac{8+4}{2})$ which gives you the correct midpoint of (5,6). Choice (A) confuses *C* as the midpoint. The other answer choices do not use the midpoint formula correctly.

10. H   Because the trapezoid is isosceles, its two vertical halves are mirror images of each other. To get from A to B requires adding 3 to the x value, and 6 to the y value of A, so to get from D to C, instead subtract 3 from the x value and add 6 to the y value of D.

11. D   To find the total average sales at each bus station, multiply the values of each column of the first matrix by the relevant row in the second matrix. $180(3) + 200(3) + 150(3) + 60(2) + 120(2) + 70(2) = 2,090$. Choice (A) finds the number of tickets sold and choice (C) multiplies that total by $2.50, the average of the two fare rates. Choice (B) gives only the peak fare sales. Choice (E) finds the total if all of the fares were bought at the peak $3 price.

12. F   The sum of the exterior angles of a regular polygon = 360°. If you have trouble remembering this rule, use the supplemental angles in the problem. Because $a° + 35° = 180°$, $a = 145°$. Find angle b the same way: $b° + 45° = 180°$, so $b = 135°$. You can now find the third angle in the triangle: $180° - 35° - 45° = 100°$. Now you know that $c° + 100° = 180°$, so $c = 80°$. $a + b + c = 145° + 135° + 80° = 360°$.

13. B   Use the words in the problem to create an equation: *percent* means "divide by 100," *of* means "multiply," and *what number* means "use a variable." The equation is $\dfrac{x}{100} \times 300 = 60$, so $x = 20\%$. Choice (A) is the percent of purple jellybeans. Choice (C) is the percent of red jellybeans. Choice (D) is the percent of orange jellybeans. Choice (E) confuses the number of green jellybeans and the percent of the sample consisting of green jellybeans.

14. H   Set up a proportion: $\dfrac{75\ red}{300\ total} = \dfrac{x}{25,000\ total}$, and $x = 6,250$. Choice (F) is the estimate for the number of purple jellybeans

in the barrel. Choice (G) is the estimate for the number of green jellybeans. Choice (J) is the estimate for the number of orange jellybeans. Choice (K) assumes that the 75 red jellybeans in the sample is the same as the percentage of red jellybeans and finds 75% of 25,000.

15. E To find the central angle, first find what fraction of the sample is composed of orange jellybeans: $\frac{120}{300} = \frac{2}{5}$. The central angle for the orange sector is $\frac{2}{5} \times 360° = 144°$. Choice (A) is the central angle for the purple sector. Choice (B) is the central angle for the green sector. Choice (C) is the central angle for the red sector. Choice (D) confuses the number of orange jellybeans with the degree measure of the central angle.

16. G Because E and F are both midpoints, draw a line between them and you divide the rectangle into 4 equal parts. Quadrilateral $AECF$ contains 2 of these 4 parts, or (G). Choice (J) shows the ratio using $\triangle ABE$ instead of quadrilateral $AECF$, while choice (F) shows the ratio of the quadrilateral to the other half of the rectangle. Choice (H) assumes the 3 parts in the original diagram are equal. Choice (K) divides the rectangle into 5 parts.

17. D In the slope-intercept form, $y = mx + b$, the slope of the line is $m = \frac{1}{2}$. Parallel lines have the same slope, so the answer is choice (D). Choice (B) is the slope of the perpendicular line to the given line. Choice (A) is the y-intercept. Choices (C) and (E) are the opposite and reciprocal, respectively, of the correct slope.

18. **K** Given that the ratio of the two sittings is 3:5, you can make the equation: 3 × x minutes + 5 × x minutes = 120 minutes, so $8x$ = 120, and x = 15. The longer sitting is $5x$ = 5 × 15 = 75 minutes. Careful not to choose choice (H), which is the shorter sitting or choice (G), which is the value of x.

19. **C** Find the square root of each answer choice on your calculator until you find a value between 11 and 12. $\sqrt{140} \approx 11.83$. Choice (B) is 11 exactly; the question asks for something greater. The value of choice (D) is just more than 12, too big. Choice (A) adds the numbers from the problem without answering what is asked for, and choice (E) = 23, the sum of the numbers in the problem.

20. **H** The area of the entire space of the garden is 10 × 16 × 3 = 480 ft². The rectangular plot for beans is 4 × 6 = 24 ft², and the rectangular plot for lettuce is $2\frac{1}{2}$ × 5 = 12.5 ft². Subtract the spaces for beans and lettuce from the total space for tomatoes. 480 – 24 – 12.5 = 443.5 ft². Since the maximum number of square feet that can be covered by a packet is 200, estimate $\frac{443.5 \text{ ft}^2}{200 \text{ ft}^2 \text{ per packet}} > 2$ packets. Susan will need to buy a minimum of 3 packets.

21. **E** First, bring the 12 to the left side of the equation, so the whole equation is equal to 0 (i.e., $x^2 + 4x - 12 = 0$). Factor the equation by thinking of what two numbers when multiplied together = –12 and when added together = 4. 6 and –2 satisfy those conditions. Make the equation $(x + 6)(x - 2) = 0$, then set $(x + 6) = 0$ and $(x - 2) = 0$ and solve for x in both cases. x is either –6 or 2. You can also try the numbers from the answer choices and see which ones satisfy the equation.

22. J   To divide, subtract the exponents of common terms. To visualize

what's happening, you can write out the expression as $\dfrac{x \cdot x \cdot x \cdot x \cdot y \cdot y}{x \cdot x \cdot y \cdot y \cdot y \cdot y}$.

Cancel matching terms in the numerator and denominator to get $\dfrac{x \cdot x}{y \cdot y}$,

or $\dfrac{x^2}{y^2}$. Choices (F) and (G) negate the value of the entire expression,

and Choice (K) flips the numerator and denominator. Choice (H) in-

correctly assumes $x^2 = y^2$.

23. E   If point A must have at least one positive coordinate value, it could
be located in any quadrant except for III, or choice (E). Points in
quadrant III have negative x-coordinates and negative y-coordinates.
Choice (C) incorrectly assumes the point has exactly 1 positive coordinate. Choice (A) assumes the point has exactly 2 positive coordinates,
while (D) assumes it cannot have 2 positive coordinates.

24. H   If the fixed cost each day of the company is $1,600 and the variable
cost is the additional cost each day of producing each box. The equation then would be the fixed cost plus the variable cost, which is 1,600
+ 4.75b, or choice (H). Choices (F) and (K) switch the fixed and variable costs. Choices (G) and (J) find the difference between the variable
costs and the fixed cost instead of adding them to form the total cost.

25. D.   The sides of similar triangles are proportional in length. To find how

many times larger the larger triangle's perimeter is than the smaller

triangle's, divide the two known perimeters $\dfrac{576"}{9.6"}$ = 60 times larger.

$\overline{AC}$ will also be 60 times larger than $\overline{XZ}$: 3.2" × 60" = 192".

26. **K** Multiply the fractions on the left so that $\dfrac{6\sqrt{11}}{x\sqrt{11}} = \dfrac{3\sqrt{11}}{11}$. You can then cross multiply to get $66\sqrt{11} = 33x$, which simplifies to $x = 2\sqrt{11}$. You can also substitute the answer choices in for x and see which works in the equation. Choice (J) is half the value needed and choice (G) is its square. Choice (H) is 11^2. Choice (F) is a number from the problem that does not answer the given question.

27. **D** Set up an equation for each runner, with the number of seconds to get to the crossing point, as well as the number of feet from point "0 feet" being equal for both runners. Jonathan starts 150 feet in from what we will say is "0 feet" on the track, or at the 150 ft. point, and he runs at a speed of 9 ft./second for x seconds, covering y feet: 150 ft. + 9 ft./second × (x seconds) = y feet. Natalie starts at 1,300 feet and runs in the opposite direction at 12 ft./second for x seconds, covering y feet: 1,300 ft. – 12 ft./second × (x seconds) = y feet. Since both equations = y, set them equal to each other and solve for x seconds. 150 + 9x = 1,300 – 12x, 21x = 1,150, x = 54.8 seconds. If you're not sure how to set up the equation, try working backwards from the answer choices. In this case, each of the answers is a possible value for the time—use this time to figure out how far along each runner is on the track, and pick the answer that gets them the closest. It won't give you the exact answer, but it can help you to eliminate some answers that give values that are either much too large or much too small.

28. **G** For each of the 3 possible ice-cream flavors, there are 2 possible types of syrup: so multiply 3 × 2. For each of those 6 possible orders, there are 6 possible kinds of candy toppings, so multiply 6 × 6 = 36 total possibilities.

29.   B   The width of the box is half its length, so if its length is 12 cm, its width is 6 cm. The width is also twice the box's height, so the height is 3 cm. To find the volume, you multiply all three dimensions ($V = lwh$): $12(6)(3) = 216$. Choice (D) incorrectly calculates the sides as *6, 12,* and *24,* and choice (E) incorrectly calculates the sides as *12, 24,* and *48.* Choice (A) neglects to multiply by the depth. Choice (C) finds the surface area of the box.

30.   J   Substitute the values into the equation given, and you'll get $D = \$2,155(1 + 0.13) + 10(2)^2$, which is equal to $\$2,475.15$, or approximately choice (J). Choice (F) forgets to calculate the interest rate. Choice (G) forgets to add the $10(2)^2$, while choice (H) adds only 20. Choice (K) incorrectly calculates the interest rate at 14%.

31.   D   The equation for surface area is given as the expression $\pi r^2 + \pi rs$, where r is the radius and s is the slant height. The radius in the figure is half of the diameter, which is given as 30. The slant height is 30. By plugging these into the equation you get $(15)^2\pi + (15)(30)\pi$, or 675π, choice (D). Choice (C) is the result of forgetting to square the radius. Choice (E) uses the diameter instead of the radius in the equation. Choices (A) and (B) each result from evaluating only half of the expression.

32.   F   To solve a composite function, work inside out starting with the value of $g(a)$, then taking the function f of $g(a)$. $g(a)$ is given as $2a^2 + 1$, so $f(g(a)) = f(2a^2 + 1)$. Substitute $2a^2 + 1$ for a in the $f(a)$ equation to get $f(2a^2 + 1) = 3(2a^2 + 1) - 4$. Distribute the 3 within the parentheses to get $6a^2 + 3 - 4$, which simplifies to $6a^2 - 1$.

33.   D   To find the average, you need to find the total of all stars given to the movie and divide by the number of students surveyed: $\frac{1(51) + 2(18) + 3(82) + 4(49) + 5(62)}{262} \approx 3.20$. If you don't have time

for the calculations, cross out answer choices that are too large or too small to be the average and take a reasonable guess. Choice (A) is much too small and choice (E) is much too large. Choice (A) flips the numerator and the denominator. Choice (E) divides 262 by the sum of the column on the left and its answer is rounded to only the nearest tenth. Choices (B) and (C) each drop one of the components of the numerator when calculating.

34. **G** Two angles are supplementary if the sum of their degrees measures is 180°. To create supplementary angles when two lines are intersected by a third line, the two lines must be parallel. Since $\angle x$ is supplementary to angles 8 and 11, lines q and s must be parallel. Since angles 4 and 6 are not necessarily supplementary to $\angle x$, lines q and r need not be parallel, eliminating choices (F) and (K). Since angles 7 and 5 are not necessarily parallel to angles 8 and 11, lines r and s need not be parallel, eliminating choice (H). Lines p and q intersect so they cannot be parallel, eliminating choice (J).

35. **E** Choice (E) reflects the correct rules of exponents: The numeral inside the parentheses (4) gets *raised to the power* of 4, then the exponents inside the parentheses are *multiplied by* 4. Choices (B) and (C) incorrectly multiply the numeral by 4, and (D) incorrectly adds 4 to the variables' exponents. Choice (A) divides all the numbers by 4.

36. **F** In order to solve this problem you need to isolate x. By doing this you get the equation $x < -11$, thus the correct answer is (F). The other choices solve the inequality with the wrong direction of signs (choice (G)) or incorrect algebra.

37. **E** Since you are looking for a point that is rotated counterclockwise, the point should be in Quadrant IV with a positive x-value and negative y-value, eliminating choices (A) and (B). A 90° rotation means you can use the line perpendicular to $\overline{AL}$. Find the slope of $\overline{AL}$ by counting the rise over the run from A to $L = \dfrac{6}{-8}$. The perpendicular slope will be the negative reciprocal $\dfrac{8}{6}$, so you want to go 8 units down and 6 units left from the center of the circle: $(10 - 6, -2 - 8) = (4, -10)$.

38. **F** First, use the Pythagorean theorem to find the third side of the triangle. $(12)^2 + b^2 = 16^2$, so $b = \sqrt{72}$. SOHCAHTOA tells you that $Cosine = \dfrac{Adjacent}{Hypoteneuse}$, or $\dfrac{\sqrt{72}}{16}$. Choice (J) is the sine of the angle, and choices (G), (H), and (K) all find other trigonometric functions of the angle.

Also, note that to solve this problem, you don't need to solve for the angle θ.

39. **C** Since $\overline{CA}$ bisects $\angle BAD$, $\angle BAC$ and $\angle CAD$ are equal, and since $\overline{DA}$ bisects $\angle CAE$, $\angle DAE$ and $\angle CAD$ are equal. Since $\angle BAC$ and $\angle DAE$ are both equal to $\angle CAD$, $\angle BAD = \angle DAE = \angle CAD$. Given that there are 180° in a straight line, $\angle CAD = \dfrac{1}{3}(180°) = 60°$.

40. **H** To find the volume of the container, set up the equation

$$\frac{6\times10^8\ molecules}{x\ cubic\ inches}=3\times10^4\ molecules\ /\ cubic\ inch.\ \ \ \text{So,}\ \ \ x=\frac{6\times10^8}{3\times10^4}=2\times10^4.$$

Remember to subtract the exponents when dividing quantities with like bases. Choice (F) is $\dfrac{3\times10^4}{6\times10^8}$. Choice (G) is the result of dividing the exponents. Choice (J) is the result of multiplying the numbers in the problem. Choice (K) is $(3 \times 6) \times (10^{4\times8})$.

41. **B** Choice (B) correctly calculates the value of $\angle C$, which is $360 - 250 + 30 = 140$. Choices (A) and (D) use the wrong angles, 30 and 250 respectively. Choice (C) incorrectly calculates $250 - 30$, while choice (E) calculates $250 + 30$.

42. **J** The number halfway between $\dfrac{1}{4}$ and $\dfrac{1}{6}$ can be found by averaging the two numbers. $\dfrac{\frac{1}{4}+\frac{1}{6}}{2}=\dfrac{5}{24}$, which is a real number, making Choice (K) the correct answer. The other answer choices are real numbers but are not halfway between the two values. Choice (G) is between the two values, but it is not halfway.

43. **D** Find $\angle DEB$ by subtracting all other angles in $\triangle ADE$ from 180°. $\triangle ADE$ and $\triangle EBA$ are congruent because they have congruent sides: both triangles share $\overline{AE}$, $\overline{BA}$ and $\overline{DE}$ are each half the length of congruent sides, and diagonals $\overline{DA}$ and $\overline{BE}$ are equal. Therefore,

$\angle EBA$ = $\angle EDA$ = 95°, and $\angle DAE$ = $\angle BEA$ = 35°. $\angle DEB$ = 180° – $\angle EDA$ – $\angle DAE$ – $\angle BEA$ = 95° – 35° – 35° = 15°. Choice (A) either simply subtracts the two angles given from 180° or is the measure of $\angle DEA$.

44. **H** x is the side of the large square table minus the side of the small square table. Since $A=s^2$, $\sqrt{A}=s$. The side of the large square table is $\sqrt{108}=\sqrt{36\cdot3}=6\sqrt{3}$. The area of the small square table is $\frac{108}{9}=12$, so its side is $\sqrt{12}=\sqrt{4\cdot3}=2\sqrt{3}$. $x=6\sqrt{3}-2\sqrt{3}=4\sqrt{3}$. Choice (F) gives the side of the small square table instead of x, and choice (K) gives the area of the small square table. Choice (G) subtracts terms with a common radical incorrectly. Choice (J) subtracts the two areas and then takes the square root of the result, instead of first taking the square root of each area and then subtracting the results.

45. **E** A rational number is one which can be expressed as a fraction. Only choice (E) can be reduced to integer values in the numerator and denominator: $\sqrt{\dfrac{81}{25}}=\dfrac{\sqrt{81}}{\sqrt{25}}=\dfrac{9}{5}$.

46. **G** Pick a value for both x and y. If x = –5 and y = –3, then $|-5+(-3)|=|-8|=8$. Choice (G) is also 8. Choice (F) is –8. Choice (H) is –2. Choice (J) is 2 and choice (K) is $\sqrt{34}$.

47. **E** In order to figure out what Jane must get on her next game, you need to figure out how many points total she has earned on the first 5 games and how many points total she must get in order to average 85 in 6 games. To find the total points she needs on the six games, multiply her desired average by the number of games: $85\times6=510$. To find the number of points she has already gotten, multiply her average on the first 5 games by the number of games which is $5\times83=415$. The

difference between these numbers is the score she must get in order to get an average of 85 on the 6 games, which is 95, or choice (E). Choice (C) is the score she would have to get in the next two games for an average of 85. You could use Process of Elimination to rule out choices (A) and (B) since she wants her average to go up, and thus, she must get a higher score on the next test.

48. **G** Since the modulus is $\sqrt{a^2 + b^2}$, then the quadrant that the point is found in is negligible since all points are squared. Thus, the point with the greatest distance from the origin will have the greatest modulus, and the point with the shortest distances from the origin will have the smallest. You could use sample points to test this. Thus, choice (G) is the answer since it is the closest to the origin, and thus has the smallest modulus.

49. **B** Since $9 = 3^2$ and $27 = 3^3$, make $9^{x-4} = 27^{3x+2}$ into $3^{2(x-4)} = 3^{3(3x+2)}$. The equation now reads: "3 to some power = 3 to some power." Therefore, the exponents are equal: $2(x - 4) = 3(3x + 2)$. Distribute the 2 and the 3 to get $2x - 8 = 9x + 6$. Subtract $9x$ and add 8 to each side of the equation to get $-7x = 14$. Divide by -7, $x = -2$.

50. **J** A sine curve is an odd function, so choice (J) is correct. If you didn't know this, test each answer choice against the graph and the function, eliminating those not supported. If you can draw a horizontal line through the function that crosses it at two or more points, you have found multiple x values for the same y value, meaning the function is not 1:1 as defined. The horizontal line $y = 0$ crosses the graph of the function three times, eliminating choice (F). This also tells us that y, another name for $f(x)$, is 0 at $x = 0$, eliminating choice (G). The arrows at either end of the function's graph tell you that the domain (set of all x values) extends infinitely in both directions beyond -6 and 6 respectively, eliminating choice (K). Test values to find the remaining incorrect answer. You can approximate that $(-3,-2)$ and $(3,2)$ lie close

to function. $f(-3) \neq f(3)$ because $-2 \neq 2$, eliminating choice (H). You are left with choice (J): $f(-3) = -f(3)$, because $-2 = -(2)$.

51. B Make a list of the integers from 299 through 1,000 which contain 1 as a digit. 301, 310, 311, 312 ... 319 = 11 integers. 321, 331, 341, 351 ... 391 = 8 integers. 11 + 8 = 19 integers from 299 through 399. Since this pattern will repeat 7 times from 299 to 999: 400 to 499, 500 to 599 ... to 999, multiply 19 × 7 = 133. Finally, add 1 for the number 1,000 = 134 integers.

52. G You can immediately eliminate choices (J) and (K) because line $\overline{LM}$ increases as x increases, which means it has a positive slope. Because $\overline{NL}$ is parallel to the x-axis and $\triangle NLM$ is isosceles, the slope of $\overline{LM}$ is the negative of the slope of $\overline{MN}$. Find the slope of $\overline{MN}$ by rewriting the equation $y + \dfrac{2}{3}x = 2$ as $y = -\dfrac{2}{3}x + 2$, where the slope m is $-\dfrac{2}{3}$. The slope of $\overline{LM}$, therefore, is $\dfrac{2}{3}$.

53. A The notation $\sin^{-1}\left(\dfrac{x}{\sqrt{x^2+y^2}}\right)$ means find the angle that has a sine value of $\dfrac{x}{\sqrt{x^2+y^2}}$. Recall that the sine of an angle is $\dfrac{opposite}{hypotenuse}$. The side marked x is opposite $\angle ACB$ so that's the angle in question. Now, use SOHCAHTOA to find that $\tan(\angle ACB) = \dfrac{x}{y}$.

54. H The area of a circle is πr^2, which in this case is $\pi (12)^2$, or approximately 452. Choice (F) incorrectly calculates the circumference ($2\pi r$). Choice (G) creates a square by forgetting to multiply by π. Choice (J) calculates $2\pi r^2$, while choice (K) shows $\pi^2 r^2$.

55. E   The general equation for a circle is $(y - h)^2 + (x - k)^2 = r^2$ (in which h and k are the x- and y-coordinates of the center of the circle, and r is the radius). You can eliminate choices (A), (B), and (C) because they are not in the correct equation form. Since the radius 12 must be squared, the correct answer is (E).

56. F   If the 2 anchors are 30 feet apart, and Joy's dog is on a 20-foot leash, it can get within 10 feet of Melissa's anchor ($30 - 20 = 10$). Melissa's dog can run 12 feet from its anchor, so there is an overlap of 2 feet. Choice (G) is the difference of the two dog leashes. Choices (H) and (J) subtract each dog leash length from 30. Choice (K) is the sum of the two leashes.

57. D   Look at the graph of the two equations. Find the x-values where the y-value of the equation $y = -(x+1)^2 + 4$ is greater than the y-value of the equation $y = (-x+1)$. According to the figure, the parabola has a higher y-value than the line between the x-values –2 and 1, making choice (D) the answer.

58. J   Test numbers to answer this question. Because you need two-digit integers, and you want the maximum value for $(y - x)$, y should be the larger value, and x the smaller. Say $t = 1$ and $u = 9$; that makes $y = 91$ and $x = 19$, and $(y - x) = 72$. The answer choice that yields the greatest value is (J).

59. C   Use the formula for the area of a parallelogram *Area = base × height*. Find the length of the base by calculating the length of $\overline{AB}$: $8 - 2 = 6$. Find the height by dropping an altitude perpendicular to the base from point D to point $(4, -4)$, which has a length of 2. *Area* $= 6 \times 2 = 12$. Choice (D) incorrectly uses side $\overline{AD}$ with length $2\sqrt{2}$ for the height.

60. **G** To determine the sixth term, you first need to find the common difference between consecutive terms in the sequence. Use the given formula to solve for x_1: $145 = 5\left(\dfrac{x_1 + 48}{2}\right)$, so $x_1 = 10$. The common difference in an arithmetic sequence is basically the slope of a straight line: $difference = \dfrac{x_n - x_1}{n-1} = \dfrac{48 - 10}{5 - 1} = 9.5$. The sixth term, therefore, is 48 + 9.5 = 57.5. Choice (F) calculates $n + 1$, rather than x_{n+1}. Choices (H) and (K) use averages, rather than a common difference. Choice (J) incorrectly adds the difference to the sum, rather than x_5.

TEST 3 READING EXPLANATIONS

1. **A**   The narrator describes a volcano that lacks *air vents* as a potential outlet for the heat and pressure building internally, leading ever closer to an eruption. Choice (A) identifies the purpose of the figurative imagery as a way of depicting the friend's frustration toward the thoughts building up uncomfortably inside of him. Choices (B) and (D) are incorrect because the narrator is describing his friend's struggle, not attempting to offer consolation or advice concerning it. Choice (C) is incorrect because the metaphor does nothing to explain the physical impairment of the friend's speech but rather it describes the psychological effects of the impairment.

2. **H**   The passage is consistently focused on the ongoing process of the narrator attempting to help his friend deal with a speech impairment. Choice (H) captures that and correctly identifies the exchange of letters between the narrator and his friend as a main source of ideas the passage discussed. The passage tells us nothing about the narrator's friend other than his speech impairment, so the passage is not a *detailed character study* as choice (F) suggests. The overwhelming voice of the passage is that of the narrator, so it is inaccurate to say that the narrator and his friend *take equal turns* debating the issue as choice (G) states. The passage is not focused on the narrator's legal career, nor does it mention any struggles related to being a lawyer as stated in choice (J).

3. **D**   The narrator compares his friend's speech to *an oceanic cloud of dust and debris* and his friend's writing to *an omni-directional lava flow*. Choice (D) correctly points to speech and writing as vocal and non-vocal expression. Choices (A) and (C) are almost synonymous pairs of nouns, making either one a very unlikely correct answer. The passage does not indicate a contrast between simplicity and complexity, so you can eliminate Choice (B).

4. **H** The narrator's *sympathetic* and *encouraging* attitude is revealed via his ongoing concern for his friend's frustration and goal of giving him a positive outlook on it; the friend shows his *anxiety* and *despondence* by saying *I fear I will eventually choke on my own thoughts* and by watching the narrator's speech with a *mix of pride and pain in his eyes*. Because the narrator is chiefly concerned with making his friend feel better, choice (F) is not correct to call the narrator *jaded* or *indifferent*. Although the friend occasionally disagrees with the narrator on points of their discussion, there is nothing *scornful* about his tone, making choice (G) incorrect. The friend is physically unable to speak his mind, but that does not make him *shy* or *reclusive* as choice (J) states.

5. **C** Little detail is provided about Cyrano de Bergerac other than that he *enlisted the help of a friend to speak his thoughts aloud* to a woman he was trying to woo. Choice (C) is supported by that detail. Choice (A) involves knowing the woman is *the love of his life*, which we do not. Choice (B) involves knowing that Cyrano had a physical impairment, which we do not. Choice (D) involves knowing that Cyrano was unable to express his emotions, which we do not.

6. **H** The passage states that pirates *share a common destiny but no longer pledge allegiance to any sovereign entity*, providing support for choice (H). Choice (F) is not known; pirates may have stringent rules of conduct for each other. Choice (G) is misleading language, borrowing the word *confusion* from the next sentence but presenting an unsupported idea. Choice (J) ignores the specific purpose of the pirate simile and merely relates pirates to the main topic of the passage.

7. **A** The details in the passage that indicate what the friend values in vocal speech come in the final paragraph. The friend *deeply misses the expressiveness that a human voice can add to the meaning of words* and he prevents the narrator from speaking *too mechanically*. Choice (A) identifies that an expressive tone is something the friend values. Choice (B) is contradicted by the friend's distaste for overly mechanical speech,

and choices (C) and (D) are not ingredients of vocal speech that are ever discussed in the passage.

8. **G** Choice (G) is correct because the friend says *I fear that I will eventually choke on my own thoughts.* This reflects an expectation of suffering due to his inability to speak his mind. A fear of embarrassment is never discussed, making choice (F) incorrect. A concern of interfering with the narrator's legal career is never mentioned, making choice (H) incorrect. The friend never questions his capacity for creating well-orchestrated thought, as choice (J) suggests; he only clarifies that both written and vocal speech are capable of expressing it.

9. **D** The narrator's mention of a puppet is an expression of his desire to allow his own voice to be used by his friend. Choice (D) correctly identifies the usage of puppet as a surrogate voice. Choices (A) and (C) are trap language based on other associations with the word *puppet*, and choice (B) relates to the subject of speech but does not correctly identify that the narrator would be a passive vehicle for his friend's ideas.

10. **F** The narrator describes a look of *pride and pain* in his friend's eyes, knowing that his friend is enjoying the legal proceedings but wrestling with the fact that the narrator can express himself *more lucidly than* the friend *may ever be able to again.* This combination of delight and deprivation justifies choice (F). Nothing in this paragraph suggests confusion, as choice (G) suggests, or overbearing annoyance to the narrator, as in choice (H). While the friend experiences pain and longing for his lost abilities, to say that he is *bitter* or *resentful*, as choice (J) does, is too strong.

11. **A** The passage states that no one before has been able to directly link human behavior to ice-shelf breakup. Choice (A) must be correct because the passage states that human behavior has been proven to be connected to the rise in temperature that causes the collapse. Therefore, human behavior is both a considerable factor and a previously

unproven one. Choice (B) is incorrect because while glaciological influences do contribute, nowhere is there evidence that human behavior is insignificant. Choice (C) is incorrect because there was no discussion of prior evidence showing human activity to be a more influential factor than is suggested by current evidence. Choice (D) cannot be correct because it's reiterated many times in the article that there are many factors contributing to ice shelf collapse, not just one.

12. **J** Choices (F), (G), and (H) reflect information presented in the concluding paragraph of the essay. Only choice (J) is NOT listed as an effect of sea level rise but rather as a cause of sea-level rise, thus making it the correct answer to this question.

13. **A** Choice (A) is the best answer because paragraph three discusses Dr. Marshall's study and cites evidence that climate change was a major factor in the collapse. In the following paragraph, lines 66–67 in reference to Glasser and Scambos, the passage reads as follows: *they acknowledge that global warming had a major role in the collapse.* Choice (B) is incorrect because all of the scientists agree that climate change was a contributing factor. Choice (C) can't be correct because while the scientists didn't find the same things, both studies found evidence to explain the collapse. Choice (D) is incorrect because while structural evidence is cited as a factor in one of the studies, it's not a common factor, nor was it the cause of the collapse.

14. **H** In the lines to consider, the author quotes the scientist's two observations: one, that this is the first time anyone has demonstrated a human process linked to the collapse of a shelf, and two, that climate change doesn't impact the planet evenly—*as evidenced by the significant increase in temperatures in certain geological areas.* This most clearly agrees with choice (H). Choice (F) is the opposite of the point being made in these lines. Choice (G) is incorrect because there is no evidence in the passage on which to base the conjecture that the observed local phenomena would extend to the entire earth. Choice (J) isn't correct because there is no connection made between sea level and human activity.

15. C The last sentence of paragraph two says, *the collapse of the Larsen B ice shelf seemed to be one of the most obvious and stunning signs of worldwide climate change,* making choice (C) the correct answer. Choice (A) hasn't yet happened, at least on the scale presented in the conclusion, (B) and (D) may happen as a result of climate change, but neither melt water nor increased temperature was called *a stunning sign.*

16. J Lines (65–69) say *the shelf was already teetering on the brink of collapse before the final summer, and though...global warming had a major role in the collapse...it is only one of a number of atmospheric, oceanic and glaciological factors* and then goes on to give an example of location and spacing of crevasses and rifts, showing that choice (J), a combination of factors is the best answer. Choice (F) is incorrect for two reasons: one, it talks about glaciers, not ice shelves, and two, the lines ask about the purpose of the findings; the findings say that global warming was not a cause, but a contributing factor. Choice (G) has no evidence to support it, and choice (H) is the opposite of the argument in the paragraph.

17. D The third paragraph discusses how human activity contributed to the collapse, which makes choice (D) the best answer. Choice (C) is a phrase found in the paragraph, but it is not the main idea. Choice (A) contradicts the evidence in the passage, and choice (B) is a main argument in the fourth paragraph, not the third.

18. J (F), (G), and (H) are all given as contributing factors to the ice shelf's collapse in the passage. Deep ocean currents are never mentioned at all.

19. B Choice (B) is clearly stated in lines 38–41...*stronger westerly winds in the northern Antarctic Peninsula, driven principally by human-induced climate change, are responsible for the significant increase in summer temperatures....* Choice (A) is disproven in the paragraph, as it is stated that the winds contribute to the warming, which contributes to the collapse of ice shelves. Choice (C) is not stated in the passage, and choice (D) is a detail unrelated to winds. Sea level has to do with glaciers speeding up after the shelves collapse.

20. **H** The remark comes just after a statement about how weather changes don't affect the planet evenly. Therefore, the specific information about the increases in temperature in that particular region is an example of how weather changes are more extreme in certain places. Choice (F) is incorrect because there is no support in the passage for the idea that scientists are prone to exaggeration. Choice (G) might be tempting because the paragraph was about how human behavior causes warming patterns; however, the remark was not intended to make people change their behavior. It was an example of the point made prior to that sentence. Choice (J) is incorrect because there weren't any misconceptions being discussed.

21. **A** The first paragraph introduces Rushdie and gives a little bit of information about his writing. It mentions where some of his books take place (India, Pakistan, and England), the fact that magical events sometimes occur, and that he is a *virtuosic*, or talented, writer. It does not, however, state what his intentions are as a writer, making choice (A) the best answer.

22. **G** The second paragraph states when and where Rushdie was born and raised. It then goes on to mention that he draws on all of these experiences in his writing. Although the passage states that Rushdie's parents were Muslim, it does not discuss his *personal faith*, as in choice (F). The passage mentions that there was a struggle between the Hindi and Muslim populations but it does not give any details as to the reason for that, as in choice (H). Although the paragraph mentions that Rushdie does eventually immigrate to England, it does not state his reasons for doing so, making choice (J) incorrect.

23. **C** The passage begins by mentioning how well-known Rushdie's life story is and then proceeds to explain some of the events in his life that seem to have influenced his work. Therefore, the best answer is

choice (C), as that is the only answer that directly connects Rushdie's life experiences with his writing. Choice (A) incorrectly refers to Rushdie's *personal failings,* which are not mentioned in this passage. Choice (B) incorrectly focuses on the partition of India rather than Rushdie himself. Choice (D) incorrectly focuses on one of Rushdie's books instead of Rushdie himself.

24. **H** The description of Bombay, as seen by Rushdie, is in the beginning of the third paragraph. The author explicitly refers to the smells, colors, and people, but nowhere is the weather mentioned, making choice (H) the correct answer.

25. **C** The fourth paragraph deals with the book *Midnight's Children* and how it mirrors Rushdie's life and exemplifies some of his feelings about life in India and Pakistan. His focus, according to this paragraph, is on the struggle that the two countries have in trying to exist together yet create individual identities after the partition. Nowhere does the passage state that Rushdie's writing has a sense of *futility* or *sadness,* as in choices (A) and (B). The passage does mention a sense of *longing* but in the third paragraph, not the fourth.

26. **J** Although the passage refers to Rushdie's work repeatedly, nowhere does it give a precise number and only one book is mentioned by name. Choice (F) is answered in the first paragraph, when the author refers to the places that Rushdie describes, and is also mentioned throughout the passage. Choice (G) is answered in the third paragraph. Choice (H) is answered in the first sentence of the second paragraph.

27. **B** The second paragraph gives Rushdie's basic history and it states that *he immigrated to England to attend school.* Although he may have attended school in India, where he was born, the passage does not specify, making choice (B) the better answer.

28. **H** Most of the descriptions of Bombay are in the third paragraph, where it is described as *a raucous place, filled with colors, scents that assault the nostrils, and people thronging the…teeming with life and all that life*

entails. The best match for that is choice (H). Although some people might find Bombay *frustrating* or *chaotic,* nowhere does the passage imply that Rushdie feels that way. Choice (J) incorrectly identifies a word used to describe Pakistan's beauty (*stark*) with a city in India.

29.   A   The line being referenced (*As interesting as his subjects are, it is the way that his prose draws readers into his world that makes his work so enduring*) serves as a way for the author to transition from a discussion of Rushdie's subject matter to his actual skill as a writer. The passage does not imply that Rushdie is too dependent on historical fact; the author of the passage seems to enjoy the historical nature of Rushdie's writing. Eliminate choice (B). The paragraph also goes on to state that Rushdie is likely to remain well-known for many years, making choice (C) incorrect. Choice (D) goes too far, although the author does state that it is Rushdie's skill rather than his subject matter that makes him great; nowhere is the subject matter called *uninteresting.*

30.   H   The final paragraph states that *certainly the way his prose draws readers into his world has been the essential factor in making his work so enduring.* Choice (F) is incorrect because it is too specific to Pakistan. Choice (G) incorrectly focuses on the partition of India, which is mentioned but is not part of Rushdie's contribution to literature. Choice (J) is incorrect because the passage deals more with the writing's ability to speak to readers than its literal beauty.

31.   D   Hypnotic analgesia *re-evaluate* and *manage a painful stimulus,* which is best reflected in choice (D). Choice (A) is a literal misinterpretation of *essentially change their brains.* Choice (B) suggests that hypnotic analgesia can be used to treat those diseases, rather than managing the pain felt from those diseases. Choice (C) is not supported by any evidence in the passage.

32.   G   The question asks you about the detection of pain, which according to the passage follows four pathways. Choice (G) correctly summarizes the first three pathways: *sensory neurons* detect stimuli from *damaged*

tissues, the signals are transmitted to the spinal cord, and then the *information is relayed to structures of the brain.* The sympathetic nervous system is not mentioned in this process, so eliminate choices (F), (H), and (J).

33.   B   The exercise routines mentioned in the first paragraph *involve more than cardiovascular activity* by focusing on the breath and mental imagery, which is said to *improve overall health,* but *nutritious diet* is not mentioned. Choices (A), (C), and (D) are supported in the discussions of mindful movement exercises.

34.   F   With the sentence *When the central nervous system perceives a threat, the sympathetic nervous system is engaged,* the nervous system is described as triggered, so choice (F) is the best answer. Choices (G), (H), and (J) do not fit the context of the passage.

35.   C   The limbic system is *the brain center for emotion, memory, and autonomic nervous system* as well as *central representation;* choices (A), (B), and (D) are all true. Muscle movement was never mentioned directly in the passage.

36.   H   The passage states that the researchers have begun to *delve deeper into mind-body therapy efficacy,* thus choice (H) is the supported answer. The passage states that biomedicine has been *slower to embrace* these therapies, but not that it has *rejected* them, so eliminate choice (G). The passage states that mind-body therapy is *increasingly popular,* but does not indicate it is being used *in place of biomedicine,* so eliminate choice (F). Although research has shown prolonged beneficial effects from mind-body therapy, there is no evidence cited in the passage to show that these therapies have been successful in *curing* many diseases and conditions, so eliminate choice (J).

37.   D   Mind-body therapies may *alter responses to stressors* so that the *parasympathetic nervous system* is engaged, rather than the *sympathetic nervous system,* which activates the so-called *fight or flight* response, choice (D). The passage states that mind-body therapies may

provoke positive reactions, but they do not impede the actual biological responses of the nervous system, so choice (A) should be eliminated. Effective mind-body therapies engage the parasympathetic, not the sympathetic, nervous system, so eliminate choice (B), and because these therapies do not act on the stressors themselves, only on our responses to them, choice (C) should be eliminated.

38. F As stated in paragraph 4, fight-or-flight responses had adaptive functions in ancestral conditions. Such responses are *automatic* and would be expected to provoke the processes discussed in Paragraph 3: The sympathetic nervous system releases stress hormones, such as cortisol. Thus, choice (F) is the credited response. Threats are perceived by the *central nervous system*, not stress responses, so eliminate choice (H). *Prolonged* stress responses may result in *negative* health consequences, such as *suppressed immune activity*, but the passage does not suggest that they directly lead to suppressed activity, eliminating choice (G). Decreased muscle tension results when the parasympathetic nervous system is engaged, and is mentioned in the passage as a benefit of conscious mind-body responses to stressors, so eliminate choice (J).

39. C The final paragraph states that *more investigation is needed* to determine the influence of a number of possible outside factors. Thus it can be inferred that research into mind-body therapy could be *affected by external variables*. Because *more investigation* is needed to determine the influence of *outcome expectations*, these factors may not be presently controlled for. Therefore, choice (C) is the best answer. There is no evidence to support choice (A), which implies that researchers should manipulate their results to make their studies look good. Although the Western therapies have researched mind-body therapies, the passage does not state that research results are valid *only* for Western therapies, so eliminate choice (B). Mind-body therapies *alter* pain experience and stress responses, but they do not *eliminate pain* or *fight stress*, so eliminate choice (D).

40. H The fifth paragraph states that mind-body therapies help to regulate stress by engaging the parasympathetic nervous system, which counteracts the negative effects of the fight-or-flight response. If the therapies were ineffective, then the parasympathetic would not be engaged, eliminating choice (G). There is no evidence to support the increase or decrease in pain detection or spinal cord activity, eliminating choice (F) and (J). Choice (H) is the best answer because the fight-or-flight reaction is a stress response, the prolonged effects of which can result in negative health consequences.

TEST 3 SCIENCE EXPLANATIONS

1. **C** The moon blocks the transmission of the Sun's rays over a range of 0.52 degrees. The lunar orbiter at Point P is located within this range of 0.52 degrees, so he or she is able to view only the moon and the Earth. Therefore, choice (C) is the best answer.

2. **F** Figure 1 shows that during a solar eclipse, the moon does not allow the transmission of the Sun's rays to the Earth. Therefore, the Sun's rays stop transmitting forward and do not continue to the Earth's surface, so choice (F) is the best answer.

3. **B** The water level is highest on the first day at around $t = 0$ hours. The water level is highest on the next day at around $t = 26$ hours. The difference in time between these instances is 24 hours, so choice (B) is the best answer.

4. **G** According to Figure 2, during the 60-hour period, the ocean surface level had a maximum of 6 feet above mean sea level and a minimum of 1 foot below mean sea level (-1 feet). Of the choices provided, only the month of March shows this exact range, so choice (G) is the best answer.

5. **D** Figure 2 indicates a water level of 6 feet at $t = 0$. The water then falls until about $t = 8$ hours when it reaches about -1 feet. Then, the water level rises again, reaching about 2 feet at $t = 12$ hours. Thus, choice (D) is correct.

6. **G** Examine the shale layer in Figure 2 closely—given the choices in the answers, find which site or city has the thickest layer of shale. The shale layers at Middleton at Site 1 clearly go deeper than those at Site 3 and West Union, so you can eliminate choices (H) and (J). Between Middleton and Site 1, look closely to see that the highest and lowest extremes in Site 1 are farther apart—the best answer is choice (G).

7. **A** From Figure 2, the limestone layer appears to increase in thickness as you move from Site 2 toward Site 3. Therefore, answer choices (B), (C), and (D) may be eliminated.

8. **H** Examine Figure 2; the shale layer at Site 2 is slightly thicker than that of Site 3, eliminating answer choices (F) and (J). A comparison of the shale thickness at Sites 1 and 2 shows that the shale layer at Site 2 is slightly less thick than that of Site 1, eliminating choice (G).

9. **A** Based on Figure 3, at greater depths below the surface the number of counts of uranium decreases. Therefore, the greatest counts of uranium should be observed closest to the surface as seen in choice (A).

10. **G** Examine Figure 2: Site 2 exhibits 8 counts of Uranium in the deepest layer. Using the equation given in Figure 3, the age of the rock at Site 2 is most nearly 8 (64/8) times 700 million or 5600 million years. Of the answer choices, only choice (G) matches this age.

11. **C** There is no mention of distance shot in Experiment 3, therefore answer choices (A) and (B) can be eliminated. Choice (D) is irrelevant to the experiment's results. As described, the results of Experiment 3 center around the visibility of bubbles in the cola, so choice (C) is best.

12. **J** For this question, look at the *before shaking* column of the two tables. Trials 3 and 5 both have distances of 6.42 meters.

13. **D** Experiment 2 asks you to determine how shaking the water gun affects how far the water gun shoots the flat-tasting cola. Neither density nor bubbles are addressed. In Table 2, compare the columns labeled *before shaking* and *after shaking*. In both trials listed, shaking the water gun decreased the distance shot.

14. **H** If you're not sure whether to answer *Yes* or *No*, make sure you look at the reasons presented in each answer choice. In Trial 5, before the water gun was shaken, it had been 1 hour since the gun had last been shaken. Experiment 3 addresses how quickly the bubbles generated by shaking the water gun disappear. It suggests that 10 minutes after shaking, some bubbles are still present, but by 1 hour after shaking, the bubbles have all disappeared. Therefore, choice (H) is correct.

15. **D** In this hypothetical trial, the cola is shaken, let sit for ten minutes, shot, shaken, and shot again (Trial 4); then let sit for an hour, shot,

shaken, and shot again (Trial 5); and finally let sit for another hour and shot with the distance of the shot measured (the hypothetical test in this question). By comparing Trial 5 before the gun has been shaken with Trial 4 after the gun has been shaken, you know that letting the flat-cola-filled water gun sit for an hour after shaking it eliminates the effects of any previous shaking. This is to say that in the hour between Trial 4 after shaking and Trial 5 before shaking, the distance shot goes from 5.49 meters to 6.42 meters—back to the same distance as never having been shaken at all (cf., Trial 3 before shaking). Therefore, after an additional shaking and hour sitting, you should expect the cola to travel 6.42 meters.

16. **G** From Experiment 3, bubbles are visible 10 minutes after shaking and not visible 1 hour after shaking. Similarly, from Trial 4, you know that 10 minutes after the gun has been shaken, the bubbles still reduce the distance of the shot. From Trial 5, you know that the bubbles do not reduce the distance of the shot 1 hour after the gun has been shaken. Therefore, the time necessary for the bubbles to stop having an effect on the distance shot must be between 10 minutes and 1 hour—choice (G).

17. **D** According to Figure 1, the greatest reflectance for blue-green algae occurs around 550 nm. According to Table 1, a wavelength of 550 nm is associated with the color green, making choice (D) correct.

18. **H** Photosynthesis is the chemical reaction that identifies autotrophic organisms, which make their own food, specifically sugar. Binary fission is the asexual reproduction of bacteria. Condensation is the transition of water from gas to liquid. Respiration is the opposite reaction of photosynthesis, breaking down glucose rather than making it.

19. **A** Choice (A), 400 nm, is the only choice where the green algae curve is higher than the diatoms curve. For all of the other choices, the diatoms curve is higher than the green algae curve, so the relative reflectance is higher for diatoms.

20. **J** Protists are organisms which cannot be classified as plants or animals. They can be one or many celled, but are always simple in construction. Choice (J) is correct because all algae are protists.

21. **B** The first paragraph of the passage tells you that as the amount of algae in a water sample increases, the water sample reflects light more like the algae so you know that all you need to do with this question is look for the algae that reflects light like the water sample. The best way to figure out this question is to quickly locate the high and low points on the water sample graph. The water sample has peaks at 550 nm and 0.08 reflectance and at 700 nm and 0.07 reflectance. The water sample has low points at 350 nm and 0.03 reflectance and at about 660 nm and 0.04 reflectance. Now, look at the algae graph. Once you match those points to the algae graph, it is easy to see the choice (B), diatoms, is the correct answer.

22. **H** To get through this question quickly, you can try to estimate. Because temperature is rising as you go down Table 1, and density is falling, the additional sample would be a new line under Sample V. Solution mass is falling in the table, so eliminate choice (J). To decide among the remaining choices, note that the falling solution mass, while not linear, declines in relatively small increments and never more than .5 g. Thus, a reasonable guess would be choice (H). To be certain of the answer, focus on the density, which we know by looking at Experiments 1 and 2 together is the more important factor (mass fell even when temperature was held constant). In Experiment 1, 150 mL of each solution is measured in the graduated cylinder. Multiplying this volume by the density of the solution will give the mass.

$$density = \frac{mass}{volume}$$

$mass = (density)(volume)$

$mass = (1.018 \text{ g/mL})(150 \text{ mL})$

Either solve by long multiplication, or eliminate choices (F) and (G) by expanding the above expression:

mass = (1.018 g/mL)(150 mL)

mass = (100 g/mL)(1.5 mL) + (1.8 g/mL)(1.5 mL)

The last product above works out to 2.7 g, so only choice (H) is possible.

23. **A** All samples in Table 2 are at 10°C according to the description of Experiment 2. Salinity of 2.50% is not directly listed, but it does fall between those of samples VI and VII. Given that all samples are at the same temperature, the density of the proposed solution will fall between that of samples VI and VII.

24. **H** According to Experiment 2, where all water samples have a temperature of 10°C, the given salinity of 2.35% matches up most closely with the salinity in Sample VII. Looking at the results of Experiment 3 for Sample VII, U3 sank and X2 remained afloat. This eliminates choices (G) and (J). Since the claim in the question states that U3 will function well at the *surface* of the water, the data do NOT support this. U3 will sink in this environment and therefore cannot operate at the surface, eliminating choice (F).

25. **D** According to Table 3, all prototypes show a pattern of floating in samples toward the top of the table, and sinking in samples toward the bottom of the table. R5 has the same results as choice (A), X1 and X2 each have the same results as choice (B), and U3 has the same results as choice (C). However, a similar pattern to choice (D) cannot be found. If the new prototype did not float in water samples IV and V, it cannot possibly float in samples VI and VII because these water samples are less dense.

26. **H** According to the description of Experiment 1, the graduated cylinder was used to *measure 150 mL of the solution*. A mL is a unit of volume. Graduated cylinders are primarily used for accurate and precise measurements of volume. Mass is best assessed with a balance, eliminating

choice (F). Salinity is typically measured indirectly through electrical conductivity, eliminating choice (G). Thermometers are used to measure temperature, eliminating choice (J).

27. A   In Table 3, prototype U3 floated in Sample V but sank in Sample VI. The density of an object must be less than that of the liquid for the object to float. If the density of the object exceeds that of the surrounding liquid, it will sink. Therefore, the density of U3 must be between the densities of Samples V and VI. The density of Sample V is 1.022 g/mL according to Table 1, and the density of Sample VI is 1.020 g/mL according to Table 2. Only choice (A) lists a value between these limits.

28. J   According to Table 1, only the haloarchaeal and bacterial cells show + signs for either acid or CO_2 presence under green light. Therefore, choice (J) is the best answer.

29. B   A plant cell alone produces only CO_2 and absorbs most of the light (i.e., has low transmittance) in the presence of red light. A haloarchaeal cell alone produces only acid and absorbs most of the light (i.e., has low transmittance) in the presence of green light. Since these two cell types do not interfere with each other, they will most likely continue to have production of CO_2 and low transmittance in the presence of red light, as well as the production of acid and low transmittance in the presence of green light. Choice (B) summarizes this.

30. G   Only the plant and bacterium produce CO_2 in the presence of red light, so you can immediately eliminate choices (F) and (H). Then, under the green light, the bacterium produces both acid and CO_2 and the plant produces neither, making choice (G) the best answer.

31. C   According to Experiment 1, the production of acid is a sign of growth. According to Experiment 2, low transmittance indicates that light is being absorbed by pigments to generate energy. The evidence that haloarchaea use light to generate energy and grow must include production of acid and low transmittance. These are both seen only in the presence of green light, so choice (C) is the best answer.

32. G In red light, the plant cell *Rosa carolina* will produce CO_2 but not acid. When CO_2 is present, a gas bubble appears above the solution. If acid is not present, then the solution appears colored. The illustration in choice (G) best represents this.

33. C The results of Experiment 1 show that bacteria and haloarchaea produce different products in the presence of red and green light. The passage does not mention any other relationship between haloarchaea and bacteria. Therefore, the best answer is choice (C): The two types of cells show different growth patterns, so we cannot conclude that they are closely related.

34. G The second sentence of the last paragraph for the 3-Domain Hypothesis implies that the more different the genetic sequence of rRNA, the farther back in time two groups of organisms diverged or split on the evolutionary tree. Similar genetic sequences would imply more closely related species, eliminating choice (F). A relationship between ester or ether linkages and divergence is not discussed in the passage, eliminating choices (H) and (J).

35. D Phospholipids have membranes but are not organelles themselves, eliminating choice (A). Ribosomes are not described as membrane-bound organelles in the passage, and the introduction implies that the Archaea have ribosomes because they have rRNA, eliminating choices (B) and (C). Nuclei are membrane-bound organelles found only in eukaryotes.

36. J The last paragraph states that eukaryotes and prokaryotes have ester linkages in their cell membranes, eliminating choice (F). The introduction defines the difference between eukaryotes and prokaryotes as the presence or absence of membrane-bound organelles, eliminating choice (G). Prokaryotes reproduce asexually as mentioned in the 2-Domain Hypothesis, eliminating choice (H). All of the organisms described in the passage are composed of cells.

37. **C** The scientist supporting the 2-Domain Hypothesis opens the argument by defining the Archaea as prokaryotes. The introduction states the Archaea contain rRNA, eliminating choice (A). Although ether linkages are found in the Archaea, this is an argument proposed by the scientist supporting the 3-Domain Hypothesis, eliminating choice (B). Protein synthesis can occur in the cytoplasm of all living organisms, and is not mentioned as a defining characteristic of any of the domains in the passage, eliminating choice (D).

38. **F** The observation of cellular metabolism similar to that found in eukaryotes discredits the arguments mentioned in the 2-Domain Hypothesis, eliminating choices (H) and (J). Since the metabolic process is similar to eukaryotes, choice (G) is also eliminated.

39. **C** Neither scientist makes the claim that the Archaea have membrane-bound organelles, eliminating choice (A). Microscopes play a vital role in accurately describing organisms, and this is not mentioned one way or the other in the passage, eliminating choice (B). The distance in relationship between eukaryotes and the Archaea is not the primary argument of each scientist. They are arguing more about whether to break up prokaryotes into bacteria and the Archaea, eliminating choice (D). The fact that the Archaea have ether linkages instead of ester linkages is mentioned by the scientist arguing for the 3-Domain Hypothesis as a significantly distinguishing characteristic, which allows the Archaea to occupy harsh environments.

40. **G** Phospholipids are described in the passage as having a water-soluble subunit and a water-insoluble subunit. Therefore, it makes the most sense that the water-soluble subunits (circles) would arrange in a manner such that they were exposed to water while keeping the water-insoluble subunits (lines) away from the water.

WRITING TEST

Essay Checklist

1. The Introduction
   Did you
   o start with a topic sentence that paraphrases or restates the prompt?
   o clearly state your position on the issue?

2. Body Paragraph 1
   Did you
   o start with a transition/topic sentence that discusses the opposing side of the argument?
   o give an example of a reason that one might agree with the opposing side of the argument?
   o clearly state that the opposing side of the argument is wrong or flawed?
   o show what is wrong with the opposing side's example or position?

3. Body Paragraphs 2 and 3
   Did you
   o start with a transition/topic sentence that discusses your position on the prompt?
   o give one example or reason to support your position?
   o show the grader how your example supports your position?
   o end the paragraph by restating your thesis?

4. Conclusion
   Did you
   o restate your position on the issue?
   o end with a flourish?

5. Overall
   Did you
   o write neatly?
   o avoid multiple spelling and grammar mistakes?
   o try to vary your sentence structure?
   o use a few impressive-sounding words?

SCORING YOUR PRACTICE EXAM

Step A

Count the number of correct answers for each section and record the number in the space provided for your raw score on the Score Conversion Worksheet below.

Step B

Using the Score Conversion Chart on the next page, convert your raw scores on each section to scaled scores. Then compute your composite ACT score by averaging the four subject scores. Add them up and divide by four. Don't worry about the essay score; it is not included in your composite score.

Score Conversion Worksheet		
Section	Raw Score	Scaled Score
1	_____/75	_____
2	_____/60	_____
3	_____/40	_____
4	_____/40	_____

SCORE CONVERSION CHART

Scaled Score	Raw Score			
	English	Mathematics	Reading	Science Reasoning
36	75	60	39–40	40
35	74	59	38	39
34	72–73	58	37	38
33	71	57	36	—
32	70	55–56	35	37
31	69	53–54	34	36
30	67–68	52	33	—
29	65–66	50–51	32	35
28	62–64	46–49	30–31	33–34
27	59–61	43–45	28–29	31–32
26	57–58	41–42	27	30
25	55–56	39–40	26	29
24	52–54	37–38	25	28
23	50–51	35–36	24	27–26
22	49	33–34	23	25
21	48	31–32	21–22	24
20	45–47	29–30	20	23
19	43–44	27–28	19	22
18	40–42	24–26	18	20–21
17	38–39	21–23	17	18–19
16	35–37	18–20	16	16–17
15	32–34	16–17	15	15
14	29–31	13–15	14	13–14
13	27–28	11–12	12–13	12
12	24–26	9–10	11	11
11	21–23	7–8	9–10	10
10	18–20	6	8	9
9	15–17	5	7	7–8
8	13–14	4	—	6
7	11–12	—	6	5
6	9–10	3	5	—
5	7–8	2	4	4
4	5–6	—	3	3
3	3–4	1	2	2
2	2	—	1	1
1	0	0	0	0

NOTES

NOTES

NOTES

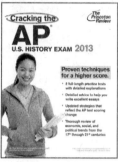